EMIL AND KATHLEEN SICK SERIES IN WESTERN HISTORY AND BIOGRAPHY

With support from the Center for the Study of the Pacific Northwest at the University of Washington, the Sick Series in Western History and Biography features scholarly books on the peoples and issues that have defined and shaped the American West. Through intellectually challenging and engaging books of general interest, the series seeks to deepen and expand our understanding of the American West as a region and its role in the making of the United States and the modern world.

Japanese Prostitutes in the North American West, 1887–1920

Kazuhiro Oharazeki

Center for the Study of the Pacific Northwest
in association with
UNIVERSITY OF WASHINGTON PRESS   *Seattle and London*

Printed and bound in the United States of America

20   19   18   17   16   5   4   3   2   1

Center for the Study of the Pacific Northwest
http://cspn.uw.edu

University of Washington Press
www.washington.edu/uwpress

Cataloging information is on file with the
Library of Congress

ISBN 978-0-295-99833-6

The paper used in this publication is acid-free and
meets the minimum requirements of American
National Standard for Information Sciences—
Permanence of Paper for Printed Library Materials,
ANSI z39.48–1984. ∞

To the memories of Jiichan and Mii

CONTENTS

ACKNOWLEDGMENTS

I have incurred many debts over the years. My biggest debt is to Professor Tom Dublin, who has guided my study since I began graduate study in history. He has devoted a great deal of time to reading my writings and has helped me overcome various challenges. This book would not have been published without his unfailing support. I am grateful to Professor Kitty Sklar and Professor Herbert Bix for introducing me to the fields of U.S. women's history and modern Japan and teaching me the importance of good questions and good writing skills.

In the course of research, I have profited from the help of many people and institutions. I thank David Takahashi and Mike Hidalgo, King County Superior Court, Seattle; Blair Galston, United Church of Canada British Columbia Conference Archives; E. Brooks Andrews, Hideo Hoshide, and Yosh Nakagawa, Japanese Baptist Church of Seattle; Barbara Nagaoka and Pearl Yamamoto, Blaine Memorial United Methodist Church, Seattle; Trevor Livelton, City of Victoria Archives; Pat Johnson and the staff at the Center for Sacramento History (formerly Sacramento Archives and Museum Collection Center); the staff at Special Collections, University of Washington Libraries, at British Columbia Archives, at the Diplomatic Record Office, Tokyo, and at the National Diet Library, Tokyo; John M. Hendricks, Charles L. Miller, and the staff in the National Archives at San Francisco and the National Archives at Seattle; Helen Insinger, Laurie Kolosky, and the staff at Binghamton University's Bartle Library. Special thanks go to Professor Sakaguchi Mitsuhiro at Kyoto Women's University, who responded to my questions and helped locate key Japanese-language sources. Binghamton University's History Department generously provided financial support, including semester fellowships and a Dubofsky Grant, which helped me complete my research in Japan and the Pacific Northwest.

Parts of chapters 2, 3, 4, and 5 were previously published as "Listening to the Voices of 'Other' Women in Japanese North America: Japanese Prostitutes and Barmaids in the American West, 1887–1920," *Journal of American Ethnic History* 32:2 (Summer 2013): 5–40; © 2013 University of Illinois Press. Chapter 6 was originally published as "Anti-prostitution Campaigns in Japan and the American West, 1890–1920: A Transpacific Comparison," *Pacific Historical Review* 82:2 (May 2013); 175–214; © 2013 University of California Press. I would like to thank the publishers for permission to reprint them in revised form and the editors of the journals, John J. Bukowczyk, David A. Johnson, Carl Abbott, Susan Wladaver-Morgan, and seven anonymous reviewers for suggestions and constructive criticisms. I am grateful to the staff at the University of Washington Press, especially Ranjit Arab, senior acquisitions editor, for finding potential in my book project and guiding me through all the stages with care and encouragement, and Thomas Eykemans, designer, for the beautiful book jacket. I thank Laura Iwasaki, for her meticulous copyediting; Tim Roberts at Field Editorial, for overseeing the process of copyediting and the creation of final files; and PJ Heim, for preparing the excellent index for my book with great care. I am greatly indebted to three anonymous reviewers for the University of Washington Press who offered truly useful criticism and advice that helped improve the quality of my analysis.

I would like to thank the descendants of the Asaba family (the natal family of Yamada Waka, a prominent social reformer in Taishō and Shōwa Japan), including Asaba Kiyoshi (grandson of Yamada's eldest brother) for sharing the family tree of the Asaba family and explaining the history of the family in Kurihama. It was my great good fortune to have been able to meet Yamada Yaheiji (Yamada's grandson) at his home, and I would like to thank him for sharing wonderful stories about his social work and helping me understand the legacy of Yamada Waka. I very much appreciate Professor Imai Konomi at Kwansei Gakuin University, Yokota Hajime, and Kishimoto Takami for making these meetings possible.

I would also like to thank the professors who have offered encouragement: the late Shigeno Akira, Mark Willis, Rebecca Calman, Kohiyama Rui, Yasutake Rumi, Ishii Noriko, Katō Yōko, Fa-ti Fan, David Stahl, and Arleen de Vera. Thanks to Shimauchi Taiken and

Daisy, Kawakubo Fuminori, and Satō Hiroki for their friendship over the years. My coworkers in a warehouse where I had worked for half a dozen years before and after receiving my Ph.D. deserve special recognition for teaching me that there is something important to learn outside academia.

Finally, let me thank my parents, maternal grandmother, aunts, and little brother for their continuous support. This book is dedicated to the memories of my late grandfather, Oharazeki Shigetada (1927–2013), a good storyteller and a friend with whom I had lots of enjoyable times, and my late cat, Mii, who was with me for five years.

In writing Japanese names, this book follows East Asian practice: surnames precede first names. Names that appear according to Western practice in archival records, published writings, and English-language sources have been left as published, with first names preceding surnames and without macrons. I use pseudonyms for the women who engaged in prostitution and the men related to them, except those whose real names have already been published widely in books, articles, and newspapers. Pseudonyms are also used for prostitutes and the men related to them who appear in the titles of primary sources, including the records of the Japanese Foreign Ministry, United States federal courts, civil and criminal courts in Pacific Coast cities, and newspaper articles; therefore, readers who wish to locate the documents and articles should rely on such information as case numbers and dates, not titles.

Japanese Prostitutes in the
North American West,
1887–1920

Introduction

Yamada Waka, a pioneering feminist writer in Taisho and Showa Japan, was born in a small farming-fishing village near Yokosuka, Kanagawa Prefecture, in 1879. Her parents produced sugar beets and other products to feed their eight children. As the fourth daughter of a struggling farmer, higher education was beyond her reach. After graduation from elementary school, she started working with her parents in the fields while caring for other children, and at the age of sixteen, she married Araki Hichijirō (also pronounced "Shichijiro"), a commodity broker in Yokosuka, who was ten years her senior. At the time of her marriage, her eldest brother, Fukutarō, was struggling to keep the lands he had inherited from their father. Yamada often implored Hichijirō to give financial assistance to her brother, but he ignored her pleas.[1] Yamada did not write about this incident publicly, but in a fictional story she wrote later in her life, she created a female character exactly like herself who married a commodity broker at sixteen. In her description of the protagonist's husband, Yamada wrote: "Moneymaking is the only purpose in his life. He had nothing to think about except money. . . . When the woman's family was struggling to keep their remaining land, he indicated that if [she] asked him for a loan, he would not mind divorcing the wife who had shared their life for almost twenty years."[2] The marriage ended shortly afterward, and she moved to Yokohama, a growing international port city, alone.[3]

In her semiautobiographical essay, Yamada wrote that after coming to Yokohama, she met a "woman from America" telling stories

3

of riches in the United States where her husband had "reached high social standing." Yamada followed her directions and crossed the Pacific alone around 1897.[4] The ship first carried her to Victoria, British Columbia, where she met the husband of the woman in Yokohama, "a good-looking gentleman slightly over forty years old," and was then taken to Seattle. After arriving at "an impressive seven-story building," she was assigned "a room with a bed, table, and portable stove" and began to work as a prostitute under the name "Oyae of Arabia."[5] "Yae" was the name of her elder sister, the second-oldest in the family after Fukutarō.[6]

At the end of the nineteenth century, Seattle was a growing regional center of trade and commerce, catering to the needs of migrant laborers at farms, lumber mills, construction sites, and mines in the region. Prostitution was rampant, with the tacit consent of local authorities, and women were coming to the city from all parts of the country and the world. With the advent of regular transportation services between Seattle and Asian ports, Japanese migrants were beginning to increase in the city, and Japanese women were found in brothels in the southern part of town. In the red-light district crowded with men and women of diverse ethnic origins, Yamada soon become one of the most popular "white birds" in the quarter, serving primarily white customers. A local Japanese-language newspaper praised her beauty, portraying her as Takao, one of the most famous prostitutes in Japan during the Tokugawa period, and describing her popularity in a *tanka*: "Yae cherry blossom is in full bloom; delighted men are crowding around her."[7] Despite her reputation, she never viewed her days in Seattle in a positive light. In her autobiographical essay, she wrote: "For some years after [becoming a prostitute], I had lived without knowing anything about your country, not to mention the political system or the ethnic backgrounds of the people, only getting a corner of your country dirty like a worm."[8]

After working for about five to six years as a prostitute, she left that life behind. In 1903, she escaped from the Seattle brothel with Tachii Nobusaburō, a newspaperman from San Francisco, which became a well-known scandal in the Japanese immigrant community in the prewar period.[9] After moving to that city, however, she was sold by Tachii to a local brothel for $150. She escaped from her brothel once again and entered the Chinese Mission Home, a Presbyterian mission built primarily for former Chinese and Japanese prostitutes. During the two years of her stay there, Yamada learned English and sewing, key skills that missionaries considered essential for former prostitutes' economic independence. She also accepted Christianity as a guiding principle in her life. She adopted a new English name, "Hanna," which indicated her determination to start afresh, leaving her former life in brothels behind.[10] Yamada recalled:

> Living among the Japanese in America, I searched for a world where men, animals devouring the flesh of women, could not set foot. I escaped into a kind of convent that forbade men to enter. After moving in, I was told that it was a Christian church. . . . [In Chinese Mission Home] I could learn letters which, I had thought, belonged to the world removed from us. And it was the Bible [from which I learned]. When I was taught that God, who ruled the world, existed and that all people were equal in the eyes of God, I looked up at the sky and forgot everything on the earth for a while.[11]

Affirming women's equality with men in the eyes of a transcendent God, she devoted the rest of her time in Chinese Mission Home to rescue work in order to free other Japanese women from brothel-keepers. She also met a local Japanese teacher of English, Yamada Kakichi, and married him. When the earthquake hit San Francisco in 1906, the couple decided to return to Japan.

Beginning a new life in Tokyo, Yamada joined a foremost feminist group, *Seitō* (Blue Stocking), dedicated to the enhancement of women's status in Japan. Using language skills that she had learned from her husband, she translated the works of Western writers, including Ellen Key and Olive Schreiner, and published several books and articles by herself. In 1931, she became a columnist for *Tokyo asahi*, a leading newspaper in Japan, answering readers' questions on topics ranging from family affairs to love and sexual problems. From the 1920s to the 1930s, as a strong supporter of the idea of the "protection of motherhood" (*bosei hogo*), she played a substantial role, along with major figures in Taisho-era women's movements such as Hiratsuka Raichō, in the passage of the Mother and Child Protection Act of 1937.[12] She established the Hatagaya Woman's Home and Nursery School in 1939, and after World War II, she worked with women who had been selling their bodies to American soldiers, providing them with domestic skills and preparing them for marriage, very similar to what she had learned at the Chinese Mission Home in San Francisco earlier in the century.[13]

When I learned about Yamada's life, I was puzzled about how it would fit into the standard narrative of Japanese immigration history with which I was familiar—Japanese men came to the United States to work; after establishing themselves as farmers or small-business owners, they decided to stay and sent for their wives from Japan; Nisei children were born, and Japanese American families and communities developed. In this narrative of migration and settlement, Japanese women were described primarily as wives and mothers who faithfully supported their husbands' work, caring for their children while performing their daily chores, with some working outside the home, participating in a variety of social activities, and contributing to the welfare of the family and the development of the ethnic community. Like these immigrant women, Yamada was born in a rural village and may have dreamed of various opportunities in America. She did not come, however, within a well-defined migration stream sustained by the emotional bonds of families and friends. She first moved alone to a nearby city to work and earn money for her family, and her transpacific journey was arranged by procurers who intended to turn her into a prostitute. Her migration pattern was more similar to those of working-class women of the Meiji period (1868–1912) toiling in textile factories and licensed brothels and of Japanese sex workers serving laborers and soldiers in the Pacific Rim region.

Yamada's story also directed my attention to the diversity in the experiences of Japanese women in both the immigrant community and larger American society at the turn of the century. After coming to the United States, she lived and worked in a social space set apart from those of other Japanese women, and the particular hardships she experienced as a racial minority in the red-light district and as a "woman engaged in an ugly trade" (shūgyōfu) despised by other Japanese immigrants shaped her decision to break away from her master or boyfriend, turn to an American religious institution (a Protestant rescue home), accept Christianity, and devote her life to the improvement of Japanese women's status first in America and later in her homeland. I wished to know more about this marginalized group of women in Japanese American history. What was it like to live and work as alien prostitutes of Asian ancestry in a multiracial world of Western prostitution? What was their place in the Japanese immigrant community that was beginning to develop in Pacific Coast cities? How did other Japanese prostitutes and barmaids engage with various religious and legal institutions in North American society?

These "Other" women have been a largely invisible or hidden subject in Japanese American and Canadian history. Nonetheless, their historical experiences are important because they not only serve as a critique of the "settler" narrative in Japanese immigration history but also reveal the significant role these deviant women played in the development of the Japanese ethnic community and gender systems in the North American West at the turn of the twentieth century.

Finally, Yamada's life as a reformer whose work expanded across the Pacific provides an opportunity to think about her place in the history of Japanese American social reform. When she was working as a helper in the Chinese Mission Home from 1903 to 1905, antiprostitution reform was growing in the Japanese immigrant community. The reformers attempted to eliminate gambling and prostitution in their community and demonstrate their ability to assimilate by adopting American or Canadian values. Their goal was to improve the general image of the Japanese among middle-class whites and smooth the process of Japanese adjustment to North American society as settlers. Initially, Yamada's work appeared to be part of this broader immigrant reform movement, but her feminist approach to the problem of prostitution set her apart from immigrant reformers whose primary concern was the sound development of the Japanese ethnic community. How did Japanese reformers handle the issue of gender oppression within their community while dealing with racism in American and Canadian societies? Although reformers were motivated by their particular concerns as a racial minority in Canada and the United States, were they also influenced by the work of other reformers who were organizing against licensed prostitution in Japan and trying to stop sex workers' overseas migration during the same period? Yamada's life as a prostitute and a reformer on both sides of the Pacific challenges scholars to think about Japanese immigrant social reform broadly, especially in relation to various developments occurring in the ethnic community, North American societies, and the Pacific region.

Thanks to Yuji Ichioka and other historians who since the 1960s have painstakingly collected and examined Japanese-language sources related to Japanese immigrants, we now know more about their lives before World War II: their work experiences in various industries, their fight against discriminatory laws at the state and federal levels, and their strong connection with their homeland government.[14] Since the 1980s, social historians have shed light on family lives and gender issues within the ethnic community by drawing on oral histories.[15] More recently, a new generation of historians has shown the internal dynamics of the Japanese immigrant community, exploring class, status, and gender conflict within it.[16] We view Japanese immigrants no longer as simply victims of oppression or a primordial folk who clung to their cultural traits but as individuals with varied identities and emotions—lonely migrant laborers struggling to achieve economic independence and gain manhood, parents concerned with the future of their American-born children, members of ethnic organizations and labor unions trying to advance the welfare of fellow countrymen, men and women from marginalized groups in Japanese society who wished to make new lives in North America, and sometimes ardent nationalists struggling to find a legitimate place for themselves amid changing international relations during times of war. All these studies show that scholars must approach the history of Japanese immigrants from the immigrants' perspectives. This is the basic approach I follow in analyzing the experiences of Japanese prostitutes in North America.[17]

From early on, however, I became aware of the difficulty of my undertaking. Japanese sex workers left few written accounts. The records written by those who opposed their existence were not a great help.[18] I began by collecting the accounts of individual prostitutes and barmaids that surfaced in vernacular newspapers published in Pacific Coast Japanese communities in the early twentieth century and information about smugglers, procurers, and alleged prostitutes prosecuted for violating the laws in Japan and North America in the records of the Japanese Foreign Ministry in Tokyo and in U.S. federal court case files in Seattle and San Francisco. As I exhausted these records, I began to look at local sources in various West Coast cities— the records of Protestant mission homes, police reports, divorce court files, marriage and death records, census manuscripts, and probate files of former prostitutes. As the research progressed in Japan, Canada, and the United States, I noticed that some individuals appeared in multiple records, and by linking these fragmentary pieces of information together, I could reconstruct the lives of these men and women to a fair extent. This type of record-linkage approach, which has often been used by social historians since the 1970s, appeared to be useful in exploring the lives of Japanese sex workers from childhood to adulthood and the sequence of events that affected their identity.

But this is easier said than done. The record-linkage approach often proves successful when scholars focus on a single community in a region, because the concentration of sources in one place makes it possible to trace individuals from property records to company payrolls to census manuscripts to newspaper articles and to describe changes in their lives over time. In the case of Japanese prostitutes, sources were scattered throughout Japan, Canada, and the United States, and the women moved constantly from country to country and from one city to another in order to avoid falling into the hands of law-enforcement officials. Thus, the historical analysis of these migrant sex workers' individual lives and actions presents a particular challenge, and it is necessary to pay careful attention to the different racial, gender, cultural, and class dynamics of each society or country where they stayed. But this individual-level analysis provides an opportunity to apply transnational and comparative approaches to explore how these factors actually played out in each person's life.

The next challenge was how to present Japanese women's experiences. Scholars' views of prostitution or prostitutes have varied considerably and have changed over time. In the study of prostitution in the American West and western Canada, scholars informed by second-wave feminism corrected the earlier idealized vision of the prostitute as an independent woman living in luxury or "the hooker with a heart of gold," revealing various forms of violence against and exploitation of women engaged in prostitution.[19] In the past two decades or so, post-feminist or third-wave feminist scholars have had different takes on prostitution, arguing that in the "real world," women do not always see sex as a sign of men's domination over women; rather, they see sexuality as a source of self-confidence and pleasure or a means of expressing their own selves and identities.[20] Indeed, recent sociological and anthropological studies of prostitution based on firsthand contact with sex workers demonstrate that many women do not see themselves as victims of coercion and instead regard prostitution as a form of work in which they simply exchange their services for money.[21] In the study of this kind of sensitive subject, we cannot be completely free of our own biases or the influence of public debates in our own age, or as Marion S. Goldman writes, "we are members of our own culture."[22]

Yet, while acknowledging the need to be engaged with actual women living in society and to take their words seriously, it is also important in a historical study to approach the experiences of

Japanese prostitutes within the context of time and their lives. To do so, we need to read sources "against the grain" by paying full attention to the biases of their authors and the contexts in which these sources were produced. This is especially important because my sources were written mostly by men of power who were often critical of these women. But a critical use of these sources makes it possible not only to show male assumptions about the prostitutes but also to describe their behavior in detail and find some clues to understanding why they took (and did not take) certain actions.

Still, I must acknowledge the limits of my research and analysis, because this kind of approach requires scholars to be not only objective but also knowledgeable about life experiences *as women*. As feminist writer Yamazaki Tomoko, the author of influential biographies of former overseas Japanese prostitutes, writes: "I am not one, of course, who thinks women only are qualified to write women's history: I have no such prejudice. I believe, naturally, that men can participate positively as readers and researchers of women's history; but I am convinced that, where the study of prostitution is concerned, there are a great many points which only a woman is in a position to clear up."[23] This passage often came to mind at various stages of research and writing, and considering the lack of these qualities on my part, I have found it necessary to address this issue seriously. At the same time, however, as Joan Wallach Scott writes, a history of women is a study of the social relationship between women *and* men.[24] Therefore, by paying attention to the experiences of men involved in the lives of prostitutes, scholars can be in a better position to reexamine various assumptions about these women and develop a deeper understanding of their lives.

A history of Japanese prostitutes in North America is also a study of migration, and I benefited from analytical perspectives offered by a growing number of transpacific and transborder migration studies in Asian American history. First in the 1980s, sociologists Lucie Cheng and Edna Bonacich offered a broad theoretical model of Asian migration, illuminating Western imperialism as the structural cause of underdevelopment in Asia and labor immigration from these regions to the United States.[25] Subsequently, historians empirically demonstrated the transnational flows of goods, people, and information between migrants' native villages in Asia and their overseas communities that continued to influence Asian American experiences over generations.[26] More recently, studies of Asian migrations across the

U.S.-Canadian border have illuminated the role of non-state actors—ethnic merchants, labor recruiters, shipping companies—in circumventing legal and racial restrictions and aiding migrants entering the country, working in various industries, and contributing to the capitalist development of the North American West.[27] These studies pointed to the need to examine Japanese sex workers' journeys as part of social and economic developments on both sides of the Pacific and pay close attention to the role of human networks of varying scale that expanded across national boundaries.

In the course of gathering sources relating to Japanese sex workers' backgrounds, I also recognized the importance of understanding the social and cultural contexts of the country they had left behind. Many Japanese women who became prostitutes in North America entered the trade via processes similar to those by which Japanese women began working in brothels in Japan, and the conventions and customs in Japan's pleasure quarters influenced the organization of Japanese sex businesses and their initial development in North America. Therefore, I decided to examine the history of Japanese prostitution in the North American West not only in a local context but also in relation to Japanese women's domestic and international labor migration and the development of ideologies about women and sexuality in Meiji Japan.

Indeed, recent studies have revealed the ways in which our understanding of Japanese immigrants can be advanced by taking the social and cultural contexts of Meiji Japan seriously. Members of the former samurai class, for instance, viewed Christianity as an attractive alternative to the Neo-Confucian ethics that had sustained the social and class system in the earlier Tokugawa period. Some migrated to the United States to learn about Western cultures and acquire Western knowledge, and many maintained the high social and economic standing that they had been losing in Japan.[28] Those in the former outcaste class in Japan moved to North America not only for economic reasons but also with an expectation that they would have more freedom from various constraints that continued to oppress them in Japan despite the Meiji government's promise to modernize the country by abolishing feudal practices.[29] Similarly, the meaning of the word "opportunities" for Japanese women who became prostitutes in the North American West will become more clear by examining their experiences in light of their premigration backgrounds in Japan.

Finally, the study of the Japanese context provides an opportunity to examine Japanese prostitutes' experiences in North America from a cross-national comparative perspective. As I learned more about prostitution in Meiji Japan, I wondered how Yamada Waka's life would have turned out if she had not migrated to the American West but had worked in a licensed brothel in Tokyo. Were there any advantages or disadvantages to working in North America? Did reformers respond to the problem of prostitution similarly or differently in Japan and in West Coast Japanese migrant communities? By exploring these questions, I could learn much about the nature of Japanese immigrant prostitution, sex workers' lives, and antiprostitution reform in the North American West. Indeed, through these analyses, I realized that transnational and comparative methods are not mutually exclusive but are rather complementary in the historical study of prostitution, international migration, and social movements.[30]

In this book, I argue that Japanese prostitution was an indispensable part of Meiji Japan's modernization, the growth of transpacific Japanese labor migration, and the development of the Japanese ethnic community and gender systems in the North American West. Although Japanese women engaged in the trade were exploited and despised by powerful men and women in Japan, the immigrant community, and North American societies, they struggled to survive and resisted oppression by various means available in the period and places where they lived. By applying a transpacific and comparative perspective to this previously "hidden" economy in Japanese North America, I will show that Japanese women could show levels of agency and in doing so paved the way for working-class immigrant women in the twentieth century.

Chapter 1 provides a broad overview of the social, economic, and political transformations in Japan and the Pacific Rim region that gave rise to Japanese women's domestic and international labor migration during the Meiji period. In the 1880s and 1890s, Japan witnessed growing poverty in rural areas, the rapid growth of manufacturing industries in cities, and increasing rural-urban migration. In this context, numerous young women left their villages, moved to cities, and worked in textile mills and licensed brothels under long-term labor contracts to help their struggling families back home. Outside the country, European and Japanese colonial expansion in the Pacific transformed the region, leading to increased demand for labor in mines and on plantations and battlefields that promoted mass migrations of men to these areas. As the Japanese began to join the international labor migration in the 1880s, Japanese women moved to Southeast Asia, the Russian Far East, and Japanese colonies and worked as prostitutes. As part of these processes, the North American West emerged as a major destination for Japanese women.

The second chapter shifts the level of analysis from the global to the local, exploring the social origins of North American Japanese prostitutes and their premigration experiences in Japan. The key documents for this analysis are the records of more than three hundred individuals (including procurers and prostitutes) gleaned from official reports held in the Diplomatic Record Office in Tokyo. Through the reports, this section first identifies the geographic origins of Japanese prostitutes in North America. Next, following in the path of similar studies by Barton, Kamphoefner, Chen, Kodama, Hayashi, and Geiger, I examine the economic, social, and cultural contexts of these prefectures and villages of origin by consulting local Japanese-language sources.[31] These analyses enabled me to explore various issues concerning class and status in Japan at the time when the women left their native villages. I argue that in doing so, Japanese women's migration to the North American West was a means of dealing with social and cultural pressures from the societies in which they were living.

Chapter 3 examines the actual mechanism of recruiting Japanese women and transporting them to North America for prostitution. Federal laws had not been effective at preventing the entry of procurers and prostitutes until the 1890s, and lax inspection at the U.S.-Canadian border resulted in a steady flow of Japanese women and procurers via Canada. Municipal government officials viewed prostitution as a necessary evil and tolerated it in segregated areas of their towns for the growth of cities. Structural factors alone, however, do not explain why Japanese prostitution expanded in the West. Japanese procurers and women evaded Japanese, Canadian, and U.S. officials by disguising themselves as married couples and using collaborators' passports; they filed lawsuits against federal officials if denied entry; they developed organized networks across the Pacific to facilitate systematic transportation of Japanese women to North America. By examining the various strategies procurers used, this chapter stresses the importance of human agency and networks in the growth of Japanese women's transpacific and transborder migration.

The fourth chapter reconstructs the social worlds of Japanese prostitutes in the North American West, showing that the actual operation of the trade and sex workers' lives were far more complex than
the stereotypical image of Asian prostitutes as "slave girls," as they
were characterized by the American and Canadian press. Some Japanese women worked in hotel rooms and served white, Chinese, and
Japanese men; others worked in bar-restaurants, entertaining Japanese customers with their artistic skills. Some worked in brothels in
order to send money home or repay their debts to employers; others
migrated originally as brides and later entered the trade due to economic hardships or for other personal reasons. The overall picture of
most Japanese sex workers' lives is grim. Without legal regulation of
the trade, women often suffered work-related losses: theft, holdup,
pregnancy, and violence inflicted by their customers. Before the rise
of antiprostitution reforms among Japanese settlers in the 1910s,
Japanese reformers were not powerful enough to prevent exploitative employers from manipulating the accounts of Japanese women's
debts or forcing them to work as long as possible. Corrupt local police
were indifferent to the suffering of women in brothels and permitted brothel-keepers to operate their houses as they saw fit. Japanese
women had little access to better work outside the red-light district
because of racism and their lack of industrial and language skills.

Chapter 5 explores the forms of Japanese women's responses to
sexual and economic exploitation from a local and comparative perspective. In North America, Japanese prostitutes turned to Protestant
rescue homes and filed for divorce from pimp-husbands; in Japan,
prostitutes organized against exploitation and asserted their right to
change their trade legally. The point in this chapter is not to play
down the reality of the exploitation of women; neither is it to characterize prostitutes' assertive actions in North America as a sign of
their "assimilation." By examining their responses from a comparative perspective, I will demonstrate Japanese women's growing social
independence through sex work and the central role of the state in
shaping the living and working conditions of sex workers.

The final chapter explores the emergence of antiprostitution reform
on the West Coast from a cross-national and comparative perspective. The antiprostitution movement in the American West emerged
in the 1890s from a transpacific dialogue between reformers in Japan
and on the West Coast over the implications of Japanese prostitution
for Japan's international reputation. As Japanese immigration history

entered a new phase in the 1910s, however, antiprostitution reformers became more concerned about the welfare of Japanese settlers and American-born children, whereas reformers in Japan strengthened their ties with the Japanese state, excluding prostitutes from the public sphere in order to protect Japan's national honor. Meanwhile, the center of overseas Japanese prostitution shifted to Japanese colonies in East Asia, and in the eyes of Japanese reformers, prostitution became a domestic issue at home and its colonies. By revealing the convergence and divergence of Japanese antiprostitution reforms from transnational and comparative perspectives, I will show the significance of Japanese antiprostitution reform not only in the history of Japanese immigrants in the North American West but also in the history of prostitution in Japan and Japanese expansion in the Pacific region.

CHAPTER I

Across the Pacific Rim

Global Dimensions of Japanese Prostitution in the North American West

During the Meiji period (1868–1912), with the increased mobility of capital and labor within the Pacific economies, the Japanese joined the international labor migration, and the numbers of Japanese sex workers began to increase in various cities and industrial centers across the Pacific Rim region: Tokyo, Honolulu, San Francisco, Juneau, Vladivostok, Port Arthur, Seoul, Shanghai, Singapore, and Thursday Island. At the height of the migration, in 1910, official Japanese documents recorded more than nineteen thousand Japanese women engaged in sex work outside the country.[1] In each region, Japanese women not only served the sexual needs of laborers and soldiers but also constituted integral parts of local economic and social life. This chapter provides a broad overview of the emergence of Japanese sex workers' global migration, with a particular focus on the history of prostitution in Japan, social and economic transformations in Meiji Japan, and industrial and colonial expansion in four major Pacific regions. This analysis illuminates broader cultural and economic forces behind the growth of Japanese women's international migration and the distinctive multiracial character of prostitution in the North American West.

THE DEVELOPMENT OF LICENSED PROSTITUTION IN JAPAN

Japanese women who served men sexually as part of their work appear in sources dating as early as the eighth century. The *Collection of Ten Thousand Leaves (Manyōshū)*, the earliest known anthology of poems, includes accounts of women called *ukareme* in the imperial office of Kyushu who served at dinner, performed dances, and attended officers in their bedrooms,[2] but women who exchanged sexual services primarily as a means of making a living appear in historical records in the tenth century.[3] Beginning in the mid-eleventh century, the struggle between the Taira and Minamoto clans continued for more than a century, and countless wives and daughters on the losing sides were forced into prostitution. In 1193, in order to ease the violent temper of samurai on the battlefield, the Kamakura shogunate (1192–1333) created an official position, the Steward for Prostitutes (*Yūkun Bettō*), to regulate prostitution for soldiers. The Ashikaga shogunate (1336–1573) followed the Kamakura system, hiring prostitutes to console samurai officers on the battlefield. In addition, for the first time in history, the shogunate began to collect taxes from brothel operators in order to make up for a deficit in revenue. The continuous conflict between warlords finally came to an end in the late sixteenth century, and Toyotomi Hideyoshi, chief adviser to the emperor, established the first pleasure quarter (*yūkaku*) in Osaka in 1585 and another in Kyoto in 1589, intended to serve traveling merchants and samurai officers.[4]

An even more organized system of prostitution appeared after Tokugawa Ieyasu came to power in 1603. Concerned about the increasing number of unlicensed prostitutes in Edo (present-day Tokyo), Ieyasu ordered the establishment of a pleasure quarter, Yoshiwara, in 1618, in order to drive scattered prostitutes into one place. It was part of the authorities' broader effort to maintain public order and control crime. The shogunate required brothel-keepers to report the number and names of prostitutes and strictly punished the managers of public baths who hired prostitutes secretly. As the shogunate tightened its control over the trade, the boundaries between legal and illegal prostitution became more rigid. After the great fire of 1657, the shogunate moved the pleasure quarter to an eastern suburb of Edo and renamed it New Yoshiwara. Some thirty-five pleasure quarters appeared in other parts of the country, and the number of prostitutes reached two thousand in New Yoshiwara and eight hundred in Shimabara, in Kyoto.[5] Furthermore, with the increase in traffic during the Genroku period (1688–1703), numerous commercial villages (*shukueki*) sprang up along major roads, and increasing numbers of waitress-prostitutes (*meshimori onna*) were hired at inns not only to serve at tables but also to meet the sexual needs of travelers.[6]

Japanese women's sex work operated within the Tokugawa system of regulation supported by the Neo-Confucian concept of patriarchy. First introduced by Buddhist monks in the Middle Ages, Neo-Confucianism had become firmly established as the official ideology of the shogunate in the Tokugawa period and stressed commoners' obligations to feudal lords and children's subordination to the family head. The precepts of filial piety and women's inferiority to men developed into the concept of *ie* (family) that permitted parents to sell their daughters to brothels for the maintenance of the household.[7] Within this ideological framework, women who became prostitutes were considered filial daughters contributing to the welfare of the household, not promiscuous, greedy women, as often described in writings on prostitutes in Europe and the United States. That parents handed their daughters over to recruiters in exchange for advances and that girls worked in brothels in order to pay off their parents' debts may give an impression that these women were de facto "sex 'slaves'" who had no control over their lives during their term of service. But as Amy Stanley writes, women and their families could appeal to the shogunate for protection and fair treatment in the workplace so long as the women presented themselves as filial daughters who were sacrificing temporarily for their parents.[8]

Over the eighteenth and the nineteenth century, however, the scale of prostitution expanded in the context of the development of a money economy, and the discourse on prostitutes underwent significant change. Brokers (*zegen*) traveled throughout the country recruiting young women from impoverished families. More prostitutes were sold and resold between brothels in far-off places as sexual commodities, which made it difficult for parents to negotiate contracts with brothel-keepers. Officials became more concerned with the economic impact of prostitution on the local economy than with the interests of prostitutes and their families. As prostitutes became more visible in the public space with the proliferation of prostitution and the increase in consumption and traffic, they were constructed as selfish, autonomous women who represented negative aspects of market relations. In order to survive, impoverished peasants and urban dwellers sold their daughters to brothels, and the women were trapped in debt bondage for many years.[9]

After the opening of Japan to the West, however, the taken-for-granted system of public brothels was called into question by an international incident, known as the Maria Luz Incident. In June 1872, a Peruvian ship entered the port of Yokohama carrying 230 Chinese laborers bound for Peru. One laborer jumped into the sea and asked an English captain for help. After obtaining evidence that the laborers had been abused, British chargé d'affaires R. G. Watson advised the

Japanese government to investigate the matter, indicating the inhu-
manity of the conditions on board. To demonstrate Japan's "civilized" status, the Kanagawa District Court ordered that the laborers
be returned safely to China by the Qing government. But the attorney
who represented the Peruvian minister to Japan protested, claiming
that because the Japanese government officially approved the legality of contracts that bound women into service in brothels for six
to eight years, it had no right to criticize the captain's ill treatment
of indentured laborers. The Japanese government refuted his claim,
but this incident embarrassed a group of "enlightened" bureaucrats.
Shortly thereafter, the government banned the selling of women and
ordered the release of all prostitutes and geisha throughout Japan.
After this incident, the Council of State banned the selling and buying
of women and ordered the release of all prostitutes, geisha, and "other
indentured servants" throughout the country.[10]

The liberation order disrupted the lives of men and women in the
pleasure quarters. After being released from brothels, some former
prostitutes returned to the homes of their parents, who were happy to
take back their daughters without the obligation to clear their debts.
But those who had been dissociated from their families had no place
to go; many became destitute on the streets. Brothel-keepers complained to the Tokyo government about this sudden change in policy,
reporting that liberated women began to practice clandestine prostitution or turned to former customers and that even some who had
returned to their families had been sold to other brothels.[11] Obviously, government officials, whose primary concern was Japan's international reputation, paid little attention to what the liberation order
meant for women engaged in prostitution.

The authorities responded to these immediate problems by reorga-
nizing the Tokugawa system of licensed prostitution so that the new
system would not violate the liberation order. A year after the order, in
December 1873, Tokyo governor Ōkubo Ichiō noticed a rapid increase
in the number of unlicensed prostitutes throughout the city and established new rules stating that women who "wish[ed] to work as prostitutes" would be licensed to practice and requiring them to register
with the local police, pay monthly taxes, and undergo periodic medical examinations. Osaka followed Tokyo's lead, making similar rules
that acknowledged the existence of brothels.[12] These new regulations
may have "modernized" the Japanese system of public brothels by
redefining prostitution as a trade based on mutual agreement between

prostitutes and brothel-keepers (workers and employers), but national leaders' view of prostitution as a necessary evil never changed. The authorities continued to permit poor parents to sell their daughters to brothels in exchange for money, and women continued to be trapped in a system of debt bondage.

POVERTY AND MIGRATION

In exploring the roots of Japanese prostitution overseas, one must also understand the broad socioeconomic changes during the Meiji period that created the context in which the Japanese began to migrate overseas. Japan's population increased from 35 million to 45 million between 1880 and 1900. Widespread agrarian poverty, together with rapid industrialization and the existing tradition of *dekasegi* (seasonal work away from home), induced small-scale farmers to send their sons and daughters to industrial centers in order to supplement family incomes. Japanese migration to foreign countries was an extension of labor migration at home in the early stages of industrialization during the 1880s and 1890s.[13]

After the Meiji Restoration of 1868, Japan's new leaders embarked on a program of rapid economic growth in an effort to secure financial independence from foreign powers, including Britain, France, the Netherlands, Russia, and the United States; however, the burden fell on the shoulders of farmers. In 1873, the government established a new national land tax, abolishing all tax systems that had been in effect under Tokugawa rule. The new rate was fixed at 3 percent of the assessed yield of the land. Landowners no longer paid tax in kind (in rice) but in cash. This meant that if crop prices fell, farmers had to sell more crops in order to pay the fixed amount of tax every year. The land tax became a stable source of revenue for the government, but the farmers' lives became increasingly susceptible to fluctuations in commodity prices in the market.[14]

At the outset, the inflationary trend during the 1870s benefited the agrarian sector. Government spending increased over the decade, including 86 million yen to pay stipends to former samurai between 1870 and 1874 and 41 million yen to suppress the Satsuma Rebellion of 1877, the largest samurai uprising against the new regime. The government attempted to cover the shortage by issuing paper currency, yet the oversupply of cheap paper money caused price inflation that resulted in an actual reduction in the value of land taxes paid in cash. The decrease in land tax was a serious problem for the government because this tax accounted for more than half of the fiscal revenue during the 1870s. The price inflation was beneficial to farmers because they could sell crops at higher prices. The price of rice rose from 4,700 yen per *koku* (5.12 U.S. bushels) in 1876 to 10,200 yen in 1880. Farmers enjoyed a temporary prosperity toward the end of the decade.[15]

In the early 1880s, however, the government's inadequate response to inflation led to the devastation of the agrarian sector. In 1881, Finance Minister Matsukata Masayoshi adopted a belt-tightening policy. The government withdrew paper money from the market, hoping that this would curb inflation and bring the price level back to what it had been before the Satsuma Rebellion of 1877. However, the sudden withdrawal of money from circulation caused serious deflation. During the first half of the 1880s, agricultural commodity prices decreased by 52 percent, and small-scale farmers suffered. In order to survive, farmers borrowed money, usually from landlords, but failure to pay off the debts often led to foreclosure on their lands. Between 1883 and 1890, some 368,000 people lost their land, and a large surplus agricultural population emerged in rural areas. The landless farmers began to work for landlords as tenants.[16] Numerous peasants responded by organizing collective protests against landlords, moneylenders, and prefectural governments, demanding reduction of taxes or deferment of their debts in the first half of the 1880s. These uprisings were often suppressed by the state and ended in failure. The two decades after 1883 witnessed a steady increase in the share of agricultural land under tenancy throughout the country (table 1.1).

The decline of the agrarian economy, however, coincided with a dramatic growth of manufacturing after the mid-1880s. Japan's manufacturing output more than doubled between 1890 and 1900. The adoption of steam power stimulated the expansion of mechanized industries: silk reeling, cotton spinning, mining, shipbuilding, and railroads. Thousands of people left their villages to work in factories and mines in industrial centers. Furthermore, the Meiji government abolished the feudal restriction on movement from one domain to another, and people began to move beyond prefectural boundaries in order to better their lives. Railway lines expanded significantly in the late 1880s, and the improved transportation system lowered the cost of moving goods and people, connecting rural villages to urban centers. In the three decades after 1885, rural farming regions—especially

TABLE 1.1. Japanese agricultural land under tenancy, 1873–1892

Year	Land under tenancy
1873	27.4 %
1883–84	35.9 %
1887	39.5 %
1892	40.2 %

Source: Furushima Toshio, *Shihonsei seisan no hatten to jinushisei* (Tokyo: Ochanomizu shobō, 1978), 191.

northern prefectures along the Sea of Japan—experienced a slight but steady decrease in population, whereas the population grew rapidly in urban areas (Tokyo and Osaka) and the northern mining region (Hokkaido).[17] Increasingly, peasants who had lost their land during the deflation sent their children to work in industrial centers for a limited period of time in order to supplement family incomes.

Thousands of young single women also bore a heavy burden, leaving their native villages to earn money elsewhere and contribute to the family economy. The largest industries that absorbed female labor during the Meiji period were silk reeling and cotton spinning. From the 1890s to 1913, Japan's silk output grew by 400 percent, about three-fourths of which was exported. Silk consistently made up 30 to 40 percent of Japan's exports throughout the Meiji period. By 1909, Japan produced 34 percent of the world's raw silk.[18] The cotton textile industry also grew at a similar pace. After the government abolished the protective tariff on raw cotton in 1896, textile industries began to rely on cheaper imported cotton from India and the United States, and cotton textile output and exports grew simultaneously. Japan's share of the Chinese cotton yarn market surpassed that of Britain in 1896 and reached 30 percent in 1899.[19] While men earned 0.25 yen a day in metalworking in 1892, women earned only 0.09 yen in cotton spinning and 0.13 yen in silk reeling.[20] By 1902, roughly 80 percent of wage earners in silk reeling and cotton spinning were women (table 1.2).

As industrialization progressed and the military expanded during the 1880s and 1890s, brothels increased steadily in urban areas, catering to growing numbers of workers and soldiers. In each town, the decision to establish military bases resulted in a sudden rise in land prices and the expansion of brothel quarters. The increase in local consumption and tax revenue helped local governments and

TABLE 1.2. Labor force in Japan, 1902

	Men	Women	Total
Textiles	32,699	236,457	269,156
Machine/tool manufacturing	33,379	983	34,362
Chemical engineering	38,615	43,683	82,298
Food and drink	16,837	13,316	30,153
Miscellaneous	20,729	11,579	32,308
Electric or gas utilities	475	21	496
Mining and refining	42,888	7,230	50,118
Total	185,622	313,269	498,891

Source: Gordon, *A Modern History of Japan*, 100.

businesses greatly, making them reluctant to see brothels abolished.[21] There were 3,156 licensed prostitutes in Tokyo in 1883; the number rose to 4,747 in 1887 and 6,834 in 1909.[22] After silk reeling (121,000 female workers in 1902) and cotton spinning (62,000 workers in 1902), licensed prostitution became the third-largest industry employing Japanese women.[23] The actual number of women engaged in prostitution must have been much greater if the countless women working as geisha, barmaids, and waitresses are included. The loans from recruiters, which were higher than those from factory agents, served as an incentive for impoverished parents to send their daughters to brothels rather than to textile factories.[24] U. G. Murphy, a Methodist missionary in Nagoya, estimated that in the peak years of 1898 and 1899, more than 50,000 women were working as licensed prostitutes in the country.[25] One cannot take these figures at face value because they come largely from reports compiled by opponents of prostitution; nevertheless, the sex industry did expand on an unprecedented scale in the context of rapid industrialization, urbanization, population increase, labor migration, and military expansion toward the end of the nineteenth century.

Despite the wish of some enlightened state officials to show that Japanese civilization was up to Western standards, municipal authorities throughout the country permitted practically all women to enter the trade so long as they did so "of their own will," and most national leaders believed that prostitution was necessary to protect the wives and daughters of "refined families." In an article published in the Tokyo newspaper *Jiji shinpō* in 1885, Fukuzawa Yukichi, a leading advocate of Japan's modernization programs, wrote that if brothels were closed in Tokyo, there would be increase in "illicit activities among the children of good families, or violation of lonely widows." Fukuzawa claimed that prostitutes were "great benefactors" who would "keep the animal instinct [of young men] under control." Faced with rapid industrialization and the growing urban male population, national leaders articulated the need for licensed brothels "for the preservation of order," while appealing to the anxiety of the emerging educated middle class, which was conscious of Japan's reputation outside the country.[26]

The liberal economic theory employed by state officials to justify licensed prostitution, that prostitution was a form of contract labor based on mutual agreement between willing individuals, diverted attention from the social and economic conditions that forced women into prostitution. In 1914, Yamamuro Gunpei, a leading figure in the Salvation Army, examined the background of one hundred prostitutes who entered its rescue mission in Tokyo. The majority of women came from the rural northeast and neighboring prefectures. Overall, twenty-four women grew up in "farming" families; fifteen women answered that their parents had "no job"; others were daughters of artisans or shopkeepers. Their primary reason for becoming prostitutes was to save impoverished parents and starving siblings. Fourteen women answered that "my parents had many children but no work"; twenty women decided to enter the trade because "my family had difficulty making ends meet after my father had passed away." Of course, these women had to prove economic need before they could be licensed in the first place, but their minimal educations indicate that poverty lay behind their decisions to enter the trade.[27]

Modernization affected daughters of middle- and upper-class families, and they embraced the mission of raising loyal sons for the nation as the ideology of *ryōsai kenbo* (good wives and wise mothers) was implemented as a guiding principle of women's education in the 1890s.[28] In agrarian villages, however, people's lives were still centered on farming, and basic social relations did not change much. Daughters had little say in choosing whom they would marry; after getting married, they shouldered the double burden of fieldwork and domestic chores, following the orders of their husbands and parents-in-law.[29] These family ideologies must be distinguished from similar ideologies that had existed in the earlier Tokugawa period; however, the pressure to contribute to the family welfare, together with poverty, continued to shape women's decisions to leave their households and work elsewhere during the Meiji period, serving as a basis for the persistence of the contractual labor system in both the textile and sex industries. As the revolution in trade and transportation linked Japan to lands overseas, the family ideology and rural poverty facilitated the migration of young Japanese women to foreign countries.[30]

THE GROWTH OF JAPANESE PROSTITUTION IN THE PACIFIC REGION

For Japanese women who had to shoulder much of the burden of the family economy, sex work abroad became a viable option. In 1907, when the Foreign Ministry conducted the first survey on the occupations of Japanese living overseas, eight thousand Japanese women were found to be engaged in prostitution and other related businesses (table 1.3). The migration of Japanese women to the North American West was part of Japanese sex workers' overseas migration in the Meiji period, composing about 16 percent of all overseas Japanese women in 1907.

Japanese women were first transported to Asian ports for sex work through commercial networks that had been established in the early modern period. In Nagasaki, Chinese merchants had formed liaisons with Japanese women since the Tokugawa period, and after formal trade relations between Shanghai and Nagasaki started in the 1850s, Japanese prostitutes' movement to the Chinese port increased. Around 1877, the first Japanese teahouse-brothels (tōyō sakan) opened, and Japanese women living in Shanghai increased, ranging in number from 460 to 600 in 1883 and 1884.[31] Growing Japanese prostitution in Shanghai, however, caught the attention of Japanese officials concerned about Japan's reputation. In 1884, Andō Tarō, the newly appointed Japanese consul in Shanghai, a devout Christian, summoned police from Japan, ordered them to arrest managers, and deported more than 500 prostitutes to Japan. The next year, the Council of State issued a proclamation granting the Japanese consul authority to deport women and men who violated the public order. As the regulation of prostitution became strict in Shanghai, the

TABLE 1.3. Japanese women in prostitution-related businesses overseas, 1907

	Restaurant businesses	Artistic accomplishments	Miscellaneous jobs	Total	Percentage
China, Railway Zone	1,117	283	1,457	2,857	36%
China, other areas	487	213	1,368	2,068	26%
Southeast Asia	32	5	1,069	1,106	14 %
Australia	0	0	37	37	Less than 1%
South Asia	0	0	218	218	3%
North America	642	260	381	1,283	16%
Latin America	6	0	49	55	Less than 1%
Europe	0	0	18	18	Less than 1%
Russia	43	0	290	333	4%
Total	2,327	761	4,887	7,975	100 %

Source: *Kaigai kakuchi zairyū honpōjin shokugyōbetu jinkōhyō*, 1907.
Note: This information comes from the Tables of Japanese Residents' Occupations Overseas (*Kaigai kakuchi zairyū honpōjin shokugyōbetsu jinkōhyō*), which the Japanese Foreign Ministry began to collate in 1907. One difficulty in using the tables is that they did not include the occupation category of "prostitutes" until 1912. Other categories that are most likely to include prostitutes are "artistic accomplishments" and "miscellaneous jobs." Yet extant sources suggest that a considerable number of Japanese women who had reported their occupation as "waitresses" or "barmaids" (*shakufu*) had engaged in prostitution in various capacities. Therefore, my estimate includes the number of women in "restaurant businesses" as well. The Railway Zone is composed of the areas along the southern extension of the Chinese Eastern Railway from Port Arthur to Changchun and all branches that Japan gained from Russia in the Portsmouth Treaty of 1905.

destinations of Japanese prostitutes shifted to the interior of China or other Asian port cities. The decline of prostitution in Shanghai led to its expansion in Southeast Asia.[32]

Three years after the raid in Shanghai, in 1887, there were already more than 100 Japanese prostitutes in Singapore.[33] During 1889, the Legislative Council, the local British administration that governed the Straits Settlements, issued 134 licenses to Japanese prostitutes.[34] Japanese women soon spread to various parts of Dutch East Indies and French Indochina; Japanese prostitutes numbered 300–400 in Sumatra, more than 200 in French Indochina, and over 100 in Borneo and its surrounding islands in 1897. Unlike typical overseas Japanese settlements, women constituted a majority of Japanese migrants in Southeast Asia, outnumbering men three to one.[35] By 1905, the Chinese Protectorate recorded 109 Japanese brothels and more than 600 Japanese prostitutes in Singapore.[36]

The growth of Japanese prostitution in Southeast Asia emerged within the context of European colonialism. In the early nineteenth century, Britain established its status as "the workshop of the world," producing industrial goods for other agricultural nations. By the mid-nineteenth century, however, the Netherlands and late-developing nations like France, Germany, and the United States began to compete with Britain in the market for manufactured goods and sources of primary products in Southeast Asia. Rubber, tin, cotton, sugar, and coffee were in great demand in advanced industrial nations, and the growth of large-scale plantations in Southeast Asia generated a demand for inexpensive labor.[37] Beginning in the 1870s, thousands of Chinese workers arrived in British Malaya, the vast majority of whom were male.[38] As an inevitable consequence of this overwhelming male population, hundreds of women were brought to the labor camps and plantations from poor regions in Asia to serve men sexually. Japanese prostitution expanded rapidly during this period.

Furthermore, the colonial government's prostitution policy provided a legal context for that growth. Most Japanese prostitutes in British Malaya received business licenses from the Legislative Council. From 1864 to 1869, the British Parliament passed the Contagious Disease Ordinance (CDO), which required prostitutes in garrison towns and seaports in Britain to register with the local police and undergo periodic checkups. The Legislative Council in Malaya followed the homeland government's lead, enacting similar laws in the Straits Settlements in 1870 to protect British soldiers from venereal diseases. In Britain, however, the anti-CDO movement led to the abolition of the ordinance in 1886 and in the Straits Settlements in 1888.[39] But the pro-regulation school of thought was strong among officials of the Legislative Council. British authorities prohibited British women from working as prostitutes but continued to tolerate Asian prostitution, requiring prostitutes to register and granting the Chinese Protectorate authority to force them to have regular medical checkups. The intent was to protect the health of British soldiers and the prestige of Britain, with no concern for the plight of Asian women.[40]

Similar racial double standards on the part of Western colonists contributed to the growth of Japanese prostitution in Hawaii. After the arrival of Boston merchant William Hooper in 1835, American investors transformed the islands into one of the largest sugar producers in the world. As in Southeast Asia, the emergence of a labor-intensive sugar industry created demand for a steady supply of cheap labor, which led to the recruitment of large numbers of workers from several Asian and European countries.[41] Eager to meet the immediate demand for labor, planters recruited largely male workers without concern for their family lives, and in 1882, the Hawaiian government, under the influence of planters, was restricting the entry of women by setting limits on the percentage of women in each ethnic group: 25 percent for Chinese and Japanese, 35–40 percent for Scandinavians, and 40 percent for Portuguese. The recruitment policy resulted in an imbalance in the sex ratio among the Chinese and Japanese. American planters' understanding of Europeans as settlers and Asians as "disposable" workers laid the groundwork for the growth of Asian prostitution in Hawaii.[42]

In contrast to other practices in the Pacific region, Japanese prostitution in Hawaii grew in tandem with large-scale Japanese labor migrations. Between 1885 and 1894, the Japanese government sent roughly thirty thousand government-sponsored contract laborers to Hawaiian plantations. In this early stage of migration, about 80 percent of the migrants were male.[43] The numbers of Japanese prostitutes increased shortly.[44] As in Southeast Asia, the local authorities made little effort to prevent prostitution, viewing it as a necessary outlet for male workers' sexual desires and a means of keeping them on the plantations. The police allowed women to work in segregated areas on condition that they had medical checkups and paid monthly dues to the doctors.[45] Police corruption and the absence of restrictions gave Japanese prostitution a boost. Henry E. Cooper, attorney general of Hawaii, reported the numbers of local prostitutes in 1898 as 29 Hawaiians, 5 "half-cast," 8 French, 2 British, 1 American, and 115 Japanese.[46]

The official survey recorded only 333 Japanese prostitutes in Russia in 1907, probably because of the lack of Japanese official manpower in the region, but sources suggest that Japanese prostitution prospered in the Russian Far East in the 1880s and 1890s. In order to populate the newly acquired Maritime and Amur Provinces, the Russian government granted each settler to the region 100 *desyatins* (about 270 acres) of land and exemption from taxes and conscription, and 243,000 Russian peasants migrated to the region between 1882 and 1907, mostly from the black-earth (high-fertility soil) provinces in the south-central part of Russia.[47] Rich natural resources—gold, fur-bearing animals, and agricultural land—brought thousands of Chinese merchants and laborers to the region beginning in the 1860s, and the construction of the Trans-Siberian Railway in 1891 attracted large numbers of male workers from China, Korea, and Japan. The Asian gender ratio was about four to one in the Maritime region and three to one in the Amur region in 1897.[48] Japanese prostitutes appeared in mining and railway towns in these provinces.[49]

Unlike European officials in Southeast Asia and American authorities in Hawaii, the Russian government formally acknowledged prostitution. In Vladivostok, the police required prostitutes to have checkups every day, and if asked by customers, prostitutes had to show doctors' certificates as evidence that they had been inspected. Brothel-keepers were ordered to make sure that prostitutes were living in healthful conditions, and any act of coercing women into prostitution was prohibited no matter how much money the women owed their employers. However, local policemen could be bribed easily, and lax law enforcement led to the widespread abuse and kidnapping of underage Japanese women.[50] The demand for Japanese prostitutes was consistently high among Chinese laborers, and as Russia began to increase its power in northeast Asia around the turn of the twentieth century, local officials permitted Japanese prostitutes to work in such tense border regions as Lushun in order to "console" Russian soldiers.[51]

Finally, Japanese prostitution developed in Korea and China as Japan began to exert strong control over the region toward the end of the nineteenth century. Japanese women appeared in Korea after the conclusion of the Kanghwa Treaty of 1876, mostly working as "barmaids" catering to Japanese men in their settlements. The Japanese consulate did not officially approve public brothels but did not forbid women from serving men sexually so long as they registered themselves as "barmaids."[52] During and after the Sino-Japanese War (1894–95) and the Russo-Japanese War (1904–5), large numbers of Japanese soldiers poured into Korea, and workers increased during the construction of major railroads. In 1895, the Government-General officially set up Japanese pleasure quarters in major cities including Seoul, Pusan, and Inchon. After Japan's annexation of

Korea in 1910, the Japanese administration introduced the domestic system of licensed prostitution, requiring prostitutes to register and undergo medical checkups. Japanese prostitutes numbered 2,940 in Korea in 1906 and 4,417 in 1910.[53]

Similarly, Japanese prostitution grew rapidly in Manchuria after the arrival of Japanese soldiers, and Japanese prostitutes appeared with the outbreak of the Russo-Japanese War. By the end of the war, in September 1905, there were almost 2,600 Japanese in southern Liaodong Peninsula, of whom 1,400 were prostitutes. Japanese prostitutes spread beyond southern Liaodong as well. In Dandong, a brothel was established for the exclusive use of soldiers around February 1905. Similar types of brothels for soldiers appeared in Yingkou and Tieling. The military government required all brothels to obtain business licenses, report the number and names of prostitutes to local military stations, and have prostitutes undergo periodic medical checkups. This system of regulation was basically the same as the one that existed in the homeland (naichi). Thus, the Japanese system of licensed prostitution was transplanted to Manchuria under military rule.[54]

It is also important to note that the regulation of women's sexuality in Japan's overseas territories in this period laid the groundwork for the growth of the system of so-called comfort women (ianfu) in Korea and China during World War II.[55] After the establishment of the Japanese Residency-General in 1905, the colonial government began to force Korean prostitutes to have medical checkups, which the women strongly opposed; some of them committed suicide. Thereafter, the police regulated Korean prostitution, and regulation became stronger and more institutionalized as Japan's control of the country increased in the 1910s.[56] In Manchuria, the Japanese military applied Japanese rules for regulating prostitution to Chinese women after they arrived in southern China during the Russo-Japanese War, requiring Chinese women to undergo periodic medical examinations. When civilian control of the government began in 1905, Japanese consulates took responsibility for regulating Chinese prostitution. As historian Fujinaga Takashi writes, these systems in which Japanese officials regulated the sexuality of colonized women during this period became the prototype of the comfort stations that increased rapidly at the height of Japanese militarism during World War II.[57]

THE EMERGENCE OF JAPANESE PROSTITUTION
IN THE NORTH AMERICAN WEST

Japanese prostitution in the North American West had some similarities to and key differences from practices in the Pacific region. Before discussing its growth in the late nineteenth century, it will be useful to briefly review the history of prostitution in the region. Since the sixteenth century, the vast land and natural resources had attracted English and French explorers to North America, and as these European traders moved into the interior along the rivers and into the mountains, trading posts became meeting places for European men and Native women in the North-Western Territory. Despite the characterization of these women as sexually promiscuous or slavish "squaw drudges" in European colonialist writings, historians have found that they played an important part in the development of diplomatic and trading relations between European and aboriginal traders in their roles as wives, interpreters, and guides, and, in the process, sex emerged as a key feature of these relationships. The evidence shows that aboriginal women were trafficked by aboriginal men and that some offered sexual services to European men as payment in trade; however, this cannot be categorized as "prostitution" in the conventional sense of the word as the simple exchange of money for sex. Historian Carolyn Podruchny writes that relations between European voyagers and aboriginal women were short-lived and casual and varied in local contexts. They could end when the men moved to the next post but could also develop into stable relationships; in some cases, European men handed off their indigenous women to other men in exchange for money, and the "traffick in sex" described in European colonialist writings became a reality.[58] Although these relations occurred in a region far east of the west coast of North America, they point to the key importance of sexuality in gender relations and socioeconomic development in a frontier society with few women.

By the second half of the nineteenth century, more people had moved into the western half of the North American continent, and prostitution became a larger, commercialized enterprise in the context of rapid economic development, labor migration, and military expansion. After the discovery of gold in the mid-nineteenth century, thousands of migrants moved to the West to work in mines and other sites where their labor was needed: farms, lumber camps, and cattle ranches. The construction of railroads from the 1860s through the 1890s, in both the United States and Canada, induced further labor migration from the East and Asia, and the recruitment of male laborers created an unbalanced sex ratio in the West, increasing the demand for prostitutes. Army bases also appeared on the U.S. western frontier in the post–Civil War years as part of the federal government's effort to protect western migrants from Indian attacks, leading to an increase in the military population. As cities grew in size and population, various service industries, including saloons, restaurants, and hotels, developed to meet the needs of growing numbers of residents, especially workers and soldiers away from their families. Prostitutes appeared in saloons, dance halls, and gambling houses; they also served men in cribs and shacks near labor camps and garrisons.[59]

Similar to the practices in Southeast Asia and Hawaii, prostitution was not formally acknowledged by the state governments in Canada and the United States, which left its regulation to local authorities. Prostitutes were driven off to segregated areas of western towns so that they would not disturb middle-class neighborhoods, and the police regularly arrested prostitutes and released them after collecting fines or bribes, which became an important source of revenue. The local business community, not only hotel and saloon owners but also bankers and restaurant managers, profited from prostitution and opposed an outright ban on the trade. In garrison towns, too, military officials, whose primary concern was the maintenance of order within the camp, tolerated soldiers' meetings with "camp followers" so long as the women did not interfere with the men's duties, become scandals, or contribute to the spread of venereal disease. Religious reformers and middle-class women, who wished to give stability to frontier lives, often succeeded in driving prostitutes out of public sites and keeping "innocent" wives and daughters away from their influence, and the local police responded by making occasional raids on brothels. But city officials and police rarely enforced laws rigorously enough to abolish prostitution or made efforts to decrease poverty, disease, and violence in the lives of prostitutes or increase jobs for women outside red-light districts.[60] Although prostitution rarely became an acceptable feature of civic life in western cities, the authorities acknowledged the sexual needs of men and found merit in sustaining the institution for its contribution to the economic and social development of the region.

The rapid economic growth and the expansion of the young male population drew women from all parts of the world who intended to earn money by serving lonely men. From the eastern part of the North American continent, white women followed male migrants to western cities and became the largest group of prostitutes in the West. Prostitutes from Europe, especially from France, also joined the migration to the North American frontier to seek more opportunities to earn money. As Chinese workers increased during the gold, silver, and copper strikes of the 1850s through the 1870s, procurers brought numerous Chinese women from poor rural areas to various labor camps of the American West to meet the sexual needs of Chinese men suffering from loneliness in a foreign land. Mexican women were prominent in southwestern states; black women also became a small but significant part of prostitution in the American West. Native American women had had sexual relations with white explorers and traders for a long period, but by the late nineteenth century, federal Indian policies had devastated the economic and cultural basis of their lives, and when military forts appeared in the American West, local Indian women served soldiers in these camps to earn a little cash and alleviate the poverty on reservations.[61] The sheer racial and ethnic diversity of women set North American prostitution apart from other practices in the Pacific region.

Another difference between Japanese prostitution in North America and practices in other Pacific regions was the intensity of racial hostility toward Japanese men and women. Unlike in Southeast Asia and Hawaii, there had been a large white population in the North American West from the early stage of its growth, and racial discrimination was a key element of its social development. The scale of Japanese prostitution in western Canada never became large enough to cause a stir among the local white population, but in western U.S. cities, white middle-class residents often complained about Japanese migrants and prostitutes as sources of disease or a blot on the morality of their community and consequently drove them into segregated areas where children could be kept away from their negative influence. Even among prostitutes, white native-born women constituted the majority, occupying the highest rung of the hierarchy in the demimonde and charging the highest price for their services. European prostitutes such as German and Irish followed native-born whites in terms of rank and earnings. Depending on the ethnic composition of the local population, nonwhite women—black, Mexican, South American, Indian, and Asian women—were consistently ranked below white prostitutes. Chinese women were segregated in

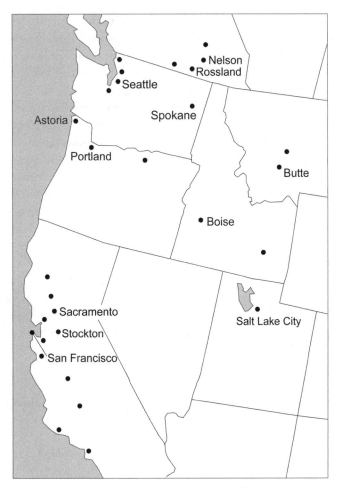

Map 1.1 Major cities where Japanese prostitutes worked in 1897–98. Sources: Report of San Francisco Consul Mutsu Kōkichi to the Foreign Ministry, August 11, 1898, and Report of Vancouver Consul Shimizu Seizaburō to Vice-Minister for Foreign Affairs Komura Jutarō, January 5, 1899; both JFMAD, no. 4.2.2.99, vol. 1.

Chinatowns, and white settlers and exclusionists called Chinese prostitution a manifestation of Chinese immorality and inability to adapt to American customs. This hostility led to the federal ban on the entry of "Oriental" prostitutes into the United States in 1875 and the Chinese Exclusion Act of 1882, which stopped the entry of Chinese laborers and their wives and children.[62] In 1885, British Columbia began to impose a head tax on each migrant with intent to deter the Chinese from coming to the province.[63] These policies discouraged family formation among the Chinese, and the unbalanced gender ratio persisted and continued to generate the demand for women among Chinese men up into the twentieth century.

After the enactment of exclusionary legislation against the Chinese in the United States and Canada in the 1870s and 1880s, Japanese prostitutes and laborers increased in the North American West, taking the place of their Chinese predecessors, especially after regular transpacific steamship service started between Japanese ports and the ports of Vancouver (1887), Seattle (1896), and San Francisco (1898) (map 1.1). With the annexation of Hawaii by the United States in 1898, Japanese migration to the West Coast increased, and continued until 1907, when a presidential order stopped the migration of Japanese via Hawaii, Canada, and Mexico, and the Gentlemen's Agreement stopped the entry of Japanese laborers as the Chinese Exclusion Act had blocked Chinese entry twenty-five years before.[64] British Columbia received a flood of Japanese migrants at the beginning of the twentieth century, especially between 1905 and 1908, due to the demand for contract laborers among Canadian companies and U.S. restrictions on Japanese migration from Hawaii to the mainland in 1907. The Hayashi-Lemieux Agreement of 1907 stopped labor migration to Canada.[65] Like the Chinese, the Japanese provided much-needed labor in mines, at railroad construction sites, in fisheries, and in lumber mills. Japanese women served not only Japanese laborers but also large numbers of Chinese men and white laborers. In the United States, Japanese prostitutes began to appear in records in the 1880s and increased in number in the 1890s. When Japanese consuls conducted surveys in 1898, Japanese prostitutes numbered 150 in California, 69 in Washington, 75 in Oregon, 23 in Idaho, 16 in Montana, and 12 in Utah. They were concentrated in trading centers and mining towns, including Seattle (35), Portland (35), Astoria (10), Spokane (20), Boise (12), Butte (10), San Francisco (38), Fresno (30), and Salt Lake City (12). In western Canada, Japanese prostitutes began to catch the attention of the Canadian press around 1890 when they were traveling to the United States via Victoria or Vancouver, but the scale of Japanese prostitution in western Canada remained small and developed not in the Japanese settlement in Vancouver but in the interior mining towns of British Columbia, such as Nelson, Rossland, Lethbridge, and Greenwood, or in the prairie provinces of Saskatchewan and Alberta.[66]

Prostitution in the North American West did not differ much from other practices in the Pacific region in that similar structural factors—industrial development, labor migration, and military expansion—spurred its growth. But central in its development was the multiracial context in which white settlers had dominated the region from the beginning, and although white settlers had despised the nonwhite women and men who were their neighbors, their lives and the region's economic development had depended heavily on the labor of Asians, Mexicans, and, to some extent, blacks and Native Americans. Japanese sex workers increased in the 1880s and the 1890s when western society excluded the Chinese but still needed an alternative source of labor that would sustain the capitalist and social development of the region.

CHAPTER 2

Hardships at Home

Micro-level Analysis of the Social
Origins of Japanese Prostitutes
in the North American West

The southern island of Japan, Kyushu, has been known as a major site of origin for Japanese sex workers in China and Southeast Asia. Yamazaki Tomoko, who explored the life of Yamakawa Saki, a former prostitute in British North Borneo, concludes that the root cause of Japanese prostitutes' migration to Southeast Asia was poverty in their native villages. Amakusa County, where Saki grew up, for example, had little arable land and few marine resources. The heavy land tax imposed by the government and population increase since the late Tokugawa period forced its residents to live on the verge of starvation. Saki, the daughter of a peasant, started working in early childhood, babysitting for a local family. None of her siblings attended school. At least twenty women from her hamlet left for Southeast Asia and worked as prostitutes.[1] What were the social origins of Japanese prostitutes in North America? From what parts of the country did they come? Were their premigration experiences similar to or different from those of Japanese prostitutes in China and Southeast Asia?

The reports of Japanese consuls in North America and prefectural governors in Japan between 1890 and 1919, in which consuls and governors often included the names of prostitutes and procurers and their addresses in Japan, permit us to identify the native prefectures, counties, and villages of Japanese prostitutes and procurers (map 2.1). Although they represent only a small portion of the hundreds of prostitutes and procurers who entered Canada and the United States (many of them unnoticed), they reveal certain patterns in the distribution of their geographic origins. The records of 137 procurers and

TABLE 2.1. Geographic origins of Japanese procurers and prostitutes in Canada and the United States mainland, 1890–1919

	Prefecture	Males	Females	Total	Proportion
1	Kanagawa	20	56	76	21.9%
2	Shizuoka	27	34	61	17.6%
3	Hiroshima	16	25	41	11.8%
4	Tokyo	10	9	19	5.5%
5	Hyogo	5	13	18	5.2%
6	Kumamoto	6	11	17	4.9%
7	Osaka	6	9	15	4.3%
8	Wakayama	11	1	12	3.5%
9	Fukuoka	5	6	11	3.2%
10	Chiba	4	4	8	2.3%
11	Shiga	3	5	8	2.3%

Sources: JFMAD, 3.8.2.12, vol. 1–2; 3.8.2.49, vols. 1, 4, 6, 8–11; 3.8.8.4, vols. 1, 2, 4, 5; 3.8.5.11, vol. 1; 3.8.5.21, vols. 1–3; 3.8.8.6, vols. 2–3; 3.8.8.10, vol. 1; 3.8.8.22, vol. 1; 4.1.4.34; 4.2.2.10, vols. 1–2, 4.2.2.27, vols. 1–3, 4.2.2.99.Note: The term "females" includes prostitutes and procurers. This categorization is problematic because it obscures the distinction between victims (prostitutes) and perpetrators (procurers), but it is difficult to draw a clear line between the two groups. Some victims (deceived women) became procurers or brothel-managers later in their lives. The evidence also shows that some women knew what they were going to do in North America before their departure.

210 prostitutes gleaned from the reports show that in the period from 1890 to 1919, 27 percent of women engaged in prostitution in North America came from Kanagawa, 16 percent from Shizuoka, 12 percent from Hiroshima, 6 percent from Hyogo, 5 percent from Kumamoto, 4 percent from Osaka, and 2–3 percent from Fukuoka, Shiga, and Chiba (table 2.1). It is well known that southwestern prefectures such as Hiroshima, Kumamoto, and Fukuoka sent the largest numbers of Japanese immigrants to Canada and the United States; therefore, it is not surprising to see some correlation between the origins of prostitutes in North America and major immigrant-sending prefectures.[2] Yet it is striking that the eastern parts of Japan, especially the areas surrounding Yokohama, the largest treaty port, sent larger numbers of Japanese prostitutes to North America. This concentration in the east provides a striking contrast to the origins of Japanese prostitutes in China and Southeast Asia, most of whom were from Nagasaki and surrounding prefectures.[3]

Map 2.1 Origins of prostitutes and procurers in Japan

Nonetheless, like the southern regions that produced Japanese sex workers in Southeast Asia, all regions where North American Japanese prostitutes came from underwent rapid social change during the Meiji period. The integration of Japan into the global economy led to the growth of treaty ports like Yokohama and Kobe and an increase in the migration of young women from surrounding farming villages to these ports, where they worked for foreigners and where some met procurers from North America. Natural disasters and a decline in the traditional ways of life in rural Shizuoka led a small number of young men to migrate to North America to earn their living, and some of these pioneering migrants started recruiting women in their native regions for prostitution in North America. Agrarian poverty and the existing tradition of *dekasegi*, or labor migration, in Hiroshima turned the prefecture into the largest source of migrants to North America during the Meiji period, and women living on the margins of these societies became targets of recruitment for prostitution in North America. Thus all these patterns of migration from specific regions occurred at particular moments when local conditions were affected by the macrostructural changes examined in chapter 1.

This chapter explores how Japanese women who became prostitutes in North America experienced these changes in the regions where they had been living before migration. This analysis of their premigration background is important, not only because it helps in understanding the causes and the mechanism of their transpacific migration, but also because Japanese ways of understanding class and status in this period continued to affect these women's lives as prostitutes in North America. What emerges in this analysis of their origins is the hardship these women had to endure that made the option of going to "America" an alternative to their hard lives in Japan.

TREATY PORTS: YOKOHAMA AND KOBE

After Japan concluded commercial treaties with the Western powers in 1858, Yokohama and Kobe, formerly small fishing villages, suddenly emerged as Japan's major ports (fig. 2.1). Foreign manufactured goods flowed into the Japanese market through these ports, and merchant vessels carried Japanese goods to various parts of the world. The opening of Japanese ports also coincided with the increasing demand for silk in the world market due to a silk blight in France and Italy in the mid-nineteenth century. Soon after the beginning of trade, silk emerged as Japan's leading export commodity, accounting for 65 percent of total exports in 1860. The export of Japanese silk to North America increased in the late 1870s. By 1890, the United States and Canada were the two largest importers of Japanese silk.[4] The opening of regular transpacific steamship routes between 1887 and 1898 connected Yokohama and Kobe with the North American ports of Vancouver, Seattle, and San Francisco, stimulating Japan's trade with Canada and the United States. On the North American side, transcontinental railroads—including the Great Northern and Canadian

Pacific—transported Japanese silk and tea from the western seaboard to the eastern market with remarkable speed. For instance, the first cargo of Japanese tea loaded on board the Canadian Pacific Railway steamship in Yokohama in 1886 reached Montreal in just forty-seven days; it arrived in New York City two days later.[5]

The movement of goods was accompanied by the movement of people. Japanese migrants increased in the Pacific Northwest after the Canadian Pacific began to provide regular service between Yokohama and Vancouver in 1887, working primarily in agriculture, railroad construction, and domestic service. In California, a small number of students appeared in the San Francisco area in the late 1880s; most worked as domestics and hoped to receive some degree of American education. They were soon joined by large numbers of agricultural laborers who came via Hawaii and worked in rural areas.[6] The United States census of 1890 recorded less than 1,500 Japanese in three western states (Washington, Oregon, and California); the number increased to 18,000 in 1900.[7] In 1901, the Canadian government confirmed the presence of some 4,700 Japanese residents in the country.[8] Prostitutes also constituted a part of this first migration stream to North America, and they quickly caught the local media's attention in Seattle and San Francisco beginning in 1890.

Another consequence of trade with the West was the growing interaction between Japanese and foreigners in treaty ports. In Yokohama, as the number of foreign males grew, Japanese women became engaged in prostitution catering to merchants, officials, and sailors from China, Europe, and North America. Streetwalkers, whom people called "nightjars" (yotaka), met foreign sailors at night on the streets. In the early 1860s, the Tokugawa shogunate constructed brothels for foreigners and recruited barmaid-prostitutes (meshimori onna) from local inns. Combination brothel-teahouses sprang up on the Sidewalk for Foreigners (Gaijin Yūhodō), where foreigners were allowed to walk without restrictions; some of the waitresses became mistresses of foreign merchants and officials. Western-style bar-brothels (chabuya) increased in the 1870s and 1880s, catering primarily to sailors. In 1887, American, British, and German consuls asked the local police to strictly punish unlicensed prostitutes in order to prevent the spread of venereal diseases among sailors; however, prostitution continued to increase.[9] By one estimate, about a thousand women worked as prostitutes for foreign residents in Yokohama in 1903.[10]

Figure 2.1. Hasegawa Sadanobu II, *Sesshū Kōbe kaigan banei no zu, sanmai tsuzuki*, work no. KCM000037. Photo credit: Kobe City Museum / DNPartcom

In Kobe, there had been a sizable number of prostitutes called *ochara* since the Tokugawa period. They either worked as mistresses for specific men or took customers on the streets. As Kobe grew in size after opening to foreign trade, prostitutes increased rapidly, catering to growing numbers of dockworkers, sailors, and merchants. As early as 1868, the governor of Hyogo Prefecture built an official pleasure quarter in Kobe and prohibited women from selling sex outside it. Numerous women, however, obviously ignored the regulation. Some continued to practice prostitution secretly, and others became the mistresses of Western sailors and merchants.[11] The latter were particularly difficult for Japanese officials to regulate because the Japanese police were not permitted to enter foreigners' residences to get evidence of prostitution. The treaties concluded with the foreign powers in 1858 deprived Japan of its right to judge foreigners under Japanese law. If foreigners committed crimes in Japan, they were tried in consular courts under their countries' laws.[12] Exemption of Westerners from local jurisdiction certainly contributed to the expansion of prostitution in both Yokohama and Kobe until the system of extraterritoriality was finally abolished in 1899.

Unlike conventional Japanese brothels, brothels for foreigners were in Western-style buildings and had English names like "America House" and "Liverpool House."[13] Nectarine No. 9 (fig. 2.2), the largest brothel for foreigners in Yokohama, had a hall where customers could dance and drink. "The interior part of Nectarine No. 9 is magnificent," one observer wrote in 1903; "it has a dance hall, smoking room, and restaurant. Rickshaws and horse-drawn carriages arrive one after another all day. The brothel is thriving."[14] In exchanges with customers, Japanese women learned Western cultural and communication skills that would enhance their opportunities to work in foreign countries. As Fujimoto Taizo described them in 1910: "In the girls of Yokohama, there are some who can hardly speak and understand European languages, and it is very funny to hear their Yokohamatic English or German, chattering boldly among young Japanese and foreign dandies." Similarly in Kobe, prostitutes "[understand] manners and customs of Europeans, and are well experienced in treatment of them by their skillful diplomatic ability." Many of them lived in "houses built in very neat and fashionable form, dotting the landscape full of green trees, extending at the foot of the mount."[15] Some of these live-in-servant–prostitutes accompanied their European, American, and Chinese masters abroad.[16] Relations between

Japanese women and foreign men sometimes continued for a long time after the men repatriated. In May 1918, *Rafu shinpō*, a Japanese-language newspaper in Los Angeles, reported that a white man named Wheeler visited the Japanese consulate in Los Angeles to ask for a help in finding the whereabouts of a Japanese woman living in Yokohama. According to him, his father had stayed in Yokohama for eighteen years more than ten years ago and during that time had formed personal relations and lived with a woman named Kotani Kayo. After his father died in 1906, the son had followed his father's order to send Kotani twenty dollars a month. In the previous year, however, when his sister visited Japan, she could not find Kotani's place, and they began to suspect that a Japanese man who had been receiving the money on her behalf may have embezzled it. Four months later, *Rafu shinpō* reported that the Japanese Foreign Ministry had sent the results of its investigation to the Japanese consulate in Los Angeles, which proved that Kotani was still alive and in good health in Yokohama and had received the money via the Yokohama Specie Bank every month. She was now fifty-six years old. Similarly, other women in Yokohama had formed intimate relations with foreign men, and the connections kept Japanese women linked to these men and their families in foreign lands.[17]

According to the reports of Japanese consuls in North America and prefectural governors in Japan, thirty-six prostitutes had former addresses in Yokohama and seven came from Kobe. How many of them had been engaged in prostitution before migration could not be confirmed, but several sources suggest connections between the women from Yokohama and prostitution in North America. Out of twenty-three North American Japanese prostitutes from Yokohama whose addresses are known, six had addresses in Ōgi, eight in Moto, and one in Kotobuki. There were more than ten Western-style bar-brothels in Moto around 1892–93, and seven to eight in the area including Ōgi, Furō, and Kotobuki in the early 1910s.[18] Indeed, one procurer, after being arrested by the Yokohama police, observed that she recruited three girls for a Japanese man who was planning to open a Western-style bar-brothel in Canada.[19] Thus, before they migrated to North America, the women had addresses in areas in Yokohama where prostitution for foreigners thrived.

The material success of former prostitutes or mistresses in North America was well known among the local people. For instance, in 1898, the *Asahi shinbun* newspaper reported the return of a Japanese

Figure 2.2 Prostitutes in front of Nectarine No. 9, Yokohama, sometime before 1903. Pedlar, *Yokohama Ehagakisho*, 132.

woman from America. She originally had worked as a waitress in Yokohama and later became the mistress of an American. When her master repatriated, she followed him; thereafter, she regularly sent her father a large sum that allowed him to start a new business and later buy large plots of lands. Four years later, she returned to Japan "stylishly dressed in western fashion" and "wearing jewelry worth over 10,000 yen."[20] Similarly, five years later, *Asahi shinbun* reported on the return of two former prostitutes to Yokohama from North America. Shortly after their arrival, they visited a local brothel and went on a drinking spree, inviting prostitutes and geisha to join them and spending about 90 yen. Both women had 500 yen in hand and 1,000 yen more in their bank accounts. When stopped by a policeman, they challenged him, claiming that they had worked hard to make money and that he had no right to question how they spent it.[21] The editor was critical of these women's habit of spending so much money on a drinking spree, which was unusual for women of their age, and their assertiveness in communicating with the police. This article could also be read as a reflection of the editor's anxiety over the autonomy of local prostitutes who had been exposed to new communication styles through their contact with foreign customers. At the same time, the existence of this kind of article suggests that there were similar "success" stories of former mistresses and prostitutes who returned to Yokohama after spending some time in North America. It seems likely, therefore, that these examples served as a powerful force in the decisions of Yokohama women to travel to America, just as similar success stories led young Japanese men to migrate to North America in hopes of earning good wages.

Sources in Canada and the United States also provide evidence that Yokohama was the place to turn to when brothel managers decided to start a business in North America. Araki Kojirō, one of the founders of Japanese brothels in Seattle, opened his house in 1889 and hired four prostitutes from Yokohama. Later, in the mid-1890s, he opened the first Japanese brothel in Nelson, British Columbia. Once again, he recruited Yokohama prostitutes, one of whom was a woman named Okatsu, a former prostitute at Nectarine No. 9, the largest brothel for foreigners in Yokohama.[22] In 1907 and 1912, *Shin sekai*, a Japanese-language newspaper in San Francisco, reported on two Yokohama women associated with prostitution, a former geisha and a brothel-keeper's daughter, who attempted to smuggle themselves into San Francisco.[23] Yokohama was connected to North America through trade and transportation networks, and local prostitutes' familiarity with Western customs would have made the transition from Yokohama to North America easier for them.

Yet one should not hastily conclude that all the Japanese prostitutes from treaty ports were born there. For instance, when brothel-keepers received girls from their parents in exchange for advances, the brothel-keepers' families often adopted and raised the girls until they were old enough to serve customers. Furthermore, procurers from North America often passed their women off as their "wives" or made them use other women's passports to enter Canada or the United States. Thus the addresses reported by consular officials and governors were more likely to show the addresses of their workplaces or those written on passports confiscated by officials, not the actual places where the women originated. It will be necessary, therefore, to turn to other sources to know more about these women and their origins.

Two newspaper articles published by the *Shin sekai* newspaper in San Francisco give a sense of how women came to treaty ports and ended up becoming prostitutes in North America. The first is an exposé of a failed plot by a Japanese man and woman to migrate illegally from Yokohama in September 1907. The man, Sano Ino-kichi, purchased a married couple's passport to the United States from another man at an inn in Shizuoka and moved to Yokohama, where he was introduced to a woman, Sawada Tomi, who had worked in a *machiai* (rented rooms where geisha and their customers met) since the year before last and wished to go to the United States. When they boarded the Canadian Pacific Railway ship as a married couple, they were arrested by the harbor police. The editor of the article suspected that the ringleader of the plot was a brothel-keeper in San Francisco who came to Japan regularly to recruit women.[24] This article suggests that women were often contacted by procurers while working in Yokohama and lured into taking illegal passage to North America.

The second story published in June 1909 reported in more detail on a woman who was lured into going to North America from Kobe. The woman, Fujii Naka, was the daughter of a Buddhist monk in Tokushima Prefecture. After her parents divorced, her mother had a hard time making ends meet and apprenticed her second daughter, Fujii, to a restaurant in Kobe. Later in 1897, fourteen-year-old Fujii met a female customer with nice clothes. Noticing that Fujii was impressed by her clothing, the woman was reported to have told her: "If you want to wear clothing like me, why don't you come to America? Now I can live in luxury because I went there." The exaggerated story of wealth prompted Fujii to follow the procuress across the ocean using another woman's identity, but she ended up working as a prostitute in a San Francisco brothel. After she wrote to her brother-in-law in Japan in 1907, he appealed to the local police for help but failed to secure any aid. Only after the *Shin sekai* reported on her brother-in-law's struggle in June 1909 did Fujii visit the Japanese consulate accompanied by a woman who had once managed the brothel.[25]

The editors indicated their indignation with the procurers and sympathy for the women induced to take ships to North America or tricked into becoming prostitutes there. The *Shin sekai*'s exposé of these incidents in 1907 and 1909 must be understood in the context of this period, when growing anti-Japanese sentiment among Canadians and Americans led to the implementation of the Gentlemen's Agreements between Japan and both Canada and the United States, which ended Japanese labor migration to these countries, and Japanese immigrant leaders were trying to improve the image of the Japanese in their host societies by abolishing prostitution in their

communities.[26] But considering the pattern of recruitment described
in these articles and the "success" stories of returnees, it is possible that young working-class Japanese women in Yokohama were
often influenced by positive visions of "America" that played a role in
their decisions to migrate to the North American West. For a better
understanding of these visions, we need to further contextualize these
women's lives before they came to Kobe or Yokohama, including the
constraints they faced because of their gender, class, and status.

RURAL-URBAN MIGRATIONS WITHIN
KANAGAWA PREFECTURE

Although it is extremely difficult to identify where in the country Japanese prostitutes were born, villages near Yokohama provided the
bulk of prostitutes mentioned in the reports of consuls and governors.
Excluding the women who had addresses in Yokohama, twenty-one
women came from other areas in Kanagawa Prefecture, and three
eastern counties—Kōza, Kamakura, and Miura—in particular sent
larger numbers of women to North America for prostitution than
other counties did (map 2.2). Farming families composed 91 percent
of the total number of families residing in Kōza. The proportion was
81 percent for Kamakura. In Miura County, 48 percent were farming families, and 25 percent were fishing families.[27] Silk cocoons, rice,
wheat, soybeans, rapeseed oil, sweet potatoes, and mulberries were
the major agricultural products cultivated in Kanagawa in general
and in the three counties in particular.[28] Clearly, the eastern half of
Kanagawa was an overwhelmingly agricultural region.

Yamada Waka, a former prostitute on Seattle's King Street, also
grew up in a farming and fishing village in Miura County. In her
analysis of Yamada's genealogy, Yamazaki Tomoko wrote that her
natal family, the Asabas, had originally been headed by a "well-to-do
farmer" with large plots of lands and forests. Before Yamada's marriage to Hichijirō, she had been courted by a poor youth in her village, but her family opposed their marriage because "[his] family was
no match for the Asabas."[29] It is difficult to know, at this point, the
Asabas' economic situation at that time, but according to Kiyoshi
Asaba, the grandson of Yamada's eldest brother, the family has inherited fairly large plots of land, and the main house from the time of
Yamada Waka, which still stands in her native town, suggests that
the family was not among the "lowest" in status in the village. By

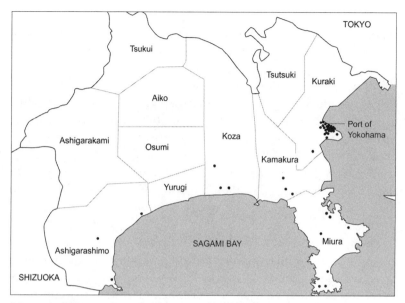

Map 2.2 Origins of North American Japanese prostitutes from Kanagawa Prefecture

the time she married Hichijirō, however, her family's financial situation was certainly on the decline. In her memoir, Yamada recalled the hardships her family was facing in this period:

> It was very sad to see the haggard face of my eldest brother struggling to maintain our family business. . . . After selling that hill and this field handed down from our ancestors, how much of the land has remained? If this remaining land ceased to be the property of my brother, he will not be able to support his large family. . . . We needed a sizable sum of money to keep the remaining land in the hands of my brother. I decided to shoulder a part of his burden without thinking about what I could do at that time. But when I became determined to do so, I could feel that I have worth and a purpose in life.[30]

Thus, her decision to leave the village and find a way to earn money was influenced by not only economic necessity but also a wish to help her family maintain the land and status in their village that they had inherited from earlier generations.[31]

Yamada's move to Yokohama should also be understood in the context of young women's rural-urban migration within Kanagawa Prefecture in the late nineteenth century. Yokohama's population increased dramatically after it opened to foreign trade: from 28,000 in 1859, to 58,000 in 1877, to 150,000 in 1893. The cigar-making, textile, and shipbuilding industries expanded rapidly, and the number of factories grew from five in 1885 to fifty-six in 1893. However, agricultural production stagnated in surrounding farming villages.[32] By 1885, the agricultural land under tenancy reached 45 percent in Kanagawa, surpassing the national average of 39 percent.[33] From 1902 to 1904, the Kanagawa Agricultural Commission investigated conditions in farming villages and reported that small-scale farmers could not survive solely from farming. In order to earn additional income, they did side businesses such as straw work and sandal making. During the slack season on the farm, their sons and daughters migrated to Yokohama or Tokyo, where they worked as errand boys, domestics, or cotton spinners.[34]

From the perspective of local social history, one could argue that these farming families experienced declines not only in economic but also in social terms. In Sagami Province (the western and central parts of present-day Kanagawa Prefecture), for instance, occupations such as making and repairing sandals and osa (a movable frame fitted with reed used for enhancing the density of a woven fabric), disposing of animal carcasses, working with leather, and serving as village guards had long been associated with members of outcaste communities, who were distinguished from samurai, peasants (hyakushō), and townspeople (chōmin). With the issuance of the so-called Emancipation Edict of 1871, the earlier status system was abolished, but former members of the outcaste class came to be called "new commoners" (shinheimin); they lived in "special communities" (tokushu buraku) and were forced to undergo new forms of prejudice based on the public's view of them as "base people" (senmin) as well as new "scientific" ideas about race and public hygiene.[35] As the Meiji period progressed, economic hardships forced struggling farmers to sell their land, the source of their pride as members of the second-highest class in the Tokugawa status order, and to engage in jobs that had been considered the work of outcastes, and accordingly, they may have felt a decline in both economic and social status. Yamada's wish to keep the remaining land "handed down from [her] ancestors" makes more sense when considering it within the social contexts of Kanagawa in that period.[36]

The conditions of small-scale farmers, however, became more serious over time. Farmers decreased steadily in rural Kanagawa during the two decades after 1890. From 1890 to 1898, the female agricultural population decreased by 10 percent, while the rate for men was 7 percent. After famine and natural disasters struck in the late 1890s, out-migration from farming villages increased. From 1898 to 1908, the female agricultural population decreased by 16 percent, far surpassing the figure of 1.3 percent for men.[37] On the one hand, the male labor force was essential on the farm, and parents expected their sons to stay. Girls, on the other hand, had worked outside their homes since the Tokugawa period, doing housekeeping for other families in exchange for room and board. As the Meiji period progressed, they left villages for factories to earn money. In the city of Yokohama, while a large pool of male migrant workers provided essential labor on the docks, the growing light industries, like cotton textiles, relied on a steady supply of inexpensive female labor. Consequently, daughters of farming families in decline became candidates for migration to Yokohama during the slack season.[38]

For young women from rural households suffering from a lack of money, serving Chinese masters in their households in Yokohama was one of several limited options. In July 1899, the *Asahi shinbun* published a series of articles on Chinese residents in Yokohama, which reported that Japanese women typically were hired by male Chinese merchants as domestics and were paid extra for sexual services. These Japanese mistresses came largely from two counties on the Bōsō peninsula (present-day Chiba Prefecture, connected to Yokohama by boat across Tokyo Bay) and three surrounding counties in Kanagawa Prefecture (Miura, Kōza, and Kamakura), overlapping the origins of Japanese prostitutes in North America reported by consuls. The editor reported that these women had been "tanned country girls clothed in cheap cotton cloth," but after serving their Chinese masters, they returned to villages "wearing impressive three layers of clothing." The villagers, "ignorant of the real conditions [of work]," sent their daughters to Chinese homes in Yokohama, "believing that the service would be an avenue to social advancement."[39] The editor's biases against the working class and Chinese are clear, and he chided these women and their parents for their ignorance of the implications of serving foreigners sexually. There was a significant population of foreign male merchants who wished to have domestic and sexual services in Yokohama, and young women in surrounding villages fulfilled this need to earn money and help their parents financially.

The *Asahi shinbun* editor declared that these women became domestics and sexual servants of foreign masters primarily to earn money and escape poverty. But other evidence suggests that their reason for doing so was not only economic. Since the arrival of foreign ships, authorities had been concerned about controlling sexuality in treaty ports, and shortly after the ports opened to foreign trade in 1858, the Tokugawa shogunate ordered the construction of brothels for foreigners. But it was not easy to recruit women willing to serve foreigners, not only because foreigners were considered enemies who imposed unequal treaties on the country, but also because they engaged in the "dirty" practices of eating animals and wearing leather shoes that had often been associated with the former outcaste community (*buraku*).[40] The shogunate first ordered the owners of local inns to manage the brothels, expecting that the barmaid-prostitutes hired there would serve foreigners. But the managers could not meet the demand for women among foreign men and began to recruit women from communities of the former outcaste class near Yokohama and from the lower class in the provinces of Sagami and Musashi (present-day Tokyo, Saitama, and part of Kanagawa Prefecture).[41] As Japanese historian Fujino Yutaka and others write, the idea behind this policy was the biased view that women in former outcaste communities were suited to sexual service for foreigners, work despised by ordinary Japanese women.[42]

This policy appears to have shaped the basic structure of prostitution in Yokohama and persisted well into the middle of the Meiji period. In 1903, half a century after the arrival of Commodore Matthew Perry, the *Yokohama shinpō* newspaper company published a book titled *The Prosperity of Yokohama* in which the editor wrote about prostitutes serving foreigners: "What is their genealogy? Needless to say, the majority of these women were daughters of *eta* [outcastes] or lazy farmers and fishermen. So they were completely ignorant. In addition, they decide to enter the trade out of their desires for luxurious lives surrounded by beautiful things. So there is no use preaching to them. To make matters worse, they are corrupting good morals; I am at a loss as to what to do with them."[43] By this time, prostitution for foreigners had been imagined as work for women from marginalized groups including local outcastes and poor farmers and fishermen. Furthermore, the women were blamed for becoming prostitutes and corrupting public morals even though their sexual services were helping the wives and daughters of "good" families avoid sexual violation by foreigners in treaty ports. This perception of prostitution for foreigners as immoral work suitable for marginalized women, combined with the prevailing rural poverty, played a role in creating a sociocultural context in which women from marginalized communities entered the trade in Yokohama.[44]

Thus, several factors facilitated women's migration from farming villages to Yokohama in the 1880s and 1890s. The growth of Yokohama as an international port and industrial center served as a "pull" factor, and the general poverty in rural villages, together with various kinds of family problems, induced peasants' daughters to move to Yokohama to make their own living or seek a way of earning money and help their families. Furthermore, from the mid-1880s, numerous Japanese men were beginning to travel by ship to the United States, a country that guidebooks often described as a "veritable human paradise,"[45] and such positive information about the United States or Canada could have spread from the port to surrounding villages, reaching the ears of women like Yamada Waka who believed that migration to North America would help solve various problems in their lives.

SHIZUOKA PREFECTURE: THE ORIGIN OF PROCURERS

Nevertheless, proximity to treaty ports was not the only factor that shaped the migration of women who became prostitutes in North America. For example, it is a little surprising that Shizuoka Prefecture, lying between Tokyo and Osaka, became the second-largest supplier of prostitutes in North America (see table 2.1). It was not a major point of origin for Japanese immigrants in Canada and the United States (except for one famous "immigrant village" along the Pacific Ocean, Miho, a major origin of migrants to Hawaii and North America during the Meiji period).[46] Yet the largest share of procurers reported in official records, 20 percent, came from Shizuoka, and their origins were concentrated in the areas along Suruga Bay (map 2.3). Among the native towns of procurers, two villages—Kanbara and Heda—appear most frequently in immigrant accounts and official documents. By examining the conditions of Shizuoka Prefecture in general and the two villages in particular, one can see that information brought by the pioneers, rather than the distance from treaty ports or economic changes, had significant impact on migration from this prefecture.

Of course there were "push" factors that created conditions under which people were forced to leave this prefecture. During the Tokugawa

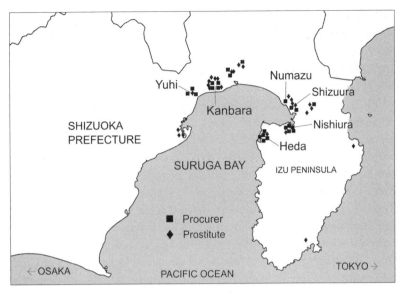

Map 2.3 Native villages of procurers and prostitutes from Shizuoka Prefecture

period, farmers in the Tokai area (present-day Aichi, Mie, and Shizuoka Prefectures) produced sake, soy sauce, textiles, and indigo for the neighboring urban markets of Kyoto, Osaka, and Nagoya. After the opening of treaty ports to foreign trade, however, the importation of cheap foreign cotton and indigo gradually displaced native growers, and Shizuoka's traditional products, like Japanese tung oil, cotton, and indigo, lost their economic value. Some farmers began to grow new commercial crops, including tea and oranges, but others chose to leave Shizuoka temporarily in search of work. Until 1899, Shizuoka's registered population surpassed the actual population, indicating that people were more likely to move out of the prefecture than come into it. The pressure to migrate began to ease after the turn of the century, when both rural industries and cities became large enough to absorb the prefecture's surplus population.[47] Before the turn of the century, migration was a viable option for those who failed to adjust to the new economic order.

In addition to the general hardships in the prefecture, economic conditions temporarily worsened in the villages of Kanbara and Heda. Before the Meiji Restoration of 1868, Kanbara had been dependent on the heavy traffic on the Tōkaidō, a major road that connected Edo (later Tokyo) and Osaka.[48] As a so-called post station (*shukuba*),

Kanbara served the needs of traveling merchants and samurai officers, and local farmers grew agricultural products for the inns and stores at post stations. The Tokugawa shogunate ordered the post stations to supply goods and services for traveling samurai officers free of charge, which was a burden on the residents; at the same time, however, the system also gave the villagers certain privileges, including financial assistance from feudal lords.[49] After the Restoration, the Meiji government abolished the post station system, and people were forced to seek new ways of making a living. Moreover, the opening of railroad service between Tokyo and Kobe in July 1889 made post stations of little importance. In 1890, when the construction of a railroad station began in the center of Kanbara and local families were moved out, the people protested, claiming that the railroad's arrival would lead to the town's decline; however, the station was constructed on the outskirts of the town.[50] The event reflected the residents' fear of machines that would undermine their traditional safeguards.

In the village of Heda, the majority of migrants to North America came from Ida, a northern hamlet in the village. Since the Tokugawa period, Ida had been a poor area without major industries or rich farmland, and its people had eked out a living by farming small plots of land and fishing in Suruga Bay. Also, because Ida served as a major quarry for the shogunate and other eastern fiefs, the hamlet's stonemasons often migrated back and forth between Ida and Edo. In 1893, however, the hamlet experienced the worst natural disaster in its history: "On March 5, 1893, a fire broke out in the hamlet of Ida and destroyed all forty-three houses. Food, clothes, and necessary goods for daily use were all destroyed. It was difficult to describe the wretched state of the village. The people constructed temporary places to live by using remaining boards. . . . The people were struggling to survive on a daily basis."[51] The hamlet plunged into a state of crisis that made it necessary for some to seek work elsewhere.

Economic hardships and natural disaster certainly provided reasons for the people of Kanbara and Heda to leave their villages to make money elsewhere, but they do not explain why men and women from these towns became procurers and prostitutes in North America. Natural disasters like tsunami, flood, fire, and cold weather could happen in all parts of Japan, and economic problems were seen throughout the country during the 1880s and 1890s, when the rich landowning class emerged in farming regions and the land under tenancy increased dramatically. To explain migration from Shizuoka, therefore, we must consider other factors, particularly the work of pioneering emigrants who established vital links between their villages and North America.

Hirakawa Tōkichi, a major procurer and brothel-keeper in the Pacific Northwest, was originally from Kanbara. Tōkichi, a "poor farmer," migrated to the United States with his wife and daughter in 1889 or 1890. There, his wife and daughter were reported to have earned money from prostitution. In fact, his name appeared as "Hirakawa Tōkichi—five [women]" on the list of brothel operators in Seattle made by a Japanese official in 1891, suggesting that he managed a brothel with five prostitutes.[52] Around 1892, Tōkichi and his wife returned to Kanbara and built a "huge tile-roofed house with large white walls," spending more than 10,000 yen. Furthermore, the money permitted him to buy "many fields without regard to their price," and he lived "like a wealthy farmer." In 1900, the average daily wage of farmhands ranged between 0.2 yen and 0.5 yen (between $0.10 and $0.25), and the average monthly wage of a primary-school teacher was only 11 yen (or $5.49).[53] These figures suggest how enormous 10,000 yen was in the early 1890s. Little wonder that his fellow villagers, admiring Tōkichi's success, called his home "the American House" (Amerikaya).[54]

Tōkichi's success induced fellow villagers and family members to follow in his footsteps. His younger brother Chōtaro, a dyer (konya), left Kanbara and went to Yokohama; from there he sailed for the United States at the end of 1894 or early 1895. In December 1895, a Japanese resident in Butte, Montana, sent a letter to the Shizuoka prefectural police stating that a group of Japanese men and women from Shizuoka were operating brothels in the town and "disgracing the reputation of the Japanese." The name Chōtaro appeared on the list of these men and women, suggesting that he became a brothel operator there.[55] Saitō Yoshi, a sixteen-year-old woman living near the home of the Hirakawa brothers, was another Kanbara migrant. After working as a domestic in Yokohama for a short period, she migrated to the United States and became a prostitute in Butte. Yoshi sent money from her earnings to support her family. When a local police officer visited Kanbara, he reported that her father, Toshikichi, "made a large fortune recently . . . and looks like a wealthy farmer."[56] As in the cases of women in rural Kanagawa, the examples of fellow villagers shaped her decision to seek work in Yokohama and overseas.

A similar story survives from the hamlet of Ida in the town of Heda. In the early 1980s, Kudō Miyoko investigated the background of Ueda Torajirō, a major procurer whose name appeared in a survey on Japanese prostitution in Canada published in 1909.[57] Born in Heda in 1858, Torajirō grew up with foster parents in the village.[58] After his foster parents had their own child, Torajirō left the household. According to the story Torajirō himself provided, he first moved to Hokkaido (Northern Island) and worked on a seal-hunting boat. The boat was caught in a storm one day, drifted for more than a month, and washed up on the Canadian shore. In Canada, he made a fortune working in a salmon fishery.[59] Another oral tradition says that he met an American in Yokohama and migrated to Alaska, where he made a fortune mining gold.[60] About twenty years after he left, Torajirō came back to Heda, wearing impressive "Western clothes and a gold chain." His nephew-in-law observed, "Thereafter, Torajirō-san helped other villagers migrate to Canada."[61] Torajirō returned at around the same time the fire hit the hamlet, leaving many residents on the verge of starvation.[62]

Vancouver consul Yada's report provides more concrete information about what Torajirō did in Canada. According to the report, he first arrived in Canada in 1885 and worked at a sawmill and a fishery. Three years later, he married his first wife, Yamashita Take, and became a naturalized Canadian citizen. During the next twenty years, he remarried three more times in Japan, brought several women to Canada as wives, and sold them into prostitution. He worked primarily for a brothel-keeper in Saskatoon, Saskatchewan, where Japanese prostitution expanded in the latter half of the 1890s. His career as a procurer ended in May 1909, when he was arrested by a Canadian official who reported that Ueda had obtained naturalization papers "in a very questionable way" and divorced his wives on every return to Japan. The official decided to deport him in the best interests of the Japanese consul and residents.[63]

Tōkichi's and Torajirō's examples seemed to have given impetus to subsequent migrants from their native villages. In 1903, for example, three villages—Miho, Kanbara, and Heda—sent substantial numbers of migrants to foreign countries from Shizuoka Prefecture. Some 106 migrated from Miho, a well-known immigrant village, another 65 went from Kanbara, the hometown of Hirakawa Tōkichi, and 56 migrated from Heda, the native village of Ueda Torajirō.[64] As in other districts, migrants from these communities were overwhelmingly male. All from Miho were men. Just over a third of migrants from Kanbara and Heda were women.[65] A significant majority of Kanbara migrants went to either the United States or Canada, and many of them migrated as married men and women. Passing themselves off as married men and women was a common practice among procurers and prostitutes who entered the United States.[66] No doubt, information brought by the procurers played a critical part in recruiting women in Kanbara and Heda.

The procurers' desire for money and their economic success often loom large in the reports of officials and written accounts of their families, relatives, and villagers. But one must also be attentive to the procurers' marginalized positions in their villages. Before his migration to the United States, Hirakawa Tōkichi was reported to have been "an extremely poor farmer," "having no property or financial resources" (*musan mushiryoku*) in his village, who may have belonged to the class of declining farmers or been a member of the outcaste class who traditionally had been engaged in farming on marginal land.[67] His brother Chōtarō was a dyer, a status often considered lower than that of farmers because the dyer's livelihood depended on skills, not on land, the source of taxes for officials and of pride for farmers ever since the Tokugawa period.[68] In the case of Ueda Torajirō, his marginality had nothing to do with his livelihood, fishing, because the whole village depended on the fishery for a living. More important factors in his case were that he had been a foster child and that his foster parents happened to have their own child after he grew up, which would have increased his feeling of isolation in the family and community.[69] Therefore, like Japanese women who became prostitutes in North America, procurers also came from social classes suffering from poverty and prejudice in Meiji Japan.

The impressive stories of returnees, including one who constructed a "huge tile-roofed house" and another who came back wearing "Western clothes and a gold chain," prompted some young men and women in their native regions to make money from prostitution despite negative perceptions of the work. In June 1908, Usui Kotaro, a young man from Kambara, made a statement before a U.S. immigration official in 1908 that about a year ago, he had met a fellow villager, Konagai Shuzo, a native of Kambara, who had "the reputation of having made a large amount of money," and was asked if he was willing to become the "nominal" husband of a woman and go to the United States with her. He told Inspector F. N. Steel that he had been aware of the illegal nature of passage, but he had been "very desirous of coming to the United States." In early 1908, Konagai arranged for him to be adopted into a local family, and he moved to Tokyo. After receiving a passport, he left Japan for Seattle with a woman named Tasaka Fusa, a native of Kambara, and later moved to San Francisco, where the woman's uncle was managing a brothel.[70]

Fusa, the eighteen-year-old woman who became the nominal wife of Konagai and migrated to Seattle with him, stated before an immigration official that she had little knowledge of what was intended for her at her destination. Konagai was a distant relative, and she followed the order of her parents who made arrangements with Konagai for her to live with her uncle in San Francisco. She observed: "I have never heard, nor do I believe that my uncle, Ohashi Seiji, is engaged in so disgraceful [a] business as that having to do with a house of prostitution. . . . My father on account of sickness is not able to work. . . . I did not know what I was to do and don't know yet, but I thought there would be some thing to do [after] seeing my uncle, such as sewing or washing or any kind of work in order to earn money to send to my parents." Her account indicates that although the opportunity to help her sick father prompted her migration, she had not intended to work as a prostitute. She viewed prostitution as a "disgraceful" business, as many people did in this period.[71]

In the case of Toki, the fourth "wife" of Ueda Torajirō, migration was an attractive alternative to her laboring life. She later told the Yokohama harbor police that she had grown up in a village in eastern Shizuoka helping her parents with farming until the age of eighteen. In the next five years, she worked as a servant for nearby families or in restaurants in Tokyo and Kobe. In 1908, when she was learning sewing in Numadu, Shizuoka, she met Ueda Torajirō, who was staying at the same inn, and accepted his marriage proposal. She noted: "I have heard that Ueda has been making his living from fishing and I had not decided what to do [in Canada]." The real reason for her marrying Ueda is unclear, but the fact that Ueda had been engaged in fishing, like many other fellow villagers, gave her assurance that she would be doing something associated with his work and status, not prostitution.

The two women's decision to migrate to North America could also be analyzed in relation to the idea of domestic work that prevailed during the Meiji period. In agrarian villages, daughters of peasants were engaged in work inside and outside the household, helping their parents with strenuous work such as cutting trees and removing stones in addition to the domestic duties traditionally assigned to women.[72] It was customary for girls, as early as the age of ten, to enter domestic service under contract in other families. In the larger Japanese society, the image of domestics was both positive and negative. On the one hand, they were looked down upon by middle- to upper-class people, called *jochū* (denotes "maids" or "female domestics") or *gejo* (literally means "low woman"), both implying persons of the subordinate class.[73] On the other hand, domestic work was considered a respectable, often ideal, job for women of humble origins, because it gave them the opportunity to learn domestic skills or go to school and served as good preparation for marriage. Indeed, their term of service often ended with marriage.[74] Tasaka Fusa's statement that she had intended to do "sewing or washing," not a "disgraceful" business like prostitution, may have reflected her wish to continue to be a respectable working-class woman while helping her father financially.

But domestic work itself was hard for all women. In Japanese families in the Meiji period, domestic work was not defined as clearly as it was in the United States. Women did all kinds of work for the families who employed them, not only household duties but also delivering goods, running errands, doing piecework, and helping out with their employers' businesses. Domestics in urban areas were subject to sexual danger, and servants working in restaurants were often forced into prostitution.[75] Despite various positive and negative images of domestic service, the work itself remained hard for all women. Therefore, in considering Ueda Toki's decision to marry and migrate to Canada with a well-off returnee, one must take into account the hardships she may have experienced as a peasant's daughter who had helped her parents and worked as a servant in other households and in restaurants before meeting the procurer.[76]

Examination of the origins of procurers and a prostitute in Shizuoka Prefecture demonstrates that the factors of class, status, timing, and contingency all played a role in the emergence of their migration patterns. The pioneering procurers had occupied marginalized positions in their native villages due to their livelihood or status. The women or men who agreed to take passage to North America with these procurers also came from struggling families. The information brought by these procurers had a profound impact on these young people's decisions to migrate. It seems likely, therefore, that first, men holding rather marginal positions in their villages left to seek opportunities, ended up in North America by chance, and learned to make money from prostitution; after they returned to their villages in glory, fellow villagers followed their example. It is not that people in this particular region had little moral prohibition against sex work or viewed prostitution as honest work. Poverty, contingency, and the work of pioneers all must be considered in analyzing the connections between these villages and North American brothels.

HIROSHIMA PREFECTURE: THE ORIGIN OF JAPANESE IMMIGRANTS

Japanese women's migration from Hiroshima Prefecture to North America did not occur in isolation. It was part of the larger stream of labor emigration from this prefecture during the first decade of the twentieth century. Japanese migration to the U.S. mainland increased after regular steamship services started up between Yokohama and Seattle in 1896 and between Yokohama and San Francisco in 1898. The Japanese population in the United States grew rapidly, from six thousand in 1895 to thirty-five thousand in 1899. In Canada, the Japanese numbered six thousand by 1906.[77] In this era of Japanese migration, Hiroshima stood as the largest source of overseas Japanese. Of all passports issued between 1899 and 1910, about 22.5 percent were issued to people from Hiroshima. Kumamoto (12.4 percent), Yamaguchi (10.7 percent), and Fukuoka (9.6 percent) followed.[78] Therefore, it is not surprising that Hiroshima sent at least twenty-nine prostitutes and procurers, or 12 percent of the total number, to Canada and the United States (map 2.4).

As past studies of immigration have shown, poverty did not automatically cause people to move to foreign countries.[79] In Hiroshima, the largest numbers of overseas migrants came *not* from poor counties with high proportions of agricultural land under tenancy (50 percent or more) but from areas where land was widely distributed among the residents—Asa, Aki, and Saeki. These immigrant-sending counties, however, experienced important changes in their economic and social structures in the 1880s and 1890s. In this area, formerly the domain of Aki and Bingo, the commercialization of agriculture had already begun, with an increase in individual farming toward the end of the Tokugawa period, but after the opening of Japanese ports to foreign trade in the 1850s, competition from foreign goods increased, and major cash crops other than rice—such as indigo,

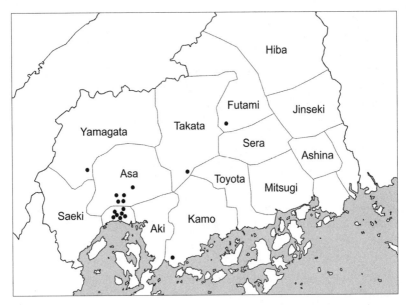

Map 2.4 Origins of North American Japanese prostitutes from Hiroshima
Prefecture

hemp, and orchids—were in decline. Small landowners were not able
to support their families solely from farming; however, these counties
had no industries that could absorb the surplus agricultural labor that
emerged in farming villages, and there were no side businesses to supplement peasant families' income other than the production of *yasuri*
(files or rasps) or *tatami* mats. Faced with declining opportunities in
their villages and increasing tax burdens, young men and women left
their families and moved to Osaka and places as far away as Hokkaido and Hawaii.[80] The largest number of Japanese prostitutes in
North America, six, came from Asa County, the major source of
overseas Japanese migrants between 1896 and 1919.[81] These women
were most likely the children of small farmers who needed additional
income.

Because there were several factors that pushed people out of their
villages in this prefecture, the migration of women from Hiroshima
must also be analyzed in relation to domestic labor migration as an
extension of continuing *dekasegi* practice in the region since the
Tokugawa period.[82] Hiroshima Prefecture's out-migration rate had
always exceeded its in-migration rate throughout the Meiji and Taisho
periods (1868–1926). This tendency was common to all counties in

Hiroshima except the urban centers of Kure and Onomichi and the city of Hiroshima.[83] Hiroshima Prefecture also produced more out-migrants than did other prefectures. In 1899, for example, about 8 percent of Hiroshima's registered population was living outside the prefecture. This out-migration rate stood second highest among twenty-seven prefectures in Japan in the period from 1898 to 1901. Even when overseas migrants are excluded, the number of domestic labor migrants, who had addresses outside their native villages, 90,491, was still the third largest among all prefectures.[84] These statistics demonstrate that Hiroshima was heavily dependent on the earnings of migrants who left their homes temporarily to work elsewhere.

Without a doubt, the easiest place to find a job was the city of Hiroshima, the bustling center of commerce and manufacturing, the third-largest city in the western half of Japan. Hiroshima had been known as a major producer of cotton yarn since the Tokugawa period, and in 1878, the Meiji government constructed the first state-operated spinning company, the Hiroshima Spinning Mill, which became the major job provider for the surplus population in and outside the city in the coming decades. Moreover, the Sino-Japanese War broke out in 1894, increasing Hiroshima's importance as a strategic foothold. The government established the Imperial Headquarters in the city, and shipbuilding factories sprang up in nearby Kure between 1891 and 1903. The Sanyō Railroad reached Hiroshima in 1894, transporting manufactured goods to the larger markets of Kobe, Osaka, and Kyoto.[85]

The expansion of industry and commerce enriched capitalists and merchants, but it also produced a large urban working class that constantly suffered poverty and unemployment. As part of the military-led city planning, large numbers of laborers were needed for building roads, bridges, and infrastructure facilities, and displaced men and women from surrounding farming areas and small towns moved there to meet the demand. Many lived in such slum areas as an outcaste community in the western part of the city, where the residents engaged in butchering and leatherwork as well as miscellaneous urban jobs like construction workers, carpenters, rickshaw men, and storekeepers.[86]

At least two of the six prostitutes mentioned in consular reports came from poor families in the city of Hiroshima. For instance, the family register of Nemoto Fumi, a woman sold to an English madam in Vancouver in 1895, recorded her as "the eldest daughter of Nemoto

Seno, a shopkeeper selling candy and notions," indicating that she had no father in her family and that her mother was the sole provider. Before leaving for North America, she had been working as a prostitute in the city of Hakata, Fukuoka Prefecture, and at the age of twenty-one, she was induced by Arase Kantarō, a native of Hiroshima, to move to Canada.[87] Another prostitute in Seattle, Miura Shime, was also the daughter of a single mother who worked as a "day laborer" in the city of Hiroshima. In December 1900, when she was a live-in servant for a restaurant owner's family, she met a procurer and sailed with him for Seattle from Yokohama.[88] The absence of fathers left the two women few options except selling their labor. These young working-class women were the most likely to catch the attention of procurers.

Other Japanese women who became prostitutes in North America migrated from farming villages in Hiroshima Prefecture, first to the city of Hiroshima and later to North America. In 1908, the *Shin sekai* newspaper in San Francisco published an article about Okame, a barmaid working in the city, that provided a concrete description of her background in Hiroshima. She was born to a rickshaw man and his wife, who did laundry on a wage basis in the village of Yoshida in central Hiroshima, where, the editor wrote, "the business of tanning leather for making sandals (*setta no kawa tataki*) was prosperous," indicating her family's connection with the outcaste community.[89] Her elder brother and sister died when she was ten years old, and the family had a hard time making ends meet. Okame left school to help her mother and began to earn money by doing laundry and babysitting for other families. When she turned fourteen, her relatives found her a job in a spinning mill, most likely in the city of Hiroshima. Sometime after beginning to work in the mill, the editor reported, Okame heard from a person there that "America is a country where people can earn a lot of money," which made her wish to go there and make money. With a man's help, she passed herself off as his wife and journeyed to Seattle, where she was later cajoled into becoming a prostitute on King Street. The editor was full of contempt for the outcaste, the poor, and women. He attacked her "vanity" (*unubore*) and selfishness as the reasons for her becoming a prostitute.[90]

The story of Okame was probably not an exceptional case among women born in former outcaste communities. Zendō Kikuyo, a well-known former prostitute from Hiroshima who worked in Southeast Asia during the Meiji and early Taisho periods, was the last of eight children born in an outcaste family in Mukunashi (present-day Daiwa) in southern Hiroshima.[91] Their parents had no land and engaged in tenant farming, supplementing their income by doing errands for landowners and making sandals. The elementary school she attended was not a comfortable place for the children of outcastes. One of her classmates later recalled the days when Zendō was telling her classmates "let me in" and being left out. After her mother's death, she was forced to quit school and was sent to a family in Okayama Prefecture, where she did babysitting, made *hana-goza* (figured mats), and worked occasionally in a spinning mill. When she was sixteen, an older coworker in the mill told her about a moneymaking opportunity in Kobe. After following her coworker to Kobe, she was put on board a ship with girls of similar ages and shipped to Klang in Malaysia, where she was forced into prostitution.[92]

Except for their outcaste origin, another commonality between Okame and Zendō, which was not emphasized in the *Shin sekai* article or the biographies of Zendō, was their work experience in spinning mills. The mechanization of work made the textile industry the major work open to daughters of peasants in Japan during the last two decades of the nineteenth century, and as many scholars have shown, working conditions in cotton-spinning mills were brutal. Japanese cotton-spinning mills soon adopted twenty-four-hour-a-day operations, and women worked on twelve-hour night or day shifts with two short breaks and one meal break (which were often ignored). The quality of meals was low—a bowl of rice of inferior grade with a few pickles and a thin soup were the norm—which forced the women to use their meager earnings on sweets sold by the company for profit. The thick dust in the air and the unsanitary conditions in the mills made the workers vulnerable to respiratory diseases, and those who contracted tuberculosis were sent home and were often put in a storeroom until their deaths. They were often sexually harassed and verbally and physically abused by their supervisors (slow workers were beaten with sticks, and some were stripped naked as punishment).[93] It was perhaps these brutal working conditions in the mill, not Okame's "vanity" or desire for money, that made her fall into the hands of a procurer.

Working outside the home was probably a way of life for sons and daughters of struggling farmers in Hiroshima at the turn of the century. Facing diminishing opportunities and prejudice, many young men and women left their families in search of work elsewhere.

Industrial work offered them a chance to free themselves from economic and cultural constraints and breathe the air of cities, where
they met new people and experienced new ways of life. From 1896
to 1907, overseas migrants from Hiroshima quadrupled;[94] there was
abundant opportunity for young people to acquire a taste for foreign
goods and cultures through American returnees or letters sent from
their families and friends in North America. But all these desires for
new experiences and money and the decision to follow procurers must
be understood together with the hard realities in rural farming villages, the existing tradition of *dekasegi* in the region, and the problems of poverty among urban slum dwellers and members of outcaste
communities.

All in all, the evidence suggests that Japanese prostitutes in North
America came from the lower strata of Japanese society in both economic and social terms. Their parents typically worked as farmers, day laborers, shopkeepers, rickshaw men, or washerwomen,
and some came from outcaste communities that continued to face
prejudice. They often grew up in one-parent households, and poverty forced them to quit school and start earning wages as domestics,
mill hands, washing girls, barmaids, or prostitutes. In a sense, their
hopes for better lives in "America" resonated with Japanese immigrants who sought better opportunities overseas. But it was not just
the elusive promise of a better life that made these women decide
to leave their native villages and move to North America but also
the particular hardships they had experienced as members of marginalized social groups and their wish to contribute to the welfare of
their families. Yet what distinguished their experiences from those of
other poor people was that they had lived or worked in areas that had
strong connections with the North American West through commercial, transportation, and personal networks. Large structural changes
and various events in women's personal lives certainly created conditions in which they were likely to leave their homes in search of better
opportunities elsewhere. But they could not make the journey to the
North American West without the assistance of procurers and procuresses. The next chapter looks at the process of their recruitment
and migration to North America, in particular the role of transnational networks created by various actors on both sides of the Pacific.

CHAPTER 3

Recruitment and Passage

Transpacific Migration of Japanese
Prostitutes to the North American West

In 1896, a Japanese-language newspaper in San Francisco offered a graphic account of Oteru-san, who was lured by a procurer's "American story":

> Oteru-san was a person from Ejiri in Shizuoka Prefecture. A wealthy returnee from America was doing business in Ejiri at the time. Young people always clustered about him because he had lots of money and told unusual stories. When they did, he said, "If one went to America, even children could earn four to five dollars per day, and with a little more work one could make up to ten to fifteen dollars in a day." He also told them about the wonders of city life.
>
> For young people already given to idle dreams, they naturally wanted to go to America where things were so beautiful and earn such money. Upon asking him how to get there, he said that he could help them since he had acquaintances on ships and any number of friends in America. Then he started to play his hidden cards. This well-to-do man had actually made his money in prostitution in America. On the surface he was engaged in a legitimate business, but in reality he was the boss of a kidnapping ring. Sometimes Oteru-san visited him with two or three other girls. In the end they were taken in by his words. On a village festival night, they sneaked out of their homes and went to Yokohama with his assistance. From there they sailed for Seattle.[1]

Procurers visited one village after another, looking for young women who wished to escape from stifling village lives, hard labor, and limited job opportunities. The procurers often had legitimate businesses in their native villages, and their Western clothing and luxury items made their American tales of riches credible and appealing to women like Oteru-san.

Yamada Waka, who had been a prostitute in the United States and had been similarly lured to migrate by a "woman from America" in Yokohama, recalled the time when she had just escaped from a San Francisco brothel and entered a Presbyterian rescue mission: "When I emerged from the underground, I was burning with hatred for people, especially for men. I kept wondering what I could do to get revenge on those devils who'd taken advantage of a poor woman and had sucked her blood. I thought of pouring gasoline on their heads and setting them afire."[2] These intense emotional words are rare among her usual feminist writings based on theories and rational thinking. But her words must be taken seriously, considering the gap between what she heard from the procuress and the realities she faced after coming to Seattle.

Like ordinary Japanese migrants, these women came to North America via well-organized human networks across the ocean, but their stories did not fit into the conventional narratives of immigration as successful adjustments of families and individuals to changing socioeconomic conditions in the Old and New Worlds. The recruiters' primary interest was not in the welfare of women or their families but largely in the value of women's sexuality and labor in the North American market. Like other Japanese migrants and brides, these women were attracted by the prospect of earning money, receiving an education, or having a "civilized" life, and they generally cooperated with agents in entering Canada or the United States through legal or illegal means. Nonetheless, most women were not well acquainted with actual conditions at their destinations, and the procurers took advantage of their lack of knowledge to exploit them. These women's migrations hardly represent the general experience of Japanese immigrants but illuminate the role of the transpacific networks that facilitated their migration flow, the economic importance of prostitution in the Japanese ethnic economy, and the distinctive social and political character of the North American West at the turn of the twentieth century.

FROM CONTACT TO MIGRATION

Surely not all women were duped into coming to North America. For instance, Fumi Naito migrated from Yokohama to the United States with Y. Mukai in April 1904. Five months later, she was arrested in a Seattle brothel. Naito indicated in federal court that she had asked Mukai to take her to America "to study tailoring." A letter that she wrote to Mukai from prison, however, revealed that after arriving in Seattle, she chose to work as a prostitute: "I do not know how I could express a proper apology, because the trouble was brought about by that I persistently asked and appealed you to do what was the cause of all, for you refused me at first. . . . [If] we were allowed to stay in this country, we will decidedly assure you not to do again the business we heretofore followed. With this assurance, we desire you to appeal in behalf of us, the immigration officers to give us their permission to stay in the country." This letter served as evidence that she had worked voluntarily in the brothel, and the jury returned a verdict that Mukai was not guilty of importing and holding her for the purpose of prostitution.[3] The context of Naito's decision to follow Mukai was not clear, but for some women, especially daughters of poverty-stricken farmers or members of marginalized groups, becoming sex workers in North America was a means of dealing with various problems in their lives.

But it is important to note that these women did not necessarily see prostitution as the same as other work. Indeed, the moral prohibition against prostitution and their sense of respectability often influenced the process of becoming prostitutes in North America. Aki Takase, a Seattle prostitute, observed in federal court that her parents in Japan belonged to the "farming class," and that she had been "working housework" in Japan when a procurer induced her to come to America. "[I] went to a friend and he told me that there was a man [who] wanted [a girl] to come to the United States and [asked] if I didn't want to come, and then I became desirous about coming," she noted. Although she was asked to work as "a girl to sell wine," after arriving in Seattle, she was pressed into prostitution. She persistently denied that she had come to the country to engage in prostitution.[4] Her claim to respectability derived from her membership in the farming class (the second highest among the four historical categories of status in Tokugawa Japan), but her wish to maintain the reputation of a respectable woman made her vulnerable to a procurer who promised her respectable work as a salesgirl.

Although Japanese women often admitted that poverty was a cause of their migrating to North America and becoming prostitutes, they often made efforts to prove their respectability if they were suspected of immorality by federal officials. When Sumi Teshima was arrested for prostitution in 1910, she told the immigration office that "my parents were poor, and I did not go to school," and she had been a "farm laborer" from "childhood until I was twenty-two." Asked if she had sexual relations with men other than her husband before marriage, she declared: "No, I was not that kind." Although she eventually became a prostitute in San Francisco, her initial decision to marry a man who had worked as "a school-teacher" in Japan and a "farm laborer" in the United States reflected her wish to prove that she was a woman of respectable origin who wished to maintain that status when she reached her destination.[5] Despite the declining economic status of farmwork, these women often took pride in their membership in the farming class in Japan. For farming-class women who ended up as prostitutes, migrating to North America was a way of maintaining their status and respectability in Japan, not making a big material advancement or leading a luxurious life.

The notion of respectability for women in the context of Meiji Japan also helps in understanding why daughters of families that were relatively stable financially became prostitutes in North America.[6] Omatsu, for example, was the daughter of a well-off family managing a sake brewery in Kanbara, Shizuoka Prefecture. A procurer named Hayashi had known her parents for a long time. Around 1905–6, when Hayashi returned to Shizuoka, he happened to hear about Omatsu, who was then a student who wanted to study in the United States. Hayashi told her of various opportunities to learn English while working in the country, promising that he would help her achieve her goal. Lured by his stories, Omatsu decided to cross the ocean, and her parents let her go with Hayashi. After arriving in Canada, however, Omatsu was taken to Edmonton, Calgary, where she was forced into prostitution in a teahouse. For Omatsu, the lure of an educational opportunity in the United States that was unattainable in Japan was too strong to resist. Sadly, her parents, not knowing what their daughter was doing in Canada, sent her such magazines as *Jogaku sekai* (Schoolgirls' world) to her brothel every month.[7]

Around the time when Omatsu came to Canada, educational opportunities for women were beginning to grow in Japan. In 1899, the Regulations Concerning Women's Higher Schools was established, and high schools for women increased from 52 in 1900 to 193 in 1910. The magazine that Omatsu's parents sent her, *Jogaku sekai*, first issued in 1900, was one of the journals published for young women in this period. According to Ishiwata Takako, who studied the contents of *Jogaku sekai*, the editor and contributors generally emphasized women's role as mothers who stayed at home and used women's unique characteristics to contribute to the household and raise their children for the country, following the idealized vision of women as *ryōsai kenbo* (good wives and wise mothers) advocated by the government and leading educators of the period. But they also taught readers, primarily students from middle-class families, that expanding educational and job opportunities for women would permit them to have jobs after graduation, and even after marriage, and contribute to the family budget, introducing such possibilities as working as journalists, telegraph operators, bookkeepers, nurses, and midwives. The journal also introduced the conditions of women's education and work abroad with such titles as "Women's Colleges in Europe and America," "American Female Students Earning Their Own Living," and "Women's Work in America." Ishiwata writes: "It is possible that these articles on examples [of work and education] from Europe and the United States became objects of adoration for readers."[8] Omatsu may have been one such reader dreaming about an education in the United States and trying to find a way to attain that goal.

Japanese women who became prostitutes in North America also included a fair number of ordinary Japanese brides who joined their husbands. One such woman was Nishida Yoshi from Ehime Prefecture, who shared her experiences with a *Shin sekai* journalist in a prison at Angel Island before deportation in April 1911. She observed that after graduating from high school, a matchmaker introduced her to Nishida Haruzō, a fellow villager who was then working in the United States. Her parents opposed her marriage with a man whom she and they had never met. Deeply impressed by the photograph of Haruzō sporting a mustache in the Western style, however, she did not want to pass up this chance to live in her dream country. She added: "I have been attracted by the United States since my high school days. I didn't hear what my parents said." After coming to San Francisco, she found that Haruzō was just a servant working for a white family. She quickly disliked him and proposed a divorce. Haruzō then demanded payment of the money he had used for bringing her over and ordered her to work in a local bar-restaurant. When arrested on the charge of prostitution in 1911, she told the newspaperman: "Please tell picture-brides to take care that they won't repeat my mistake."[9]

From the mid-1880s, numerous men and women had taken ships
to the United States, with their own versions of "America" in their
minds. For many, the United States was a country where they could
earn a lot of money and have the opportunity to study at schools if
they wished. Those active in the People's Rights Movement or labor
movements came to the United States to continue their activities away
from oppressive Japanese authorities.[10] To young women with much
ambition but few resources, "America" presented itself as a country
of dramatic opportunities where they could live free from various
restrictions prescribed for them in Japan, and these idealized visions
of the United States made the women easy targets for procurers.

CONTRACTUAL AGREEMENT

The labor contract became a central feature of Japanese prostitution in the North American West shortly after its appearance around
1890, but unfortunately, few have survived.[11] The local American
press often lumped the contractual relation between Japanese prostitutes and procurers together with the similar system prevailing among
the Chinese as "Hideous Slavery."[12] To get a sense of the nature of the
contract, it will be more useful to turn to the reports compiled by
Japanese officials who were making efforts to understand the actual
workings of this system so as to prevent further migration of Japanese women for sex work. In March 1907, Shiga Prefecture governor Kawashima Sumitomo reported that about a year before, Kishida
Tomi, a procuress, entered into a labor contract with Terai Saki, "an
illegitimate child of Yanaka Kume," who lived in the same village,
telling her that she could work in her husband's restaurant in Vancouver. Kishida bought Western clothes, a hat, and a pair of shoes for
Terai and took her to Kobe. After giving Terai a passport, passage,
and seventy-five yen, she let the girl embark at Kobe alone. Once Terai
reached Vancouver, the procuress's husband attempted to send her
to a brothel in the interior of British Columbia. The Japanese consul
detected this plot, and authorities in Japan arrested the procuress for
violating the Japanese immigration law that prohibited agents from
recruiting laborers without licenses.[13]

The fact that Terai was an "illegitimate child" (shiseiji) deserves
consideration. Since the early Tokugawa period, keeping mistresses
had been a commonly accepted practice among the samurai class as
a means of producing heirs and maintaining the household. In the

Meiji period, rich merchants and politicians kept mistresses, mostly the daughters of poor families, by entering into work contracts with their parents.[14] The general status of mistresses remained low. In the revised legal code of 1882, the Meiji government ceased to acknowledge the legal status of concubines (*mekake*), and the Civil Code of 1898 limited their rights of inheritance—common-law wives had no right to inherit the property of their common-law husbands, and their children could inherit only half the share of legitimate children.[15] It is not clear whether or not Terai was aware that she would work as a prostitute in Canada, but her mother's decision to send her daughter to a procurer in exchange for an advance must be considered in relation to the general hardships experienced by common-law wives and women born out of wedlock.

The lack of information about the actual conditions at their destinations made these women vulnerable to exploitation by procurers. In June 1902, in Yokohama, a young couple, Yoshii Mitsu and Saburo, met an agent dispatched by Yamamoto Kisuke, a brothel-keeper in San Francisco, locally known as a "proprietor of a bamboo shop and a carpenter house." The agent provided them with tickets, the fee for quarantine, and cash worth 262 yen, and the couple signed a labor contract that stated: "I, hereby, promise to work for you for four years [*sic*], and shall obey your command, and shall not breach this agreement" (fig. 3.1). Once they arrived in San Francisco, Mitsu was placed in a brothel managed by Yamamoto. She escaped shortly and turned to a local "Japanese Christian Mission" for help.[16] The contract itself was not extraordinary considering that it was a common practice in Japan for women to sign labor contracts, get advances, and agree to work under the command of lenders. However, the absence of a clear definition of "work" in the contract gave the employer freedom to interpret the word as he saw fit and order Mitsu to work in his brothel.

After women started to work in brothels, their employers often used the contracts as a means of generating as much profit as possible from their labor. In the red-light districts that journalist Osada Shōhei visited in 1908–9, most Japanese women were indebted to their masters and working in their brothels to repay their debts. Theoretically, the women and masters were equal, and the women would be free from contractual obligations after clearing off their debts. In reality, however, women were often exploited in this system. According to Osada, indentured women (*kakae*) were required to give half

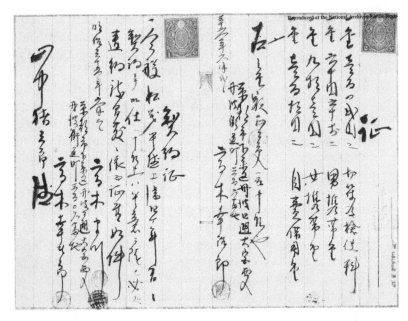

Figure 3.1. Labor contract between a Japanese couple and a brothel-keeper.

their earning to their masters, and out of the other half, they paid off their debts and bought necessary clothes and goods. So it was quite difficult for these women to pay off the $400–500 they owed their masters.[17] There was no place where the women could complain about the manipulation of accounts of their debts, because the police were protecting the interests of brothel-keepers in exchange for fines or bribes. The women's lack of information and language skills, and the absence of laws against the exploitation of prostitutes (or no enforcement of antiprostitution ordinances, to the benefit of their masters), permitted employers to use the contracts to exploit the women.

The existence of contractual agreements between procurers and prostitutes was also reported by Lucie Cheng in her study on Chinese prostitution in California. According to Cheng, Chinese women entered into a contract of four to five years and received no wages during the term. The contract required them to work at least 320 days per year, and sickness or pregnancy often forced them to take days off, which were added to the terms of service.[18] The fact that Japanese women received wages seems to show that their contracts included more elements of a work contract than the Chinese contracts, which allowed total domination by masters. But in both cases, employers used contracts to keep the women in brothels as long as possible by increasing the amount of debt. It is important to distinguish the Chinese labor-contract system from the Japanese one, because each contract was specific to the time, region, and circumstances of the signers. However, we must refrain from seeing the existence of contracts between women and their employers as evidence that the relationship between both parties was always equal or mutually beneficial.

LEAVING JAPANESE PORTS

Like Chinese prostitutes in California, Japanese women were also smuggled into Canada and the United States. Because procurers and prostitutes were often captured by Japanese officials before passage, Japanese government records include relatively concrete information about their plots. In May 1894, for instance, an English ship prepared to sail from Yokohama for Tacoma, Washington. The harbor police, while examining the freight, heard cries from two pieces of Western leather luggage. When they opened them, they found two teenage girls packed with clothing in each. The police also found two dubious trunks with two other girls inside, both almost dead from suffocation. Ichikawa Kihei, a passenger, was detained on the charge of smuggling the girls, and the examination revealed that Ichikawa came from the United States to hire prostitutes and asked his female accomplice in Yokohama to locate women. The woman, in cooperation with the wife of another procurer in the United States, recruited three girls from villages in Shizuoka and Kanagawa and the city of Yokohama. All were found guilty and fined for violating the Japanese law that forbade unlicensed agents to recruit laborers.[19]

In the process of transporting Japanese women to North America for prostitution, Chinese men played key roles. Chinese merchants had purchased the sexual services of Japanese women in Nagasaki since the Tokugawa period. After four other ports were opened for foreign settlement in 1858, they began to hire Japanese women as servants or concubines and secretly brought some of them back to China.[20] It was often difficult for Japanese officials to prevent the outflow of Japanese mistresses, because the masters dressed the women in Chinese clothing and made them look like their daughters.[21] Chinese sailors were also reported to have helped procurers and women board ships secretly.[22] Yuji Ichioka was probably correct in writing that some of these women would have been transported later to Chinese labor camps in North America for prostitution. Otherwise, one cannot explain the presence of Japanese prostitutes in Denver, Colorado, in the 1860s and Butte, Montana, and the Los Angeles area in the 1880s.[23] Only after the opening of direct service between Yokohama and Vancouver in 1887 did Japanese prostitutes begin to draw the attention of Japanese consuls.[24]

Regular reports on similar smuggling cases by the Japanese press in the 1890s indicate that smuggling was a common means of transporting Japanese women to Pacific Coast cities in the early stage of the development of Japanese prostitution in the North American West.[25] However, it is actually difficult to estimate the scale of Japanese smuggling accurately, because procurers evaded the eyes of Japanese officials, and the majority did not appear in the records of the Foreign Ministry. One can say only that smuggling was a risky business. Procurers and brothel-keepers could maximize their profits without paying for the women's passage. But they could lose all the money they used for arranging this undertaking just by being discovered by captains or officials. This measure thus worked well when it was organized by small groups of trusted collaborators in the early phase of migration in the 1880s and early 1890s.

As Japanese officials began to examine departing women rigorously in the 1890s, procurers turned to another tactic—passing Japanese women off as their "wives" by using other women's passports. As a general rule, the Japanese government did not issue passports to young single women;[26] therefore, a fraudulent marriage was the easiest way to get passports and leave Japanese ports. Vancouver consul Nosse Tatsugorō, in a letter to the Foreign Ministry, reported that since he had started his new job in January 1895, every ship from Japan brought five to six prostitutes to Victoria. Nosse explained that "[a]t first, a Japanese procurer and his wife appear in person at the prefectural office to receive their passports. Then, the procurer's wife gives her passport to a girl, having her memorize all the information on it so that she can answer the harbor police's questions. In another case, a girl goes on board with a procurer's wife as a person seeing her off. . . . When the ship starts sailing, the procurer's wife disappears in the crowd and gets off the ship." After their arrival in North American ports, the procurers sent the passports back to their accomplices in Japan and reused them to import other women.[27] Procurers also purchased other women's passports or asked fellow villagers to take their prostitutes to North America.[28]

EVADING CANADIAN AND AMERICAN LAW

Typically, procurers and prostitutes arrived in the United States via Canada, more specifically, Victoria and Vancouver, British Columbia. Before 1906, the Canadian government did not regulate the entry of immigrants as strictly as the U.S. government did. It established the first Immigration Act of 1869 primarily for ensuring safe passages and promoting the settlement of immigrants in Canada. It prohibited the entry of migrants likely to become public charges and those with a physical disability or a criminal tendency, but because many migrants passed through Canada and moved to the United States, these restrictions were not strictly enforced.[29] Furthermore, deportation in Canada from the 1890s to 1906 was, according to historian Barbara Roberts, "under-reported, informal, and ad hoc." There were certainly cases in which officials decided to exclude some kinds of aliens whom they deemed undesirables, including the injured, the incapable, and those deemed "immoral," but "[t]he role of government was essentially passive" in the period, Roberts writes.[30] Canada's lax attitudes toward immigration and deportation of aliens made British Columbian ports major way stations for Japanese procurers and prostitutes moving to the south. This pattern continued at least until 1906, when Canada revised the immigration law and implemented a more rigid deportation practice.[31]

At the provincial level, however, officials did take action to exclude Japanese prostitutes and procurers before 1906 in response to requests from Japanese consuls in Vancouver. In July 1904, for example, W. H. Bullock-Webster, acting immigration officer for British Columbia, in his letter to Charles Wilson, K.C., attorney general of the province, wrote that, in response to the Japanese consul's request, he had refused to allow the landing of six Japanese women and a man by drawing on the British Columbia Immigration Act of 1904, which prohibited the entry of those who failed to pass a European-language test. He ordered the ship captain to take them away from the province. Subsequently, the group hired a Canadian lawyer to file for writs of habeas corpus, arguing that the British Columbia Immigration Act was "ultra vires." Bullock-Webster agreed to bring the group ashore, and according to the *Victoria Daily Colonist*, the chief justice issued writs of habeas corpus.[32] At the same time, however, Bullock-Webster sent a telegram to the Japanese consul to request his attendance at the Supreme Court, where the passengers would be prosecuted for violating the provincial code criminalizing the procurement of women for the purpose of prostitution.[33] As Andrea Geiger and others have written, the provincial power to refuse entry to the Japanese was severely restricted in this period due to existing treaties between Britain and Japan—especially the Anglo-Japanese Treaty of Commerce and Navigation in 1894, which permitted British and Japanese "to enter, to travel or reside in any part of the dominions and possessions of the other contracting party"—and the federal government's intention to assert its power over the province.[34] It was not until the implementation of the Lemieux Agreement in 1908 that the Canadian government started exercising its federal power to severely restrict the entry of the Japanese.

Canada's federal power over naturalization also created a context in which Japanese procurers could bring over Japanese women by circumventing provincial attempts to restrict their entry. Unlike the U.S. government, which had restricted citizenship to "free white persons" (by the Nationality Act of 1790) and "persons of African nativity and descent" (by the Nationality Act of 1870), the Canadian government permitted alien residents to apply for naturalization after three years of residence in Canada, and after swearing allegiance to the country and satisfying notaries public that they were persons of "good character," applicants were granted citizenship.[35] British Columbia opposed this practice, responding to local white fishermen's complaints about Japanese fishermen who had applied for naturalization and received licenses in increasing numbers; the provincial legislature appealed to the federal government to revise the act to make it difficult for Asians to be naturalized.[36] The federal government revised the Immigration Act in 1914, extending the residency requirement from three to five years and requiring applicants to show proficiency in English or French;[37] however, the country kept naturalization open to foreigners.[38] As immigration officials examined women who arrived as wives of migrants more closely after 1906, procurers made their women carry copies of their naturalization papers to ensure their safe passage.[39] Thus, despite white Canadians' general opposition to Japanese immigration and growing federal restrictions placed on the entry of aliens (especially laborers), naturalized citizens and their wives were not, in the eyes of the law at least, "immoral" or members of the excludable class.

The migration of Japanese procurers and women across the Canadian border must also be understood as part of the transborder migration that had been growing since the last years of the nineteenth century. The Committee on Immigration and Naturalization set up in the 51st United States Congress (1889–91) reported that there was "no inspection whatever" on the Canadian border in the late nineteenth century. In the six months from July 1890 to January 1891 alone, some fifty thousand had crossed the U.S.-Canadian border, including large numbers of those excluded by earlier legislation, such as contract laborers, convicts, and paupers.[40] Although the majority of these migrants entering the United States from Canada were Europeans, a fair number of Chinese, Japanese, and South Asians joined this migration stream and found work in various industries in the Pacific Northwest.[41] As Yukari Takai writes, the emergence of this transborder Asian migration pattern was due in part to the absence of Canadian laws preventing Asians from entering the country as well as the agency of migrants. The Chinese were fined upon entering Canada, but their entry was not prohibited; the Japanese were free to come, at least until 1908, when the treaty with Japan began to restrict the migration of laborers to Canada and President Theodore Roosevelt's executive order (effective in summer 1908) made it illegal to enter the country via Hawaii, Canada, and other insular U.S. possessions; South Asians were not welcome but were permitted to come, at least before 1908, when the Canadian government passed an order-in-council requiring continuous passage from countries of origin. After entering Canada, some of these Asian migrants who wished to move to the United States but would be excludable under U.S. immigration law bought passports from fellow countrymen on the U.S. side, walked without documents through the thick forests along the border, or hired guides who helped them journey to U.S. labor camps.[42]

Working closely with local residents, ship captains, and steamship companies, Japanese procurers skillfully crossed the border with Japanese women. Okawara Tomikichi, a brothel-keeper in Salt Lake City, for example, took a seal-otter hunting boat at Hakodate and smuggled two women into Victoria; from there he crossed the Canadian border into Washington in 1901.[43] Similarly, Yokota Yasaburo and his accomplice in San Francisco first let their women steal passage to Victoria in 1904, and upon securing a fishing boat in New Westminster, they proceeded to the state of Washington late at night.[44] Vancouver consul Morikawa Kishirō reported in 1906 that Dodwell & Company steamships frequently carried Japanese prostitutes from

Vancouver to Tacoma.⁴⁵ Typically, the steamships, upon arriving at Vancouver or Victoria, declared Canada as the final destination of their passengers; after going through formalities, the passengers boarded the same ships again and moved on to Seattle, Tacoma, or San Francisco. For their part, steamship companies preferred to disembark passengers at Canadian ports rather than pay the four-dollar head tax for each migrant landing at U.S. ports. They also wanted to avoid the burden of deporting excluded migrants to Japan when they were refused entry at U.S. ports. The migrants were also aware that Canada would offer them transit privileges, allowing them to stay in Canada even if they were denied entry by U.S. officials for medical reasons, and many of them later moved to the United States.⁴⁶ The transborder migration of Japanese procurers and prostitutes was thus part of broader strategies employed by Asian migrants to cope with the power of the nation-state at the turn of the century. At the same time, as Erika Lee and others write, their challenge to national sovereignty and security surely contributed to the construction of Asians as "illegal" "smugglers," leading to stricter regulation of Asians entering the two countries after the turn of the century.⁴⁷

This migration pattern points to the complex interaction between race, economy, and the law in the Canadian borderland, challenging our understanding of race relations. As Kornel Chang and William H. Siener have shown, despite the growing antipathy toward Asian laborers in the Pacific Northwest (represented by the expulsion of Chinese laborers from Bellingham, Washington, in 1885), local industries— milling, logging, salmon canning, and railroad building—continued to generate demand for labor, and Asian laborers continued to come with the help of middlemen, providing American capitalists with much-needed labor. Chinese merchants gave laborers fraudulent documents and coached them for interviews with immigration officials, seeking to evade the Chinese Exclusion Act of 1882, which prohibited the entry of Chinese laborers for ten years (it was extended for another ten years in 1892 and made permanent in 1902). They collaborated with local American and Canadian guides and ship companies in passing Chinese laborers across the border on ships and on foot, subsequently transporting them to labor camps.⁴⁸ Following these examples, Japanese procurers paid immigration officials and local white residents sizable sums that secured smooth passage across the border.⁴⁹ Thus, in the border region where "illegal" migration became a lucrative business, social relations were not clearly defined by race, and to understand the nature of this migration pattern, it is necessary to see the Canadian border region as a creative space where various social and racial groups interacted with one another and sometimes worked together to achieve their goals.

When procurers and women reached U.S. ports, strict examinations awaited them, and they had thoroughly prepared for the exams. In May 1896, for instance, two procurers, Fukada Kojiro and Omura Kumakichi, arrived in Seattle via Canada with their "wives" and three girls. Immigrant inspectors detained them and referred them to the U.S. district court in Seattle. All the women denied the charge of coming to the country to work as prostitutes. Fukada, Omura, and their "wives" similarly denied that they had induced the girls to come to the United States under labor contracts, observing that they had never known the girls until they became acquainted with them in Yokohama. By saying that, they denied the charge of violating the Page Act of 1875, which banned the entry of any immigrant who had entered into a labor contract "for lewd and immoral purposes" before arrival and "Oriental" women imported "for the purposes of prostitution."[50] When Fukuda was asked why he had paid for passage from Victoria to Seattle for the three girls, he answered that he had done so "as a small act of kindness." Then the three women showed in court that they had twenty to thirty-eight dollars each to support the claim that they were not likely to become public charges. The juries found the detainment of these women unlawful, and all the men and women were released.[51] As Roger Daniels writes, Japanese labor contractors often furnished their laborers with so-called show money as proof that the workers were financially independent;[52] Japanese procurers also made their women carry a certain amount of money and pose as laborers or wives, instead of appearing as destitute migrants or prostitutes under labor contracts.[53]

As Yuji Ichioka's study revealed, procurers turned to the U.S. district court when officials prevented women from landing at U.S. ports. In May 1890, two Japanese women, Chiyo and Shina, arrived at the port of San Francisco, and immigration officials detained them as people likely to become public charges (fig. 3.2). Genji Hasegawa, who had summoned them, appealed to the federal court to secure writs of habeas corpus. His accomplice, George Wakimoto, persuaded the court to release the two women, providing evidence that they had come to work in Hasegawa's store. The women were released and actually began to work in the store. After four weeks, however, they were discovered in a brothel on St. Mary Street.[54] Once again, a year later, Hasegawa sent for four women from Japan and filed for a writ of habeas corpus on their behalf when they were denied landing by Inspector W. H. Thornley. Commissioner Houghton refused to accept the petitions, stating that the court had no right to review the actions taken by federal inspectors appointed by the federal government. Hasegawa then appealed to the U.S. Supreme Court. By a decision in January 1892, the court decided to deport two women who had no skills and permitted the other two women, who would be able to earn their living through embroidery, to remain in the country.[55]

One should not take these women's court performance as evidence that they had intended to work as prostitutes in the United States, however. Note that when they attempted to enter the country, they claimed before officials that they had come to the country to join their husbands or engage in work other than prostitution, but as discussed earlier in this chapter, when the women or their procurers were found guilty and sentenced to deportation, Japanese women often explained in court that they had been deceived by procurers into coming to the country or forced into prostitution after their entry. Therefore, it is not entirely clear what these women had intended to do in the United States at the time of their entry. Surely, some would have intended to work as prostitutes and performed in front of officials so that they would be allowed to enter the country. Others would have simply been responding to officials' questions as they had been coached by procurers before arrival. There were both possibilities.

In analyzing the use of habeas corpus petitions by Japanese procurers, the influence of earlier Chinese examples is not negligible. In August 1874, for example, the state of California denied the landing of twenty-two Chinese women at San Francisco based on the state law that required those suspected of being paupers, convicts, and "lewd or debauched women" to post a $500 bond (another California statue enacted in 1870 made it unlawful to bring over persons without evidence of voluntary emigration and good character). The procurers submitted habeas corpus petitions to the federal court, and the women claimed that they had come to join their husbands. The court found the California statute unconstitutional on the grounds that it violated the equal protection clause in the Fourteenth Amendment. According to Rev. Otis Gibson, who had provided testimony against these women in court, these women, except one whose case was referred to the U.S. Supreme Court, were subsequently sent to

Figure 3.2. Two Japanese women imported
for prostitution by Genji Hasegawa in
1890. Courtesy of the National Archives
and Records Administration, San Bruno,
California

local brothels.[56] As Lucie Cheng has explained, American lawyers collaborated with procurers to allow these women to land, and agents in China had instructed women on how to respond to immigration officials' questions through the use of coaching papers.[57] In 1882, the Chinese Exclusion Act restricted immigration of Chinese women to the wives of merchants and naturalized citizens,[58] thereby making it extremely difficult for procurers to bring over Chinese women for prostitution by this means. Thereafter, the Japanese succeeded the Chinese in prostitution on the West Coast, following the example of their predecessors in dealing with immigration restrictions.

LOCAL CONDITIONS IN THE NORTH AMERICAN WEST

The ineffectiveness of federal laws restricting the entry of prostitutes and the agency of procurers do not explain everything about their migration processes. One must also consider the local conditions of the North American West under which Japanese prostitution expanded. From the late 1840s, discoveries of gold, silver, and copper brought thousands of miners to California, and later to British Columbia, Montana, and Idaho; the constructions of lumber mills and canneries in the Pacific Northwest and the building of the Great Northern and the Canadian Pacific Railroads facilitated further migration of male workers to the North American West. After the opening of regular routes from Japan to Vancouver, Seattle, and San Francisco between 1887 and 1896, Japanese male laborers flooded into the West. These developments created societies in which men far outnumbered women. The skewed male-female ratio distinguished western cities from eastern cities in both Canada and the United States (see table 3.1).

This unbalanced gender ratio shaped the industrial and political character of western towns. After the Klondike gold rush of 1897, Vancouver, Seattle, and Portland grew by supplying goods and services to miners making their way north, and prostitution and outfitting businesses expanded rapidly in these cities.[59] Publicly, municipal governments generally opposed prostitution and enacted ordinances against it. However, because prostitution was an indispensable element in the economies of western towns, authorities permitted women to practice prostitution in segregated red-light districts. In Spokane, for example, authorities declared prostitution illegal in 1889, but the police rarely enforced the law. They

TABLE 3.1. Numbers of men per hundred women in eastern and western North American cities

	1890–1891	1900–1901	1910–1911
Halifax	92.9	98.5	92.7
Toronto	94.9	87.7	98.1
Winnipeg	109.6	107.5	120.7
Calgary	124.7	124.6	155.0
Vancouver	187.5	144.8	149.9
Boston	94.4	96.1	96.7
New York	97.4	98.5	99.9
Philadelphia	97.3	94.7	96.4
Butte	201.7	147.7	132.4
Spokane	199.5	134.9	122.7
Seattle	166.8	176.7	136.2
San Francisco	131.5	117.1	131.6
Portland	167.6	142.4	134.5

Sources: Fay Farraday, "The Debate about Prostitution: A History of the Formation and Failure of Canadian Laws against the Sex Trade, 1867–1917" (M.A. thesis, University of Toronto, 1991), 115; Department of Interior, Census Office, *Report on Population of the United States at the Eleventh Census: 1890*, part 1 (Washington, D.C.: Government Printing Office, 1895), 452, 460, 467, 471, 476, 478, 483; Department of Interior, Census Office, *Twelfth Census of the United States, Taken in the Year 1900*, vol. 1, Population (Washington, D.C.: Government Printing Office, 1901), 610, 620, 631, 637, 639, 645; Department of Commerce, Bureau of Census, Thirteenth Census of the United States Taken in the Year 1910, vol. 1, Population (Washington, D.C.: Department of Commerce, Bureau of the Census, 1913), 263, 283, 286.

customarily arrested prostitutes for charges not related to prostitution, such as "vagrancy," and released them after collecting fines. Protestant reformers did protest against this system, but the regulation school of thought was strong among authorities who viewed prostitution as providing a necessary sexual outlet for men, especially those living without spouses. Moreover, the city's business community—including bankers, restaurant managers, and the owners of buildings where prostitutes worked—profited from prostitution and strongly opposed an outright ban. Viewing prostitution as a vital part of the local economy, authorities developed the system of confining and fining, which became a common feature of mining towns and service centers supplying goods and services to miners in the North American West. Japanese prostitution grew in this political atmosphere of the western frontier. In Spokane, Japanese women constituted the largest group (23 percent) of prostitutes who paid fines in the police court between 1889 and 1910.[60]

Similarly, in Seattle, economic considerations resulted in the development of the fine system, but in the creation and application of antiprostitution laws, nonwhite women were picked out in ways white women were not. In 1861, John Pennell from San Francisco built the first brothel in the town to serve the needs of laborers working in the sawmill established by Henry Yesler and recruited local Native American women to work in his house. Prostitution developed hand in hand with local industries thereafter. In 1884, responding to the requests of residents who opposed these developments, the city established an ordinance titled "Dissolute Indian Women, Soliciting Prostitution" restricting the movement of Native women at night and making "soliciting prostitution upon any of the public streets, alleys, wharves or other public places of the city" a punishable offense, although by this time, the majority of prostitutes were white and Asian.[61] While directing attention away from white and Asian prostitutes and strengthening the image of Native women as "dissolute," the police demanded that Asian women pay them "fines" in return for not enforcing antiprostitution ordinances. The criminal docket book for King County, Washington, recorded that in the period between 1892 and 1903, twelve Japanese criminal cases reached the superior court in Seattle. Only one Japanese woman, named "Mabo," was prosecuted on the charge of living in a "house of ill fame" in 1892.[62] Japanese officials were frustrated with the reputation of the Japanese in American society. Secretary Fujita Toshirō, who visited Seattle in 1891, complained that the "fines" collected by local police from Japanese brothel operators were bribes that made the prosecution of Japanese brothel-keepers and prostitutes under existing city ordinances extremely difficult.[63] Seattle consul Abe Kihachi reported that before 1910, Seattle had been "wide open" and "brothel-keepers placed [corrupt] policemen in front of their houses and operated their business openly."[64]

In San Francisco, from the mid-nineteenth to the early twentieth century, the economy of the city's flourishing red-light district was closely tied to prostitution. Hotel managers, liquor salesmen, and theater managers, for example, all depended on prostitutes as customers. Prostitutes also spent their money on luxury items—like jewelry and fashionable clothing—and regularly visited physicians for checkups or abortions. Brothel-keepers bribed the mayor, policemen, and judges so that the police would protect prostitutes from arrest, and the authorities ensured that prostitutes could continue to work. Reformers' attempts to eliminate prostitutes from their community ended in failure.[65] After the arrival of Chinese laborers in the mid-twentieth century, prostitutes increased in the city's Chinatown, where prominent white citizens owned most of the estates and leased them to Chinese brothel-keepers, charging rents two or three times higher than those paid by whites. As Lucie Cheng wrote, the high rents, together with the fines paid to the police, caused brothel-keepers to exploit Chinese women more severely in order to generate profits.[66] The Page Act of 1875 and the Chinese Exclusion Act of 1882 limited the migration of Chinese prostitutes and wives of laborers but also increased the need for Japanese women among both the Chinese and increasing numbers of Japanese laborers who replaced the Chinese.

In western Canada, Japanese prostitution did not develop in the Pacific Coast cities of Victoria or Vancouver but in inland towns, especially in the Kootenays, a major mining region in the southern part of British Columbia. In the 1880s and 1890s, a series of silver and copper strikes attracted large numbers of miners to this region, and by 1900, the construction of railroads across the Canadian border carried rich ore from the Kootenays to smelters in the United States and facilitated the migration of miners from the U.S. side of the border.[67] As an inevitable result of the overwhelming predominance of males, prostitution became a lucrative business in the region.[68] Japanese prostitutes increased in Nelson, Rossland, Revelstoke, and Greenwood in the late 1890s, and according to a consular report, the majority of them came from Spokane, Washington.[69] By 1908–9, when Osada Shōhei did a survey on Japanese prostitution in Canada, Japanese prostitutes had been working throughout mining towns and trading centers along the Canadian Pacific Railway in British Columbia, Alberta, and Calgary. The scale of Japanese prostitution was smaller and its development slower than in the United States, but the evidence suggests that Japanese prostitution continued until the late 1910s or later in Canada as the U.S. government tightened its regulation of prostitution during the first two decades of the century.[70]

Although Canada's Criminal Code of 1892 had criminalized the seduction of women between fourteen and sixteen years of age and procurement of women for prostitution in and outside Canada,[71] the system of fining and confining was an accepted practice in western Canada, too. Of course, not all residents were willing to accept the practice. In Nelson, for instance, in August 1896, a grand jury criticized lax morality in the town and submitted an indictment for vagrancy against two Japanese living with unmarried women. The judge was unsupportive of this move, however. According to the *Nelson Miner*, "His Lordship proceeded to discuss the question of abolishing houses of ill fame, and while undoubtedly those badly conducted ought to be suppressed, it was an open question whether society would be benefited by closing them all," attributing the non-enforcement of the vagrancy law to the fact that "there were not enough constables in [Nelson and Rossland]."[72] Western Canada was less populated than the American West in the early twentieth century, and the lack of manpower made it difficult to enforce antiprostitution laws. The authorities adopted the policy of segregation, arguing that it would protect respectable women from prostitution and prevent prostitutes from spreading throughout the city.[73] When Osada Shōhei visited Nelson in 1908–9, he witnessed Japanese brothel-keepers and prostitutes being protected from arrests in exchange for the fines they paid regularly to the police. He wrote: "There is no place like Nelson where [prostitution] is operating in such an orderly manner."[74] The combination of these political, demographic, and social factors contributed to the persistence of Japanese prostitution in the inland of Canada after the turn of the century.

Thus Japanese prostitution developed in this peculiar social, cultural, economic, and political environment of the turn-of-the-century North American West. Both the authorities and reformers agreed that prostitution was not a legitimate way for women to make living, and the authorities enacted ordinances against prostitution, ordering the police to raid brothels, especially those of Asians, as a form of lip service to reformers who wanted more order in their community and white laborers who opposed growing numbers of Asian laborers in the West. Yet they also acknowledged the importance of prostitutes, who increased local consumption, enriched local businesses, and served Asian workers who were providing much-needed labor for the extractive and construction industries. This led to the unofficial recognition and regulation of prostitution through fines and segregation. Japanese prostitution thus developed as part of racial and class formations in the North American West, where Asian laborers and prostitutes were not welcomed but were considered indispensable for social and economic developments in the region.

ORGANIZATIONAL NETWORKS

In the early years of Japanese prostitution in North America (the late 1880s to the 1890s), most migrations of procurers and prostitutes were small-scale, individual undertakings. By the turn of the century, however, as the U.S. and Canadian governments began to examine the entry of "undesirable" aliens more strictly, the processes of recruiting and transporting Japanese women to the North American West had become more organized, involving actors on both sides of the Pacific. Federal investigations of corruption in the immigration service in 1900 and 1907 graphically revealed the operation of these systems. In October 1900, Customs Inspector Frank Barry in San Francisco denied the landing of three Japanese women, charging them with coming to the country for prostitution. Immediately, James Kimura and Robert Lyons, an attorney, headed to the ship and showed the inspector passes for the women signed by Albert Geffeney, Deputy Immigration Commissioner. Charles Geffeney, an acting Japanese interpreter and also Albert's brother, became suspicious of his brother's behavior and later discovered that Albert had received money from procurers and agreed to help them land their women. He then decided to file a corruption charge against his brother. "It was like sticking a knife into my own flesh," Charles told a newspaperman, but "I had to defend myself from unjust implication." His testimony proved strong enough to force Albert to resign from office.[75]

According to a letter sent from a Protestant church member in San Francisco to the governor of Kanagawa Prefecture in 1906, James Kimura had been known as the "leader of Japanese smuggling ring" in San Francisco. He had established his office on Pine Street in 1898, and ever since, he "had worked with Chinatown brothel-keepers, kidnapped naïve wives of laborers from Hawaii, and forced them into prostitution."[76] Kimura's connection with Albert Geffeney continued even after Geffeney was forced out of service. He followed Geffeney to Seattle, where Geffeney was reinstated as an inspector in the immigration service and helped Japanese women enter the country. In May 1906, Seattle consul Hisamizu Saburō reported that since Kimura had come to Seattle, it had become easier for prostitutes to land, and brothel-keepers were forming "undesirable relations" with immigration officials.[77] The presence of Geffeney and Kimura thus gave Japanese prostitution in Seattle a boost.

Geffeney's reign did not last long, however. From September to October 1907, immigration inspectors investigated corruption charges against him, and he was forced to leave his position. The investigation disclosed that Geffeney had frequently received loans from Aiyū Sha, a Japanese insurance company that compensated its members if they were deported from Seattle.[78] But in reality, Japanese procurers used this insurance system as a vehicle for importing Japanese women for prostitution in Seattle and other places. Japanese procurers purchased the insurance in Yokohama; in Seattle, Geffeney permitted those wearing the emblem furnished by Aiyū Sha to land. As Lucie Cheng wrote, as more provisions were added to the immigration law from 1891, the inspection of immigrants at ports took more time to complete, and this created more opportunities for corruption and the need on the part of procurers to give officials larger bribes meant to ensure the smooth entry of the women and themselves.[79]

Therefore, immigration officials were often in a stronger position than procurers in negotiating the amount of a bribe. As Aiyū Sha became more dependent on Geffeney for the importation of women, he began to demand a larger sum for his work. He forced members of the insurance company to lend him money, and from July to August 1907, he took a vacation trip to Japan at the company's expense, and its members in Japan arranged a welcome party for him and paid for amusement expenses worth $115. As a hotel owner observed, "Mr. Geffeney, understanding the Japanese customs, manners and language so well, some immoral Japanese are afraid of him."[80]

Ostensibly, members of Aiyū Sha were known as leading businessmen in Seattle's Japantown; these included hotel owners, an investor, the vice president of a trading company, a laundry owner, and a dealer in general merchandise. At the same time, however, they were making large profits from prostitution by managing brothels or leasing their buildings to brothel operators. According to Takeuchi Kōjirō, the former editor of the *Taihoku nippō* in Seattle, Hirade Kuranosuke, a major figure in the business community in Seattle's Japantown, originally arrived in Seattle in 1891 and worked as a migrant laborer. After accumulating capital by selling fruit to Japanese prostitutes, he established himself as a leading businessman, serving as the vice president of the Oriental Trading Company. But he continued to profit from prostitution by leasing one of his buildings to the owner of the Aloha House, a major brothel in Seattle. In 1906, Hirade, in cooperation with other businessmen, constructed a building for another brothel.

His plan ended in failure due to the sudden relocation of the red-light district by the city.[81] In the early days of the Japanese community in Seattle, Japanese businessmen had close connections with prostitutes and brothel-keepers.[82] Takeuchi described the place of prostitution in Seattle's Japantown in its early days: "When Japanese men were still struggling to find a way to make a living in a foreign land, Japanese women made a fortune so quick. It was an undeniable fact that these women were the providers for fellow countrymen."[83]

In the federal court case against Geffeney, one of the pieces of evidence submitted was the diary of a procurer, Matsunaga Chubei, who arrived in Seattle with his "wife" and two other girls in June 1907. It described the whole process of his migration with prostitutes from Yokohama to Butte, Montana, where he opened a brothel. From the diary, we can see that Matsumura took a Great Northern Railway ship, SS *Minnesota*, at Yokohama, on May 24, 1907. Fifteen days later, the ship arrived at Port Townsend and reached Seattle the next morning. Matsunaga's entry for June 7 says: "At 6 A.M. through with medical inspection. At 10 arrived at Seattle. At 2. p.m. pictures were taken. At 4 P.M. got through with the questions from the immigration officers and landed. *From (or through) Mr. Fuda communicated to Geffeney and sent twenty dollars as compensation* [emphasis added]. Put up at Eureka Hotel." He exchanged money in Japantown, and the party took a train to Spokane on June 9. He met two individuals at Spokane Station on June 10 and arrived in Butte on June 11. In the next seven days, Matsumura located a room and ordered kimonos for the two girls. He started cooking, cleaned the room, and attended to one of the girls, Hama, who had caught a cold. Finally, he "opened the house" for prostitution on June 18.[84] His well-structured and smooth migration process from Yokohama to Butte demonstrates that the *Aiyū Sha* network extended back to Japan, and the importation of women required collaboration with local Japanese businessmen as well as U.S. federal officials.

To ensure the smooth operation of their businesses, procurers planned the procurement of women carefully. In September 1906, a Japanese procurer named Hayase was arrested in Nagoya, Japan. According to Rev. U. G. Murphy, who reported this incident, in the past five years, Hayase had sent large numbers of Japanese women to Seattle, where his brother Yoshitaro sold them to brothels. Like many other procurers, he reused passports that were originally issued to other

women. Hayase had received $15,000 for recruiting prostitutes dur-
ing the past five years and owned a large farm near Nagoya. When he
was arrested, he had a letter sent from his brother in Seattle. Murphy
translated it as follows:

> As far as possible send poor girls from the country who had never had
> anything to do with men. The last lot is giving me much trouble and I
> am afraid that I shall not even get the bargain money out of them. They
> are too common. I intend to work them a while and then cast them
> off. You must not be too strict on girls *en route*. If after landing they
> should run away to some distant interior place it would be difficult to
> catch them again. Of the lot before the last *Koto* has a good face, is
> strong and takes well with white men—Americans. She has already
> caught several lovers and is having a jolly time. *Shizu*, of the same lot,
> is weak and is in the hospital at present. It may be necessary to give her
> some *rough treatment* [kill her] and settle her case.[85]

Obviously, a group of women sent by Hayase had given his brother
in Seattle "much trouble," as indicated in the reference to the difficulty of catching women if they escape into the interior. The brother's request for women who knew nothing about men suggests that
the women who were used to dealing with men, or who had already
engaged in sex work in Japan, were more likely to escape from brothels with customers or lovers. Also important is that in the Seattle
procurer's eyes, a woman who had a good appearance and many customers was having "a jolly time," and a sickly one who could not get
customers and did not generate profits must be disposed of. Thus his
view of women was determined primarily by their profitability and
had nothing to do with how they were feeling. The fact that the letter was translated by a Methodist minister who had opposed Japan's
licensed prostitution cautions against generalizing about the recruitment methods used by procurers in the North American West. But
the letter provides a glimpse into a world of Japanese prostitution that
operated much like any other business governed by the principles of
experiment and profit making.

   The scale of smuggling is difficult to estimate accurately because
successful cases of smuggling simply did not appear in official records.
However, it did continue to be a method that procurers used to import
Japanese women for prostitution, and as immigration officials investigated the movement of migrants and ships across borders after the turn
of the century, it became a more organized undertaking that required
close collaboration. Two letters obtained by the U.S. government in

a smuggling case in December 1909 illustrate this point. In the first letter, dated April 20, 1908, the author (the procurer) in Yokohama was responding to an order from Portland for a prostitute, informing the purchaser that "the market price of a woman is about $500." He promised to send a woman once he received a deposit of $300 from the purchaser. In the second letter, dated July 1, the procurer notified the Portland man that he had received the deposit, a postal money order for 202.1 yen, via a man in Yokosuka (a port city neighboring Yokohama), saying that "you may set your mind at ease about [the order]." He proposed a plan directing his man to transport the prostitute to the vicinity of San Francisco and asked the purchaser to "go out to meet them [with money]" and "hear from them about the details of how to land them." The letters show that several men were involved in the process of transporting a woman from Yokohama to San Francisco: the boss who arranged the exportation of a woman, a man who transferred a deposit from the purchaser to the boss, and a man who transported the woman to the United States. The cost of passage, commission paid to collaborators, and other expenses added up to $500, and this sum became the woman's debt to the purchaser.[86]

Finally, women procurers, oftentimes former prostitutes, played key roles in the recruitment of young women in Japan. Kawaguchi Matsu, a major procuress arrested by the harbor police in Yokohama in March 1911, is an example. According to information that appeared in newspapers and journals in Japan and San Francisco, she was the daughter of a navy officer in Shinagawa, in Tokyo, who left her home at the age of sixteen to escape from an arranged marriage, followed a Japanese man to Hawaii, and became a common prostitute. She later moved with another man to San Francisco, where they managed a brothel. In 1911, at the age of thirty-six, Matsu returned to Yokohama to recruit girls, and, according to the *Shin sekai* newspaper in San Francisco, she had become a procuress, "stylishly dressed in Western clothing."[87] Working under another major procurer in Hong Kong, she was reported to have been "living in luxury, owning impressive mansions in Hong Kong, and keeping men in several places."[88] In these accounts, the source of information about her background is not entirely clear. Some clearly was from the story she had presented to Japanese officials at the harbor police station; some was from rumors among those who had known her work. The description of her background is highly subjective indeed. The newspaper editors' focus on her "criminal" activities suggests not so much their concern with the facts of her activities as their anxiety over a woman who used her sexuality to gain power and exert a strong influence over girls as well as men (both her subordinates and those she had kept as paramours). At the same time, however, these accounts indicate that these "stylishly dressed" procuresses with large sums of money played a major role in persuading young women to follow their example.

The transportation of Japanese women to the North American West was an enterprise that developed under these particular conditions in Japan and the North American West around the turn of the twentieth century. In Japan, cultural constraints and economic hardships women had experienced created a context in which recruiters succeeded in luring them to North America with tales of work, educational, and marriage opportunities. The existing tradition of indentured servitude and arranged marriage also made the recruitment process smooth. In Canada and the United States, the contradiction between the ideology and the reality—societal opposition to the view of prostitution as a legitimate work for women but reliance on it for regional economic development—resulted in less rigid regulation of national borders and tacit recognition of prostitution through the system of fining and confining in the period before the turn of the century. In this particular context, the importation of Japanese women for prostitution became a lucrative business in which various actors—procurers, procuresses, Chinese sailors, steamship companies, local whites, immigration officials, municipal authorities, property holders, and immigrant entrepreneurs—invested on both sides of the Pacific.

CHAPTER 4

Racialized, Exploited, and Excluded

The Lives of Japanese Prostitutes and
Barmaids in the North American West

Remembering Seattle around the turn of the twentieth century, Tamesa Uhachi observed:

> Some [prostitutes] couldn't stand their lives and attempted to escape. But [pimps], in cooperation with a gang, would leave no stone un-turned until they found the women and punished them by striking and kicking them. Later, *Fujin Home* [a Protestant rescue mission] was founded, and women could escape the lives behind pink curtain [in brothels] by entering the institution. Pimps threatened women say-ing "If you escape to there, I will hire rascals to kill you."
>
> I heard that a number of women were actually killed [by their pimps]. Probably, the victims were . . . those who tried to escape not only one time but two or three times. They would have been killed as a warning to others. The way of killing them was unusual. It would cause trouble if the dead bodies were found. So they, as far as I heard, cut the women's bodies into five pieces or so, grinded their flesh and internal organs, liquefied them by using a chemical, and poured them down the drain. What these men did was thoroughgoing.[1]

This is what Tamesa told Yamazaki Tomoko, who was researching the life of Yamada Waka in Seattle and was obviously sympathetic to these women, who were being exploited by pimps. While this account revealed some common features of Japanese prostitution in turn-of-the-century Seattle, we must also be aware that he was trying to give Yamazaki the kind of information she wanted. All pieces of histori-cal evidence reflect the authors' values and their attitudes toward the subject, and the circumstances in which they were created influence what was presented. In this chapter, I would like to contextualize

various pieces of evidence concerning Japanese prostitution in the
North American West to explore key issues in Japanese women's lives
as prostitutes or barmaids. My research suggests that these women
had to deal with pressures not only from white Canadians and Americans but also from fellow countrymen in their community.

THE WORLD OF PROSTITUTION IN THE WEST

Toward the end of the nineteenth century, growing numbers of
"respectable" people from the East were settling on the western frontier, and as law and order became more established in these societies,
the line between good women and bad women was clearly drawn.
The dominant ideology of womanhood in the nineteenth century,
which had ideological roots in East Coast societies, continued to
hold men and women to sexual double standards in the cities of the
American West. As Marion S. Goldman writes, "good women" were,
first of all, mothers, caretakers, and moral guardians who stayed at
home and were subservient to their husbands. Those engaged in work
outside the home or in suffrage movements risked losing respectability and the protection afforded to women of their class. At the same
time, the ideology of womanhood of that era created a need for "bad"
women who would help men of all classes satisfy their sexual desires,
which led to the establishment of red-light districts where sex was
exchanged for money. Despite their service to middle-class men, these
"bad" women were prohibited from entering the spheres in which
respectable people resided. They were confined to segregated areas
and kept away from daughters of respectable residents.[2]

Japanese women were also working in such areas created for "bad"
women in West Coast cities and inland towns (e.g., Front Alley in
Spokane, Rose Street in Walla Walla, and Brooklyn Place in San Francisco). In Seattle, brothels prospered in the area around King Street,
the two blocks between Weller and King Streets, and Fifth and Seventh Avenues in the International District. Called Deadline, this district was a place where all vices, including gambling and prostitution,
were tolerated by the local police.[3] The streets were reported to be
"ablaze with many colored lights displaying the names of notorious
ones," and "painted women in a half-nude condition came out openly
on the streets . . . to solicit passers-by."[4] Okina Kyūin, a Japanese
migrant who visited Seattle in 1911, characterized the district as "an
international flesh market," where almost five hundred women from

various European and Asian countries were working as prostitutes.[5] Black and Japanese prostitutes were concentrated in the area along lower Jackson Street.[6] Major hotels with Japanese "cribs," or cheap brothels, included the Eureka House, Aloha House, Tokyo House, Diamond House, Yokohama House, Eastern House, Paris House, and Washington House, each of which accommodated from five to more than twenty Japanese women.[7]

The seemingly multicultural world of Western prostitution was in fact racially segregated. Jay Moynahan writes that in Butte, Montana, French women were "in great demand" among the residents, and German, Scandinavian, and Irish women were ranked "in the middle of the scale." Mexican and South American women were "below them," and the Chinese were "consigned to be at the lower end of the rung" along with Native American and African American women.[8] This racial hierarchy was clearly reflected in the prices that men paid for the services of each group (e.g., $1.00 for native-born girls, $0.75 for French women, $0.50 for Chinese, Japanese, and black prostitutes, and $0.25 for Mexican women in late-nineteenth-century San Francisco).[9] Furthermore, Asian prostitutes were often relegated to slum areas with Latino prostitutes, and the low price charged at their brothels drew a variety of customers, including common laborers and drinking men, who often treated the women harshly.[10]

Race also affected one's sexual access to other racial groups. Japanese prostitutes served men of all racial groups and were divided into groups according to the customers they served: "Japanese birds" (*nihonjin tori*), "Chinese birds" (*shinajin tori*), and "white birds" (*hakujin tori*). The houses of "white birds" put up a placard saying "white only" and refused to sell their services to men of color.[11] As Yuji Ichioka noted, this division shows the prejudices of both whites and Japanese—white men disliked prostitutes catering to Asians, and Japanese men disliked women serving Chinese men.[12] But it must be added that the whites had more power in controlling their and others' sexuality: as customers, they had access to women of all racial groups, and as prostitutes, they often refused to serve Asian men. Sources suggest that Chinese and Japanese men could purchase the services of some white prostitutes, but as a former Japanese sawmill worker in Spokane recalled, "High-class white prostitutes rejected to meet the Japanese as customers," and "Japanese customers were allowed to have the service of 'third-grade' white women, who charged $2.00."[13]

This, in turn, pressured Chinese and Japanese women to serve men of their own ethnic groups. Thus Asian men and women had fewer options as customers and workers in this racially stratified market.

An exclusive focus on race, however, obscures class stratification among prostitutes. In most western towns, from West Coast cities to inland mining towns, scholars find that at the highest end, elite women, usually whites, had only a few customers a night and the right to refuse to serve certain customers, worked in well-furnished rooms or parlor houses, and sold both sexual services and companionship. The majority of women, both white and nonwhite, however, belonged to the class of common prostitutes, working on the streets or in cribs, found in clearly defined areas like San Francisco's Barbary Coast.[14] There was also stratification within each ethnic group. In late-nineteenth-century San Francisco, Lucie Cheng wrote, "the best Chinese brothels in San Francisco . . . catered only to Chinese, because Chinese men believed that the most degrading thing a Chinese woman could do was to have sexual intercourse with a white." Chinese prostitutes on the lower end served both Chinese and whites, including laborers, teenagers, sailors, and drunkards, working in sparsely furnished rooms with only a bowl, a chair, and a hard bunk bed. So "[t]he distinction between higher- and lower-grade brothels was one of both class and race."[15]

In the case of Japanese prostitution, "class" was a complicated matter defined by women's material conditions, the cultural meanings associated with their trade, and the customers they served. In both Japanese and North American societies in this period, prostitution was generally considered stigmatized work. But Japanese prostitutes in North America served non-Japanese customers and were despised for this reason as well. In a consular report returned to the Foreign Ministry from San Francisco in 1898, Deputy-Consul Mutsu Kōkichi reported on an "unsightly" location on the outskirts of Chinatown, where there was an "ugly den" (*shūkutsu*) of Japanese prostitutes catering to the Chinese, informing Tokyo of an incident in which Japanese women had been forced to leave the street because "they might pollute (*kegasu*) good families surrounding it."[16] Although whites were viewed as "civilized" people by the Japanese at the time, some of their cultural practices, like working with leather or eating meat, were considered polluting and similar to what outcastes were doing for a living in Japan;[17] prostitutes serving white customers in Yokohama were often women from marginalized social groups and were despised by the public for serving enemy aliens and being engaged in "dirty" work. Many Japanese women in North America who had white customers also internalized the idea that they were doing "dirty" work, as Yamada Waka recalled in her memoir addressed to "American ladies": "I was living without knowing anything about your country . . . only getting a corner of your country dirty like a worm."[18] Japanese leaders typically distinguished those working in hotel rooms and serving men of all racial groups from barmaids working in Japanese bar-restaurants and serving Japanese customers, calling the former "women engaged in an ugly trade" (*shūgyōfu*) and the latter "barmaids" (*shakufu*). There was an indication that prostitutes deserved to be criticized for engaging in "dirty" work, further tainting their bodies by serving non-Japanese while staining the reputation of the Japanese among the white population. Barmaids could escape this criticism by serving primarily the Japanese and were somehow considered a part of the Japanese community. In the North American context, therefore, the "class" of Japanese prostitutes was not only a matter of material conditions. It was also defined by Japanese perceptions of work and by customers who were considered either lacking in civility or barbaric in custom.

Both white and Asian prostitutes worked in segregated areas of western cities and were subject to city ordinances criminalizing prostitution and associated activities. Importantly, however, the police often enforced the law on nonwhite women more strictly. In April 1891, for instance, the Seattle police arrested thirty-six women for vagrancy, ordering each Japanese woman to pay the $25 bail while releasing white women without bail "after a long interview with the chief." Similarly, in Salt Lake City, eight women were arrested for prostitution, and whereas six women paid the $8.50 fine, the two Japanese women were charged $25 "for the same offense."[19] Jef Rettmann, in his study of prostitution in Spokane, found that Japanese women paid the largest fine to the police, which constituted 23 percent of all prostitutes paying fines in the city from 1899 to 1910. The amount of the fine reflected, to some extent, the scale of Japanese prostitution in the town, but it may also suggest that the police enforced the law more vigorously against Japanese than native-born and white European prostitutes, as had been the case in San Francisco in the earlier period.[20] Asian prostitutes were required to pay larger fines and bribes to the police out of their earnings, which were less than the earnings of white women.

Japanese brothel-keepers and women were constantly subject to police harassment. In December 1909, the *Seattle Star* reported on the charge filed against policemen misusing their position to force local pimps and boardinghouse-keepers to pay them a certain amount regularly. Pimps collected money from their women and passed it to the police, and the group of women who paid the largest sum were Japanese. "Foreigners were controlled by their men, who were powerless in the police's hands," the newspaper reported. Of course, not only Japanese but also black and white women paid bribes to the police. But considering that this case reached the ears of judges only after an Italian policeman and a white prostitute had reported it to a grand jury, the weak position of nonwhite men and women in this system of graft is noticeable.[21] Thus, Japanese women were exploited not only by their employers but also by local policemen who took advantage of the official nonrecognition of prostitution to supplement their incomes with fines or bribes from nonwhite women.

Japanese prostitutes were subject to various forms of criticism, including mockery and ridicule, by the American press. When a fire broke out in a Seattle brothel in 1893, for instance, the *Seattle Post-Intelligencer* reported: "[Japanese] women picked up their things and were running out of the house like scared animals."[22] The same year, the *San Francisco Chronicle* reported that Japanese prostitutes in the city were "not as a rule of the best class, but unmistakable types of the race, and when Clement Scott [a *Chronicle* writer] speaks of ugly, expressionless, piggy eyes, coarse, dairymaid cheeks, shuffling gait and black, coarse hair done up in most unbecoming fashion, we cannot bring ourselves to say him nay."[23] The rendition of Japanese prostitutes was similar to that of their Chinese counterparts. Both groups of women were reported to have been sold or kidnapped by procurers and forced into a "life of shame."[24] They were characterized as victims of "Asian slavery," a manifestation of "Oriental secretiveness" and "Oriental cunning."[25] American reformers' efforts to rescue Chinese and Japanese "slaves" from brothels were covered in depth and often depicted as heroic efforts, but otherwise, newspapers assigned the women negative images as "immoral" women or, at worst, the source of pollution.[26]

The perception of prostitution as "immoral" or "dirty" work was not limited to Japanese prostitution. In Canada and the United States, the idea of prostitution as immoral led members of the respectable community to oppose it in order to protect their families and children from its negative influence and reformers to associate prostitutes with other immoral conduct such as heavy drinking.[27] Prostitution was considered not only the lowest rung of the occupational hierarchy but also "dirty" because of its association with human wastes and the perception of prostitutes as sexual outlets.[28] The attack on prostitution from the medical community came from physicians' concerns about the spread of disease or women's sexual transgression and also from their anxieties over foreigners who were arriving in massive numbers around the turn of the century.[29] As Alan M. Kraut writes, U.S. immigration laws that developed beginning in the 1890s focused on the regulation of disease among European and Asian immigrants in response to growing concerns about their impact on public health.[30] Following the lead of the United States, the Canadian government revised its immigration law in 1906 to restrict the entry of those "afflicted with a loathsome disease" as well as those who had been "convicted of a crime involving moral turpitude."[31] In Canada and the United States around the turn of the century, white prostitutes suffered from existing views of prostitution as "dirty" and "immoral" work; white immigrant women could also be attacked for their alleged association with disease by nativists who opposed the entry of immigrants.

At the same time, the conflation of morality, health, and place of origin in writings about prostitutes in this period must also be analyzed at the local level in relation to increasing public concern with epidemics as well as anti-Asian sentiments in Pacific Coast cities. San Francisco, for instance, had experienced outbreaks of such epidemic diseases as smallpox and plague since the 1870s, and the authorities considered Chinatown the source of disease and a threat to the health of white Americans. In these discourses, Chinese prostitutes were accused of spreading syphilis to young white men and degrading the morality of the city and the nation.[32] These negative opinions of Chinese people's health and morality were later directed toward the Japanese. In 1893, for instance, a local newspaper in Salem, Oregon, attacked Chinatown, where Chinese and Japanese brothels were concentrated, as "a fruitful source of disease and moral degradation," claiming that the city must force them to "conform to sanitary laws as well as moral laws."[33] Comparing Japanese prostitutes to animals like pigs and magpies evokes the image of wastes that were often considered the cause of disease threatening the health of the white population.[34] In 1900, after a Chinese was suspected of dying of bubonic plague in San Francisco, the police chief shut down Chinatown, ordering both Chinese and Japanese residents to be vaccinated and forbidding those who were not to leave town.[35] Certainly, Chinese and Japanese prostitutes were two different groups and should not be mixed. In the eyes of the general public, however, Chinese and Japanese were often lumped together as "diseased" and "immoral" Asian Others.[36]

Equally important, within the Japanese immigrant community, however, prostitutes were also subject to the gaze of fellow countrymen, which was as harsh as that of white Americans. Prostitution was constructed as "dirty" and "immoral" work in Meiji Japan; therefore, Japanese migrants often saw prostitution in the United States through that lens. A Japanese traveler who visited Reno, Nevada, in 1914, for instance, observed that it was "a matter of great shame" (*ichidai chijoku*) to allow the existence of these vices in "the United States, reputed for its [high level of] civilization." At the same time, by calling the city an "outcaste village" (*eta mura*), he emphasized the seriousness of the problem by associating it with outcaste communities that were despised in Meiji Japan.[37] Elite Japanese could not stand the prevalence of prostitution in Pacific Coast Japanese communities. Secretary Hanihara Masanao, who visited Fresno in 1908, described local Japanese prostitutes as "women engaged in an ugly trade" (*shūgyōfu*): "They construct crude hovels of two nine-by-nine-foot rooms in several filthy three to four feet wide alleys wedged in a slum area and accessible by side and rear entrances. When evening sets in, they show off their 'wares' by leaving the doors open and wearing grotesque, bright Japanese or Chinese garments with beds by their sides."[38] Japanese prostitutes were despised by elite fellow countrymen whose views were shaped by existing perceptions of prostitution and marginalized social groups in Meiji Japan.

Aside from the image of immorality, dirt, and disease, the "exotic" image of "Oriental" women was also prevalent in American society, and Chinese and Japanese brothel-operators shrewdly drew on it in order to market their services. Chinese brothels in San Francisco, for example, were often decked in the "Oriental" style, with rooms furnished with bamboo products, embroidered hangings, silk cushions, and traditional paintings.[39] Several accounts suggest that Japanese brothels similarly attempted to create the atmosphere of the "Orient." A Presbyterian missionary described a Japanese brothel in San Francisco's Brooklyn Place in 1899: "[Japanese] girls were exhibited in a kind of cage. Each dressed in a gaudy red garment. Each had painted cheeks, and a peculiar wreath-like ornament upon the head, which instead of being the crown of a pure and noble womanhood was the emblem of shame."[40] This is reminiscent of *harimise*, the Japanese practice of displaying prostitutes in a room exposed to the streets in order to attract customers. Importantly, in the American context, Japanese managers adopted this style to serve white and Chinese men, their principal customers.[41] On Brooklyn Alley, according to Herbert Asbury, Japanese cribs serving white men adopted "several ancient customs of the Yoshiwaras." When a customer arrived, he was "required to remove his shoes at the threshold; and when he departed, he received a gift, usually a good cigar, while his shoes were returned to him cleaned and polished."[42] Clearly, Japanese brothel-keepers were aware that non-Japanese customers would pay good money for this Orientalist fantasy of "geisha" created by the American press in this period, and they strategically capitalized on it to generate profits.

Among the three groups of Japanese prostitutes' customers, the Chinese appear most frequently in immigrant accounts and public records. The Chinese began to arrive in the western regions of the United States in the mid-nineteenth century, and as an inevitable result of the lack of women, prostitution prospered in their settlements, reaching its heyday around 1870.[43] The growth of Chinese prostitution was in part the result of the Chinese family system that discouraged respectable women from traveling abroad so that they would be available to provide care for parents-in-law and ensure regular remittance from their husbands abroad while permitting migration of prostitutes. In this sense, the Chinese sexual ideology divided women into "good" and "bad" women as the American one did. Yet, as Lucie Cheng and Judy Yung wrote, it is difficult to ignore the factor of anti-Asian sentiments of the day. After the enactment of the Page Act of 1875 (prohibiting the entry of "Oriental" prostitutes) and the Chinese Exclusion Act of 1882 (restricting the immigration of Chinese women to allow only merchants' wives), it became difficult for brothel-keepers to import women from China. The rising cost of recruiting women, together with the dwindling supply of females in China, pushed the price of a prostitute up to as much as $3,000 by the 1890s.[44]

In British Columbia, the presence of a relatively large number of Chinese prostitutes had roused white Canadians' indignation at "young ladies from the Celestial Empire" since the 1870s, and both white and Chinese residents had called for the abolition of Chinese prostitution.[45] This made it difficult for procurers to bring over women from their country. Moreover, the head tax on Chinese migrants made it difficult for Chinese men to accumulate money and bring over their families from China, increasing the demand for Japanese prostitutes among the Chinese. At the same time, there was no immigration restriction targeting Japanese prostitutes except the Page Act, which procurers could evade without much difficulty by bringing over prostitutes as their "wives." The steady supply of women from impoverished agricultural areas in rural Japan kept their price at about $500–600 each.[46] As a result, more Chinese visited Japanese brothels, and it was no coincidence that Japanese brothels sprang up on the outskirts of Chinatowns.[47] By the end of the nineteenth century, Japanese brothels outnumbered Chinese establishments in San Francisco's Brooklyn Place.[48] In the early twentieth century, when Osada Shōhei visited Japanese brothels in western Canada, he reported that "[Japanese prostitutes] never serve the Japanese but only whites and the Chinese."[49] The capitalist economy of the West, which needed Asian labor, and hostility toward Asians resulted in the enactment of laws that prevented family formation among Asians, and the subsequent decline in Chinese immigration and prostitution created a peculiar relationship between Japanese women and Chinese men in the 1880s.

Certainly, race was not the only cause of Japanese prostitution in North America, because buying the services of prostitutes was a leisure activity for working-class men regardless of their ethnicity. A Japanese sawmill worker at Port Blakely told a traveler in 1899: "How do we use money? You can drink and buy women in Seattle. . . . It's better to enjoy as much as possible before you die. Drink, gamble, and buy women. Then you can use up all the money in a minute."[50] Japanese laborers suffered from loneliness, and going to the red-light districts was an easy way to relieve it. A former fruit picker in San Jose recalled his laboring days in the-mid 1890s: "After finishing work, we [laborers] go back to the apartment. . . . After the dinner, each starts hanging around the town. Some go to theater houses, others go to bars. Our little home becomes empty." The town had "all kinds of vice institutions—theaters, storyteller's halls, brothels, and gambling houses." As he became accustomed to an American life, he began to smoke, dress up, and go to bars. "Women also began to catch my attention," he wrote.[51] Some Japanese men probably considered alcohol, prostitution, and gambling as part of their workingmen's culture and remedies against the boredom associated with their monotonous laboring lives.

At the same time, however, one must also note that this Asian men's working-class culture emerged in a context in which Asian men had difficulty forming their own families. California outlawed marriage between a white and a "Mongolian" as early as 1880, and after the Chinese Exclusion Act banned laborers from bringing over their wives in 1882, working-class Chinese men were forced to live alone in a foreign land, so they socialized with other men or met prostitutes in brothels.[52] Compared to the Chinese, Japanese men had an easier time starting their own families, because the strong standing of their homeland government in the international community enabled Japanese officials to negotiate the right for their subjects to bring over their wives from Japan with the U.S. and Canadian governments in 1907–8. Nevertheless, they faced the same ban on interracial marriage as the Chinese did, and unless they had enough resources to support their families, they had to continue to live alone in a foreign land. Even in Washington and British Columbia, which placed no restrictions on interracial marriage, Japanese and Chinese men who attempted to marry white women faced strong criticism from the Canadian and American public.[53] The large pool of unattached Chinese and Japanese workingmen created by racist measures and attitudes contributed to the persistence of prostitution in both ethnic communities well into the twentieth century.

BAR-RESTAURANTS: "A CENTER OF JAPANESE SOCIAL LIFE"

Brothels were not, however, the only places where Japanese women were engaged in prostitution. Some worked in Japanese restaurants as barmaids (*shakufu*). According to consular reports, Japanese bar-restaurants began to appear in the late 1890s. In Seattle, for example, they numbered three in 1899, ten in 1902, and twenty-two in 1905.[54] By the end of 1906, restaurants were the largest employer of Japanese women in Seattle's Japantown, hiring fifty-eight women, of whom twenty-three were listed as managers or proprietresses.[55] When Secretary Hanihara Masanao came to the Japanese community in Seattle in 1908, he is reported to have seen streets where "strange" signboards and lanterns were displayed in front of Japanese stores and restaurants, calling the view "dark and obscene" (*in'an hiwai*). He added that "what is undesirable about Japanese residents in Seattle is that the numbers of barmaids and prostitutes among Japanese women are larger than those in other regions."[56] Overly sensitive to white exclusionists' response to the "dark and obscene" view in the Japanese community, he probably exaggerated the number of prostitutes and barmaids. In fact, bar-restaurants existed in almost all Japanese settlements on the West Coast in the early twentieth century: forty-one in Seattle, twenty-one in San Francisco, and twenty in Los Angeles in 1910; at least five in Spokane between 1907 and 1912; fifteen in Vancouver in August 1908; and eight in Denver, Colorado, in February 1911.[57]

The interiors of these bar-restaurants looked like "traditional Japanese restaurants" (*ryōtei*) (fig. 4.1). Immigrant Inspector F. N. Steele, while investigating a bar-restaurant in Spokane in 1908, visited the Asahi Tei restaurant, where he found "four Japanese girls and a number of well dressed Japanese men seated around a table eating and drinking," and "[o]ne of the girls present, known as 'May' made haste to inform me in English that she was a 'good' girl now, she stating that she had quit the 'business' and that she did not even have a sweetheart." He added: "This place differed from other Japanese restaurants in that the front windows were glazed so that one could not see in from the outside and each table is in a room or box separate from the others." This was a relatively high-class restaurant where well-dressed customers were served by waitresses in private rooms divided perhaps by shoji serving as sliding doors and fitted with *tatami* mats. Common laborers and immigrant journalists patronized bar-restaurants of a lower grade.[58] For all classes of Japanese men, these bar-restaurants were important places to meet their friends and relax. The Immigration Commission, when it conducted a survey in 1909, characterized these establishments as "a center of Japanese social life."[59]

The barmaids' primary job was to entertain customers: serving food and alcohol, talking to them over drinks, and dancing and playing *samisen* (three-stringed Japanese musical instrument). Some literate women exchanged *tanka*, traditional Japanese poems, with customers. Japanese barmaids were similar to geisha in that they not only sold sexual favors but also entertained customers with artistic skills. The precise number of women who turned to prostitution while working as barmaids is subject to debate. Yuji Ichioka, who produced

Figure 4.1 Barmaids in the Maneki restaurant, Seattle, date unknown. Itō Kazuo, *Zoku hokubei hyakunen-zakura*, 89.

a pioneering study of nineteenth-century Japanese prostitution in the United States, wrote that "[n]ot all prostitutes worked in brothels. Innumerable small bar-restaurants, which hired *shakufu* or barmaids, proliferated in inchoate immigrant communities in the 1890s. Not every *shakufu* was a prostitute, but some were, and they worked in these bar-restaurants rather than brothels."[60] Indeed, the boundary between barmaids and prostitutes was indistinct. The number of barmaids increased as prostitutes were transferred from brothels to restaurants around 1907–10, when the U.S. government revised laws against prostitution and began to deport foreign prostitutes.[61]

Yet the work of barmaids was not simply a form of sex work. It is true, in most cases, that economic considerations played a key role in their decision to become barmaids, and they faced constant pressure from both employers and husbands to sell sexual services in exchange for money. But their work was different from that of prostitutes in that they managed their emotions in order to please their customers, for example, making their stressed-out customers (Japanese men) feel proud of themselves by listening attentively to their stories or making them relax and enjoy themselves by singing and dancing. Moreover, the kinds of services barmaids offered depended on both the needs of customers and the willingness of the women to offer them. Decisions on whether or not to offer sexual services could be influenced by such factors as women's attitudes toward prostitution, the amount of debt they owed their employers or "husbands," and the number of families they had to support in Japan or North America. Therefore, it is important not to draw a clear line between the work of prostitutes and that of barmaids; their work experiences were intimately tied to their social relations with husbands, employers, customers, parents, and children.

Typically, barmaids were married women who entered the trade due to financial and family problems that developed after they arrived in North America. The immigrant press printed their stories usually as a caution, suggesting that any wife could have such misfortune if a husband failed to support her. In the case of a barmaid who went by the name of "Ochiyo," it was poverty and her husband's unemployment that forced her to work in a restaurant. Like thousands of Japanese brides, around 1908–9, Ochiyo journeyed from Yokohama to Seattle to meet the husband chosen by her parents, Kunitarō. He had come to Seattle in 1907 and worked as a bartender in order to save money to set up his own family in the United States. In the course of time, however, he began to frequent a local Japanese bar-restaurant to see his favorite barmaid Fumiko and spent a large share of his income there. By the time Ochiyo arrived in Seattle, he had lost all his money and had to borrow $150 from his friend to buy new clothing for her. Having a hard time getting by on his low income as a bartender, he barely supported his wife. Tragically, their married life began in a cheap local hotel; their property consisted of a gas stove, a bottle of soy sauce, two dishes, and two cups. And what was worse, Kunitarō was dismissed from his job and was unable to pay their rent. Economic hardship finally forced Ochiyo to become a barmaid in a local restaurant, Matsunoe.[62] The ways in which Kunitarō was caricatured in this article suggest that he had failed to live up to the ideal of the hardworking, family-centered husband that prevailed in the Japanese immigrant community in the 1910s.

In the case of Fujimoto Haruye, her husband's debts forced her to work as a barmaid. In 1911, when she exchanged photographs across the Pacific and migrated to the United States, her husband, Umetarō, was managing a farm in Walnut Grove, California. After moving to Agnew's Village, they continued farming, but as a result of a business failure, their debts kept mounting, and Haruye was forced to work in a local bar-restaurant to supplement their income. She probably entered the trade intending to leave it after repaying their debts; however, the birth of her child increased family expenses, and she had to continue to work to make ends meet. Even worse, her husband had a gambling habit and began to take advances on her salary. She also needed to pay the expenses of bringing up her child, who had been placed with another family. Haruye later decided to file for divorce from her husband.[63] As in the case of Ochiyo and Kunitarō, her husband's inability to provide was the key factor behind her decision to become a barmaid. This means that although newspaper editors and Japanese leaders promoted the image of successful family formation in the community, actual immigrant couples encountered various problems in the North American West. Because of the stress of poverty or unemployment and a sense of powerlessness, husbands often turned to alcohol or gambling, and some became dependent on their wives' earnings from their jobs in bar-restaurants.

Japanese women had little difficulty finding work in restaurants in Pacific Coast cities where information on jobs was readily available. But there was also a demand for them in small towns or rural areas, and managers of bar-restaurants placed advertisement in newspapers published in West Coast cities (fig. 4.2). In 1908, for instance, the *Shin sekai* newspaper in San Francisco carried an advertisement for a barmaid in San Jose, which read: "Wanted, Barmaid for Taniguchi Restaurant, $30/Month."[64] The *Shin sekai* also carried a want ad for a restaurant in the rural town of Cheyenne, Wyoming, which said: "We need barmaids between 18 to 25 years. . . . Women with artistic skills are preferred, but if you cannot play samisen, we will offer free lessons. The salary is $30 a month regardless of one's skill. We will cover travel expenses from wherever you come."[65] In seeking a barmaid, a restaurant in Ogden, Utah, promised to cover travel expenses, send a person to meet the woman, and offer a position to her husband as well.[66] Unlike in western Canada, the Japanese settlement in the western United States spread into the interior region (1,300–2,000 resided in Montana, Idaho, Colorado, Wyoming, and Utah in 1910); the male-female ratio there (25:1) was much more unbalanced than in the three Pacific states (6:1).[67] The variety of benefits restaurants offered to bring women to inland areas indicates a substantial demand for women as well as the profitability of the bar-restaurant business.

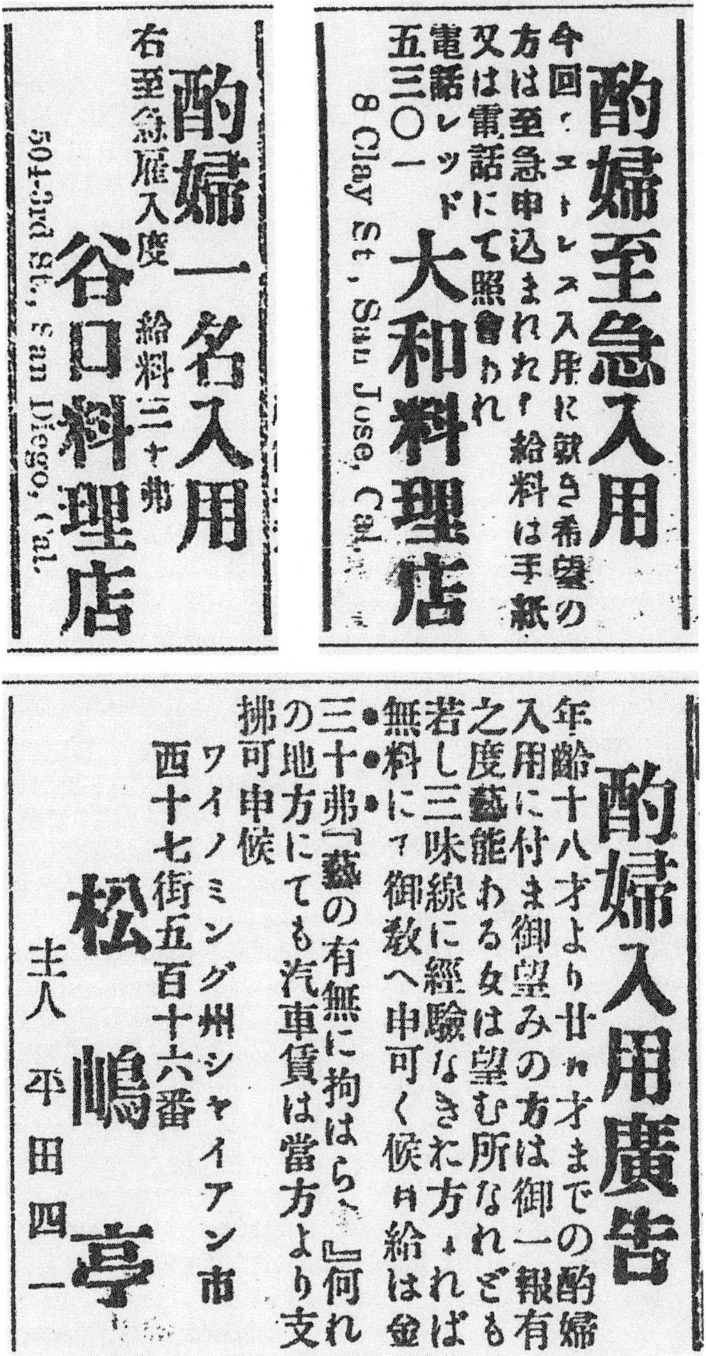

酌婦至急入用
今回、ウエトレス入所に就き希望の
方は至急申込まれ〻給料は手紙
又は電話にて照會れ
電話レッド
五三〇一
8 Clay St, San Jose, Cal.
大和料理店

酌婦
一名入用
右至急雇入度
給料三十弗
谷口料理店
504-3rd St., San Diego, Cal.

酌婦入用廣告
年齢十八才より廿ゝ才までの酌婦
入用に付ま御望みの方は御一報有
之度藝能わる女は望む所なれども
若し三味線に經驗なき方ナ給は金
無料にヽ御敎へ申可く候
三十弗「藝の有無に拘はらヽ」何れ
の地方にても汽車賃は當方より支
拂可申候
ワイオミング州シャイアン市
西十七街五百十六番
松嶋亭
圭人 平田四一

Figure 4.2. Advertisements for barmaids in San Diego and San Jose, California, and Cheyenne, Wyoming. *Shin sekai*, October 26, 1908, October 23, 1909, and January 14, 1911.

As opposed to the practice in brothels, barmaids catered exclusively to Japanese men. What factors drew Japanese men to bar-restaurants? The first incentive was to meet their favorite barmaids. When Nagai Kafū, a Japanese novelist, visited Seattle in 1903, he described the conversation of Japanese men in front of Nihontei, a bar-restaurant in Jackson Alley:

> "Damn! She is drinking and making merry tonight, too."
> "It's Oharu. She's playing a *samisen*. She is too good to be in America."
> "I have never seen her, but is she so lovely?"
> . . .
> "When did she arrive? It should have been quite recent."
> "She came on the last steamship *Shinano*. I've heard she's from Hiroshima."[68]

The *Shin sekai* reported the excitement when a popular barmaid arrived in the Japanese community in Walnut Grove in 1911: "When she arrived on a boat last night, over ten Japanese men came to see her, accompanied her to Asahitei, and competed for first place as her customer. With her popularity, which is even greater than that in Sacramento, she will have the mob twisted around her little finger."[69] Gossiping about barmaids was one of the favorite pastimes of Japanese men. The immigrant press carried readers' columns in which male readers exchanged information about women who debuted in local restaurants.[70]

Moreover, the accounts of Japanese immigrant men often suggest that they visited bar-restaurants not only for satisfying their sexual desires. Overcome with homesickness, the customers, mostly unskilled migrant laborers, were naturally attracted to the Japanese *sake*, food, and songs in these establishments. One immigrant, Hirade Kametarō, recalled the dishes served free of charge in local bar-restaurants on the New Year holidays: "Every customer was treated. They grilled large sea bream ordered from Japan with salt and placed them on the tables. They served a variety of dishes, from traditional New Year dishes to Chinese dishes to all sorts of delicacies." Songs were also essential parts of the social gathering. Hirade continued, "[Customers] paid waitresses tips and asked them to sing *okesa bushi* [a traditional folk song] and popular Japanese songs. 'Japan' was alive [in bar-restaurants]. It was an exhilarating spring day."[71] Their memories of their native villages in Japan did not fade easily. It was even strengthened when they faced strange customs and discrimination outside their community. In this sense, bar-restaurants were one of the few places where immigrant Japanese could relax and socialize with fellow countrymen without feeling ill at ease.

Some Japanese men preferred Japanese bar-restaurants to American brothels. Nishikata Chōhei observed why young literary men (*bunshi*) went to these places: "At that time [early twentieth century], men came to America with high hopes, but the reality was too hard. . . . [E]ven if they wanted to sing the praises of youth, there were no Japanese women to go out with. Even if they sought sexual outlets in the red-light district, the American style was boring. So they went to Japanese restaurants and talked of their vague love-longings to married barmaids."[72] In brothels, customers simply received sexual services in exchange for money. In bar-restaurants, men could relax by eating Japanese dishes, drinking sake, and enjoying conversations with barmaids in Japanese. They probably felt "at home" there.

In thinking about why bar-restaurants prospered in Japanese communities, one must also understand that American lives often damaged Japanese men's self-esteem. The majority of Japanese were unskilled laborers working for low wages at railroad construction sites, lumber camps, and canneries. Many did menial work such as domestic service in white families, which often contradicted their status in Japanese society. The account of Okina Kyūin, who worked as a schoolboy (a person who attended a school while working as a live-in domestic) in a white family, probably speaks to the feelings of many: "One day, I found myself reflected in the mirror in the drawing room working in an apron and sweeping the room with a broom. . . . He had a dirty look with black hair, high cheekbones, and pale skin. What an insignificant-looking man [I am]. . . . How did I ever get into this mess? This is the demeaning work that Japanese people look down on as 'girl-servants' job' (*gejo hōkō*)."[73] Like Kyūin, early male Japanese migrants came to the United States with the hope of earning a college degree, but many ended up doing what was considered girl-servants' jobs in their native country. They were denied access to "respectable" jobs and services in white-owned restaurants and hotels. The weak position of Japanese men in the larger society thus created the need for bar-restaurants where they were treated like "men."[74]

Surely the men could enjoy Japanese sake, folk songs, and conversations with women in bar-restaurants, but they could not escape the loneliness. Japanese migrant men left numerous *tanka* that express their complex feelings about their lives in the United States. Miyauchi Jishirō, a young man who came to Seattle to earn money and pay off his father's debts, spent years wandering from one place to another, working first as a section hand and later as a member of an itinerant troupe. In the course of his travels, he had friends who were dismissed from work or lost all their money gambling. He also often got drunk and left several love *tanka* about a barmaid he met in a restaurant:

> This woman always smiles but does not talk much;
> So many men have lost their hearts to her.

> I told her my feelings about her, knowing she had received me warmly
>   for money;
> I felt miserable when realizing it.[75]

The ultimate source of his and other migrants' misery was the instability of their status as single men in a foreign land. Here is what Miyauchi wrote:

> I have declared that I will not get married;
> My friend started persuading me that I was wrong.

> A friend took a wife and appeared to spend days happily;
> I have come to envy him nowadays.[76]

Marriage was an important step toward finding one's place in the community, but it was difficult to undertake without any prospect of owning a farm or shop. As late as 1920, almost half the Japanese men in the United States were still living alone.[77] Bar-restaurants offered them consolation, and there they could feel like family heads served by women. Yet they were often dismayed at the end to realize that they could not possibly marry these barmaids, because the majority were strictly controlled by their pimp-husbands. Many migrant men shared the feeling expressed by Nakajima Shozan, who wrote in his *tanka*: "Time passes without any sound; when will my wandering days end?"[78]

The experiences of Asian migrants have often been described in narratives of putting down roots in America. Japanese men came to the United States for necessities, and with the arrival of brides and the birth of children, they decided to make the United States their permanent home. As Nayan Shah writes, however, scholars have often failed to recognize temporal, intimate, or sexual relations among Asian transient workers in the history of the North American West and their search for companionship among their own groups and across

ethnic lines under the gaze of a state that had constantly attempted
to exclude cultural and sexual deviants from citizenship.[79] Japanese
transient men also formed relationships with other workers and barmaids in order to have a sense of self-worth and dignity. Their lives
illuminate the gendered and class features of racial formations and
help reconceptualize mobility and transience as major issues in Asian
American history.[80]

THE ECONOMICS OF JAPANESE SEX WORK

An economic analysis of sex work is essential to understanding the
lives of both prostitutes and barmaids because sex was exchanged to a
varying degree as a commodity, and the values attached to it directly
affected their earnings, careers, and relations with their employers.
The lack of evidence makes it hard to estimate exactly what Japanese
prostitutes charged, but accounts provide rough figures. Takasaki
Aki, who worked in a Seattle brothel in 1904, noted that she earned
$3–10 a night (roughly $81–270 today).[81] A former sawmill worker
observed that a Japanese prostitute, who had worked at a lumber
mill in Oregon around 1908–9, charged Japanese workers $5 for one
meeting. He observed that "when our [sawmill workers'] net income
was $20–25 a month, [prostitutes] earned $10–15 a night. It was not
a bad business."[82] In Canada, a 1908 observation notes that the average charge was $2 for a short time, and if men stayed with prostitutes
all night, it cost them $10.[83] There are few sources showing how many
customers Japanese women served per night. Lucie Cheng estimates
that a full-time Chinese prostitute met four to ten customers a night.[84]
If Japanese women had seven customers a night and worked twenty-
six days a month, they served 182 men a month. If they earned $8–10
a night and worked the same number of days, each Japanese prostitute
could have generated $208–260 a month. These figures permit one to
estimate that their average earnings probably ranged between $200
and $300 a month (about $5,400–8,100 today), quite a large sum
considering that in 1900, the average monthly wage of a primary-
school teacher in Japan was only 11 yen ($5.49).[85]

But prostitutes themselves, whites and Asians alike, received only
a small share of their earnings. In the frontier towns of the American
West, as Anne M. Butler writes, prostitutes had to make regular pay-
ments at the police station to keep working, and they paid hotel owners exorbitant rents or were charged for room and board by madams

or pimps. The police often punished them for stealing money from their customers, but for the women, Butler writes, it was a means of improving their dismal economic circumstances.[86] In the case of the Chinese, Lucie Cheng found that in the early years of prostitution in the mid-nineteenth century, some women who made a significant sum from prostitution bought brothels or returned to their home country with a large sum. As the trade became more organized in the late nineteenth century, most Chinese prostitutes worked under contract, during which time they had to pay off loans advanced to their families in China and received little or no earnings. The contract required them to work 320 days a year at minimum, and if they failed to do so, they had to work an additional year. Thus the system operated so as to ensure that women would work four to five years for no pay regardless of how much profit their labor generated. This system allowed brothel owners to make a handsome profit. For instance, Cheng estimated that the owner of a Chinese brothel with nine low-grade prostitutes could make about $7,650 a year in 1870.[87]

The Japanese were also subject to this type of exploitation. Similar to the Chinese, they often owed their procurers for advances for their passage and other expenses. Osada's survey revealed, for instance, that women in Canada gave half their earnings to their masters to pay off their debts and used the other half to buy goods and clothes and pay fines to the local police; therefore, only a small amount would have remained as their income.[88] If the women were not in debt to procurers and had simply followed them across the ocean of their own volition, they could have a more regular income, which certainly allowed them a partial sense of freedom and control over their own labor. Yet, because of their lack of English proficiency and the local labor conditions, they often failed to understand the value of their labor in local currencies. Consider a description of the relation between a procurer and five prostitutes in Nelson in the 1890s: "Taking advantage of the women's inability to communicate, Iseoto deceived them into signing an absurd contract that each woman would receive a monthly salary of $20. The women, however, worked without complaining about their salary, appreciating [his generosity] by saying that $20 is equivalent to 40 yen in Japan."[89] Four months' salary for a primary-school teacher in Japan was $40 yen in this period, but $20 was what a Japanese domestic could earn in a month in the United States.[90]

In contrast, the earnings of brothel-keepers were enormous. If they received $100–150 a month (50 percent of earnings) from one prostitute, they could make $1,200–1,800 a year. Even after they used some of the money for the cost of maintaining the women and paying fines to the police, their profits were still considerable. Added to their income from prostitution, masters often charged prostitutes so-called consolation money (*tegirekin*) when the women wished to quit working for them. The amount of consolation money varied from prostitute to prostitute, depending on the contracts between the women and their employers, but evidence from newspaper articles suggests that in the early twentieth century, it typically ranged from $500 to $600 in the San Francisco area.[91] For popular prostitutes like Osuzu of the Banka House and Oteru of the Akebono House, the consolation money came to as much as $2,000–2,700.[92] These figures were not so different from the amount of debt reported by Lucie Cheng, $400–1,800, for Chinese prostitutes in the late nineteenth century.[93] These earnings enabled brothel-keepers to hire procurers and import more women from Japan after prostitutes repaid their debts.

Certainly, Japanese prostitutes working in North America generally understood the content of the contracts they had entered into with procurers, but they became angry when they realized that their earnings were small relative to those of their masters. In 1898, the *Asahi shinbun* newspaper in Tokyo published a letter it had received from a group of prostitutes in Chicago reporting on the malpractice of a female procurer, Matsuoka Yoshi. According to the letter, Matsuoka first worked as a prostitute in San Francisco and made 10,000 yen from prostitution, which permitted her to buy a house in Yokohama and live a "comfortable life." A few years before, she had started managing brothels in Seattle and Chicago, hiring prostitutes recruited by her sister and her husband in Japan, and she was now planning to return to Japan to recruit more girls. In the letter, the women warned: "Parents who have daughters in Tokyo and Yokohama, beware. . . . Women receive only 30 percent of the charge from customers, and 70 percent goes to the repayment of debts and other fees. After buying necessary things from the 30 percent, little remains at the end of the month. We are really angry about that."[94] The context in which they decided to write this letter was not entirely clear, but the letter revealed not their wish for help in escaping sexual exploitation but their claim to a share of the profits derived from their hard labor. These women came to understand that they had been deceived or exploited as they realized the value attached to their sex labor that generated much profit for their master.

At the same time, however, one must acknowledge that if prostitutes paid off their debts and became brothel-keepers, they could also earn a considerable income. The case of Kato Yasu serves as one example. Her probate file says that Yasu, a former resident of Nelson, British Columbia, died in Tokyo in August 1907, leaving two buildings and furniture valued at $4,000. In her will, she left one of the buildings to her two sons in Tokyo and the other to a man named Charles Waterman in Nelson. The furniture was divided among her husband and two sons. She asked Waterman to pay "the rents and profits issuing from such buildings" to her sons for a period of five years.[95] The will does not mention her former occupation in Nelson, but it seems likely that she worked as a prostitute or madam. When Osada Shōhei visited Nelson in 1908–9, the only Japanese women he found were prostitutes; there was no other occupation that would have enabled a Japanese woman to earn such a large sum of money in this period.[96] The value of Yasu's estate was enormous considering that Japanese sawmill workers in Canada earned $0.90 a day in 1902 and relatively well-paid Japanese miners received $1.37 a day in 1905.[97] Yasu may well have been a madam who hired and supervised a couple of Japanese girls.[98]

The system of payment for barmaids was a little different from that for prostitutes. Unlike prostitutes, who gave most of their earnings to their masters, barmaids received wages. Different sources provide varying estimates of their earnings. In 1911, the Immigration Commission reported that in Seattle, "waitresses," who worked in Japanese restaurants, earned $25 a month with board plus tips from customers, which averaged $10 a month. This figure may not represent the earnings of barmaids because the commission did not distinguish barmaids from "waitresses."[99] An anonymous barmaid, in an interview with an *Ōfu nippō* reporter, provided more precise figures in 1915: "Our basic salary is $20–25 a month. If barmaids get good customers, the boss secretly gives them a bonus. Those who need to constantly carry *sake* to dinner tables are paid extra." The greater part of their income, however, came from tips. She continued: "we get tips, on average, $2 a day, $60 a month. In good times, we get $90, but this month is not so good. People think that the amount of tips depends on the quality of women, but if we check with each other at the end of the month, the difference is usually within $10."[100] One can infer from these figures that barmaids typically made $80–85 plus extra for getting regular customers or doing extra work. Considering the data acquired in other locations, it appears that barmaids usually made about $100 a month during the 1910s.[101]

The earnings of Japanese barmaids were more than those of contemporary male Japanese migrant laborers. In interviews conducted in the Seattle area in the 1960s, former railroad workers recalled that they typically earned from $1.30 to $1.60 a day in the early twentieth century. Former unskilled sawmill workers observed that they earned $1.25 a day in 1905 and $1.50 a day or less in 1908–9. Although the jobs were seasonal, workers in the Alaskan fishery and cannery industries could earn more than railroad and sawmill workers, averaging $80–150 a month during the same period.[102] The Immigration Commission reported that male Japanese barbers in Seattle received $13–35 a month with room and board in 1911. Male laundry workers earned from $1.10 to $1.40 per day with board and lodging.[103] One can infer from these varied sources that male Japanese workers earned roughly $1.10 to $1.60 a day between 1900 and 1920. If they worked twenty-six days a month, they earned $30 to $40 a month. Briefly put, barmaids earned three times more than male Japanese workers did.

In discussing the earnings of prostitutes and barmaids, one must remember that they were judged by their conduct and, most likely, appearance. From the 1890s to 1910s, Japanese-language newspapers regularly carried readers' columns in which the contributors (mostly men) wrote about the reputations of local Japanese prostitutes and barmaids. In 1901, for example, a Seattle newspaper published an article titled "Selection of Beautiful Women in Seattle," praising the physical beauty of seven women chosen from Japanese brothels on King Street.[104] From Vancouver to San Francisco, the Japanese-language press occasionally held beauty contests, inviting votes from readers. Typically, barmaids were rated for their "looks," "conduct," "arts," "charm," "popularity," and "hospitality."[105] None of the criteria in the contest were related to intelligence or personality. Prostitutes and barmaids were portrayed primarily as entertainers and sex objects.

Post-feminist or third-wave feminist scholars often view women's participation in beauty contests as a positive assertion of their beauty or evidence for their empowerment. Certainly, winning prizes resulted in an increase in Japanese women's earnings; they could gain many regular customers, earn a large sum in tips, and have a higher chance of being redeemed by customers. One must remember, however, that these contests did not necessarily lead to improvement in the lives of Japanese sex workers as a whole. Fierce competition based primarily on physical appearance often undercut their sense of "sisterhood," preventing the creation of the camaraderie that often became a basis of collective action against exploitation in licensed brothels in Japan.[106] Furthermore, the women could assert their youthful attractiveness only when they were young. It did not guarantee that they would maintain as much power when they became older. Finally, because they were not expected to assert qualities such as individuality or intelligence, their freedom of expression was actually limited. These contests even led to the perpetuation of the image of Japanese women as sex objects, and their masters could capitalize on it to make profits.

WORKER-EMPLOYER RELATIONS, WORK-RELATED LOSSES, AND CAREERS AS PROSTITUTES

The relations between prostitutes and pimps described in immigrant accounts were mostly exploitative. Okina Kyūin, who worked as a writer in the Seattle area from 1907 to 1915, wrote of Japanese pimps: "*Amegoro* [which means 'American thugs'] were behind the women, men who had been in abject poverty in Japan or who had come to America with ambitions, but abhorred honest work and had gone the wayward path. To carouse and gamble, they duped women and forced them into prostitution. The worse ones fraudulently married several women and sold them off to the Chinese."[107] Prostitutes had various reasons for staying with their pimps. Most women were bound by the contracts they had entered into with their pimps before coming to the United States. Prostitutes were often lonely and emotionally dependent on their pimps. Because the police offered no protection and there were no regulations related to the trade, they also needed men who could force their customers to pay the charges and protect them from violent customers.[108] More realistically, these women had few options except to obey the orders of pimps. It was extremely difficult for them to find work outside Japantowns, and if they attempted to escape, they would meet with physical retribution from the men. Women who had been smuggled into the country or had used other women's identities to enter were living in fear of being deported every day. For various reasons, most of the women probably found it more practical to adjust to these constraints—building good relations with their masters and making their lives a little more bearable—until they could pay off their debts.[109]

It is also important to note that prostitution was a key part of the economy of the Japanese community in the early stage of its development. As Yuji Ichioka's study revealed, some pioneering Japanese entrepreneurs advanced their careers by exploiting prostitutes. Tanaka Chūshichi, a former fisherman, took a Seattle prostitute to Ogden, Utah, where he forced her to sell her body to laborers. In 1891, he handed her to a Chinese labor contractor in exchange for the right to subcontract a railroad building for the Oregon Short Line. What happened to her is not known. Even her name is not recorded in the historical account of this incident. Setting up headquarters in Nampa, Idaho, Tanaka became one of the earliest Japanese labor contractors in the Rocky Mountain region.[110] Two major labor contractors in San Francisco, Hasegawa Genji and Wakimoto Tsutomu, operated brothels along with their "legitimate" business.[111] Furuya Masajirō, the owner of the largest business establishment in Seattle, started his career as a tailor taking orders from Seattle prostitutes in April 1890. As he gained the confidence of prostitutes, he began to keep their earnings, serving as a kind of private banker for them. Moreover, Furuya was financially supported by his mistress Ohama, who worked as a prostitute. By December 1892, he had accumulated enough capital to open a grocery store in Seattle.[112]

To protect their business interests, brothel managers sometimes organized. In January 1908, the *Ōfu nippō* published articles in which the editor expressed his support for campaigns against the Sacramento Club, which had functioned as a kind of a mutual-aid society for local Japanese brothel-keepers. According to the articles, the club's monthly dues were $5 for brothel-managers, $3 for pimps, and $1 for prostitutes. The club also required managers of new brothels in town to make a one-time payment of $300 for insurance. The money collected was used as "emergency funds" to pay the bonds of arrested members or to compensate members for damages if the police ordered them to shut down their houses. The club also regularly held gambling parties, and its profits covered any deficit in revenue.[113] The immigrant press could reveal the nature of this type of "vice" institution openly only in the context of growing reform activities and family formation in the Japanese immigrant community during this period. But until then, not much restriction had been placed on the activities of this type of organization, which had enabled brothel-keepers to

continue doing business without interruption. In other words, by paying the police regularly, Japanese brothel-managers had allied with
white authorities in maintaining the system of informal regulation
that led to the exploitation of women.

Internally, the masters exerted tight control over the women's earnings and schedules to ensure steady profits. Takasaki Aki, a Japanese
prostitute arrested in Seattle in 1904, observed that she stayed in her
master's house and commuted to the Aloha House on King Street
every day. She left the house around eleven o'clock in the morning
and returned to the house around two o'clock the next morning. At
the end of each day, she gave all her earnings to an old woman named
Tori in the brothel.[114] Tightly controlled prostitutes had little control
over their wages or hours of work. Tamesa Uhachi, a former shipping
agent in Seattle, observed: "Most women rented and lived in apartments [with pimps]. They left their apartments around four or five
o'clock in the afternoon and went to their rooms behind *pinku kāten*
['pink curtain,' a Japanese term for a brothel]. It is painful to listen
to, but plain women who couldn't get many customers went to their
rooms behind pink curtain as early as eleven o'clock in the morning.
They returned to their apartments at midnight. When they had good
customers, they stayed there all night."[115] Prostitutes were forbidden
to go outside freely and, in some cases, even to write to their families
in Japan.[116] Women had little say over how long they would work and
whom they would serve.

Like the Chinese prostitutes studied by Lucie Cheng, Japanese prostitutes escaped from brothels and turned to local courts, rescue missions, and lovers, and their employers went to a great deal of effort to
capture these women by hiring members of extralegal organizations
or using the local court to file charges against them and force them to
return to their places of work.[117] In December 1892, for instance, the
Seattle Post-Intelligencer and the *Butte Anaconda Standard* carried
articles on a Japanese woman named Jennie who escaped from her
master in Butte, Montana, and went to Spokane, breaking the three-
year labor contract she had signed before coming to the United States.
The editors reported that a police officer in Butte, compensated for
his travel expenses by the Japanese master, visited Spokane to take
Jennie to Butte and make her resume work and pay off the remaining debt of $600. Jennie claimed that she had no wish to return to
work in the brothel, adding that in Butte, several other women had
been deceived into prostitution and bound by similar contracts. Then

the "best legal talent in the city" demanded Jennie's release, and the governor of Washington refused to issue a warrant. She was allowed to stay in Spokane.[118] The story was framed in the repeated narrative of a fight for women's freedom from sexual "slavery" carried on by reformers (judges, local residents, and a governor) against a perpetrator (the master). The result of this campaign is not known due to lack of evidence.[119] The articles suggest, however, the difficulty masters had in controlling the movement of prostitutes within the U.S. legal context: Masters could appeal to the court for the return of money, but because prostitution was not recognized as a legitimate work, they could not force women to work in brothels to repay their debts. They probably had no option except to withdraw their suits, fearing that additional investigation would lead to the wholesale deportation of women and procurers.

Of course, not all women simply broke their contracts with their masters; the evidence suggests that Japanese prostitutes who did so typically had worked for particularly abusive masters who extracted an unreasonable amount of profit from their labor. For example, Ogawa Haru, who borrowed $200 from a Japanese brothel-keeper in Portland, began to work as a "Chinese bird" to repay her debt in April 1908. Within two months, she returned $350–360 to him and stopped working as a prostitute because she was pregnant. In August, after the baby was born, however, the master ordered her to resume working in his brothel. When Ogawa resisted, the master had "friends threaten to kill me if I refused to resume practicing prostitution," she observed before federal officials. Her husband brought the matter to a local Japanese reform society, and immigration officials arrested the Portland master.[120] It was possible that Ogawa exaggerated the criminality of her master in order to receive protection from the authorities and ensure a successful prosecution. The master's repeated demands for continuation of work, however, suggest that his intention was to extract profit from women's labor as much as possible, not to abide by his contract with Ogawa. The absence of laws regulating the sex trade exacerbated the problem considerably.

The lack of laws regulating prostitution also exposed prostitutes of all races and ethnic backgrounds to many dangers in their workplaces. In the inland mining towns Anne M. Butler and Marion S. Goldman studied, the local press and the police court recorded many instances of violence in brothels such as fighting, drunkenness, and murder, and prostitutes were often assaulted and robbed by customers.[121] Accounts of brutal murders of Japanese prostitutes also appeared in the local American press. In May 1899, Katsu, a prostitute in the Yokohama House, was strangled to death and robbed of her money and two gold rings. "[Her] face was of a livid purple hue, her eyes were closed but swollen and suffused with black blood, and her neck and face were bruised in several places," the *Seattle Post-Intelligencer* reported.[122] In these descriptions of violence in Japanese brothels, the press focused on valuable items the women had, like "a pair of gold bracelets," as well as the brutality of murders exemplified in such phrases as "[a victim's] throat was cut from ear to ear" or such titles as "Jack-the-Ripper Murder."[123] They also tended to exaggerate the criminality of the Japanese by describing a man who extorted money from a woman as a "blackmailer in an artless Japanese way" or another man who forced a woman to work in a brothel as a "very smooth all-round rascal."[124]

A similar focus on violence in brothels and racial biases shaped the police attitude toward Japanese prostitution in British Columbia. In the murder case of Jennie Kiohara in Revelstoke, British Columbia, a chief constable from Nelson visited the spot and reported that "the body of Jennie lying on the bed room floor covered with a blood stained blanket. The throat was cut, the head was cut in numerous places, and there were stabs and gashes on all parts of the body." According to his report, Jennie and her husband acquired a brothel from Wah Chang, a local Chinese merchant, with partial payment, and after making full payment, they pressed him to transfer the brothel to the couple. On the day Chang finally agreed to do so, the murder took place. The constable believed that "[t]he fiendish manner in which the murder was committed points to the murderer being Oriental," but he found no evidence of the guilt of the suspects and returned to Nelson because he was busy with other duties.[125] The police investigated murders, but their reports did not indicate that they had serious concerns about the problem or took active measures to protect prostitutes from violence, leaving the operation in the hands of Japanese masters or pimps. Two local newspapers, the *Revelstoke Herald* and the *Railway Men's Journal*, described the incident as the "most blood-thirsty and awful crime in the history of the city or the west" and a threat to the "good name of this city and of British law and order."[126]

Japanese prostitutes who became victims of violence or extortion committed by customers and masters did not receive much sympathy from their fellow countrymen, either. As Andrea Geiger writes, Osada Shōhei, in his account of the Kiohara case, offered grotesque details of the murder from a police report, including that her throat was slit from ear to ear and the skin had been peeled off her face. By doing so, Osada used this brutal murder case as a warning that women engaged in such despised work as prostitution would meet the same fate.[127] On another occasion, Osada described, in a highly sarcastic tone, the fate of Akagi Tomi, who made a large sum as the manager of a thriving brothel in Cranbrook and was extorted of all the money by a Japanese man she had hired as a traveling companion on her return to Japan.[128] Implicit in these writings is the message that prostitutes deserve their fate because of their work. Thus, Japanese women were oppressed under the burdens of both racism and prejudice against their work within the Japanese community. Criticism of these women became stronger as antiprostitution movements developed among Japanese reformers in the 1910s.

Japanese-language sources are useful in understanding leaders' and reformers' assumptions about prostitutes, and they also provide good detail on the actual lives of these women. From newspaper articles on the murders of prostitutes, for instance, we learn that these women were often victims of jealous men—both husbands and customers—who failed to win their hearts. In September 1910, a manager of a San Francisco bar-restaurant discovered that his wife, Yukie, had eloped with another man. First, he agreed to let her go with her lover, but as the couple started a new life, he became consumed with jealousy and shot her to death. He later told a newspaperman: "I was offended by her decision to run away with another man."[129] As another example, a labor contractor in Sacramento used most of his savings to see his favorite prostitute, Katsu, and asked her to marry him several times. As she continued to take no heed of what he said and started preparing to return to Japan, he shot her to death.[130] Sawada Otomatsu in Isleton, California, also spent a large sum of money to redeem a barmaid, Kikue, from her husband, but after their relationship deteriorated and she committed adultery with another man, he killed her.[131] The unbalanced gender ratio certainly enabled Japanese women to use their sexuality to attract customers and earn large sums, but it also made men compete for a small number of women. Inevitably, a barmaid's rejection often incurred their ill will.

Prostitutes often became victims of extortion for the simple reason that they had no secure place to keep their money. Fujioka Shirō recalled why Japanese prostitutes in Seattle put their money in the care of Furuya Masajirō, a tailor who took orders from them: "After going through many hardships and saving money in America, prostitutes wondered how to take care of the money. . . . They could not deposit money in a bank because they were not allowed to go out. . . . [Prostitutes] kept their money in the drawers of their bureaus or on the bottom of their trunks. Some hid it inside the mattresses of their beds. But none of the women felt secure. After pondering a way to solve the problem, they consulted a familiar face, 'Tailor Masa,' about the matter."[132] If they did not know anyone whom they could trust, they had to protect their property by themselves. Takahashi Kiyo, a former prostitute in Canada, kept all her money in a hotel room in Vancouver. At the age of eighty-eight, she decided to return to Japan, but shortly before her departure, someone broke into her room and stole all her money.[133] She passed away not long after the incident.[134] Considering the extralegal means by which she earned money, she must have been wary of depositing it in banks.

Pregnancy was an inevitable problem associated with the trade, although women no doubt used contraceptive devices. Newspaper articles on pregnant women suggest that they were rarely allowed to take maternity leave or receive care during pregnancy. Fujita Yoshi, a prostitute, after conceiving a baby, was ordered by her husband to continue to sell her body to customers. When she resisted the order, she was confined in a room, beaten, and refused food for three days. The beating resulted in the death of her baby a few days after the delivery.[135] Working during pregnancy was physically dangerous for women, because drunken customers got violent and often played nasty tricks on them. One night in August 1915, a few customers in a San Francisco bar-restaurant were waiting for Oyasu, a pregnant barmaid, to pour beer into their glasses. When she was about to sit down to pour the beer, the men moved her chair and made her fall backward. The damage to her hips forced her to give birth to her child in the seventh month of pregnancy. A newspaper reported that the men tried to appease her husband and Oyasu by arranging a dinner party and giving her some money.[136] Oyasu may have needed money, but it did not bring her around. Although the baby was healthy, her condition suddenly worsened, and she died in October of that year.

Although women could choose to have abortions, the pregnant prostitutes reported in Japanese sources often bore their children.[137] But how could they raise their children while working in brothels?

Typically, they made arrangements with other families and placed the children in their care. For example, Owaka, in Cranbrook, British Columbia, who appeared in Osada Shōhei's account, conceived while serving white customers. She left the child in a local Canadian family's care, paid them $16 a month, and visited her daughter every Sunday. Similarly, Omaki, in Calgary, Alberta, had the child of a black customer and placed the boy with a local black family. Maimie, in Fernie, British Columbia, did not wish to raise her baby born out of wedlock and attempted to sell her unwanted daughter to a Chinese man, but the negotiations ended in failure because the man did not want a racially mixed child.[138] The decision to give up her own child must have been difficult, but placing the child under the care of others—even if they were non-Japanese—may have been the best choice she could make as a mother, because the child was more likely to be provided with nutritious food, a better education, and health care in a normal family than in a brothel.[139]

But a more important issue in considering the decision of Owaka and Omaki to place their children with foster parents who were racially related to their children was racial attitudes within the Japanese community. Osada, in his description of Omaki's case, used a derogatory Japanese word for African Americans, *kuronbo* (meaning "black boy"), to describe her black husband. As Andrea Geiger writes, Japanese immigrants' usage of this word exemplified their anxiety that they would be placed in a low position similar to that of African Americans in American society, which was equivalent to the status of the outcaste in Japan.[140] Some Japanese immigrants also found the children of Japanese women and white men distasteful. In Japan, racially mixed children of Japanese prostitutes and foreign customers became targets of prejudice, as the editors of the *Yokohama shinpō* wrote in 1903: "If you visit the village of Chigasaki or the outskirts of Odawara, you will often see young racially mixed children being excluded by their playmates and crying."[141] In the North American Japanese community, too, whites were not always regarded in a positive light, as indicated by a word some Japanese used to describe whites, *ketō* (meaning "hairy barbarian").[142] Owaka's decision to place her child in a white family's care may have reflected her fear that the child would be subject to prejudice from other Japanese as well as her wish to be connected to the child.

In addition to pregnancy, venereal diseases were an unavoidable problem for Japanese sex workers. Although Japanese prostitutes also contracted venereal diseases in the regulated context in Japan, the Canadian and U.S. governments' reluctance to recognize prostitution and implement compulsory medical checkups for prostitutes appear to have exacerbated the problem of venereal diseases among the Japanese in the North American West.[143] In a federal investigation conducted in Seattle in 1907, Dr. Uyematsu Tatemaru told an official from the Bureau of Immigration and Naturalization: "You also must investigate the Japanese restaurants where they keep female Japanese waitresses; they are very bad; very many men come to me with chancre, bubo and syphilis contracted in these places."[144] A considerable number of advertisements for medicines for curing gonorrhea appeared in the Japanese press, suggesting that Japanese men did frequent brothels and contract the disease.[145] The development of Neosalvarsan, a new treatment for syphilis, was of considerable interest in the Japanese community. In January 1911, the *Shin sekai* carried an article, "Good News to Syphilis Patients," reporting that the medicine would soon become available in California.[146]

The immigrant press's treatment of venereal diseases deserves consideration, because these articles show that the women who had contracted disease rarely won the sympathy of fellow countrymen. In August 1910, the *Shin sekai* editor, in his report on the repatriation of a Japanese woman after she had made $4,000 from prostitution, wrote that a serious disease that she had contracted "spread throughout her body . . . hollowed her cheeks, and reduced her to a skeleton." While describing her condition as "pitiful," the editor called her fate a "rust from her own body" (*mikara deta sabi*), meaning that it was the consequence of her own deeds.[147] Anyone who purchased sexual services in brothels ran the risk of contracting a venereal disease, but women were blamed for the infection. In 1906, the *Ōfu nippō*, in reporting the spread of gonorrhea among local Japanese men, attributed the cause to prostitutes who failed to take medicine or see physicians regularly.[148] Absent in these writings is any reference to the hard reality of these women's lives, including that, even after contracting diseases, their masters or pimps forced them to continue taking customers.

The predicaments faced by Japanese prostitutes become more revealing when understood in the context of their careers. In 1910 and 1913, the governors of Kanagawa Prefecture reported on the return of thirty-eight Japanese prostitutes who had been deported from Seattle and San Francisco. Almost 80 percent were thirty years old or older, and more than 30 percent were in their late thirties or forties.[149] This age profile comes into focus when it is compared with that of prostitutes in Japan during the same period. According to a Japanese government survey conducted in 1900, 66 percent of licensed prostitutes were between eighteen and twenty-five years of age. Two decades later, more than 70 percent of Tokyo prostitutes belonged to the same age group.[150] Furthermore, prostitutes in Japan usually worked for only a limited period before marriage. Of prostitutes in Tokyo surveyed from 1921 to 1923, 70 percent had worked less than three years, and those who had worked more than six years accounted for only 7 percent.[151] This figure supports a social survey-or's contention that "it is the custom [in pleasure quarters] that prostitutes were released from masters on the completion of the term of service regardless of the amount of their debts."[152] Japanese women engaged in prostitution in North America were typically older and worked longer than their counterparts in Japan.

Consul Abe Kihachi's brief biographical sketches of seventeen prostitutes deported from Seattle in 1910 illuminate characteristic features of Japanese prostitutes' careers. The vast majority arrived in Hawaii or North America when they were in their late teens or early twenties, and their careers spanned eight to ten years on average. Their places of work included not only the coastal port cities of Seattle, Portland, and San Francisco but also smaller interior towns in the Pacific Northwest, including Pendleton, Aberdeen, Kalispell, Idaho Falls, White Fish, and Walla Walla. The majority were accompanied by their "husbands," who were obviously living off their wives' earnings from prostitution. Yet even after the husbands died or deserted them, many of the prostitutes continued to barter sexual favors until they were arrested in 1910. None acquired jobs outside the red-light district during their years in North America.[153]

One could argue that these features of Japanese prostitutes' careers—migrancy and limited occupational mobility—were typical among prostitutes of all ethnicities. As past studies of prostitution have demonstrated, in the North American West from the Rocky Mountain region to Pacific Coast cities, in both the United States and Canada, many white-collar (and well-paying) jobs were limited to men, and women had to accept lowly paid work as domestics, laundresses, and sewing women, more so in the West, where industrial wage work in factories or positions as salesgirls were less available. Most prostitutes came from working-class families, and, certainly, some women

viewed prostitution as a means of getting expensive items such as clothing and cosmetics that they could not afford otherwise. But for the
majority of women, most scholars agree, prostitution was not a trade
that they entered willingly but a last resort. The records of criminal
courts showed that problems of poverty, alcoholism, and homelessness
often permeated the lives of white prostitutes arrested by the police.[154]
Japanese prostitutes, too, came from poor agricultural regions and
often grew up in households with problems. They also had to give up
school to work for wages or for their parents' businesses. They had no
industrial and language skills that allowed them to find white-collar
jobs in the North American labor market. The causes of prostitution,
therefore, can be attributed to general problems of poverty and gender
inequalities in Japanese, Canadian, and American societies.

However, it must also be remembered that in the United States, Japanese women had fewer job options than white women did. According to the 1900 census, 57 percent of employed Japanese women were
domestics, 21 percent were service workers, and those who held cleri-
cal and professional jobs accounted for less than 2 percent.[155] Given
that most service workers were employed in Japanese establishments,
one can infer from these figures that except for domestic work, the
opportunity to earn wages outside Japanese communities was rarely
available to Japanese women. The same can be said for Chinese
women. Judy Yung shows that in late-nineteenth-century San Francisco, Chinese women who wished to work had few options except
doing piecework such as sewing, washing, and making cigars or sandals; a very large portion of Chinese women were listed as prostitutes
in the federal census, 86–97 percent in 1860 and 71–72 percent in
1870.[156] White women were also placed in disadvantaged positions in
the labor market, but at the same time, it must be acknowledged that
language difficulties, unfamiliarity with local customs, an unusually
unbalanced sex ratio created by immigration policies, and racism limited Asian women's access to jobs available to white women and made
it more difficult for them to *choose* to get in and out of prostitution
as their life circumstances changed. But both white and Asian prostitutes had to deal with the stigma attached to prostitution while being
used as sexual outlets for men whose access to women's sexuality was
protected by double standards in the dominant sexual ideologies of
both Japanese/Asian and North American societies.

The idea of prostitution overseas as "seasonal work away from
home" (*dekasegi*) may have postponed the women's decision to

repatriate. Yet despite the recognition they received from their families, the stigma attached to the occupation often prevented them from
beginning new lives in their homeland. A woman named Kiyo, for
example, made $2,000 during two years in the United States as a
prostitute and returned with her husband to their native village in
Yamaguchi Prefecture in 1906. By then, however, the fact that she
had made money from prostitution became widely known, and, "sickened by being ignored by fellow villagers, they could not but leave,"
the Ōfu nippō reported. They migrated to Hawaii, and Kiyo started
practicing prostitution again. Later in 1908, they moved to the mainland to start a bar-restaurant.[157] As an occupation, prostitution was
legal in Japan, and the economy of rural agrarian villages and of the
nation was dependent on money sent from overseas prostitutes; however, their filial piety and contributions to the state were not always
rewarded by the people who profited from these women's labor. Thus,
the fear of bringing shame to their families and being isolated in their
ancestral villages, along with the continuous demand for their labor
in the North American sex market, may have prolonged Japanese
sex workers' stays in the United States and Canada. Fear of rejection
could be a reason for some to start new lives elsewhere rather than go
back home.[158]

But it does not mean that those who remained in the North American West had easier lives. Suicides of Japanese prostitutes were sometimes recorded in both English- and Japanese-language newspapers,
but unlike the American or Canadian press, which often focused on
brutal murders, the immigrant press tended to offer more personal
stories. Watarai Toki, a Fresno prostitute, for example, shot herself
fatally with a pistol in June 1912 after living as a prostitute for several years. According to the Ōfu nippō, she had lost all hope when
she was sexually abused and forced into prostitution by her uncle.[159]
In September 1916, the editor of the Tairiku nippō in Vancouver, in
its report on the death of Ohana, a Vancouver barmaid, described
her troubled married life. She had married three different men after
coming to Canada. When relations with her third husband deteriorated in September 1916, she drowned herself off Port Moody.[160]
Sickness made it difficult for women to pay off debts and plan for life
after leaving the trade. In September 1909, San Francisco's Shin sekai
reported that Yazawa Tomi, a prostitute in Merced, California, who
committed suicide by drinking poison, had been "anxious about her
future because of the sickness she had suffered for years."[161] These

articles show that suicide did occur among women who found the life too stressful to endure.

Due to their unfamiliarity with the language and social systems in their host societies, some Japanese women were trapped in extremely difficult situations. The story of Ishida Chiyo, which appeared in Osada Shōhei's account, is revealing. The author, usually sarcastic in his attitude toward prostitutes, spent fourteen pages on a detailed description of her predicament, calling her case one of the "ugly, despicable examples" (shūrō naru jitsurei). He wrote that Chiyo was "a woman of extraordinary beauty," not yet twenty years old, equipped with sewing skills, when she was persuaded by a Japanese man to travel to Vancouver with him in 1905. Shortly after she moved to Nelson and began to work in a brothel, local residents protested against the practice of permitting a handicapped woman (she was lame) to work as a prostitute. Later, she was transferred to Michel, then to Lightbridge, and then to Calgary. She became pregnant and delivered a baby.[162]

In Calgary, Chiyo attempted to run away with a Chinese customer who had proposed to her; however, she was caught and brought back to the brothel. Her master decided to sell her back to a brothel in Michel, but she resisted fiercely, insisting that she would never return to sex work. Fortunately, the Salvation Army intervened in this case and took her into its care; however, a brothel-manager from Saskatoon, Saskatchewan, persuaded Salvation Army officials to hand Chiyo over to him, lying that he had come to take her to her brother who was staying in Vancouver. She was then pressed into prostitution in Saskatoon. Despair drove her to drink and ruined her health. She later died of an illness, leaving behind her child.[163] Her powerlessness in the hands of brothel-keepers and her death reveal a negative feature of the turn-of-the-century North American West—the absence of consistent efforts to abolish prostitution on the part of local authorities who were concerned primarily with economic development and order in their communities often enabled the powerful to dominate the weak.

THE SUBCULTURE OF PROSTITUTION

In studies focused primarily on white prostitutes in western mining towns of the United States at the turn of the twentieth century, scholars have found that relations among prostitutes were rarely harmonious.

The insecurity of jobs and the limited social mobility outside brothels placed women in constant competition with one another, and women often internalized the stigma attached to their work by society and viewed women in the same trade with hate and suspicion. These factors led them to fight or verbally abuse one another in public, and accounts of these conflicts surfaced in local newspapers and criminal docket books.[164] At the same time, cooperation was sometimes necessary in times of hardship, because they could rarely create trusting relationship with anyone. As sexual deviants excluded from "normal" family lives, they sometimes lived and traveled together, helping one another in escaping the dangers associated with their work, caring for one another in times of illness, or introducing customers to one another.[165] Japanese women were more tightly controlled by pimps and brothel-keepers than white prostitutes were, and their relationships were limited to women in the same trade. We can find instances of such interactions among these women and their own voices in vernacular newspaper articles and the writings of Japanese immigrants. Although filtered through the eyes of male authors, these sources provide a window into the daily lives and subcultures of Japanese prostitutes.

In their spare moments, Japanese women sought consolation in leisure activities. One of them was *shibai* (the Japanese theater), a popular form of entertainment in pre–World War II Japanese immigrant communities. In Seattle, it began in the 1890s, when amateur actors organized theatrical companies. The performances included *kabuki* (traditional Japanese drama), *shishimai* (a dragon dance), and Japanese melodramas popular in Meiji Japan. In the early years of Seattle's Japantown, the majority of the audience consisted of prostitutes.[166] In San Francisco, too, prostitutes were the major customers of *shibai*, always occupying the best seats and "showing their attractive faces and figures under the light."[167] It was a rare occasion when ordinary immigrants could see these women in a public place, but the immigrants often viewed the women as objects of curiosity and scorn. Maeno Kunizō, who graduated from a junior high school (equivalent to today's high school) in Japan and came to the United States with the hope of entering Stanford University in 1903, remembered the first time that he went to the theater in Seattle: "Barmaids and madams of bar-restaurants were watching the play in a group in the boxes on both sides of the stage. Large plates of *sushi* were carried into the boxes during the intermission. . . . If I characterize the scene in one word, I would say 'gaudy.'"[168] On another occasion, Maeno characterized the "white birds" as "gaudily dressed in clothing with deep colors that cannot be described either as Japanese or as Western but was peculiar [to these women]."[169] As an educated youth, he shared Meiji officials' contempt for women engaged in entertainment work and prostitution, who were considered low in class and status in Japan, as well as their concerns about the reputation of the Japanese in American society.[170]

Japanese prostitutes and barmaids were not, however, simply objects of curiosity or scorn. From newspaper articles and immigrant accounts, we see that they actively engaged in theatrical activities. For example, Kyōraku Ren, a theatrical company in Seattle, was started in 1904 by two barmaids, Omasa and Kotaka, together with local artisans. They performed twice a year in a hall located in the red-light district, drawing large numbers of spectators including prostitutes and barmaids.[171] Japanese women also financially supported theaters. In 1911, local literary men presented a series of plays to make money for the construction of a library in Seattle's Japantown, and twenty barmaids from major bar-restaurants were some of the largest contributors to this charity.[172] The same year, a contributor to the *Taihoku nippō* reported that six barmaids were planning to put on a one-act play with a local theatrical company to congratulate a barmaid on her marriage and retirement.[173] The managers of bar-restaurants were generally supportive of their employees' participation in the plays, closing their businesses temporarily for special occasions and making monetary contributions to theatrical companies.[174] The employers certainly saw the merits of exhibiting their women in the spotlight at public events, because it would draw more male customers to their restaurants.

Most Japanese prostitutes and barmaids were allowed to have some free time during afternoons before work. In British Columbia mining towns, according to Osada Shōhei, women got up around noon, cleaned their rooms, and had lunch, usually dishes made with Japanese foods ordered from Vancouver. Osada described the conversation among Japanese prostitutes during lunchtime in a fictional account:

> "The Chow Mein that a Chinaman treated me to last night was delicious."
> "I like Fu Rong Dan [a Chinese dish using scrambled eggs] more than Chow Mein."

"If you say that, I will tell my *reko* [sweetheart] all about it."
"I don't care. I want to go back to Japan and have *soba* [buck-wheat noodles] and *unagi no donburi* [grilled eel bowl]."

The lunch was followed by singing. Then some read novels, and others asked their pimps to go downtown and get fruit and candy for them. They sometimes went out for gambling in Chinatown or shopping downtown.[175]

One of the most graphic accounts of barmaids' everyday lives is found in an anonymous Japanese woman's diary, which first appeared in a local Japanese paper in Stockton and was reprinted in the *Shin sekai* in January 1911. In publishing this diary, the editor of the press added a note: "I happened to have found [her] journal and am going to print some parts that I found interesting. Keep this a secret from her." From today's perspective, this is a violation of privacy for which the press would be liable. In the context of the Japanese immigrant community in this period, however, the civil rights of "women engaged in an ugly trade" (*shūgyōfu*) were not taken so seriously as today, and editors often published private writings exchanged between or written by men and women whom they considered a shame on their community and not deserving of being treated with respect. The publication of such writing usually served as a punishment for these individuals and a means of telling readers how they should behave. In this particular case, however, the editor did not appear to be so critical of what the woman did or wrote. Considering that this memoir was published on New Year's Day, perhaps the editor just wanted to deal with an unusual topic that would draw the attention of readers and decided to publish a barmaid's diary that happened to include a good deal of information about her daily life.

According to the diary, she worked from Monday through Saturday, during which time she had to deal with a number of difficult customers. She wrote in her entry for Monday: "We have only cheap customers nowadays. Some order only two small bottles of sake and talk whatever they like. I gave them a nickname 'one order group.' Another group of four rustic men came down to the kitchen to complain that we had left them unattended for too long. When I drew closer to them and tell them to touch my legs, their expression softened, and they had a smile all over their faces and returned [to their room]. I really hate these men."[176] She was also annoyed with a customer who tried to make advances to her. In another entry, she wrote: "Mr. _____ came [again]. People say that he is in love with me, but I really hate him. So after receiving a tip, I try to keep away from him."[177] Their kindly manner and smiles notwithstanding, their work was a source of stress and frustration for barmaids.

In her free time, however, she could do what she wanted. She had a friend and colleague named "Hana-chan," and they went to a public bath (*sentō*) after finishing the day's work at midnight. She spent her money on her favorite foods, including roasted chestnuts, mandarin oranges, candies, and peanuts, and lottery tickets. The following is her entry for her day off: "Today is Sunday. The restaurant is closed. I can enjoy myself fully. I woke up around eleven o'clock and began to put on makeup. I couldn't wait until one o'clock when the movie would begin, so I went out with Hana-chan. We played Box Ball. . . . [Later] we went to the Oriental Hall to watch a *kabuki* play. A tear rolled down my cheek. I knew that everyone would tease me for that from tomorrow, but I couldn't stop crying."[178] Only on Sundays, could she do what she wanted without having to think what would please her customers.[179]

Barmaids wrote *tanka*, which were published in newspapers and appear in oral history collections. They provide a glimpse of what was on their minds. One barmaid, Hayashi Hideko, was a well-educated daughter of a doctor who married a Japanese migrant to the United States. After arriving in Seattle, Hideko realized that her husband was a mere laundryman. Begged by the poor husband, she decided to work at Maneki, a high-class Japanese bar-restaurant.[180] Her poems express hardships associated with this trade:

It is disgraceful to powder my face three times a day;
I powder my face to brush the disgracefulness away.

Men praise me with thousands of words;
They approach me and force me to kiss them.[181]

Itō Kasumi, perhaps a barmaid, sang of her sadness to be working in a bar-restaurant:

I cannot drown out my sorrows in the sound of *samisen*;
I remain intoxicated and sad.

I feel pain even if I sing loudly, I feel lonely even if I drink sake.
There is no place for me to go.[182]

Barmaids were often married women with higher levels of education than their laborer husbands. The poems indicate their sense of shame and discontent.

Was there anyplace where women could talk to one another outside their place of work? Shopping was an opportunity for prostitutes
to socialize with other women in the trade. One of the daily destinations of Tamesa Uhachi, a former deliveryman in Seattle, was the Satō
Grocery Store, where prostitutes from King Street came to shop and
chat with the wife of the owner, who used to work as a prostitute.
Tamesa recalled: "Women of King Street, the so-called red-light district, often came and chatted with other prostitutes there. They may
have felt secure because the madam was a former prostitute. Yamada
Waka-san was also one of the women of King Street who shopped
at the Satō Grocery Store. . . . Waka-san liked Mrs. Satō, calling
her 'Sister, Sister.' . . . They got along well, probably because they
were from the same prefecture."[183] The store would have been one of
few places where they could spend time without worrying about the
watchful eyes of other Japanese or being interrogated by policemen
or reformers.

In the limited time before and after work, Japanese prostitutes and
barmaids found some comfort in a variety of activities: reading novels, gambling, eating favorite foods, watching plays, shopping, going
to public baths, and chatting with other prostitutes. As the forms of
these pastimes indicate, however, their world was confined to brothels and certain places in the Japanese community. In the eyes of ordinary Japanese immigrants, prostitutes were "women engaged in an
ugly trade" (shūgyōfu) who should be distinguished from "persons
engaged in honest work" (seigyō-sha).[184] Barmaids received recognition through their service to their customers but did not receive much
sympathy when they got injured or suffered from diseases. These
women internalized the negative perceptions of their work and rarely
revealed their real names or what parts of Japan they were from.[185]
These leisure activities may have lessened the emotional burdens associated with their work but, at the same time, must have reinforced
their sense of isolation from North American societies and the Japanese immigrant community.

Breaking the Shackles of Oppression

*Japanese Prostitutes' and Barmaids'
Response to Sexual and Economic
Exploitation*

Kojima Tomi, a woman working as a barmaid in a local Japanese restaurant in Sacramento, filed for divorce from her husband in superior court in March 1917. She observed in court that before marrying him, she had "lived with her parents in Japan, and was in comfortable circumstances as her parents were well to do" and "was unaccustomed to hard labor and was never required to do such by her said parents." When Shinjiro, a returnee from America, met her and her parents in Tomi's home in Hiroshima, he represented himself as "a wealthy man and possessed of considerable property in California." In proposing marriage, he said that "when they were married, they would remove to California where [he] would have plenty of servants to do all labor and all that [Tomi] would have to do would be to assist defendant in managing his property." She did not tell how she had responded to the marriage proposition but continued: "[A]fter said marriage [Tomi] and [Shinjiro] remained in Japan visiting friends and relatives and living a life of ease and comfort" and later in March 1916 "left Japan for Seattle." After arriving in Seattle in April, they moved to Sacramento.[1]

Tomi claimed, however, that shortly after starting their married life in Sacramento, she realized that Shinjiro was not a wealthy landowner but a mere employee in a local grocery store. He then took Tomi to a restaurant on L Street, telling her that "you would have to go to work in said restaurant as he was not able to keep her unless she helped in the support by working herself." Stunned by the change in his attitude, Tomi "grew angry and demanded of the defendant an explanation of the representations made to her by said defendant prior to their marriage in Japan." Shinjiro then "threatened to kill plaintiff if she did not immediately go to work and obey his command." Tomi had no choice except to obey his orders but made clear that "[she] [was] a young woman of the age of nineteen years, refined, educated and unaccustomed to labor in public places, and by reason of her youthful and attractive appearance [she] has been sought by the customers of said restaurant," emphasizing that "the attentions paid her at said restaurant by said customers were distasteful and unpleasant."[2]

Although Shinjiro forced Tomi to work in the restaurant, he became jealous of her relations with her customers. Tomi observed: "[Shinjiro] constantly appeared at said restaurant and watched [her], waited for her to finish her work for the day and accompanied her to their home. . . . [A]lmost every night after retiring to their said home, [he] would find fault and quarrel with said plaintiff and accuse her of attempting to make appointments with the customers in said restaurant." Before long, he transferred Tomi to another restaurant so that she would not become too close to particular customers. And yet, in March 1917, he once again accused her of "being too familiar with one of the customers . . . and attempting to make an engagement with one of the said customers." Shinjiro beat her, "knocking her down and again drew a knife and threatened to kill plaintiff if she made another complaint." One morning, she left the home, hid herself with the help of her friends, and filed for divorce in superior court, to separate from her husband who "inflicted upon [her] great and grievous mental pain and anguish and physical suffering."[3]

Parts of this story were certainly exaggerated. Tomi did not tell how she, a sixteen-year-old at the time of the marriage, decided to go with Shinjiro, twenty-two years her senior, narrating her experiences as if she and her parents were tricked into marriage by an evil old man who misrepresented his economic circumstances in the United States. By presenting herself as an innocent woman coerced into working as a barmaid by a parasitic husband and stressing that she was from a well-off family without financial constraints, she was careful not to give the impression that she was a selfish woman who wanted to live a luxurious life in California or a promiscuous woman willing to become a barmaid to earn more money. Her story, therefore, should be taken as a means for her to obtain a divorce rather than an accurate description of what happened.

At the same time, however, it is difficult to deny that Tomi studied the divorce laws carefully and manipulated the system and assumptions about women seeking divorce to her advantage. Her attempt to assert her "respectability" before the judge and the careful preparations she must have made before the trial challenge us to reconsider the conventional portrayal of Japanese barmaids as powerless women who fell into lives of servitude and were controlled by abusive husbands. Most existing sources about Japanese prostitutes and barmaids demonstrate the hardships they experienced, but while reading these sources, we sometimes encounter women who did not act according to the rules of behavior set for them by male power holders. Analyzing a variety of responses of Japanese prostitutes and barmaids and men's responses to them in the contexts of their lives produces a deeper understanding of gender relations and power structures in the early Japanese immigrant community in the North American West.

PAYING OFF THE DEBT

Most Japanese women owed passage and loans to masters or husbands upon arriving on American shores; therefore, for those who wished to end their relations with these men, redeeming their debts was the surest way of gaining their freedom. Otaka was one woman who resorted to this means. She journeyed to Seattle in October 1912 to join her husband, Takahashi Masajirō, who had preceded her. Shortly after her arrival in the United States, Otaka began to discuss a divorce with her husband. The two concluded that Otaka would work as a barmaid in a local bar-restaurant, Maneki, in order to pay Takahashi her consolation money (*tegirekin*) for the divorce, $700. According to a Japanese-language newspaper, Otaka had planned to get a divorce from Takahashi upon her arrival and marry Naitō Toranosuke, a clerk for the *Nippon Yūsen* steamship company. The editor summarizes Otaka's letter to Naitō:

> [Otaka's] letter is written in a very complex manner, but its main points are as follows: I am writing to let you know that I arrived in America safely. I recently broached the issue of divorce with Takahashi. I have the backing of a few influential men, so I feel secure. I owe Takahashi $700. We have fixed that I will pay him $400 in cash and will repay the rest of the debt by working at a bar-restaurant, Maneki. When I have solved this problem, I will be relieved of a heavy burden. I am looking forward to seeing you.[4]

The editor's decision to disclose the contents of this personal letter and Otaka's personal matters with her husband and lover reflects, to some extent, his intention to use this incident as a moral lesson, warning readers that a loose woman who used her marriage as a means of joining a boyfriend in the United States deserved to be punished for her conduct. By summarizing the contents of the letter rather than transcribing it, the editor may have emphasized some aspects of her behavior to present her as a shrewd woman twisting men around her finger. Despite the editor's wish to present her as a bad woman, her actions as described in the articles also demonstrate that she had well understood the immigration law and customs related to marriage and divorce that would permit her to achieve what she wanted. She migrated as a married woman (rather than a barmaid) to ensure her safe entry into the country and, once reaching Seattle, negotiated a divorce with her husband. She offered to pay him $700 as compensation and knew "a few influential men" who would help conclude this negotiation. She had certainly planned a strategy carefully before migration.[5]

The consolation payment was a kind of compromise between Japanese women and their employers or husbands. Masters agreed to release prostitutes with the understanding that the consolation money would offset the loss of expected income and their initial investment in purchasing the women (the money also allowed them to hire procurers and import other prostitutes from Japan). Similarly, husbands of barmaids agreed to let their wives go, typically with their boyfriends, upon receipt of consolation money that would compensate for the cost of arranging marriages and bringing the women over. Women were required to pay off their debts before leaving employers or husbands, but the burden in these arrangements was probably light for them, considering that their boyfriends would help pay the consolation money. Interestingly, the consolation payment practice was more popular among Japanese migrants in western Canada than in the western United States because of the difficulty of getting a divorce under Canadian law and highly negative societal attitudes toward divorce in Canada.[6]

One could also argue that the consolation money payment was an extension of local practices in Japan, because extralegal dissolutions of marriages were common in the nineteenth century. Japanese parents allowed sons and daughters of marriageable age to cohabit and marry casually, to see if they got along well. If not, the couples dissolved their marriages and reported divorces to the municipal office. This practice of "trial marriage" resulted in a high divorce rate in Japan, which surpassed that in other industrialized nations, including France, Germany, Sweden, and the United States, in the period before 1910. The Meiji government sought to stop the practice of casual marriage, and the Civil Code of 1898 required couples to dissolve their marriages either by mutual consent (*kyōgi rikon*) or by filing for divorce in the courts (*saiban rikon*). Although the divorce rate began to decline thereafter, few couples used the courts to dissolve marriages. Between 1900 and 1940, more than 99 percent of divorcing couples dissolved their marriages by mutual consent as they had done in the late Tokugawa and early Meiji periods.[7] Regardless of changes in the laws, government arbitration in marital disputes was infrequent in Japan. Given the popularity of private settlement of marital disputes in Japan, dissolving an unhappy marriage through the payment of consolation money would have been a reasonable option for married Japanese prostitutes and barmaids in North America.

However, one must also remember that not all prostitutes and barmaids were fortunate enough to be redeemed by their customers or suitors. The consolation money, commonly $500 to $600, was a large sum for male laborers. There were many couples who had no money and dared to risk their lives by running away. In most cases, however, the pimps and their friends tracked the couples down and forced the men to pay consolation money. Not surprisingly, newspaper articles on these cases indicate that redeemed prostitutes and barmaids were some of the most popular women.[8] Many other prostitutes and barmaids who could not find suitors willing to buy their freedom had to work until their debts were repaid. As Mary Murphy explains, prostitution was a competitive business. Some women with good communication skills and physical appearance could get many regular customers and earn a large sum in tips. They also had a good chance of repaying their debts quickly and marrying customers.[9] Yet we must be careful not to apply these findings, which apply primarily to white prostitutes, to Japanese women, who were heavily indebted to and more strictly controlled by husbands or masters. Most Japanese women did not have much say in negotiations between masters and lovers who claimed a right to own their bodies.

RUNNING AWAY AND REPORTING TO THE POLICE

For prostitutes who were tightly controlled by their masters, running away from brothels was often the only option available. These women often appeared in sources created by law-enforcement officials. Not surprisingly, they fit the stereotypical images of innocent victims controlled by evil white slavers. For example, in December 1909, Yamamoto Kiyo told her story before a notary public in King County, Washington. Originally she followed her cousin and her husband to San Francisco in 1904 under a promise that she would work as a waitress. After their arrival, however, she was sold to a local brothel. In 1906, when the earthquake destroyed the town, her master took her to Oregon and later to Bellingham, Washington, where she was sold to another master and soon transferred to a brothel in Seattle. A year later, she was allowed to leave the brothel on the condition that she would repay the rest of her debt later. She then moved to Seattle, where she entered a Protestant rescue mission. One day, however, she was caught on the street by a gang and ordered to work in a labor camp. She ran away and went to her old master for help. Contrary to her expectations, she was physically abused by him and confined in a hotel under constant surveillance.[10]

Fortunately, a stranger who witnessed Kiyo being beaten by her former master called the police. The master was arrested, and she was protected by the police and Japanese Protestant reformers. She entered a Protestant rescue home for women.[11] She observed in court: "I practiced prostitution four years and a half; after all this time I am penniless." The first master, who brought her to Astoria, Portland, and later to Bellingham, "took every cent I earned, and whenever I refused to give him, he threatened to kill me with a revolver, so I had to give him all the earnings." Then she appealed to the court: "I am now seeking protection, and trying to escape from this slavery, for if I am not taken care of, I will be compelled to go back and lead the life of a prostitute, or I might be killed by the gang; I want to be decent and respectable, and will work honestly to earn my living, so please help me."[12] As her accounts suggest, she was in a desperate situation. Deceived into prostitution, burdened by debts, and physically abused by her master, the only institution she could rely upon was the police.

Going to the police, however, would not have been an option for all Japanese prostitutes. Until the 1910s, when the "white slavery" hysteria reached fever pitch, the local police rarely intervened in brothel management so long as prostitutes paid fines and did not disturb middle-class neighborhoods. Japanese masters tried to make sure that prostitutes adhered to the agreements they had made with them, and if the women ran away, the masters searched for them by placing runaway notices in Japanese-language newspapers.[13] For example, the runaway notice for Shibata Kura, a Sacramento barmaid who ran away without paying off her debts, reads as follows: "Shibata Kura, a.k.a. Fujiye, from the town of Maebara, Itoshima County, Fukuoka Prefecture, disappeared on November 29. She is 5 *shaku* [30.3 centimeters] and 1 *sun* [3.03 centimeters] 5-1 tall, with double eyelids, a fair complexion, a round face, gold teeth, accompanied by a Japanese man. . . . A fifty-dollar reward will be offered for informing us of her whereabouts" (fig. 5.1). The immigrant press carried these notices not only to help employers capture these women but also to control the behavior of "vain" women who disregarded their prescribed gender role as dedicated wives.

Key to understanding these disciplinary actions against Japanese women is the ideology of *ryōsai kenbo* (good wives and wise mothers) that prevailed in the immigrant community in the 1910s. This ideology was implemented by the Meiji government in the 1890s as a guiding principle in women's higher education, which defined women primarily as homemakers who raised loyal sons for the nation. National leaders attached greater importance to *ryōsai kenbo* as the need for industrial workers and military servicemen increased in the context of capitalist development and Japanese expansionism after the turn of the century.[14]

As Kei Tanaka writes, however, this ideology of womanhood was not simply transplanted into American soil. It was redefined in a new setting. As Japanese migrants began to settle in the country in the 1910s, Japanese leaders noticed increasing numbers of picture brides who asserted individual freedom and eloped with other men. Worrying that their scandals would catch the attention of exclusionists, the leaders drew on the *ryōsai kenbo* ideology to insist that women be confined within the home and help their husbands faithfully. Thus, the ideology came to have a different meaning from the original one in Japan, reflecting the concerns of Japanese leaders who were promoting the steady development of Japanese immigrant families and communities in the United States.[15]

At the same time, the extraordinary efforts that employers, husbands, and Japanese leaders made to discipline Japanese women suggest that

Figure 5.1. Runaway notice for a barmaid, Sacramento, California. *Ōfu nippō*, December 2, 1914, 3.

they were actually having difficulty dealing with runaway prostitutes and barmaids. First, although masters required prostitutes to pay off debts by continuing to work and women often agreed to do so, these rules were not legally binding in the United States; therefore, the masters could not turn to the courts to enforce such contracts, even if the women stole away without clearing their debts.[16] Second, since the beginning of Japanese migration, Japanese consuls had been wary of "undesirable" migrants, including gamblers and prostitutes, who would damage Japan's reputation as a "civilized" nation; therefore, if prostitutes went to Japanese consuls for help in escaping from brothels, they were sent back to Japan.[17] Finally, there were several institutions that helped Japanese prostitutes to break away from their masters. To understand prostitutes' actions more fully, therefore, one must look beyond the Japanese community and explore women's relations with religious institutions and legal systems in the larger American or Canadian society.

ENTERING RESCUE MISSIONS

One key institution that Japanese prostitutes and barmaids could turn to was the Protestant rescue mission willing to offer shelter and security. Recall Yamada Waka, who escaped from her Seattle brothel with Tachii Nobusaburō, a newspaperman, and was once again forced into a local brothel after arriving in San Francisco. She then entered the Chinese Mission Home, a Presbyterian rescue mission for former Chinese and Japanese prostitutes.[18] Newspaper articles report that after selling Yamada to the brothel, Tachii attempted to meet her by calling and writing letters. However, Donaldina Cameron, the matron of the Chinese Mission Home, turned down his requests, and Rev. Sakabe, a local Japanese minister supporting the rescue work as an unpaid assistant, was reported to have told him: "[She] says that she does not want to see you. So there is nothing we can do about it."[19] Then Tachii committed suicide by drinking a bottle of poison in December 1903.[20] According to the *San Francisco Chronicle*, he sent a message to Rev. Sakabe asking, "please take good care of Hannah [Waka] after [my] death and be kind to her."[21] Yamada had never written about Tachii's death in her lifetime, but her decision to turn to the Chinese Mission Home and her refusal to see him need to be understood as results of several key events in her life—being forced into prostitution in Seattle and sold to another brothel by a man whom she had once trusted.

Yamada's escape highlights the importance of the institution to which she turned. Founded in 1874, the Chinese Mission Home, headed by its matron, Donaldina Cameron, rescued Chinese and Japanese women from prostitution with the help of the local police. Regarding Asian prostitution as a visible threat to female purity, Protestant missionaries converted the prostitutes to Christianity, inculcated them with Victorian gender values, and encouraged the women and their suitors to solemnize their marriages and make permanent homes. The Chinese Mission Home also provided former prostitutes with domestic and job skills essential to their independence from their masters. Yet the relationship between the missionaries and Asian prostitutes was not one of equality. Missionaries often exhibited notions of Anglo-Saxon and female moral superiority as they criticized the "heathen" Asian culture for such practices as foot binding and the selling and buying of women. More important, however, their attitudes toward prostitutes were different from those of anti-Asian politicians or labor leaders in that they were more concerned with Asian women's subordination within the household than with the influx of Asian immigrants.[22]

Yamada stayed at the Chinese Mission Home from 1903 to 1905 and played an important part supporting its rescue efforts. The school provided sewing and cooking lessons, and Yamada went to a nearby sewing school and learned English from a Japanese teacher, Yamada Kakichi, at his private school.[23] Eighteen months after her entry, she was also baptized and given an English name, Hanna.[24] Believing in the existence of a transcendent God and the principle of human equality, she devoted the rest of her time at the Chinese Mission Home to rescuing other Japanese women from their lives as prostitutes.[25] Cameron characterized Yamada as a "clever, interesting girl, who after sad and bitter experiences in her own life knows so well how to sympathize with, help and guide her unfortunate sisters who seek shelter in Our Home."[26] When Yamada married an English teacher and left the home in 1905, Annie Sturge, chairman of Japanese Work, observed of Yamada: "We have recently lost through marriage the help of a remarkable Japanese woman, who, because of her past experiences and unusual education, seemed to be especially fitted for such a work as we have in hand."[27] Clearly, Yamada contributed to the rescue work and received high recognition within this institution.

Japanese women in Canada also turned to rescue missions, the most famous of which was the Oriental Home and School in Victoria. In 1886, J. E. Gardner, the son of an American Presbyterian missionary in China, discovered that a considerable number of young Chinese girls in Victoria were kept in "slavery worse than the slavery of the Blacks." To save them, Gardner rented a house, appointed a matron, and began to accommodate Chinese prostitutes in 1887. As at the Chinese Mission Home, the administrators of the Oriental Home made efforts to save Asian girls from sexual slavery, convert them to Christianity, and provide them with domestic skills to prepare them for marriage. The first Japanese residents were two young women from Hiroshima, Nemoto Fumi and Miura Shime, who were sold to an English madam in Vancouver, saved by the police, and placed in the home in August 1895. Both were baptized immediately, and one entered domestic service, married, and settled in Canada. According to the institution's records, the Oriental Home accepted an increasing number of Japanese women thereafter: one in 1896, ten in 1898, six in 1899, ten in 1900, nine or ten in 1903, twenty-three in 1905, and eleven in 1906.[28]

For Japanese women, the Oriental Home functioned primarily as a temporary shelter. Otori, a barmaid who entered the home in 1909, was one of the most popular barmaids in Vancouver whose stories occasionally appeared in a local Japanese newspaper. She enjoyed a high reputation for her beauty and had won first prize in a pageant held by a local newspaper company. After changing her place of work from one restaurant to another, she became the proprietress of a bar-restaurant, Shōgetsu. Despite her successful career in the bar-restaurant business, she did not get along with her husband, Okajima. According to a *Tairiku nippō* article, on the evening of April 15, 1909, Otori had a fight with him, left their home, and entered the Oriental Home.[29] The home's record book confirms her story. It says: "[Otori] Ran away from her husband, she said he was going to sell her to a Chinaman. Real reason [is] a man in the case."[30] The "man" mentioned here was, the *Tairiku nippō* reported, a white accountant named *Kuraaku* (probably "Clerk" or "Clark" in English) with whom she became intimate while working at the bar-restaurant.[31] When Otori entered the Oriental Home, she had already conceived his baby, but the record book says that she "[g]ot rid of a baby last of Aug/09," suggesting that she had an abortion after coming to the Oriental Home. The white man visited the home several times, but Ida Snyder, the superintendent, did not allow him to see her.[32]

During her four years in the Oriental Home, Otori acquired English skills, learned cooking, and worked as a servant for a local Canadian family.[33] She was baptized in April 1911.[34] A series of newspaper articles suggests, however, that Otori had not been entirely freed from her complex relations with her husband and other men. One evening in August 1913, she went to a movie with her friend, and on her way back home, she was waylaid by her husband, Okajima, who took her watch and jewelry by force. Luckily, a railroad conductor helped her get on a train, and she was unhurt. According to a newspaper account of the incident, it was the husband's "lingering affection" for her that had made him attempt to see her in person for the past three years.[35] It is not clear exactly what happened between her and her husband, and between her and the white customer, and why her husband continued to pursue her despite her rejection. She left Canada shortly for Japan after being threatened by a man who knew of her life in Hawaii.[36] According to the Oriental Home's record book, she "[m]arried in Japan Spring of 1916."[37]

Despite white reformers' efforts to "rescue" Japanese prostitutes, Japanese immigrants were not so enthusiastic about the rescue work itself. The administrators of the Chinese Mission Home appreciated the work of unpaid male Japanese assistants, including Rev. Sakabe Tasaburō, a minister at the San Francisco Japanese Church of Christ, who offered Japanese residents Christian teachings, held marriage ceremonies, and managed a sewing school for them. No Japanese churchwomen appeared in white missionaries' reports, and the missionaries continued to express the need for female Japanese helpers who would replace Yamada Waka.[38] Similarly, in the Oriental Home, the records include only the names of a few male Japanese ministers cooperating with the reformers, including Rev. Kaburagi Gorō of the Japanese Methodist Church in Vancouver, who brought Japanese women to the Oriental Home and held marriage ceremonies for them. There was no indication of strong commitment in the local Japanese community to the rescue work.[39] As Rumi Yasutake writes, the primary concern of middle-class Japanese churchwomen and immigrant leaders from the 1890s to the 1910s was the general reputation of Japanese residents among middle-class white Americans. To protect the image of Japanese as men and women of fine moral and civic qualities, they focused on excluding prostitutes from their community or protecting "virtuous" women from falling into prostitution rather than "rescuing" women who were already working in the trade.[40]

Japanese antiprostitution reforms could be more successful when reformers responded to the broader needs of the immigrant community. In Seattle, for example, Japanese ministers and Mark A. Matthews, a local Methodist minister, organized the Humane Society (*Jindō Kyōkai*) in 1906 to save Japanese women from prostitution, place them in the Japanese Woman's Home (*Nihon Fujin Hōmu*) attached to the Japanese Baptist Church of Seattle (fig. 5.2), and prepare the women for marriage.[41] However, the administrators of the Woman's Home, including its founder, Okazaki Yoshiko, were more interested in offering newly arrived Japanese women and children a temporary residence to protect them from vice operators in the nearby red-light district. As Japanese brides increased after the Gentlemen's Agreement in 1907–8, the Woman's Home accommodated a variety of women, including picture brides who disliked their husbands, self-supporting women, and widows with children.[42] Japanese ministers also held marriage ceremonies for former barmaids who wished to marry their boyfriends after divorcing their abusive husbands.[43] These activities also met the needs of immigrant leaders who wished to solve marital problems among Japanese couples, including mismatches, domestic violence, and brides' elopement with other men (*kakeochi*), before these "scandals" reached the American public.[44] Although Japanese ministers and some church members had

Figure 5.2. Japanese Baptist Woman's Home, Seattle, ca. 1917. The sign above the porch says "Japanese Woman's Home." Courtesy of the Japanese Baptist Church of Seattle, Washington.

their own religious mission to "rescue" women from sexual "slavery," their antiprostitution reforms needed to be linked to various issues that emerged in the Japanese immigrant community when its members were trying to adapt to American society as permanent settlers.

DIVORCING THEIR HUSBANDS AND LIVING ALONE

Whereas Protestant rescue homes functioned as one common route out of prostitution and unhappy marriages, the more assertive women used the American judicial system to end their relationships with pimp-husbands. They hired lawyers and Japanese interpreters (*tsūben*) and filed for divorce from their abusive husbands.[45] Divorce cases filed by Japanese prostitutes and barmaids in Seattle and Sacramento before 1920 illustrate the point.[46]

Like prostitutes who appealed to the police for help, the women who turned to the courts typically were in a desperate situation. Kinoshita Mine, a sixteen-year-old Japanese bride in Seattle, told her story before Judge Arthur Griffin in 1908: "I meet Yasuzo in [Osaka] and my father say I marry him. I do. We come to San Francisco. He hires me out to another man. He takes me to Tacoma. [A] Chinese woman tells me that I don't be a slave in America. I run away in the night and come to Seattle."[47] She had married Yasuzo in Japan, in November 1901, and the couple journeyed to San Francisco in March 1903. Over time, she observed in court, Yasuzo was "growing tired of [her] and having no longer any love or affection for her" and sold her to another Japanese man "as if she were the slave or property of the said defendant [Yasuzo]." In early 1907, her new master took her to Portland, where she learned from a Chinese woman that "slavery in any form was not tolerated in the United States of America and that she need not and could not be held in bondage by anyone." She ran away from her master, moved to Seattle, and while working and supporting herself there, appealed to the court to grant her a divorce in May 1908. Some questions remained unanswered. Who was the Chinese woman, and what was her relationship to Mine? It might be possible that Mine created this part of story to make her escape from "sexual slavery" more dramatic after consulting her lawyer or members of local Protestant churches.[48] In any event, Yasuzo failed to appear in court, and Mine won the case.[49]

Husbands often failed to respond to their wives' complaints, and the women won the suits without difficulty; in some cases, however, husbands did not remain silent and allow their wives to win in court. Like the women seeking divorces, they also framed their stories to cast their wives in a negative light. Ōta Kimi, a prostitute in Sacramento, filed for divorce from her husband on the grounds of extreme cruelty in October 1911. She complained that her husband, Shōhei, had forced her into prostitution in several towns in Utah and California during the past three years. Every time she protested against living in a brothel, her husband took out a pistol and told her: "If you leave this house, I will kill you." The next month, Shōhei appeared in court to demur, arguing that Kimi "does not state facts sufficient to constitute a cause of action." He also claimed that she had had an adulterous relationship with a man named Higashida and "cohabited with [him] and had sexual intercourse with him." He petitioned the court not to grant her any money and reimburse him for legal expenses.[50] Although Shōhei did force Kimi into prostitution, the disclosure of her adultery was effective enough to invalidate a felony charge filed against Shōhei for violating the state law that penalized husbands for placing wives in brothels.[51]

Subsequent developments forced Kimi to go to extremes. After being discharged, Shōhei started hanging around the hotel where Kimi was staying, seeking an opportunity to talk to her. On February 19, 1912, he finally broke into her room, and the couple got into a bitter argument that developed into a gunfight. An extra edition of the *Ōfu nippō* reported in a dramatic fashion: "Three bullets went through the man's head and pushed his brain out. He died instantly in the pool of blood." Kimi was soon arrested by order of the grand jury.[52] In the following days, the *Shin sekai* newspaper carried detailed articles about this incident, which revealed that their family life had been full of conflicts and problems since their marriage. They had two children, but Shōhei had no regular job and lived off Kimi's earnings from prostitution. At some point, Kimi gave him $800, and Shōhei agreed to return to Japan. And yet, once Kimi took up with another man, he attempted to restore his relationship with her.[53] Only the killing stopped him from interfering in her life. The editor was not necessarily sympathetic to Kimi, calling her an "adulterous woman" (*kanpu*), attributing part of their marital problems to her relations with other men. Equally eager to attack Shōhei as a "shameless man" (*shūkan*) who had damaged the reputation of the Japanese community, however, the editor unintentionally gave a good account of the hardships Kimi had to endure.

Like prostitutes, married Japanese barmaids filed for divorce from their husbands, usually on the grounds of extreme cruelty and failure to provide support; however, a more important reason behind barmaids' decisions to divorce their husbands—a reason they rarely presented in court—was their relations with other men. In January 1915, the *Taihoku nippō* carried a series of articles titled "Oima's Hidden Reason for Divorce," introducing the background of a divorce case filed in the superior court. According to the press, Oima and her husband, Kunitarō, had married in Japan and managed a Western-style bar-brothel (*chabuya*) in Yokohama. They also had a thirteen-year-old son in the care of their family in Japan. After coming to Seattle, Oima started working as a barmaid and, over time, became intimate with Kawabata, a foreman at Blaine Cannery, and asked Kunitarō for a divorce. Worrying that her misdeeds would bring disgrace on him and his family in Japan, he agreed to the divorce on the condition that Oima would return to Japan. However, Oima refused and carried the struggle into the courtroom to divorce her husband.[54] The editor clearly opposed her decision, describing it in an angry tone: "[H]aunted by a heavenly devil (*tenma*), adulterer Oima is telling the people that she was planning to go to the court to end her relation with Kunitarō in an American way and live a licentious life as she pleases. I am at a loss with what to do with this fearless *ama* [a derogatory term for 'woman']."[55]

In court, Oima complained that her husband neglected to provide for her throughout the marriage, and she supported herself by working in bar-restaurants in Seattle. After coming to the United States, Oima noted, her husband became an alcoholic, physically abused her several times, and often took money from her by force. She concluded that she had "lost all love for the defendant and believes that it will be absolutely impossible for her to ever again live with the defendant as husband and wife."[56] Her husband fought back, filing a suit against Oima for adultery. A public prosecutor issued a warrant for the arrest of Oima and her boyfriend, Kawabata.[57] Two weeks later, the Japanese press reported that someone intervened in this dispute, and it was decided that Oima would be sent back to Japan.[58] Yet, contrary to what the newspaper reported, the court record reveals that Oima remained in the United States and pursued the divorce case. In the final verdict returned on May 21, 1915, Oima won the suit, getting a divorce, custody of her son, and the right to use her maiden name.[59] A year after the divorce, she and her boyfriend registered their marriage before the auditor for Pierce County, Washington, and the recorded place of residence suggests that they had moved to Tacoma.[60]

A LARGER PICTURE OF JAPANESE IMMIGRANT DIVORCES

One must not view these court struggles as exceptional cases filed by exceptional women. The actions of these prostitutes and barmaids represent general characteristics of Japanese immigrant women's attempts to dissolve their marriages in the early twentieth century.

Between 1907 and 1920, more than 160 Japanese couples filed for divorce in Seattle and Sacramento. In both locations, plaintiffs were largely women (69 percent in Seattle and 61 percent in Sacramento). Japanese women typically filed for divorce on the grounds that their husbands neglected to provide for them and forced them to seek work outside the home to support themselves and their children (mentioned fifty-two times in Seattle and seventeen times in Sacramento, overall 66 percent of all cases).[61] Some said that their husbands deserted and thereby neglected to provide for them; others claimed that their husbands did not work and forced them to seek work outside the home. These women characterized their husbands as indolent, abusive men living off their wives' earnings.

Japanese women rarely provided information about what kinds of work they did to support themselves, but local Japanese-language newspapers, which reported on these divorce cases, sometimes did. Of the twelve female divorce petitioners in Seattle whose occupations were known, eight worked as waitresses or barmaids, one worked as a domestic, one worked as a barber, one worked in a laundry, and one worked first in a restaurant and later in a barbershop. In Sacramento, five women worked as waitresses or barmaids, one worked as a prostitute, and one worked as a domestic.[62] These findings give some credibility to a vernacular newspaper account of 1909 that reported the vast majority of the wives of divorcing Japanese couples in the preceding two years were barmaids or actresses. The newspaper editor called these women "immodest persons" engaged in "frivolous occupations" (uita kagyō), denigrating them both for their conduct, which did not fit the prescribed images of immigrant wives, and for their occupations, which were considered low status in Japanese society.[63] The women who decided to file for divorce were often attacked for their "rude" behavior or "licentious" motives in the Japanese immigrant press; in court, however, they were given opportunities to narrate their stories in their own language and provide the causes of their hardships, usually desertion and extreme cruelty in relation to husbands' neglect.

The distribution of divorcing women's employment reflects, to some extent, the general pattern of Japanese businesses in the two cities. Seattle developed as a regional trading and supply center in the Pacific Northwest, and Japanese migrant laborers returned to the city during breaks in their work. While staying at cheap inns in its Japantown, they enjoyed Japanese food and conversation with barmaids over drinks in restaurants, played pool with friends, had their hair cut, and went to Japanese-style public baths (sentō).[64] Not surprisingly, according to a government survey conducted in 1909, boardinghouses, restaurants, laundries, and pool halls were the primary Japanese businesses in Seattle.[65] The situation was similar in Sacramento, a regional hub of agricultural laborers in the Sacramento Valley, a major fruit- and vegetable-producing region in the American West. As in Seattle, Japanese small businesses—including lodging houses, restaurants, and barbershops—thrived by catering to the floating male population.[66] Accordingly, there would have been good opportunities for married Japanese women to earn wages in these establishments and support their families.

We should not take these women's statements in court at face value, because they certainly would have fabricated or exaggerated parts of their stories in order to get divorce permissions; however, by considering the demands these women made in the context of their living and working conditions, we can get a sense of their growing social and economic independence from their husbands.[67] Unlike other Japanese immigrant women who contributed to the family economy in the form of unpaid labor on farms and in shops, barmaids acquired an independent source of income—wages and tips—which probably amounted to about $100 a month in the 1910s.[68] The figure was two to three times more than male Japanese workers earned during the same period ($30–40 a month).[69] Their earnings allowed them to support themselves, their husbands, and their children and hire lawyers and interpreters when they filed for divorce. Thus, as they worked in bar-restaurants, their knowledge and experiences made them realize the possibility of living without abusive husbands who drank and gambled away their hard-earned money. Their growing awareness of the value of their own labor was evident when a Seattle waitress requested that the court restrain her husband from touching the money in their bank account, or when a Sacramento barmaid asked the court to order her husband to "restore to plaintiff her gold watch."[70] Through wage-earning experiences, these women acquired a sense of social and economic independence unusual among Japanese women in the early twentieth century.

A COMPARATIVE PERSPECTIVE

These patterns of Japanese women's responses may lead some to conclude hastily that they were "assimilated" into American society.

Japanese women's elopement can be viewed as a result of the decline in the power of the community to sanction their "deviant" behavior. For some Japanese women, the rejection of their husbands and their pursuit of extramarital relationships based on mutual affection might signify the transition of the symbolic importance of their social action from "family" to "individual." Their attempts to divorce their husbands and protect their wages through Western legal means can be interpreted as an adoption of the norms of American and Canadian societies, including the concepts of marriage as a contract based on mutual consent and a married woman's right to control her property. Japanese women also sought sanctuary in religious institutions in North America (Protestant rescue missions), and some converted to Christianity and helped with the work of missionaries. One could argue that their actions were signs of their acceptance of the dominant religion (Protestantism) and gender roles (based on middle-class Anglo-Saxon ideas of womanhood that stressed piety and motherhood).[71]

In the 1970s and 1980s, sociologists and anthropologists of Japanese immigration took these models seriously, attempting to explain the experiences of Japanese immigrant groups through the dialectic of assimilation and resistance.[72] In the past two decades, however, historians have focused on the instrumental and symbolic roles of ethnicity, exploring the ways in which Japanese leaders invented a sense of natural kinship among immigrants to solve internal conflicts and deal with structural pressures imposed by the dominant society.[73] Scholars no longer rely on the assimilation model imprudently. Meanwhile, a small number of gender-conscious sociologists and historians have shown that Japanese immigrant women had to deal with not only racism but also patriarchal gender norms brought from their homeland and the danger of sexual violence from predatory men in an early immigrant society with few women. Despite these predicaments, scholars also suggest, women sometimes achieved a measure of freedom and independence through wage-earning experiences after coming to the country.[74]

Acknowledging that ethnic identity is a social construct while not denying the influence of the economic and cultural forces of the host society entirely, here I draw on a comparative perspective to highlight the nature of Japanese prostitutes' responses in North America. The vast majority of Japanese women who became prostitutes in the Meiji period did not migrate overseas; they worked in cities in

Japan, where different concepts of women, work, and the law prevailed among state officials and the population at large. As Raymond
Grew and others have suggested, comparison helps historians to see
new patterns not apparent in a single context, and a growing number of studies of prostitution have revealed remarkable national differences in the development of prostitution policies.[75] By exploring
the patterns of Japanese prostitutes' responses in the North American West in comparison with those of their counterparts in Japan,
where prostitution was regulated, I will demonstrate that both economic and sexual exploitation of sex workers were real in both Japan
and the North American West, and that the ways in which women
responded to these pressures reveal the remarkable role of the state
in shaping their behavior and living conditions in the two regions. I
also argue that in both regions, sex workers' responses could be best
understood as their quest for freedom from oppression rather than as
a sign of their assimilation into the dominant Anglo-Saxon culture
in North America or their acceptance of prostitution as "legitimate"
work for poor women.

LEGALIZED PROSTITUTION AND THE CENTRALITY
OF THE LABOR CONTRACT

Throughout the period between 1890 and 1920, the Japanese central
government officially acknowledged prostitution, and the labor contracts that prostitutes entered into with their employers were legally
binding. As in North America, prostitutes ran away from brothels when
they found the work unbearable or formed close relationships with customers who did not have the money to redeem the prostitutes' freedom
from their employers. Not often, however, did flight secure permanent
freedom for prostitutes in Japan. Employers could sue prostitutes and
their families if the women simply neglected their obligations and ran
away. The police willingly cooperated with brothel-keepers in captur-
ing employees who simply disregarded their contracts. In November
1902, for instance, the *Yomiuri shinbun* newspaper reported that a
licensed prostitute in Tokyo escaped with her lover who had no money
to redeem her; the police captured the couple quickly, and the boyfriend
was required to pay the employer a fine.[76] Couples rarely could live
together until they had paid off the women's debts.

A survey of sex workers in Japan reveals the close relationship that
developed between the state, the police, and brothel-keepers. In 1876,

the Meiji government transferred the authority to regulate prostitution to the police department, and subsequent ordinances permitted the department to collect taxes from brothel-keepers and prostitutes and apply them to the expenses of weekly medical checkups, police investigations, and medical treatment for prostitutes.[77] Because the police had the power to approve or disapprove the operation of brothels, it was essential for brothel-keepers to maintain a good relationship with them. They often permitted police officers to eat and drink at their establishments without charging them. In return, the officers helped capture runaway prostitutes and returned them to brothels.[78] Granted enormous authority by the state and financially supported by brothels, the police became the great obstacle for prostitutes who wished to leave the trade.

In neither Canada nor the United States did such cooperation develop between the sex industry and the federal government. In Canada, the Criminal Law Amendment Act of 1885 outlawed procuring and detaining women for the purpose of prostitution. The Criminal Code of 1892 made operating brothels punishable, and penalties for these charges became more severe over this period until 1920.[79] In the United States, the Page Act of 1875 declared contracts between procurers and prostitutes illegal, and subsequent federal laws of 1903, 1907, and 1910 strengthened immigration officials' power to deport foreign prostitutes.[80] Because labor agreements between prostitutes and masters were not acknowledged in North America, prostitutes who wished to quit had the option of appealing to federal officials for help. At the local level, the authorities tended to be more lenient toward prostitution. The police allowed prostitutes to work in segregated areas so long as the women paid fines regularly and did not disturb middle-class neighborhoods. However, municipal governments did not formally recognize prostitution. California enacted a penal code to punish men who forced their wives into prostitution or abducted unmarried women under the age of eighteen for the purpose of prostitution,[81] and local ordinances made it a punishable offense to solicit prostitution in public places or to rent rooms for the purpose of prostitution.[82] Therefore, if Japanese prostitutes turned to the police or local courts for help, officials were required to offer them protection and some form of assistance (e.g., filing criminal suits against pimps, filing for divorce from their husbands, or making arrangements with federal officials to send them back to Japan).[83]

Certainly, the internal code of conduct made such dramatic responses unnecessary. Many prostitutes worked under contract and acknowledged their obligation to work in brothels to clear off their debts. Married women with unemployed husbands agreed to work in local restaurants to earn money quickly and help with family finances, although they often despised the work. If prostitutes and boyfriends escaped without clearing off debts, masters and husbands tracked them down and forced the men to pay off the women's debts. Outside Japanese communities, however, prostitution and prostitution-related service jobs were not recognized as a legitimate way for women in Canada or the United States to make ends meet; therefore, if women found their work intolerable or masters too abusive, the law permitted them to end their careers as prostitutes, although the authorities rarely showed concern for the real needs of these women, punishing them with fines or excluding them from the country.

ORGANIZED STRIKES AS A MEANS OF PROTEST IN LEGALIZED PROSTITUTION

Significantly, prostitutes in Japan were more likely than their counterparts in North America to express their grievances collectively.[84] Japanese prostitutes organized strikes as early as the 1870s to protest against unreasonable treatment by their employers or negotiate their wages and taxes. Their strikes became more prominent in the 1890s, when recessions affected brothel management. To give an example, in May 1893, *Yomiuri shinbun* reported that soaring rice prices forced a brothel-keeper in Shinjuku, Tokyo, to reduce food expenses for his prostitutes. The prostitutes expressed their dissatisfaction with this treatment, claiming that they could not work all night on such a simple diet. Some prostitutes suggested that they transfer to other brothels; others proposed that they petition the owner for an increase in the charge to customers from 0.3 to 0.5 yen per meeting to generate more profits. The owner held a brothelwide meeting to promote mutual understanding, but the prostitutes did not yield an inch. On May 21, when the women did *harimise* (the practice of displaying prostitutes in a show window to attract customers) as usual, they remained silent all day, refusing to offer tobacco or make themselves agreeable to customers.[85]

These strikes in Japan, however, cannot be viewed as simply conflicts between management and labor, because prostitutes often sought to improve the management of brothels as a result of their actions. Strikes in brothels reported by Tokyo newspapers in the

1890s typically started as a complaint from prostitutes about their living or working conditions, but they also demanded that the employer increase the charge to customers in order to generate more income or dismiss incompetent managers so that more customers would be drawn to their brothel.[86] In these cases, prostitutes were willing to work with employers so as to make brothels more profitable, improve their living conditions, or increase their chances of paying off their debts more quickly. An important point to be made here is that the interests of prostitutes did not necessarily conflict with those of their employers.

A similar tendency to cooperate with employers was also found among the geisha. Unlike licensed prostitutes, the geisha did not work in their houses. They lived in geisha houses (*okiya*) and visited restaurants or entertainment rooms (*machiai*) when requested by guests. Restaurants and entertainment rooms paid commissions to geisha houses and to the geisha office (*kenban*) that mediated between them. The geisha received wages from the owners of their geisha houses, and the amount depended on the extent of their debt to their employers. Women who had entered into contracts with geisha house owners to pay off their parents' debts would receive small or no wages. Those without debts shared larger sums of money with geisha house owners.[87]

The geisha's actions in the period from 1890 to 1920 stemmed mostly from disputes over the sharing of profits among entertainment rooms, geisha offices, and geisha houses. In 1902, for instance, *Niroku shinpō* reported that entertainment rooms in Ōji, Tokyo, began to demand a 30 percent share for each time the geisha used their rooms. Geisha houses rejected the demand and stopped sending their girls to the rooms until the room owner agreed to reduce the rate to 12 percent.[88] Conflicts also occurred between the geisha office and entertainment rooms. In May 1903, *Niroku shinpō* reported that in Yokosuka, Kanagawa Prefecture, the geisha office began to demand that entertainment-room owners pay commissions twice a month, declaring that they would not arrange meetings between the geisha and customers if the owners failed to meet their demands. Concerned about a possible decline in their work opportunities, the geisha stopped working to protest the office's policy and demand that the office be more accommodating.[89] Like prostitutes, they often tried to increase the profits of their geisha houses and ensure that they could continue to work without disruptions.

In comparison, only two cursory accounts of Japanese sex work-ers' strikes in North America before 1920 are known. In one inci-dent reported by the Japanese press in Denver in July 1915, local barmaids went on strike to protest the restaurants' decision to cut wages by five dollars because of a recession, complaining that they would not be able to pay their rent, buy necessary goods, and watch movies. They soon agreed to return to work after the employers decided to increase their wages by ten dollars four months later.[90] The other strike, reported two years later in San Francisco, resulted from two incidents that angered the barmaids: (1) their master forced them to work overtime one evening to entertain his friend, and they missed their chance to see a play (*shibai*) in a theater; (2) their mas-ter refused to cover the costs they incurred to buy items necessary to entertain guests.[91] Clearly, these barmaids had recognized the value of their labor and protested unfair work arrangements as their coun-terparts did in Japan; however, these were rather rare, isolated events in the United States that Japanese-language newspapers described as "unprecedented" (*zendai mimon*) and "strange, rare, and incompa-rable" (*chinki murui*).

The key to understanding the frequency of Japanese prostitutes' collective response in the two regions is the different environments in which the women lived and worked. In North America, prostitutes lived with their pimp-husbands in apartments or hotels, and because of the restrictions placed on their mobility, they had few places where they could share their problems and concerns with other prostitutes. In sharp contrast, a communal nature characterized the lives of pros-titutes in Japan. The majority entered the trade in their late teens or early twenties and worked under labor contracts for a limited period before marriage; they lived with fellow workers in brothels or geisha houses, with the common goal of paying off their debts and leaving the trade as soon as possible. Surely, the competitive nature of this work sometimes undercut solidarity among prostitutes, but a kind of homosocial network was more likely to develop in this environment, and it served as a basis for prostitutes' collective action against their masters' unreasonable treatment.[92]

A more important factor in the collective response of Japanese prostitutes was licensed prostitution itself. Prostitutes went on strike to improve the quality of meals and the management of brothels. Gei-shas cooperated with their employers in the interests of geisha houses to secure their profits from their work. None of the participants seem to have questioned the legality of the contracts they had entered into with their employers; therefore, these strikes were more a strategy of collective bargaining than a sign of their "resistance" against their masters. This kind of consciousness as workers was much less evident among Japanese prostitutes and barmaids in Canada and the United States, where prostitution was not a "legitimate" means of survival for working-class women and Japanese women were working in the shadow of the law. The police and judges did not arbitrate disputes between management and labor in brothels. If women decided to organize in public, they could be arrested for "being a disorderly person" or, worse, deported for violating federal laws against alien prostitution. It was difficult for them to exercise their civil rights as sex workers in North America.

SUBMITTING REPORTS OF CESSATION
AND LEAVING THE TRADE LEGALLY

Because Japanese law recognized prostitutes as legitimate workers, women who were dissatisfied with their working conditions could assert their right to change their trade. It began with a well-known legal case concerning Sakai Futa, a prostitute in Hokkaido who filed suit against her employer in 1899. Just like many other prostitutes in this period, she had agreed to work in a brothel to pay off her debts, but once she started working, she found prostitution unbearable and decided to leave the trade. She prepared the report of cessation, a form required by the police to remove one's name from the official register. When her employer refused to countersign it, she petitioned a local court to permit her to leave the trade. The court declared her labor contract lawful and denied her petition to leave the brothel until she had paid off all her debts; the Supreme Court (Daishinin), however, overturned the local court's decision in February 1900 because the contract "restricts [her] freedom of body" and violated the Ordinance Liberating Prostitutes, which banned the sale and purchase of people. Sakai was free to leave the brothel.[93] Although prostitutes were still obligated to pay off their debts to brothel-keepers, they could, at least, quit working at the brothel and seek another job.

Following this case, the so-called free-cessation movement occurred throughout the country. In March 1900, Fujiwara Sato, a prostitute in Nagoya, ran away from her brothel and sought the help of U. G. Murphy, a local Methodist missionary. Murphy filed suit for her in a local court, arguing that the contract with the employer was null and void because it contradicted the principle of the Meiji Civil Code of 1898, which stated that "any legal act which is deemed contrary to the public order and good morals is null and void." The judge supported his argument and ordered her release from the brothel.[94] Six months later, for the first time in Tokyo, licensed prostitute Nakamura Yae wrote to *Niroku shimpō* to ask its help in leaving the trade. Its employees went to her brothel and helped file a report of cessation at a local police station. The precinct chief refused to accept it because it lacked her employer's signature, but the Tokyo police, which wished to settle the matter quickly, accepted her notification.[95] This series of incidents led the Home Ministry to issue new regulations in October 1900 acknowledging prostitutes' right to make a report of cessation "either orally or in writing."[96] The police could no longer refuse to accept the notification due to the absence of a brothel-keeper's signature.[97]

At first sight, this type of action by prostitutes—drawing on civil law to end their legal obligation to work for their current employers— was unique to Japan, because there was no such contract that could force women to sell their bodies in Canada and the United States; however, we must recall that Japanese prostitutes in U.S. Pacific Coast cities also attempted to leave their pimps by dissolving a different type of contract that restricted their freedom, the marriage contract. Japanese prostitutes typically arrived in North America as married women in order to elude the eyes of immigration officials, who often denied landing to single women. But many prostitutes and barmaids became close to customers at work, and when they wished to start living with these men, they filed for divorce from pimp-husbands in court. Accordingly, free cessations in Japan and divorce suits in the United States were similar in that the women attempted to sever their relations with exploitative men by turning to the civil law.

A key difference was the different conception of sex work in the two countries' legal systems. Japanese law recognized prostitution as a form of work and permitted unmarried women to practice it so long as their purpose was to alleviate poverty in their households. In the cities of the American West, authorities acknowledged the sexual needs of men and tolerated prostitution in segregated areas, but the majority of respectable residents wished to confine sexual relations within the institution of marriage, and municipal governments rarely recognized prostitution as legitimate work for women. In divorce court, judges were sympathetic to women who claimed to have been forced into prostitution and punished men who failed to support their wives and lived off their wives' earnings from prostitution.

Another difference was the ways in which Tokyo prostitutes and their North American counterparts turned to the civil law: the former were more likely to act collectively. Since the 1870s, Tokyo prostitutes and geisha had organized to protest against unreasonable treatment by their employers or to negotiate their wages and taxes.[98] Drawing on the tradition of collective protests, they learned to use cessation as a strike tool to negotiate quality-of-life and working conditions with their employers after the rise of the free-cessation movement around 1900. Like the usual strikes, free cessations started in response to employers' measures to reduce the cost of operating brothels during recessions (especially when they decreased the number of meals or lowered meal quality), and if employers denied their petition to improve their treatment, the women escaped from the brothels and submitted reports of cessation to the police collectively. Newspaper reports on these cases suggest that the women fully understood their right to leave the trade of their own will and asserted this right as other workers did.[99] Thus, the legalization of prostitution, combined with the communal nature of their living environment, served as a basis for the use of cessation as a strike tool in Japan.

FACTORS THAT LED THEM TO LEAVE THE TRADE

Notwithstanding all these differences in the responses of prostitutes in Japan and North America, the two groups shared similar motivating factors in their decision to leave the trade. In 1916, Salvation Army officer Yamamuro Gunpei studied the backgrounds of 300 prostitutes who came to the Salvation Army for help and their reasons for deciding to leave the trade. Excluding the 123 women who observed that they came for help after they "heard about the work of the Salvation Army," 171 women (96 percent) gave either increasing debt and/ or sickness as the primary factors behind their decisions. Yamamuro further studied the financial conditions of 87 prostitutes, finding that 53 women reported that their debts *increased* after working several months in brothels; for 34 women, the debts decreased while they worked, but the decrease was too slight to give them confidence that they would ever be free.[100] Obviously, they were charged exorbitant rates for maintenance and other necessities by their employers. The prostitutes who decided to submit notes of cessation were, therefore, more likely to be the ones who had worked for particularly exploitative employers and realized that their hard work would not guarantee a steady decrease in their debts.

The wish to break away from unreasonable, exploitative masters was shared by their counterparts in North America. Typically, women first agreed to become prostitutes to pay off their debts or obeyed their husbands' orders to work in bar-restaurants and contribute to the family income. In fact, due to the fear of retribution from masters and the lack of work outside Japantowns, most women had no other option; their best hope was that they would be released after a few years of service or that their "husbands" would start working seriously and support them. Yet some brothel-keepers ignored the contracts and forced the women to work even after they had repaid their debts; some husbands failed to meet their responsibility as providers, continuing to drink and gamble away the women's hard-earned money. It was these severely exploited women, as in Japan, who left their masters or husbands by turning to Protestant missionaries or civil court judges who were willing to punish men for their failure to live up to white middle-class ideals of industrious, family-centered fathers.

Examination of the fate of former prostitutes reveals another reason that Tokyo prostitutes and their North American counterparts shared. In 1917, Salvation Army officer Itō Fujio investigated the fate of three hundred prostitutes who had left the trade. After their names were removed from the official list, more than 60 percent married urban working-class men of modest income such as factory hands, artisans, and shopkeepers.[101] A former resident of the Salvation Army rescue mission told a journalist that "the reason why we [prostitutes] turn to the Salvation Army is that we want to be together with our boyfriends."[102] Rev. U. G. Murphy recalled in his memoir: "We have found that very few of the girls rescued need to be sent to the rescue home, as one half, or more, immediately marry some lover."[103] Many prostitutes, therefore, often had definite plans for what they would do after leaving the trade.

The presence of suitors and the practical use of religious institutions or the legal system reveal some important similarities between the experiences of prostitutes in Japan and North America. As the records of rescue missions revealed, most Japanese residents stayed there only for a short period, and few women, except a couple of "remarkable" inmates, embraced Christianity or assisted in rescue work. Some women used it to keep a distance between themselves and their masters or husbands, to see if the men's attitudes toward them would improve. Others chose to go with other men, simply leaving the mission or filing for divorce in court. Newspaper articles reported that barmaids often resisted deportation, and the decision to seek divorce under American law indicated their intention to remain in the country with suitors (otherwise, the couples would be charged with adultery). Although individual women's life circumstances varied considerably, they found missions and courts useful in getting out of entanglements with employers or pimp-husbands and finding security through a permanent relationship—marriage.

This comparative analysis reveals the central importance of the state in shaping the place of prostitution in society, the lives of prostitutes, and their responses to oppression. In Japan, state regulations made it extremely difficult for prostitutes to run away from brothels by breaking the contracts they had entered into with their masters; therefore, those who wished to leave the trade had to do so legally by submitting reports of cessation to local police, often with the help of reformers. At the same time, however, the legality of prostitution promoted prostitutes' consciousness as workers, which served as the basis for collective action against their masters' exploitation. In Canada and the United States, federal and municipal laws related to prostitution were far more repressive, and the government did not create a legal framework within which sex workers could work safely. With little chance to obtain work outside Japanese communities, women had to work underground, constantly harassed by the police and subject to violence from customers. In North America, however, prostitution was not viewed as legitimate work, and society expected husbands to be self-disciplined, independent men who could support their families without relying on their wives' sex work. Missionaries and judges wished to impose these concepts on racial minorities, but Japanese women used them to their advantage. In both legal and illegal contexts, a fair number of sex workers turned to available resources and could exercise a degree of control over their life situations.

But I must stress that not all Japanese prostitutes and barmaids could resist exploitation as did the women discussed in this chapter. Many were so oppressed that they had no access to venues for changing their circumstances. They were living far away from their families, who could not offer help in releasing them from exploitative masters. The stigma attached to prostitution survived in the North American Japanese community and isolated prostitutes from fellow country-men, except, of course, for customers and pimps. As members of a racial minority, they found it extremely difficult to find jobs outside the Japanese community. To get help from religious and legal institu-tions, they had to present themselves before missionaries and judges as "fallen" women who wanted to be rescued. The stigma attached to them was so strong that these former prostitutes made efforts not to reveal their past. In the 1970s, when Yamazaki Tomoko visited San Francisco, she received a midnight phone call from an elderly woman who reported having been deceived into coming to the United States and forced to work as a prostitute in Chinatown in the early twentieth century. After years of struggle, she married a Japanese laborer and was now living with her son and his family. Fearful of being heard by her son but wishing to make her voice heard, she called Yamazaki to tell her story, leaving a message in a "barely audible voice": "I hope the silly chattering of an old woman will be of some use to you."[104] The hardships that this elderly woman had to endure deserve to be remembered.

Like the elderly woman, many prostitutes and barmaids who met suitors at work also settled in North America. Certainly, the negative perceptions of prostitution continued to oppress these women after migration and even after they left the trade, but in the North Ameri-can West, the Japanese as a whole were treated as a racial group, and as Andrea Geiger writes, minorities within the community—including the outcastes—would have found it easier to define them-selves as Japanese rather than as members of specific social classes separated from others by rank or profession in Japanese society.[105] Furthermore, the lack of women and the tendency toward permanent settlement among Japanese migrants in the 1910s created an environ-ment in which former prostitutes and barmaids could find a space for themselves as mothers of American-born children. Barmaids often got married after divorcing their husbands, and in newspapers and immigrant writings, their marriages were often described as happy occasions so long as the women showed signs of becoming good housekeepers and wives.[106] Thus, in the particular conditions of the immigrant community in the early twentieth century, these women could find security through marriage.

In conclusion, by analyzing the lives of Japanese prostitutes and barmaids from below and from a cross-national comparative perspective, we can go beyond the simplified or distorted images of these women created by journalists, reformers, and social scientists. All of these women encountered new challenges and possibilities in the North American West, which was undergoing dramatic change in the early twentieth century.

The Emergence of Anti–Japanese Prostitution Reforms in the North American West from a Transpacific and Comparative Perspective

During the Meiji period (1868–1912), prostitution became a major topic of discussion among middle-class reformers in Japan and Japanese immigrant communities in the American West. The existence of licensed prostitution in Japan came to light in 1872, during an international conflict between the Japanese and Peruvian governments over the treatment of Chinese indentured laborers carried to Yokohama on a Peruvian ship. Licensed prostitution was seen as conflicting with the international movement for the abolition of slavery and the campaign against the sexual exploitation of women in the industrial era. Since the first appearance of Japanese prostitutes on the west coast of North America in the late 1880s, Japanese consuls and immigrant leaders regarded prostitutes as stains on Japan's international reputation and initiated an effort to remove them from Canada and the United States. Meanwhile, anti–alien prostitution movements also grew among Canadian and American reformers along with various reforms of this period, and the federal governments began to take steps to exclude alien prostitutes from their countries. As the Japanese began to settle in both countries in the 1910s, Japanese antiprostitution campaigns developed into community-wide projects in their struggles to deal with pressure from North American societies. By examining anti–Japanese prostitution forces in North America from the 1890s to the 1910s from a cross-national comparative perspective, one can see a major shift in the concerns of North American Japanese migrants from the country of origin to the country of settlement.

EARLY JAPANESE RESPONSES TO PROSTITUTION

Japanese consular officials and immigrant leaders were the earliest antiprostitution activists. Shortly after Japanese prostitutes began to appear in North American ports in the late 1880s, Sugimura Fukashi, the first Japanese consul in Vancouver, began to report on the arrival of Japanese prostitutes and procurers. In October 1890, Sugimura sent Tokyo a list of major Japanese brothel-keepers in Seattle, noting the presence of almost 150 prostitutes. Most of them crossed over the U.S.-Canadian border where inspection was lax, and Sugimura complained that he had no way of forbidding these "legitimate" travelers from making their way to the American side because they arrived at the ports as married couples with valid passports. He urged the Foreign Ministry to take immediate measures to prevent Japanese prostitutes from coming to Canada in order to prevent an increase in the number of prostitutes in the United States.[1]

The appearance of Japanese prostitutes quickly drew the Canadian and U.S. media's attention. In March 1891, the *Victoria Daily Colonist* reported on U.S. officials' attempts in San Francisco to prevent Japanese procurers from sending their women's passports back to Yokohama to be reused in procuring Japanese women for prostitution.[2] Next month, the *Seattle Post-Intelligencer* reported on a police raid in Jackson Alley where the cribs "swarmed with disorderly, uncleanly, lawless element." Japanese women "flew about, jabbering loudly, like a band of pursued magpies." Of thirty-seven arrested as prostitutes, thirty-one were Japanese and five were white, and "[t]he Japs all gave half English, half Japanese names, such as 'Jap Mary' and 'Jap Lizzie.'" "[A]t least 300 disreputable women live in Whitechapel," and the newspaper added, "the greater number of whom are Japanese."[3] Immediately, G. H. Ando, a leading Japanese trader in Seattle, sent the newspaper article to Consul Sugimura in Vancouver, who forwarded it to Tokyo, noting that the newspaper article "stained the honor of the Japanese."[4] Sugimura began to observe media coverage of Japanese prostitutes closely, and if he found any incorrect information in newspapers, he sent letters of protest to the editor.[5]

Sensational articles on Japanese prostitution caught the attention of officials down the coast as well. In March 1891, Consul General Chinda Sutemi in San Francisco received a notice from a Japanese minister in Washington, D.C., that the *Washington Evening Star* had carried an article on an auction of Japanese women in San Francisco, reporting that Henry Slocum was invited to a room where he witnessed "twenty Japanese girls who were overcome with shame at being viewed clad in such a paucity of clothing." "[T]he girls went off like hotcakes on a cold morning and at prices ranging from forty to five hundred dollars each."[6] The San Francisco police denied the authenticity of the article, but Chinda was badly shaken by the charges. "[This kind of newspaper coverage] is the most detestable thing that would disgrace the reputation of Japanese residents." Admitting that there were ten Japanese brothels with more than fifty prostitutes in the city and that increasing numbers of Japanese prostitutes were entering the country via Canada, Chinda urged Tokyo to prevent the departure of prostitutes from Japan.[7]

What irritated Japanese consuls were the ways in which the American and Canadian press treated Japanese and Chinese prostitution. Newspapers tended to portray both Chinese and Japanese prostitutes as "slave girls," stressing the criminal nature of the two groups without distinguishing their differences.[8] In addition, the rapid expansion of Japanese prostitution gave the impression that the Japanese were succeeding the Chinese in the sex industry. In May 1891, the *San Francisco Daily Report* carried an article titled "The Slave Trade," which linked Japanese prostitutes to their Chinese counterparts: "The Chinese are not the only people in San Francisco engaged in the slave trade. For some years the Japanese have also been busily engaged in the traffic. . . . Nearly all the Japanese women who come to San Francisco are . . . destined for houses of ill-fame."[9] The *Victoria Daily Colonist*, in May 1895, reported on two "Japanese slave girls" in Vancouver who claimed to have been "in bondage, practically the slaves of a man who had sent them." After being saved from a brothel "where they [had been] held prisoners" and protected by Consul Nosse and the police, the editor reported, they "are slaves no longer, and will be sent to Japan on the next boat."[10] The influx of Chinese laborers and prostitutes since the mid-nineteenth century had fueled anti-Chinese sentiments in the West and led to the passage of exclusionary legislation against the entry of Chinese men and women in the United States in 1875 and 1882 and the imposition of a head tax on each Chinese migrant in British Columbia from 1885.[11] Well aware of these precedents, Japanese officials worried that the presence of prostitutes would encourage a similar exclusion movement against the Japanese.

Japanese consuls' strong opposition to prostitutes came from concerns about the influence of prostitutes on Japan's international reputation, but it also probably reflected their disdain for "lower-class" Japanese more generally. In his reports to Tokyo, Vancouver consul Sugimura often complained about the presence of "uncivilized" Japanese. He wrote that Japanese migrants "cannot communicate in [the English] language and are ignorant about customs in this country. . . . If migrants have the same morals as those of the lower class, they will not obtain permanent jobs in this land." He argued that migrants should prepare themselves for permanent settlement, respect the morals and customs of the host society, attend Christian churches, and improve the quality of their lives. "If [migrants] live extremely frugal lives like the Chinese, it is inevitable that natives will look down upon [the Japanese]," he concluded.[12] His disdain for migrant laborers thus came from his conviction that these laborers who looked like "uncivilized" Chinese would harm the reputation of the Japanese. At the same time, considering his comments in relation to the tendency among Japanese officials and immigrants of this period to avoid being associated with fellow migrants engaged in certain occupations—including coal mining and prostitution—it is possible that Sugimura had opposed the migration of laborers not only because they were "uncivilized" but also because these men and women were considered "low" in Japan and their presence would be a reason for Japanese exclusion in Canada and the United States.[13]

Responding to reports on Japanese prostitutes crossing the Canadian border, San Francisco consul Chinda dispatched his secretary Fujita Toshirō to the Pacific Northwest to investigate the actual conditions of the Japanese in the region. To his surprise, Fujita found a Japanese settlement in Seattle dominated by "men and women engaged in ugly trades" (shūgyōsha). Of its 250–60 Japanese residents, 105 women were prostitutes, and 70–80 men were either their husbands or their employers. He learned that in the two preceding years, 400–500 Japanese prostitutes had arrived in Seattle, and many of them moved to interior towns including Butte, Salt Lake City, Ogden, Denver, and Chicago. Next he went to Spokane, where he found about 60 Japanese, and "all residents except four or five" were engaged in prostitution; many of them had recently moved to Butte, Montana. The situation was similar in Portland, where one half of Japanese residents were making their living from prostitution, and according to Fujita, the prostitutes were controlled by their pimps, who were typically former sailors, gamblers, or college dropouts.[14]

This Fujita report is a well-known source and has helped historians to describe general conditions in the early days of Japanese American communities,[15] but this document should be treated carefully. As Roger Daniels writes, Fujita's writing exhibits a strong bias against working-class Japanese and those engaged in prostitution and gambling, and Fujita failed to mention the hardworking small-scale entrepreneurs who appear in other immigrant writings.[16] At the same time, however, we can also learn from this report the real difficulty Fujita experienced in persuading brothel-keepers to stop operating their businesses and police chiefs and mayors to enforce the law against prostitution. The men attached to the prostitutes prevented him from meeting with the women, threatening to drive him out of town. Frightened by these "roughnecks" (*buraikan*), no Japanese cooperated with his investigation. Added to the factor of intimidation, local authorities were corrupt, as he wrote: "I met the mayor, the chairman of the city council, and a sheriff, and I asked them about prostitutes and gamblers. They said that they wanted to punish them but it was difficult to do so. . . . When I met the police chief and a vice-chief, their opinion was similar to that of the mayor. . . . Some people say that the police chief's indifference toward the removal of prostitutes was the result of the bribes [in the form of fines]." Fujita wrote that the influence of pimps and prostitutes was so strong that few "individuals engaged in legitimate work" (*seigyōsha*) wished to settle in these towns.[17]

Japanese immigrant leaders were equally concerned about the conduct of the Japanese described as "undesirables" in the American press.[18] As early as 1889, the Gospel Society, the first Japanese immigrant organization in San Francisco, petitioned the Japanese government to ban indigent persons from coming to the country.[19] In 1891, Japanese residents of Seattle organized the Society of Concerned Japanese (*Nihonjin Dōshikai*) to "purify those defiling their morality," and they shared sensational reports with consuls to bring attention to the problem.[20] As in Japan, these early reformers were largely successful, educated men, including students, church members, and businessmen who distinguished themselves from other "dissolute" migrants who indulged in gambling and drinking.[21] Many had come to the United States with high hopes of "returning to hometowns in glory" (*kin'i kikyō*), and they naturally feared that the public outcry over prostitutes would lead to an outright ban on Japanese immigration that would threaten their livelihood. Therefore, they felt a strong need to exclude "uncivilized" fellow countrymen to show that the Japanese were more "civilized" than the Chinese.[22]

TRANSNATIONAL DIMENSIONS
OF ANTIPROSTITUTION REFORMS

Significantly, the reports of Japanese prostitution on the Pacific Coast stimulated antiprostitution reforms in the homeland. In Japan, anti-prostitution reforms had first developed among "enlightened" government officials who wished to make the country stand on a par with Western powers. In the 1880s, Protestant reformers emerged as a major force in the debate over prostitution, due to their access to Western culture and knowledge. Progressive politicians and journalists joined these efforts, critiquing licensed prostitution as part of their fight for basic human rights, such as universal suffrage and workers' right to organize.[23] These reformers were largely urban, educated, middle-class men and women who had familiarized themselves with Western culture by reading books and interacting with foreign scholars and missionaries. As strong supporters of modernization, these activists shared a sense of mission to elevate the Japanese and eradicate premodern customs. In their eyes, prostitutes appeared not only as victims of the feudal family system but also as perpetrators who would tarnish Japan's reputation and discourage their efforts to establish new gender norms in Japan.

Reformers in Japan responded quickly when the *San Francisco Bulletin* reported on Japanese prostitution in early 1890. *Haishō*, an abolitionist newspaper in Tokyo, published an article in which the editor wrote: "Japanese prostitutes behaved so shamefully in the center of the United States, causing the Yankee to criticize [the Japanese]. It brings shame to Japan's reputation and a disgrace on Japan's national flag."[24] More news of Japanese prostitution came from Japanese reformers living in California. Kawaguchi Masue, a member of the Japan Woman's Christian Temperance Union (WCTU) in Sausalito, wrote that her work with local churchwomen against Japanese prostitution had yielded no significant results and urged Tokyo leaders to "share this problem with the authorities and strictly regulate [prostitutes]."[25] Before long, Tokyo leaders came to realize that, to prevent further expansion of prostitution in the American West, it was necessary to stop the departure of prostitutes from Japanese ports. Shortly after the Imperial Diet opened in late 1890, the Japan

WCTU submitted a bill for the prosecution of Japanese women who migrated abroad for prostitution and of men who took women out of the country for that purpose.[26]

At the state level, Foreign Ministry officials were the strongest supporters of stricter regulation of prostitutes' overseas migration, but other central authorities were not necessarily enthusiastic. In July 1890, for instance, Foreign Minister Aoki Shūzō personally submitted a bill for the prosecution of procurers and prostitutes who attempted to leave Japanese ports. The Cabinet accepted the bill and submitted it to the Diet, but three days later, the bill was withdrawn for unknown reasons. Frustrated, Aoki then asked the justice minister if the criminal code could be revised to permit officials to ban the departure of prostitutes from Japanese ports. The justice minister replied that "the government should not restrict [the migration of prostitutes] as long as it would not harm Japan's national interest," adding that it was illogical to forbid Japanese women to practice prostitution overseas while permitting them to do so in Japan.[27] Authorities considered licensed prostitution necessary to keep the growing male urban population under control. At the same time, overseas prostitutes were helping the national economy by way of their remittances and played a role in the settlement of Japanese migrants and Japan's overseas expansion.[28] The argument for the "national interest" continued to overrule reformers' opinions within the government in the 1890s.

Nevertheless, the Foreign Ministry began to take steps to stop the migration of prostitutes to North America. In 1893, it issued the first order to prevent men from recruiting women for prostitution and women from leaving Japanese ports without legitimate reasons.[29] It issued the Regulations for Protecting Immigrants (*Imin hogo kisoku*) the next year, and Article 14 stated that the government would suspend the business of immigration agents "guilty of conduct which is deemed injurious to public peace or morality." In 1896 the Foreign Ministry revised the regulations to permit female migrants to engage only in domestic work in foreign countries, thus banning them from other occupations, including prostitution.[30] Meanwhile, a flood of reports on Japanese prostitution in the United States made it clear that, to circumvent U.S. immigration law, procurers often let prostitutes receive passports as their "wives" or let them use other women's passports. The ministry ordered prefectural governors to check carefully before issuing passports and directed the harbor police to arrest suspicious couples before they departed.[31]

Most striking was the Foreign Ministry's severe attitude toward Japanese prostitution in Canada and the United States compared to its lenient policy in other major destinations in East Asia. In Korea, for instance, Japanese migrants and prostitutes increased in number after the opening of treaty ports in 1876, but Japanese officials did not outlaw prostitution there. As early as 1881, Japanese authorities issued regulations for Japanese prostitution in Wonsan, requiring women to register and undergo regular checkups. Publicly, the homeland government declared its intention to abolish Japanese prostitution in Korea and China (Order of 1883), and Japanese consuls banned the operation of brothels in other Korean port cities, where many other countries had consulates. Nevertheless, as long as the women reported their occupations as "geisha" or "barmaid," they were permitted to practice prostitution throughout the 1880s and 1890s. Thus, there was a double standard in the practice of the Foreign Ministry: It made serious efforts to limit Japanese prostitution in white-settler societies like the North American West, while tolerating it in East Asian countries over which Japan was beginning to exert its influence.[32] Certainly, one can call Japanese consuls' actions in the western United States more "show" than substance, because they had not paid much attention to the existence of prostitutes so long as their numbers were small and escaped the attention of the American public. But when prostitutes made a stir in Pacific Coast cities around 1890, officials identified them as a "problem" and made them subject to documentation and regulation.[33]

Accordingly, it is not surprising that the news of Japanese prostitution in the North American West disturbed reformers in Japan. Yet the significance of the reports was twofold: They not only brought a sense of national disgrace but also directed reformers' attention to licensed prostitution at home as the fundamental cause of Japanese prostitution overseas. In May 1891, when the San Francisco Bulletin carried another sensational article on Japanese prostitution, Iwamoto Yoshiharu complained about the ineffectiveness of the Foreign Ministry's measures, noting that officials had no power to prohibit the migration of Japanese women who had not yet committed any crime. More important, he argued, as long as the government permitted prostitution in Japan, overseas prostitutes would never understand why their behavior was "a national disgrace," and as a result, foreigners would continue to view Japan as an "adulterous country."[34] Like-minded politicians shared his view. Later that year, Kojima Kango, a member of a Tokyo assembly, made a motion to abolish licensed prostitution in Tokyo, arguing that, as the capital city of Japan, Tokyo could play an important role in advertising the country's clear opposition to "the act of selling sex."[35] Increasingly, reformers came to view the abolition of licensed prostitution in Japan as the key to abolishing Japanese prostitution overseas and regaining the respect of the Western powers.[36] In this sense, antiprostitution reforms at home and abroad were not two separate phenomena. They influenced each other and developed together.[37]

On the North American side, however, consular officials still found it extremely difficult to abolish prostitution on their own because of the strong influence of pimps and brothel-keepers. In his 1891 report, Secretary Fujita petitioned the Foreign Ministry to construct a consulate in Seattle so that local residents could cooperate with officials in eliminating Japanese "roughnecks" and pimps. Three years later, San Francisco consul Chinda dispatched Secretary Odagiri Masunosuke to the Pacific Northwest to explore possible locations. After visiting major Japanese settlements, Odagiri reported that the Japanese in Seattle and Portland, composed largely of prostitutes and pimps, were despised by local Americans, recommending Tacoma, where Japanese residents "gained a wide reputation" among local Americans.[38] A consulate was built there the next year.[39] Japanese officials were not successful in eliminating pimps and prostitutes from Seattle, Spokane, and Portland. The absence of regulation resulted in the further expansion of Japanese prostitution in Pacific Northwestern towns through the 1890s.[40]

THE RISE OF NORTH AMERICAN ANTIPROSTITUTION REFORMS AND JAPANESE PROSTITUTION

During the same period, antiprostitution forces were developing in North American societies as well. Propelled by growing antiprostitution movements in Britain in the 1880s, Protestant and feminist groups in Canada—including the Woman's Christian Temperance Union and the National Council of Women—led local campaigns promoting "social purity" that grew into a nationwide movement in the 1880s and 1890s.[41] Similarly, in the United States, as British reformers' sensational reports of the sexual exploitation of working-class women reached the country during the 1880s, the so-called new abolitionism, which had historical roots in the nineteenth-century social movement against black slavery, grew in tandem with various movements for the advancement of women's rights in society, and former abolitionists and members of the WCTU directed the public's attention to the problem of white slavery in their own country. In both Canada and the United States, prostitution drew the attention of many groups of reformers due to the multiple connotations of the term: to Protestant ministers, a sign of the declining morality of young women; to feminists, a sign of male domination in society; to physicians, a threat to public health. To native-born Canadians and Americans whose families had originally come from Britain and northwestern Europe and had lived in their countries for generations, prostitution represented the evil of social changes at the turn of the century—the influx of immigrants, rapid industrialization, and urbanization—that threatened existing patterns of life and the ethnic composition of the states. This anxiety provided the ground on which scattered, local activities developed into nationwide social movements. The federal governments soon began to act as agents to regulate the lives of their citizens and the morality of their nations.[42]

North American activity against Japanese prostitution emerged first among religious reformers shortly after the appearance of Japanese prostitutes in West Coast cities. In Seattle, Protestant ministers started organizing meetings to discuss Japanese prostitution in the early 1890s, urging city authorities to prosecute pimps strictly and bringing the attention of Japanese officials to the problem.[43] In a letter addressed to Consul General Chinda in 1892, A. Inwood, a representative of the Ministers' Association of Seattle, reported that seventy to eighty prostitutes were living "in virtual slavery" and kept "under a system of terrorism" by the men who had brought them over.[44] Japanese officials shared the letter with the foreign minister in Tokyo and asked the Seattle police to investigate the conditions of Japanese prostitutes.[45] Their criticisms were not influential enough to change the city's open-town policies, but they put Japanese authorities into action.

In Protestant reformers' efforts to save Japanese women from prostitution, women stood out prominently. In San Francisco, Presbyterian missionaries in San Francisco began to "rescue" Chinese prostitutes from sexual "slavery" in the 1870s, placing them in their rescue mission, converting them to Christianity, and preparing them for marriage; they began to accommodate Japanese women in the early 1890s.[46] In Seattle, Nellie Fife, a former missionary to Japan, began to take charge of the Japanese Baptist Woman's Home in 1905 and worked with Japanese helpers to prevent women and children from falling into the hands of vice operators on King Street.[47] The Puget Sound branch of the Home Missionary Society established an immigration station in Seattle, making arrangements with Rev. Yoshioka Seimei of the Japanese Methodist Church to accommodate newly arrived Japanese women who needed help "until they find a permanent home for them."[48] In Victoria, members of the Woman's Missionary Society got involved in rescuing Chinese women from its inception in 1887, and Ida Snyder and other missionaries served as matrons of the rescue home and superintendents of its Sunday school successively and made efforts to get rescued Asian women married and converted to Christianity.[49] Believing in a sisterhood based on the middle-class ideology of true womanhood, American and Canadian missionaries sought to create homes where Japanese women could become good Christians and adjust smoothly to their host societies.[50]

Certainly, Protestant reformers did not target Japanese prostitution exclusively, because campaigns against prostitution were also growing in other parts of the country. In both Canada and the United States, female reformers—especially members of the Woman's Christian Temperance Union, the National Congress of Mothers, and Parent-Teacher Associations—were seriously concerned with the negative influence of rapid industrialization on the lives of women and children. They viewed alien prostitution as a threat to the family and national morality and stepped outside the home to shape society in their own image of white Christian America or Canada. Toward the end of the century, their persistent efforts gradually moved state and federal governments to take measures to prevent women from practicing prostitution. By 1895, California, Oregon, and Washington had raised the age of consent to fourteen, sixteen, and sixteen, respectively, making it difficult for procurers to recruit young women for prostitution. In Canada, influenced by the passage of the British Criminal Law Amendment Act of 1885, which was aimed at protecting young women from sexual exploitation, the federal government revised the criminal code in 1892 and raised the age of consent to fourteen, criminalizing the seduction of "any girl of previously chaste character" and making it a punishable offense to "[procure], or [attempt] to procure, any woman or girl to become, either within or without Canada, a common prostitute."[51]

These legislative changes reflected basic societal opposition to prostitution in the two countries, but they were not necessarily effective in abolishing prostitution or stopping the entry of alien prostitutes. In western Canada, the lack of manpower made it difficult for local governments to enforce the criminal code. In the United States, local authorities adopted the system of fining and confining and permitted brothels to operate for regional economic development. At the state level, the Page Act of 1875 prohibited the importation of Chinese and Japanese women for prostitution and granted immigration officials the power to fine or imprison procurers who held women in service under contract;[52] however, it was difficult for officials to prove such prearranged contractual agreements between prostitutes and procurers at the port of entry, especially when the men and women arrived as married couples with passports. In 1903, the government revised the immigration law to confirm penalties against procurers who imported women for prostitution, adding prostitutes to the excludable classes.[53] But the revised law permitted federal officials to deport prostitutes *only* at the time of entry; officials had no way of proving that women would be engaged in prostitution after their entry. If they were not allowed to land on the charge of coming to the United States under contract or for immoral purposes, procurers submitted habeas corpus petitions to federal courts and secured their prostitutes' release.[54]

Despite the flaws in the law, federal officials in Pacific Coast cities, responding to local hostility toward Asians, extended their efforts to enforce existing laws to exclude Japanese prostitutes after the turn of the century. In October 1902, San Francisco officials indicted Yamamoto Kisuke for importing Yoshii Mitsu and forcing her into prostitution. The investigator obtained a labor contract exchanged between Yamamoto and Mitsu, and the evidence was too compelling for Yamamoto to deny the charges.[55] Two years later, Seattle officials tried Naito H., the manager of the Aloha House, a major local brothel, on the charge of importing two Japanese women for prostitution. Extensive interrogation of witnesses revealed that his collaborator brought two Yokohama women to Seattle via Canada in exchange for a $300 commission and that Naito forced the women to work in his brothel to repay the debt.[56]

Also, after the turn of the century, the U.S. government created legal frameworks within which federal officials could deport alien prostitutes and procurers more easily. In 1904, it entered into the

Canadian Agreement, which permitted U.S. officials in Canada to inspect disembarked passengers bound for the United States; it established the Bureau of Immigration and Naturalization in 1906 and the next year revised the immigration law to permit officials to deport alien prostitutes not only at the time of entry but anytime within three years after they entered the United States. From 1907 to 1910, the government investigated immigrant settlements around the country in search of alien prostitutes who were deportable under the new regulation.[57] In Seattle, an investigation led to the indictment and dismissal of Inspector A. H. Geffeney, who had frequently received loans from a Japanese insurance company in Seattle and helped the company to bring over prostitutes.[58] Seattle officials also prevented the entry of a Japanese restaurant manager who had lived off the earnings of a Japanese woman working as a prostitute during his previous stay in the United States on the grounds that he was "likely to become a public charge."[59] Increasing government efforts made it difficult for Japanese procurers and prostitutes to escape prosecution.

This federal effort to restrict the entry of "undesirable" aliens into the United States influenced the development of similar federal laws in Canada. While consistent in the effort to promote immigration so as to provide labor for the country's growing industries, the Canadian government made changes to the immigration act in 1906 and 1910, responding to growing complaints from law-enforcement officials suggesting an increase in crime, churches and charity providers working in expanding ethnic ghettos, and physicians and social scientists influenced by eugenic theories who wished to ban the entry of inferior persons.[60] The revised acts specified excludable aliens, including those who were mentally disabled and diseased, individuals "likely to become a public charge," criminals, prostitutes, and procurers. Notably, these excludable classes were almost the same as the ones defined in the U.S. Immigration Acts of 1907 and 1910.[61] But the scale of Japanese prostitution was small in Canada and because of the difficulty of enforcing the law at the provincial level in sparsely populated western Canada, Japanese prostitutes and procurers were rarely prosecuted under Canadian federal law.

In applying U.S. federal laws to the Japanese, some local officials abused their authority. For instance, in July 1901, Yamataya Masataro and his niece Kaoru landed in Seattle. Shortly after their arrival, Inspector Thomas Fisher arrested them and prosecuted Masataro on the charge of importing Kaoru for the purpose of prostitution.

To defend Masataro, Kaoru's parents and siblings appeared at the U.S. consulate in Nagasaki, Japan, and made statements to prove his innocence. The parents testified that Kaoru was a "rebellious" daughter who had met her boyfriend at night against their will. After she became pregnant, her parents decided to keep her away from her boyfriend and asked the mother's brother, Masataro, who was then in the United States, to take her there and "arrange for her to study English and sewing," furnishing him with money. A local government official in Nagasaki endorsed their statements, providing evidence that Masataro and Kaoru went through the proper channels before leaving Japan. Masataro was found not guilty.[62] The federal inspector's attempt to prosecute Masataro without thorough investigation represents the tendency among some federal officials to associate the Japanese with prostitution and bring charges without enough evidence based on the assumption that *all* Japanese women were brought over for "immoral" purposes.[63]

The tendency among West Coast officials to apply the federal law to Asians strictly, however, did not mean that they were given unlimited authority to exclude procurers and prostitutes. The case of Ogawa Haru illustrates this point. In the fall of 1906, Ogawa joined her husband, a migrant laborer, in Port Blakely and migrated from place to place, failing to secure a stable job. After arriving in Portland in February 1908, the husband began to suffer from rheumatism, and they lost their livelihood.[64] Forced by these struggles, Ogawa borrowed money from a man named Sakuma and started working in his brothel to repay the debt in early March.[65] After she delivered a child in August 1908, her master threatened her to resume prostitution. The husband then turned to a local Japanese reform society, which reported their case to the immigration office in Seattle, and Ogawa was referred to the Florence Crittenton Home in Seattle. In November 1908, Inspector J. H. Barbour issued a warrant for her arrest to hold her as a witness against the master who had forced her into prostitution.[66] In April 1909, the grand jury formally indicted the master for violating the immigration act of 1907, which criminalized the act of holding a woman for the purpose of prostitution. U.S. Attorney Walter Evans and Inspector Barbour in Portland wrote to Daniel Keefe, commissioner-general of the Department of Commerce and Labor, in Washington, D.C., to request his support for the deportation of Ogawa on the grounds that the act of 1907 permitted officials to deport alien women who practiced prostitution within three years of their arrival, although they *knew* that Ogawa had entered the country in October 1906, before the passage of the act.[67] Keefe, however, replied that the act of 1907 "is not retroactive" and "her deportability must be determined by the provisions of the law in force at the time of her entry." He noted that "[u]nder the former Act [of 1903] it was necessary to establish that a woman was a prostitute at the time of landing or that she entered for purposes of prostitution in order to render her expulsion from the country possible."[68] Ogawa came to the United States as a bride and fell into prostitution after her entry; therefore, she was not imported to the United States for prostitution. Portland officials' attempt to apply the 1907 act to her case thus violated the nonretroactive operation principle. The case was dismissed.[69]

Historians agree that during the Progressive Era, many American reformers, politicians, and intellectuals held a belief that prostitution was closely linked to immigration.[70] Immigrants did not represent a particularly large share of prostitutes in the United States, but the visibility of immigrants in urban spaces and workplaces led Americans to associate them with various evils of cities—including the growing crime rate, the decline in morality, and the spread of diseases—and become concerned about the negative influence of foreigners on the lives of native-born middle-class Americans. In this context, reformers and federal officials began to focus on working-class neighborhoods where the native-born mixed with foreigners, investigating the condition of white slavery and preventing "innocent" native-born girls from falling into the hands of French, Italian, and Jewish white slavers. As the Chinese and Japanese increased on the West Coast, reformers similarly attacked Asian prostitution as "Yellow Slavery," and Asian men were constructed as a threat to the sexual purity of white women.[71] As a result, the calls for suppression of alien prostitution developed hand in hand with demands for stricter immigration regulation on both sides of the North American continent.[72]

But it is not fair to characterize all Progressive Era reformers as "enemies" of immigrants. Unlike xenophobic writers who regarded foreigners as innately immoral, settlement workers and Protestant missionaries who worked among immigrants, including Jane Addams of Hull House and Donaldina Cameron of the Chinese Mission Home in San Francisco, saw prostitutes as victims of various structural forces, trying to shift attention from immigrants' racial traits to specific problems—including low wages, long work hours, lack of family ties and language skills, and the allure of consumer products in cities—that prompted women to choose prostitution as an alternative to their meager job options. Their ultimate goal was not to exclude immigrants but to transform them into good members of the nation as wives and mothers acquainted with American civic culture. Their inclusive and protective approach certainly had limits, because they attacked immigrants' patriarchal family traditions as detrimental to their cause of women's solidarity.[73] They were nativists in that they imposed their Victorian American and Christian values on foreigners, but they also tried to pave the way for immigrant women's future in their new country by criticizing their oppressive working conditions and the state's attempt to restrict immigration.

The drive to exclude Japanese prostitutes in this period was more linked to the growing anti-Asian feelings among the white working class on the West Coast who had long considered Asians a threat to their standard of living. As early as 1892, the Western Central Labor Union in Seattle resolved to send a petition to ask the police chief to work hard to eliminate Japanese prostitutes from the town, responding to complaints from the White Cooks' and Waiters' Union that Japanese prostitutes contributed so much to Japanese restaurants that white cooks and waiters could not get jobs.[74] In July 1907, the Seattle branch of the Japanese and Korean Exclusion League sent a note of protest to the federal government, claiming that Japanese immigrants and their collaborators in the United States were habitually committing the crimes of misrepresentation, perjury, and fraud in order to import Japanese women and sell them into a system of "slavery."[75] Established in San Francisco in 1905, the Japanese and Korean Exclusion League was at the forefront of Asian exclusion, supported by white workers along the Pacific Coast who resented Chinese, Japanese, Korean, and, from 1907, South Asian workers.[76] The growing association among white Americans of immigration with immorality served as a tool for exclusionists to drive Asian workers out of the country.

Finally, in 1910, the revised U.S. Immigration Act made the period of deportability of alien prostitutes permanent, and the White Slave Traffic Act, known as the Mann Act, granted the federal government authority to prosecute anyone for transporting women across state lines for the purpose of prostitution.[77] These legislative changes enabled federal officials to attack Japanese prostitution more effectively. In August 1910, immigration officials, in cooperation with

Japanese members of the Humane Society (*Jindō Kyōkai*) in Seattle, raided Japanese brothels, arrested ten women alleged to be prostitutes, and deported all of them.[78] Dozens of Japanese prostitutes were deported from Pacific Coast ports in 1911 and 1913.[79] Japanese men who transported prostitutes across state boundaries were also prosecuted in Seattle and San Francisco.[80] Even prominent local Japanese businessmen became targets of enforcement, including Iwata Hidekuni, the "richest Japanese in San Joaquin Valley," as described in the *Shin sekai* newspaper in San Francisco.[81] Although the act had little influence on domestic prostitution, because the local police controlled law enforcement within state lines, it gave federal officials the power to exclude "undesirable" foreigners—including prostitutes and procurers—from the country. Increasingly, the government sided with nativists in the East and anti-Asian exclusionists in the West who had alleged that immigrants had low morals and an inability to assimilate, taking active roles in protecting the moral health of the country from ethnic-racial Others.[82]

One must remember here that changes in prostitution-related immigration laws had different impacts on prostitutes of different racial groups. The act of 1910 permitted officials to deport foreign women who practiced prostitution anytime after their entry into the United States, which meant that naturalized women were not affected. In September 1910, for instance, Seattle consul Abe reported that while Japanese prostitutes were deported from Pacific Northwest ports, most other foreign-born prostitutes could avoid deportation because they had become naturalized American citizens before the law came into force.[83] Although it is impossible to tell the exact proportion of foreign-born prostitutes who had been naturalized by this time, Asian prostitutes, who were declared "aliens ineligible for citizenship" by the government, were certainly the most vulnerable racial group of prostitutes under the new regulation.

After these revisions in immigration law from 1907 to 1910, Japanese men could no longer manage brothels openly. However, it did not mean that Japanese prostitution was abolished. After the abolition of street prostitution, bar-restaurants rapidly increased in Japanese communities in cities on the West Coast. In 1909, when Japanese reformers started a campaign to eradicate prostitution by cooperating with federal officials and municipal authorities, the *Tairiku nippō* editor reported a shift in work patterns of Japanese prostitutes in a sarcastic tone: "It is well known that the authorities dealt a hard blow to brothels recently. The [Japanese] prostitutes were no longer able to play around and lead luxurious lives, and they were thrown into confusion. The panic [on King Street] resulted in the increase in the number of waitresses in Japanese restaurants."[84] Not all prostitutes became waitresses or barmaids so that they could continue to lead "luxurious lives," but Japanese restaurants did increase in West Coast cities: thirty-eight in Seattle, twenty-five in San Francisco, and thirty-eight in Los Angeles in 1914.[85] Barmaids were recorded as "waitresses" in official reports, and so long as they were not engaged in sex work publicly, the police and federal officials rarely interfered in their business.[86]

Furthermore, Japanese prostitutes did not disappear completely from North America. As law enforcement became strict, Japanese men and prostitutes moved into the interior, migrating from city to city to escape prosecution and continue to earn money.[87] Some Japanese prostitutes also went to the interior of Canada and towns along the Canadian Pacific Railway in British Columbia, Alberta, and Calgary.[88] As late as 1917–20, Japanese newspapers reported the presence of prostitutes in labor camps in Wyoming and mining towns in British Columbia.[89] Although the Japanese gender ratio became more balanced as Japanese brides increased in the 1910s, almost half of Japanese men were still living alone in 1920, and there was a persistent demand for places where Japanese and Chinese men could drink and enjoy the companionship of women after the day's work.[90]

THE TRANSFORMATION OF JAPANESE COMMUNITIES AND THE RISE OF REFORM ACTIVITIES

Simultaneously, in the first two decades of the twentieth century, antiprostitution forces gained strength among Japanese immigrants as their history entered a new phase. The Gentlemen's Agreement and the Lemieux Agreement severely restricted Japanese laborers' immigration to the United States and Canada in 1908. Subsequently, Japanese migrant men, who originally came as sojourners, decided to settle, sending for their wives in Japan or arranging marriages through the picture-bride system. Japanese women began to increase in number during the first decade of the century. In 1900, official censuses recorded only a total of 834 Japanese women in California, Oregon, and Washington (no Japanese woman was recorded by a Canadian census for that year). By 1911, however, their numbers had increased to 8,222 in the three U.S. Pacific Coast states and 1,443 in British Columbia.[91] Marriages produced children, and their numbers increased dramatically (269 in 1900, 4,502 in 1910, and 29,672 in 1920).[92] As Japanese men began to enjoy stable lives with wives and children, families, rather than bars and gambling joints, became key institutions in the Japanese community.

The presence of wives also permitted husbands to rise from the position of wage earners to entrepreneurs in the areas of farming, fishing, and store keeping;[93] however, Japanese entry into small businesses contributed to growing anti-Japanese sentiment among native-born Americans and Canadians in the West. In 1913, the California state legislature passed the Alien Land Law, which prohibited "aliens ineligible for citizenship" from owning land. In Seattle, white store managers petitioned the municipal government not to issue licenses to Japanese owners of small businesses—especially hotels, barbershops, and restaurants—during the 1910s. Labor unions pushed local wholesalers not to sell their goods to Japanese grocery stores.[94] In British Columbia, municipal officials, editors, and provincial politicians held several meetings to pressure the federal government to prohibit the Japanese from purchasing land and acquiring fishing licenses.[95] Economic competition between Japanese and whites, combined with the rising Japanese birthrate, increased white anxieties over the "peaceful penetration" of the Japanese into the West Coast.[96] Faced with opposition from the host societies, Japanese leaders acutely felt the need to show that they were lawful residents who respected the dominant white cultures in Canada and the United States. In this context, exclusion of "undesirable" elements from Japanese communities became a top priority.

The decade after 1908 witnessed the initiation of various moral reforms intended to improve the image of North American Japantowns. In Vancouver, the *Tairiku nippō* frequently criticized Japanese laborers' indulgence in Chinese gambling, and the Japanese Association of Canada campaigned against it.[97] In California, too, the Japanese Association of America attacked gamblers by publishing their personal information in newspapers and informing their families in Japan of their indulgence.[98] Heavy drinking also became the target of criticism by Japanese leaders and reformers. In Vancouver, Japanese ministers organized the Japanese Temperance Society at a local Methodist church in 1910.[99] The next year, in Seattle, a former president of the Japanese Association of North America organized the

Moral Reform Alliance (*Fūki Shinkō Dōmei Kai*) with the agenda of "improving the public morals of Japanese in America."[100] Over the 1910s, Japantown newspapers exposed excessive drinking among the Japanese, and after the U.S. Congress ratified the Eighteenth Amendment, the leaders criticized those who broke the Dry Law as a "disgrace on Japan and Japanese in America."[101] All these campaigns shared the purpose of purifying the image of Japanese and maintaining harmonious relations with white Americans and Canadians.

During World War I, Japanese leaders encouraged the Japanese to show their allegiance to their host societies as permanent settlers. The so-called 100 Percent American movement grew in the United States over the course of the decade. Progressive reformers viewed Americanization as a key to integrating immigrants into the larger society, and business leaders promoted Americanization programs as a means of taming radical foreign-born workers and smoothing relations between management and labor.[102] Similar efforts were applied to the Japanese. In 1919, white reformers visited Los Angeles's Japantown to offer Japanese women free lessons in the English language and American manners and provide them with knowledge on child care and sanitation. Although the program was proclaimed as intended for the "improvement of living conditions [among the Japanese]," reformers were not simply concerned with the welfare of the Japanese. In organizing the program, a white sanitary inspector claimed that because the Japanese were producing more than 80 percent of the food grown in California, they must pay attention to sanitary issues so as not to exert a harmful influence on public hygiene.[103] As in the previous period, the conflation of race and diseases continued to shape "reform" programs targeted at Asians.[104]

Japanese immigrants, who had been accused of the inability to assimilate, used this opportunity to show their allegiance to the government. In 1919, the Japanese Association of North America in Seattle established the Americanization Committee to encourage Japanese immigrants to respect and adopt American customs. The committee declared: "We earnestly support the United States government's Americanization Movement. To materialize the plan, [we] will strive to encourage Japanese residents to respect the founding ideals of the United States, its political traditions, manners, and customs, and foster their spirit of settlement to make themselves loyal elements of this nation."[105] As a racial minority, Japanese immigrants had to respect Anglo-Saxon middle-class moral standards and make efforts to represent themselves as members of a "civilized" race that could be integrated into national life in the United States.[106] Therefore, in this view, prostitution, a symbol of the migrant labor period as well as an uncivilized "Asiatic" custom, had to be eliminated from Japanese societies in the period of family formation and permanent settlement. The account of Inoue Orio, a Presbyterian minister in Seattle and a leading figure in the Humane Society, exemplified this sentiment clearly. In 1913, he contributed an article to a Japanese journal dedicated to antiprostitution reforms:

> Recently, California passed the Alien Land Law to make our fellow countrymen suffer a great deal. However, I am certain that we will win a victory if the Japanese in this country [the United States] stop thinking like "there is no need to worry about manners while travelling" and begin to fight for a just cause. We must do as Americans do when in the United States; stop doing things despised by Americans, believe in the Lord, eliminate all prostitutes and procurers, and build our characters so that Americans will respect us. Accordingly, anti-Japanese exclusionists in California were not Americans but ourselves. If we keep our chastity and fight in the cause of justice, they [Americans] cannot exclude us.[107]

Japanese leaders, aware of the weak position of the Japanese, promoted assimilation in order to integrate Japanese immigrants into American society.

Assimilation has been generally interpreted as a coercive process by which native-born Americans imposed their values on ethnic minorities, and immigration historians of the 1970s and 1980s viewed the phenomenon largely as a tragic sign of declining ethnicity among white ethnics. More recently, however, Gary Gerstle and others began to focus on the process by which immigrants adopted the language, culture, and civic ideals of the host society, showing that shared "American" values and ideals often helped immigrant workers forge cross-ethnic alliances in labor organizing or that ethnic identities were derived from both ethnic heritages and New World experiences.[108] Asians, however, were racially different from the dominant Anglo-Saxons and were subjected to intense racism in West Coast states; therefore, the pressure to assimilate was probably more immediate for them than for European migrants. Yet both Europeans and Asians shared the process in which once they had decided to settle in the United States, they began to identify themselves as American "ethnics" and sought ways to improve their position within the host society by asserting their assimilability. In this sense, antiprostitution reforms that occurred in Pacific Coast Japanese communities were also part of the immigrants' efforts to show their ability to assimilate American values, a phenomenon similar to what James R. Barrett calls "Americanization from the bottom up."[109]

CORRECTING FELLOW COUNTRYMEN'S BEHAVIOR

Japanese immigrant reformers began to take full advantage of the growing tide against prostitution in their host society after the turn of the century. In Seattle, in March 1906, Republican William H. Moore won the mayoral campaign with the support of local ministers, prohibitionists, and women's groups.[110] In April, at a meeting of the Japanese Methodist Church, Rev. Yoshioka Seimei and other participants endorsed Moore's policies against vice in the town and passed a resolution that they would "persuade pimps and prostitutes to either find legitimate jobs or return to Japan" and "prohibit each bar-restaurant from selling liquor."[111] The same year, Japanese ministers and Mark A. Matthews, a local Methodist minister, organized the Humane Society in order to save Japanese women from prostitution and accommodate them in the Woman's Homes attached to Japanese Methodist and Baptist churches.[112] In 1908, when a new mayor, John Miller, was elected, delegates of the Humane Society visited his office, asking for his cooperation in rescuing Japanese women from prostitution and helping them "stamp out this evil for the good of the entire community."[113] The next year, when federal officials came to Seattle to investigate a corruption charge against an immigration official, Humane Society members helped officials as interpreters and translators and broke up a Japanese trafficking ring.[114]

In Northern California, antiprostitution forces developed as Japanese leaders attempted to prevent prostitution from spreading into surrounding areas after the San Francisco earthquake in 1906. In August of that year, the *Fresno Republican* reported on the opening of a Japanese brothel on the town's outskirts, and a Japanese-language newspaper immediately reprinted the article to call readers' attention to the "disgusting, disgraceful behavior" of prostitutes.[115] In Oakland, too, a vernacular paper carried an article on Japanese brothels in February 1908, stressing the need to eliminate the "malignant tumor" from their settlement.[116]

In organizing all these campaigns against Japanese prostitution, the Japanese-language press took major roles.[117] In May 1911, the *Taihoku nippō* in Seattle carried an article, "A Theory of the Development of Japanese Women in America," declaring that the period of prostitutes and waitresses was over. The author claimed that such stories of forcing wives into prostitution had already become "old tales" and that "serious people" now constituted the majority of Japanese wives.[118] Following the publication of this article, the newspaper held a beauty contest, publishing photographs of the candidates for queen. Brief curriculum vitae attached to the photographs show that the majority of the candidates were well-educated daughters of leading businessmen. The women were dressed in Western fashions, demonstrating the degree of their assimilation into American society.[119] Similar new images of educated and Westernized Japanese women appeared in Vancouver's *Tairiku nippō,* which increasingly emphasized the community's transition to family formation, for instance, by celebrating the marriages of acculturated Japanese couples.[120]

In contrast, pimps and prostitutes became major targets of criticism in the Japanese press. From November 1908 to February 1909, the *Tairiku nippō* dispatched a journalist, Osada Shōhei, to various parts of the Canadian interior to report on the conditions of Japanese prostitution. During those three months, Osada's reports appeared in the newspaper every day and disclosed the real names of prostitutes and pimps, their work locations in Canada, and even their native villages in Japan. The next year, the newspaper company edited his reports and published it as a book, *Kanada no makutsu* (The red-light district in Canada). One theme running through the writing was Osada's eagerness to eliminate the problem of prostitution from Japanese communities in Canada. He reminded readers of the 1907 Vancouver Riot in which Canadian exclusionists attacked Japantown and broke every window of Japanese stores. He asserted that Japanese residents must pay serious attention to the cause of exclusion, declaring that Japanese pimps and prostitutes were "bacilli that prevent the sound development of the Japanese" in Canada. Osada printed the message from R. G. Chamberlain, chief constable of Vancouver, supporting this attack on Japanese prostitution.[121] Osada considered cooperation with white authority useful in eliminating the "bacilli" from the community.

Further reading of Osada's attempt to stigmatize prostitution illustrates the nature of the immigrant society in which former prostitutes had to live after leaving the trade. As Andrea Geiger pointed out in her analysis of this campaign against prostitution, Osada described the life of a former prostitute in a sarcastic tone, because, in his view, she had violated two moral codes: first by marrying a black barber, whom Osada called *kuronbo* (a derogatory term referring to an African Americans), and second as a former "woman engaged in an ugly trade" (*shūgyōfu*). He ridiculed her view of a life after death, which was still influenced by the Buddhist way of thinking, and in so doing, he denied the possibility of her becoming a Christian and being salvaged from a life of prostitution.[122] Not all Japanese immigrants viewed former prostitutes as Osada did. But the negative opinion about women who had been engaged in prostitution did not disappear instantly. Former prostitutes had to deal with the stigma attached to their former trade if they wished to continue to live in North America.[123]

This exposé of Japanese prostitution in Canada was probably a bit too radical in the context of the Japanese immigrant community in 1909. In his book, Osada attacked Nakayama Jinshirō, a major figure in Vancouver's Japantown who later compiled a major volume of Japanese Canadian history, *Encyclopedia of the Development of the Japanese in Canada* (*Kanada dōhō hatten taikan*), as "a terrible person who was known as a contributor [to the community]" but was actually "filling his pocket by secretly helping the importation of prostitutes."[124] After the publication of *Kanada no makutsu*, the publisher of the *Tairiku nippō* that had published Osada's book and articles was ostracized.[125] Therefore, it should be noted that a number of Japanese leaders were concerned that this exposé of the ills of the community would be used by anti-Japanese exclusionists as a weapon against the Japanese.[126] At least, however, the 1909 campaign signaled the beginning of reform activities among Japanese immigrants that would grow in the following decade.

In the 1910s, with new editors, the *Tairiku nippō* continued the strategy of turning the spotlight on pimps and prostitutes, and it certainly worked well in ostracizing certain individuals. In May 1915, for instance, Matsuyama Shohei, a major procurer, arrived in Victoria with his "wife." Immediately, the *Tairiku nippō* announced his arrival, publishing a series of articles on his personal history in North America, including his relations with the Aloha House in Seattle, several trips to Japan for importing young women for prostitution, and his transactions with brothel-keepers in Portland, Saskatoon, and Edmonton. The article explained that Matsuyama was "waiting for money" from brothels in the interior. Matsuyama could no longer bear being constantly watched by the press, and two days later, he suddenly disappeared from town. "Sickened by these newspaper articles, Matsuyama left Vancouver with his new wife," the editor observed.[127] What was significant about this case was not only that the procurer was excluded from the community but that his arrival was widely reported as far away as San Francisco.[128] It became difficult for procurers to escape the well-organized network of reformers that had expanded across the West Coast.

In addition to attacking pimps and procurers, the *Tairiku nippō* put the blame on Japanese businessmen who were financially dependent on prostitution not only in Vancouver but on the other side of the border. During July and August 1912, the press carried a series of articles titled "The Other Side of the New Rich in Seattle," in which the editor disclosed leading Seattle businessmen's close connections with prostitution. For instance, Takahashi Tetsuo, the president of the Oriental Trading Company, leased the Washington House, a major Japanese brothel, and subleased it to a Japanese manager, sharing profits with him. Hirade Kuranosuke, the vice president of the company, also leased the Aloha House and subleased it to other managers. In 1907, Takahashi, Hirade, and others established the Cascade Company, a stockholding company, to solicit funds for constructing a large-scale brothel in Japantown; this plan failed due to the sudden relocation of the red-light district by the city. The articles also revealed how some "established" businessmen in Seattle had accumulated money by forcing their wives into prostitution back in the early 1890s.[129] Increasingly, newspaper editors had become aware of the growth of similar reform activities in U.S. Pacific Coast Japantowns, and prostitution and the community's past relationship to it became subjects of discussion among not only Protestant reformers, Japanese leaders, and officials but also a broader audience in the community concerned with the future of their families and children in North America.

As professional prostitutes decreased after 1907, however, bar-restaurants surfaced as objects of criticism. Responding to increasing problems with noise and violence in bar-restaurants, the *Ōfu nippō* in Sacramento in 1909 published an article titled "Purify Bar-Restaurants," in which the editor stressed the need for the Japanese Association to pressure its managers to suspend their businesses after midnight and supervise barmaids more strictly.[130] In subsequent years, newspaper editors put the blame on those who were likely to catch the attention of local white residents—barmaids who walked on streets chattering loudly, those who wore Japanese zori, sashes, and kimono "untidily," and those selling and buying married women.[131]

But to the editors, the problem was not only that barmaids caught the attention of local white residents but that these particular kinds of clothing and practices would lead white people to look down on the Japanese as a whole. In the discussion of wife selling among the Japanese, for example, the editor argued that in Japan, the practice of paying consolation money at the time of a divorce was "done only among barmaids and similar kinds of people who belong to the 'lower-class society' (katō shakai)." Therefore, the editor concluded, "[i]f [our] society continues to tolerate such practice of wife selling as a matter of course, [our society] has no reason to say that we should not be criticized [by the Americans] for having no scruples."[132] In Japan, notwithstanding the national slogan "civilization and enlightenment," stricter regulations were still imposed on former members of outcaste communities, as former members of the farming class began to feel insecure about the blurring class boundaries as they witnessed increasing number of "new commoners" (shinheimin) doing what had been prohibited to them before the Meiji period, like moving beyond the designated areas of residence or wearing sandals, sashes, and certain kinds of clothing that had been reserved for the farming class.[133] So newspaper editors and Japanese immigrants opposed women of the "lower class," not only because they caught the attention of Americans, but also because they wore Japanese clothing considered inappropriate for their status and did so "untidily," which would lead Americans to believe that they represented the Japanese community. Thus, Japanese ways of considering class and status continued to shape the response of Japanese leaders to anti-Japanese sentiments in North American communities. At the same time, these articles represent a gap in attitudes toward the host society among Japanese migrants in the 1910s, with growing numbers of settlers who had achieved financial stability, become family heads, and begun to support the leaders' reforms to deal with racism and secure a place for themselves in the host society, on the one hand, and less successful migrants who were still at the stage of making money and exhibited what leaders considered the worst tendencies among the lower class in Japan, on the other.

Yet it is important to remember that while leaders wished to press fellow countrymen to be aware of the demands of Americans and

Canadians, they did not expect married women to break prescribed
gender roles within Japanese communities. The incident involving
Sasaki Toshi, a barmaid, is revealing in this regard. In April 1913,
Toshi joined her husband Minoru in Vancouver. The husband, how-
ever, had gambled away his money, incurred a heavy debt, and forced
Toshi to work as a barmaid in a local restaurant. After Minoru
returned to Japan in October 1915, Toshi entered the Central Mission
Girls Home in Vancouver and hired a lawyer to petition a Canadian
official to prevent Minoru from coming back to the United States.
Her Canadian lawyer observed that during the marriage, Minoru
never provided for her, lived on her earnings, and before leaving for
Japan "practically mortgaged her [Toshi] to a dis-reputable house";
therefore, he asked the government to prohibit Minoru from landing.
When Minoru returned to Victoria in March 1916, Canadian officials, in cooperation with Consul Abe Kihachi, arrested him and sent
him back to Japan. Angered by this treatment, Minoru petitioned the
governor of Fukuoka Prefecture to arrange his return to Canada as
soon as possible.[134]

In June 1916, Arikado Yatarō, the president of the Fukuoka Prefectural Association in Vancouver, sent a twenty-three-page note of
protest to the Foreign Ministry in defense of Minoru's position. In
this letter, he criticized Consul Abe, who cooperated with Canadian
officials in deporting Minoru. According to evidence Arikado submitted, Toshi had led an "immoral" life in Canada, committing adultery,
becoming pregnant, and having an abortion. Refuting Consul Abe's
low opinion of Minoru, he argued that Toshi "volunteered" to work
as a barmaid and that Minoru never forced her to do so; therefore,
Arikado claimed that "the grounds for deportation were not solid."
Several newspaper accounts attached to his letter criticized Toshi's
adulterous relationship with her lover, calling her "enchantress"
(yōfu), "wicked woman" (dokufu), and "flirt" (impu). Uniformly, the
stories attributed the cause of the marital breakdown to her "vanity"
(kyoeishin) without taking into account the plight of Toshi, who had
to work as a barmaid to support herself after Minoru left her alone
in Canada.[135]

While criticizing assertive women, newspaper articles of this
period often praised obedient, hardworking wives who dutifully
served their husbands. In April 1915, for instance, the *Taihoku nippō*
introduced the wife of a pool hall owner as an example of an "ideal
wife." Her parents sent her to a Japanese pool hall owner in Seattle in

exchange for 1,000 yen, but she "helped her husband's business faithfully from morning till night without grumbling about her fate." The editor claimed that "the common run of wives who have the cheek to divorce their husbands should learn from this woman's hard work."[136] The next year, Miwata Masako, a leading female educator in Japan, contributed an article to the *Tairiku nippō* in which she stressed the importance of women adopting the "good customs of the host societies" and making their homes as pleasant as possible for their husbands. In so doing, she argued, women could wipe away bad images of the Japanese in the host society and keep husbands away from vices like gambling, alcohol, and prostitution.[137] Thus, newspaper articles in this period became increasingly schizophrenic, representing idealized images of immigrant wives as *ryōsai kenbo* (good wives and wise mothers) who are submissive to husbands while reporting on a number of assertive brides who stressed individual wants over familial obligations.

The need to control women's behavior arose in part from the increase in marital breakdowns among the Japanese on the West Coast. In Sacramento, where at least fifty-six divorce cases were filed between 1908 and 1920, the *Ōfu nippō* published an article in 1909, "Collapsing Women's Moral Standards," emphasizing the need to decrease such scandals as elopements and marital quarrels. The editor claimed that in order to achieve that goal, Japanese women must acquire "the virtue of obedience" and attacked "assimilating" Japanese women who asserted women's rights and "[threw] their husbands over their shoulders" in divorce courts.[138] Japanese leaders did not oppose Japanese men's and women's assimilation entirely, because they believed that adopting such customs as wearing Western clothes and walking side by side in public would help to avoid drawing criticism from white Americans or Canadians. Within their households, however, the couples were expected to maintain the traditional gender relations of Japan, which, the leaders believed, would strengthen the order and integrity of their community.[139]

As Kei Tanaka and Eiichiro Azuma showed, efforts to inculcate the *ryōsai kenbo* ideal in immigrant women started even before the women departed for North America. For example, Shimanuki Hyōdayū, president of Rikkōkai, a Christian institution in Japan, established a private school in 1908 to train future wives of Japanese immigrants. Admission was restricted to women sixteen years or older who had received at least a high-school education. Instructors offered moral lessons that blended Japanese feminine ideals with Protestant ethics to train *ryōsai kenbo* who would support their husbands' work faithfully and diligently.[140] In 1914, Shibusawa Eiichi, a leading entrepreneur in Japan, established the Japan Emigration Society in Yokohama to teach picture brides American customs such as how to wear Western clothes or use Western bathrooms and cooking utensils. The society's guide warned immigrant women that "[white] Americans tend to find Japanese life style and customs strange, unpleasant, and even reprehensible" and that Japanese behavior "often leads to the unfortunate misconception that Japanese are unable to Americanize, undesirable, and such."[141] Japanese leaders contended that immigrant wives must be dutiful, hardworking mothers equipped with Western manners, not assertive women running away with other men or filing for divorce.

Most important, however, behind all these programs of reforming the immigrant masses in the 1910s was the hard reality that Japanese immigrants had difficulty fighting against exclusion in Canadian and American societies. Without the right to vote, they had little power to oppose discriminatory legislation—including antimiscegenation and alien land laws. Neither were they allowed to join labor unions dominated by whites. In settling in North America without these basic rights, Japanese immigrants felt pressured to adopt middle-class Anglo-Saxon norms. At the same time, North American Japantowns were entering the period of permanent settlement with increasing numbers of American- and Canadian-born children, the Nisei, born with full rights as Canadian and American citizens. The most important thing for the future of Nisei children, the leaders thought, was to maintain good relations with the host societies by representing themselves as good elements of society. Japanese leaders' opposition to prostitution thus came from their collective strategy for surviving as racial minorities in hostile lands.

Japanese prostitution steadily declined in North America over the 1910s. After changes to the federal Immigration Act in 1910, officials began to deport all alien prostitutes. Japanese procurers could no longer transport women to labor camps in the interior across state boundaries, and many frontier towns had abandoned the policy of tolerance by World War I.[142] Sources suggest that clandestine prostitution continued among barmaids, but the demand for prostitution gradually declined as the sex ratio became more balanced in the decades following 1908.[143] In 1921, growing Japanese exclusion campaigns

pressured the Japanese government to stop issuing passports to picture brides. Japanese men could no longer bring over women and
make them work in brothels or bar-restaurants. The Nisei birth rate
reached its height between 1919 and 1921 in the United States.[144] As
Takeuchi Kōjirō put it, the "prostitutes-centered era" was over, and
Japanese immigration history entered the stage of family formation
and settlement.[145] Stories of women forced into prostitution became
"old tales" of the frontier period.

A GLOBAL PERSPECTIVE

Japanese immigrant reform can be framed as a domestic response to
economic and cultural developments in American or Canadian society, but it was also influenced by developments occurring outside the
region in the same period. From the late nineteenth century, antiprostitution reforms had been developing in Europe as a response to
various problems associated with migration, urbanization, and industrialization. First in Britain, sensational reports on the white slave
trade in London led to the 1886 abolition of the Contagious Disease
Ordinance that regulated prostitution. It stimulated the growth of
similar antiprostitution forces in other European countries, including
France and Germany, where prostitution was regulated by the state.
The National Vigilance Association held the first international conference on white slavery in London in 1889, and five years later, in Paris,
sixteen European nations signed the International Agreement for the
Suppression of the White Slave Traffic outlawing the recruitment of
women for prostitution in foreign countries. Another international
agreement, signed in 1910, included clauses on punishing traffickers
who forced women into prostitution at home and abroad.[146]

These developments in Europe influenced the structure of prostitution in European colonies in the Pacific region. In the Dutch East
Indies, the colonial office in Batavia began to clear away prostitution
in its colonies after A. W. F. Idenburg, a devout Calvinist, took charge
of its administration in 1909, revising the immigration law to prevent
procurers from entering the colonies, rewriting the criminal code to
impose heavy penalties on procurers and pimps, and ordering brothel-
keepers to close their businesses by the end of August 1912. In British
Malaya, in the early 1910s, British reformers in Singapore began to
send the Association for Moral and Social Hygiene in London reports
on drug addiction and the spread of venereal diseases among local

white prostitutes, declaring them to be "a blot upon British rule and a disgrace to Christianity." Pressured by these forces, the Legislative Council ordered the expulsion of European pimps and banned white women from practicing prostitution in 1913; it continued these efforts until 1916, when European prostitutes left for other parts of Asia.[147]

Responding to the host societies' attacks on prostitution and other developments in the 1910s, Japanese antiprostitution efforts became strong in Southeast Asia. Since the 1890s, the local Japanese community's financial reliance on prostitution, together with the local administration's policy of tolerance, had made it extremely difficult for consular officials and reformers to eliminate prostitutes and procurers from the region. During World War I, however, Japanese investment in Southeast Asia increased rapidly, and more businessmen arrived in the region, replacing independent entrepreneurs who had had a stake in prostitution. In September 1915, local Japanese businessmen organized the Japanese Association and started campaigns against prostitution. Taking advantage of the British authorities' efforts to end prostitution, Japanese consuls began to restrict, with the help of the Chinese Protectorate, the entry of Japanese women for prostitution while encouraging brothel-keepers to repatriate prostitutes voluntarily. Finally in 1920, acting consul general in Singapore Yamazaki Heikichi declared his intention to exclude all Japanese prostitutes from his jurisdictions to representatives of Japanese Associations from various parts of British Malaya.[148] Official surveys show a visible decline in the number of prostitutes in Southeast Asia after 1920 (table 6.1).

As Japanese prostitution declined in Southeast Asia, the center of overseas Japanese prostitution moved to East Asia. After its victories in the Sino-Japanese War (1894–95) and Russo-Japanese War (1904–5), Japan began to exert control over Korea, Taiwan, and southern China, sending numerous soldiers to these areas. In order to protect the health of the soldiers who defended these strategic footholds for Japan's expansion in East Asia, the Japanese colonial administration established pleasure quarters, enforcing medical checkups for prostitutes and collecting taxes from brothel-keepers. The establishment of licensed prostitution created a context in which Japanese prostitution expanded rapidly.[149] Official censuses recorded 4,925 Japanese prostitutes in China in 1907 and 4,400 in Korea in 1910.[150] By 1929, prostitutes in China accounted for 85 percent of overseas Japanese prostitutes, while those in Southeast Asia and North America had

TABLE 6.1. Numbers of overseas Japanese prostitutes, 1914–1929

	1914		1919		1924		1929	
	Number	%	Number	%	Number	%	Number	%
Australia	0	0%	0	0%	0	0%	3	0.1%
China	5,264	65.8%	5,905	61%	3,728	76.3%	5,439	84.9%
Europe	0	0%	0	0%	0	0%	0	0%
Latin America	0	0%	44	0.5%	30	0.6%	3	0.1%
North America	275	3.4%	273	2.8%	267	5.5%	230	3.6%
Russia	297	3.7%	781	8.1%	290	5.9%	8	0.1%
South Asia	0	0%	495	5.1%	130	2.7%	72	1.1%
Southeast Asia	2,167	27.1%	2,187	22.6%	441	9%	654	10.2%
Total	8,003	100%	9,685	100%	4,886	100%	6,409	100%

Sources: *Kaigai kakuchi zairyū honpōjin shokugyōbetsu jinkōhyō*, 1914, 1919, 1924, and 1929.
Note: A new category, "geisha, prostitutes, barmaids, and others," began to appear in the tables from 1913; therefore the number of women in other prostitution-related occupations such as "miscellaneous jobs," "artistic accomplishments," and "restaurant businesses" is not counted. Readers should note that many Japanese barmaids in North America reported themselves as "waitresses" to consuls; therefore, their numbers do not appear in this table.

decreased to 3–10 percent. The exclusion of Japanese migrants and prostitutes from white-settler societies (Canada, the United States, and Australia) and Japanese militarism in Asia shifted the focus of procurers and prostitutes to Japan's colonies.

Japanese leaders' opinions on overseas prostitutes also had changed by the 1920s. When Japan opened its doors to the West, it had no valuable products to trade with Western powers. Japanese leaders viewed the emigration of laborers and prostitutes as a solution to the population problem in Japan and appreciated overseas prostitutes as martyrs who contributed to Japan's industrialization in the form of remittances. By the end of the 1910s, however, Japan had acquired overseas territories in Asia and joined the ranks of the Great Powers; at the same time, Japanese leaders' expectations for remittances from overseas declined in the postwar economic prosperity. Gradually, prostitutes began to take on a different meaning. National leaders no longer viewed them as martyrs but as a national disgrace that would prompt questions about Japan's ability to westernize.[151] Meanwhile, an international conference was held in 1921 in which participating nations agreed to ratify the 1904 and 1910 agreements concerning trafficking in women and children. Faced with this pressure from the international community, Japan acceded to the treaty in 1925 on the condition that the acceptable age of women engaged in prostitution would be lowered from twenty-one to eighteen and that the treaty would not apply to Korea, Taiwan, the Kwantung leased territory of Sakhalin, and the South Sea Mandate.[152] They joined consular officials and immigrant leaders in their efforts to abolish prostitution outside Japan's territories, to defend the honor of Japan, while tolerating it in Japan's colonies, so as to protect the health of soldiers and ensure Japan's control of these regions.

The continuance of prostitution in Japan's territories was closely linked to the failure of antiprostitution reforms in the metropole. As Japan experienced the Sino-Japanese and Russo-Japanese Wars, Japanese reformers began to support the government's war effort, sending care packages (*imonbukuro*) to soldiers at the front while increasingly attacking prostitutes who "corrupted" the morals of soldiers and injured Japan's reputation and campaigning for the exclusion of prostitutes from the public sphere.[153] Reformers succeeded in this area of activity by asserting their own position as defenders of soldiers, families, and the "national honor," but when they demanded the closing down of brothels, (male) authorities who supported the interests of brothel-keepers and the local business community ignored them. Licensed brothels continued to operate in Japan and its colonies in Korea and Manchuria until the end of World War II.

This global perspective on the use of Japanese women for the sake of the Japanese empire permits a better understanding of reform activities targeted at Japanese women in the immigrant communities of the North American West in the early twentieth century. In a recent article, Sidney Lu Xu showed that during the same period, Protestant reformers in Manchuria made efforts to turn former prostitutes into domestics who would help manage Japanese residents' households and thereby contribute to the growth of the Japanese settler community in Manchuria. During the same period in California, Lu wrote, the Japanese encountered intense hostility as a racial minority, and Protestant reformers and immigrant leaders attempted to eliminate prostitution that would offend the Americans, simultaneously disciplining Japanese immigrant women through education programs for picture brides and critiques of assertive married women who challenged the idealized image of Japanese immigrant women as *ryōsai kenbo*. In both regions, all these programs aimed at reforming women were justified as beneficial for the Japanese race and empire. At the same time, through these programs, Japanese middle-class women acquired dominance over the poor and racial Others and formed an uneasy alliance with licensed prostitution at home and abroad. As Lu incisively pointed out, these developments in the early twentieth century paved the way for the forcible recruitment of poor women at home and in Japan's colonies in Korea and China for sex work during World War II.[154] Antiprostitution activities in North American Japanese communities thus had broader implications for the place of women in the Pacific Rim region during the period of imperial expansion.

Conclusion

This study began as an attempt to place the experiences of Japanese prostitutes in the North American West in the context of both the country of origin and the country of reception. In Japan, the disintegration of the agrarian sector in the early 1880s forced struggling farmers to send their children to industrial centers to supplement family incomes, and the growing textile and sex industries absorbed large numbers of young Japanese women. In North America, the expansion of agricultural, mining, railroad, lumber, cannery, and service industries attracted large numbers of Asian and white laborers. From the mid-1880s onward, expanding trade and transportation networks facilitated the transpacific movement of goods and people between Japan and North America, and Japanese women became part of the trade and migration flow, moving to frontier cities and mining towns where women were scarce. This initial survey of their migration pattern convinced me that, as in the cases of Chinese and other Asian migrants, Japanese migration to North America took place as parts of diverse social and economic transformations on both sides of the Pacific Ocean.

As my research proceeded, however, I came to realize that economic changes alone did not explain everything about the transpacific migration of Japanese women and their lives as prostitutes in North America. The existing views of women from the earlier Tokugawa period continued to shape their place in Meiji society, leading impoverished parents to sell their daughters to brothels in exchange for advances on wages for the sake of *ie* (family). Despite the new government's goal of modernizing the country through the abolition of "feudal" practices, licensed prostitution continued, and for women from historically marginalized groups who continued to suffer prejudice, prostitution was one of their limited options for survival. After coming to the North American West, they faced new challenges in both the red-light districts and larger Canadian and American societies as prostitutes and racial minorities. At the same time, perceptions of class, gender, and status rooted in Meiji Japan continued to oppress them within the immigrant community, as exemplified in the attitudes of Japanese leaders and officials and the word used to refer to them, *shūgyōfu*. Thus, by expanding our focus to include the social and cultural contexts in Japan, we gain a richer understanding of social formations in the Japanese immigrant community in Canada and the United States around the turn of the twentieth century.

As I read more on the subject of Japanese women and prostitution in the Meiji period, I also learned to see Japanese prostitution in the North American West as part of broader developments occurring in Japan and the rest of the world. Japanese migration to North America was part of the larger streams of Japanese women's migration to all parts of the Pacific Rim region that occurred in the context of European and Japanese colonialism and industrial developments during what Eric Hobsbawm called the "Age of Empire" (1875–1914).[1] Anti–Japanese prostitution movements occurred in Japan and the North American West in the 1880s as part of a broader effort to protect Japan's honor in the international community but gradually diverged as reformers in the two regions pursued different interests in the context of Japan's expansion into neighboring countries and Japanese immigrants' settlement in the United States and Canada. And the decline in Japanese prostitution in the North American West resulted in part from the shift in the center of overseas Japanese prostitution from non-colonies to colonies as Japan's national leaders began to focus on military developments and the health of soldiers in Japan's East Asian colonies while attempting to abolish Japanese prostitution in white-settler societies in Australia, North America, and European colonies in Asia. These developments laid the groundwork for the so-called comfort women system that developed at the height of Japanese militarism during World War II. By looking at the link between Japanese prostitution in North America and various developments in other parts of the Pacific Rim region, this study suggests the limitations of national frameworks and the need for a broader perspective in the historical study of Asian women's migration and sexuality.

At the same time, I would like to caution readers against connecting Japanese prostitution of a century ago to similar phenomena taking place in our own age. The problems of so-called modern-day slavery and human trafficking have drawn a great deal of attention all over the world, not just because they contradict the dominant Christian idea of sex in the Western world as a private act confined to marriage, but also because they have often been framed as the negative consequences of global developments after the collapse of the Soviet Union in 1989. These include uneven economic development, an increase in regional conflicts, and the growing movement of peoples, goods, and information across national boundaries.[2] As in the turn-of-the-century Pacific Rim region, the root cause of prostitution was poverty resulting from structural changes occurring in all parts of the world. Yet these structural causes were specific to the period and places under study; in the case of Japanese prostitution in North America at the turn of the twentieth century, they include displacement of farmers caused by Meiji "reforms," continuing prejudice against women and marginalized social groups, legal and racial restrictions placed on the entry of Asians into Canada and the United States, intense hostility toward Asians in Pacific Coast cities, the sexualized image of "exotic" Asian women in North American society, the unbalanced gender ratio created by racist immigration laws of that period, and Asian migrants' lack of various social and civic rights as "aliens ineligible for citizenship." Without a sense of historical context, we may end up reproducing generalized images of women engaged in prostitution as victims of "sexual slavery" or the procurers of women for sex work overseas as members of transnational "crime groups."

Although this study started as an effort to make sense of these women's individual experiences, in the course of my research, I came to appreciate the perspectives of both women *and* men. Japanese men who were involved in the personal lives of Japanese prostitutes and barmaids—including husbands, customers, and lovers—are marginal figures in the standard narrative of Japanese American and Japanese Canadian history in which men figure as successful immigrants who became managers of farms or shops, brought over wives, and had their own families. In contrast, these men continued to hold unskilled jobs, including domestic work, which was considered a "girl-servants' job" (*gejo hōkō*) in Japan. Separated from the social world of Americans and Canadians, they frequented brothels and bar-restaurants to seek the companionship of women, drank heavily, or became dependent on their wives' earnings as barmaids. Meanwhile, women who became prostitutes or barmaids often did so to do their duty to their parents or husbands, but as they became economically and socially independent while working, some chose to leave their husbands to be with other men. By using gender as an analytical lens, this study has revealed that the transition from the "frontier" period to the "settlement" period in Japanese immigration history was not as smooth as past studies have shown but was fraught with conflict between the leaders and individual men and women who deviated from the community's norms.

Finally, as this is a study of prostitution, I would like to comment on the meaning of prostitution for Japanese women based on my findings. Prostitution had a positive impact on some women, especially when they were young and attractive. Popular barmaids won beauty contests, had regular customers, earned large sums in tips, and were redeemed by customers who desperately wanted to marry them. The money also helped some women become managers of bar-restaurants or hire lawyers to file for divorce and protect their hard-earned money. But the bright picture of their lives often turned grim as they became older: Some suffered from disease and discrimination after returning to their native villages, were robbed of all their money, or died alone in a foreign land. In recent years, sociologists and anthropologists who have interviewed women currently working in the trade often focus on women's positive comments on sex work and the opportunities that the work opened for them; some scholars even call for the legalization of prostitution.[3] But as individual stories of Japanese women revealed, the circumstances in which women were engaged in sex work, including their relations with husbands and families, could change over the course of their lives; therefore, we need to broaden our perspective to examine women's lives not only when they worked as prostitutes but also after retirement, especially in their old age, to learn how they deal with the stigma attached to the trade and how they recall their pasts as sex workers in comparison to the broader social relations they have at the present. As Raelene Frances writes, women become prostitutes as a result of a gradual "process." Some women sell sex occasionally; others do so for an extended period.[4] Therefore, understanding the varying meanings of prostitution for women who have been engaged in it requires continued examination of their individual experiences. It would be helpful to shed assumptions about these women and to see prostitution in its full complexity as a problem in its own right.

ABBREVIATIONS

BC Archives	British Columbia Archives, Victoria
CSH	Center for Sacramento History
CVA	City of Victoria Archives
IA	Internet Archive, https://archive.org/
JARP	Japanese American Research Project Collection, University of California, Los Angeles
JFMAD	Japanese Foreign Ministry Archival Documents, Tokyo
KCSC	King County Superior Court, Seattle
NARA	National Archives and Records Administration
NDL	National Diet Library, Tokyo
RINS	Records of the Immigration and Naturalization Service
SFTS	San Francisco Theological Seminary, San Anselmo, California
SUL	Stanford University Libraries
UCA	United Church of Canada, British Columbia Conference Archive, Vancouver
WOBFM	Woman's Occidental Board of Foreign Missions
WSADA	Washington State Archives, Digital Archives, http://www.digitalarchives.wa.gov/Search

INTRODUCTION

1. Yamazaki Tomoko, *Ameyuki-san no uta: Yamada Waka no sūki naru shōgai* (Tokyo: Bungei shunjū, 1978), 48–59; translated into English as *The Story of Yamada Waka: From Prostitute to Feminist Pioneer*, trans. Wakako Hironaka and Ann Kostant (Tokyo: Kodansha International, 1978).

2. Yamada Waka, "Ominaeshi," *Seitō*, 4:11 (1914): 52.

3. Yamazaki, *The Story of Yamada Waka*, 52.

4. Yamada Waka, *Renai no shakaiteki igi* (1920; repr., Tokyo: Yumani shobō, 2000), 185.

5. Ibid., 184–88.

6. The family tree of the Asaba family was compiled by Asaba Kiyoshi, the grandson of Yamada Waka's eldest brother, Fukutarō. Courtesy of Asaba Kiyoshi.

7. "Shiatoru bijin no mitate," *Nihonjin*, August 24, 1901, 3.

8. Yamada, *Renai no shakaiteki igi*, 188.

9. The oldest document on her story that I could find is "Shiatoru shussin no Yamada Wakako," *Hawai hōchi*, April 4, 1917, 2. See also Takeuchi Kōjirō, *Beikoku seihokubu nihonjin iiminshi* (Seattle: Taihoku nippōsha, 1929), 486–89; "Arabia Oyae shusse monogatari," *Amerika shinbun*, February 16, 1938, JARP.

10. Report of Donaldina Cameron, *WOBFM Annual Report*, 1904, 56–57, SFTS.

11. Yamada, *Renai no shakaiteki igi*, 108.

12. On her work from her participation in the discussion concerning the "idea of motherhood" (*bosei shugi*) in 1918 through the passage of the Mother and Child Protection Act in 1937, see Imai Konomi, *Shakai fukushi shisō toshite no bosei hogo ronsō: Sai wo meguru undō-shi* (Tokyo: Domesu shuppan, 2005).

13. Yamazaki, *Ameyuki-san no uta*, 178–242, 259–74; Imai Konomi, *Shakai fukushi shisō*, 271.

14. Yuji Ichioka, *The Issei: The World of the First Generation Japanese Immigrants, 1885–1924* (New York: The Free Press, 1988); Ichioka, "Japanese Immigrant Nationalism: The Issei and the Sino-Japanese War, 1937–1941," *California History* 69:3 (1990): 260–75; Donald Teruo Hata, Jr., *"Undesirables," Early Immigrants and the Anti-Japanese Movement in San Francisco, 1892–1893: Prelude to Exclusion* (New York: Arno Press, 1978), chap. 2; Brian M. Hayashi, *"For the Sake of Our Japanese Brethren": Assimilation, Nationalism, and Protestantism among the Japanese of Los Angeles, 1895–1942* (Stanford: Stanford University Press, 1995); Eiichiro Azuma, *Between Two Empires: Race, History, and Transnationalism in Japanese America* (New York: Oxford University Press, 2005).

15. Valerie J. Matsumoto, *Farming the Home Place: A Japanese American Community in California* (Ithaca: Cornell University Press, 1993); Linda Tamura, *The Hood River Issei: An Oral History of Japanese Settlers in Oregon's Hood River Valley* (Urbana: University of Illinois Press, 1993); Sylvia J. Yanagisako, *Transforming the Past: Tradition and Kinship among Japanese Americans* (Seattle: University of Washington Press, 1985).

16. Andrea Geiger, *Subverting Exclusion: Transpacific Encounters with Race, Caste, and Borders, 1885–1928* (New Haven: Yale University Press, 2011); Cecilia M. Tsu, *Garden of the World: Asian Immigrants and the Making of Agriculture in California's Santa Clara Valley* (New York: Oxford University Press, 2013), chap. 3. I have to add, however, that the need for "recentering" women in Asian American history had already been addressed by Gary Okihiro in *Margins and Mainstreams: Asians in American History and Culture* (1994; repr., Seattle: University of Washington Press, 1996), chap. 3. Sociological studies attentive to gender conflicts include Evelyn Nakano Glenn, *Issei, Nisei, War Bride: Three Generations of Japanese American Women in Domestic Service* (Philadelphia: Temple University Press, 1986); Yen Le Espiritu, *Asian American Women and Men: Labor, Laws, and Love* (Lanham, Md.: Rowman & Littlefield, 2008). Literary scholars have also made efforts to tease out the gender differences and sexual tensions often hidden in Asian American political writing. For instance, see Rachel C. Lee, *The Americas of Asian American Literature: Gendered Fictions of Nation and Transnation* (Princeton: Princeton University Press, 1999).

17. On the need to examine Asian-language sources in the study of Asian immigration, see Yong Chen, "In Their Own Words: The Significance of Chinese-Language Sources for Studying Chinese American History," *Journal of Asian American Studies* 5:3 (2002): 255.

18. The extreme difficulty of recovering the voices of prostitutes has been pointed out by historians of prostitution. For instance, see Gail Hershatter, *Dangerous Pleasures: Prostitution and Modernity in Twentieth-Century Shanghai* (Berkeley: University of California Press, 1997), 4.

19. Two major works that debunk the myth of the prostitute with a "heart of gold" are Marion S. Goldman, *Gold Diggers, Silver Miners: Prostitution and Social Life on the Comstock Lode* (Ann Arbor: University of Michigan Press, 1981); Anne M. Butler, *Daughters of Joy, Sisters of Misery: Prostitutes in the American West, 1865–90* (Urbana: University of Illinois Press, 1985).

20. Major anthologies in this genre include Rebecca Walker, ed., *To Be Real: Telling the Truth and Changing the Face of Feminism* (New York: Anchor Books, 1995); Merri Lisa Johnson, ed., *Jane Sexes It Up: The Confession of Feminist Desire* (New York: Four Walls Eight Windows, 2002

21. For example, Laura Maria Agustin, *Sex at the Margins: Migration, Labour Markets and the Rescue Industry* (New York: Zed Books, Ltd., 2007); Ronald Weitzer, *Legalizing Prostitution: From Illicit Vice to Lawful Business* (New York: New York University Press, 2012).

22. Goldman, *Gold Diggers, Silver Miners*, 4.

23. Yamazaki Tomoko, "From Sandakan No. 8 Brothel," trans. Tomoko Moore and Steffen Richards, *Bulletin of Concerned Asian Scholars* 7:4 (October–December 1975): 53.

24. Joan Wallach Scott, *Gender and the Politics of History* (New York: Columbia University Press, 1999), 32.

25. Lucie Cheng and Edna Bonacich, eds., *Labor Immigration under Capitalism: Asian Workers in the United States before World War II* (Berkeley: University of California Press, 1984), chaps. 1–3.

26. Yong Chen, *Chinese San Francisco, 1850–1943: A Trans-Pacific Community* (Stanford: Stanford University Press, 2000); Madeline Y. Hsu, *Dreaming of Gold, Dreaming of Home: Transnationalism and Migration between the United States and South China, 1882–1943* (Stanford: Stanford University Press, 2000).

27. Erika Lee, *At America's Gates: Chinese Immigration during the Exclusion Era, 1882–1943* (Chapel Hill: University of North Carolina Press, 2003); Mae Ngai, *Impossible Subjects: Illegal Aliens and the Making of Modern America* (Princeton: Princeton University Press, 2004); William H. Siener, "Through the Back Door: Evading the Chinese Exclusion Act along the Niagara Frontier, 1900 to 1924," *Journal of American Ethnic History* 27:4 (Summer 2008): 34–70; Yukari Takai, "Asian Migrants, Exclusionary Laws, and Transborder Migration in North America, 1880–1940," *OAH Magazine of History* 23:4 (October 2009): 35–42; Takai, "Navigating Transpacific Passages: Steamship Companies, State Regulators, and Transshipment of Japanese in the Early-Twentieth-Century Pacific Northwest," *Journal of American Ethnic History* 30:3 (Spring 2011): 7–34; Geiger, *Subverting Exclusion*, chaps. 5–6; Kornel Chang, *Pacific Connections: The Making of the U.S.-Canadian Borderlands* (Berkeley: University of California Press, 2012), chaps. 1, 2, 5.

28. Hayashi, *"For the Sake of Our Japanese Brethren,"* 24–25, chap. 3.

29. Geiger could make this major argument in her work only through the rigorous analysis of Japanese migrant lives in both Japan and the North American West. Geiger, *Subverting Exclusion*.

30. The merits of combining transnational and comparative methods in historical analysis have been pointed out by a number of scholars. For example, see Marc Bloch, "A Contribution towards a Comparative History of European Societies," in *Land and Work in Mediaeval Europe: Selected Papers by Marc Bloch*, trans. J. E. Anderson (New York: Harper and Row, 1967), 44–81; Jürgen Kocka, "Comparison and Beyond," *History*

and Theory 42 (2003): 39–41; and Deborah Cohen and Maura O'Connor, "Introduction: Comparative History, Cross-National History, Transnational History—Definitions," in Cohen and O'Connor, eds., *Comparison and History: Europe in Cross-National Perspective* (New York: Routledge 2004), 1–22. This is also a response to Gary Okihiro's call for making a "transpacific site" for Asian American history, which he made two decades ago. Okihiro, *Margins and Mainstreams*, xii. On his argument for including Asia and women in the study of Asian American history, see *Margins and Mainstreams*, chap. 3.

31. Josef J. Barton, *Peasants and Strangers: Italians, Rumanians, and Slovaks in an American City, 1890–1950* (Cambridge, Mass.: Harvard University Press, 1975); Walter D. Kamphoefner, *The Westfalians: From Germany to Missouri* (Princeton: Princeton University Press, 1987); Chen, *Chinese San Francisco*; Kodama Masaaki, *Nihon iminshi kenkyū josetsu* (Hiroshima: Keiseisha, 1992); Geiger, *Subverting Exclusion*.

CHAPTER 1. ACROSS THE PACIFIC RIM

1. Kurahashi Masanao, *Kita no karayuki-san* (1989; repr., Tokyo: Kyōei shobō, 2000), 73. The actual number would have been much larger because many were smuggled into foreign countries and most had eluded any official count.

2. Saeki Junko, *Yūjo no bunka shi* (Tokyo: Chūō kōron sha, 1987), 116–17.

3. Sone Hiromi, *Shōfu to kinsei shakai* (Tokyo: Yoshikawa kōbun kan, 2003), 12, 15–16. Amy Stanley writes that in the early medieval era, the economy was not commercialized enough that bartering goods for sex can be distinguished from receiving money for services. As commercialization progressed over the fifteenth and sixteenth centuries, sex was increasingly identified as a commodity to be purchased and sold. See Amy Stanley, *Selling Women: Prostitution, Markets, and the Household in Early Modern Japan* (Berkeley: University of California Press, 2012), 30–31.

4. Yamamoto Shun'ichi, *Nihon kōshōshi* (Tokyo: Chūō hōki shuppan, 1983), 4–5; Kim Il Myon, *Yūjo, karayuki, ianfu no keifu* (Tokyo: Yūzankaku, 1997), 11–15.

5. Sone, *Shōfu to kinsei shakai*, 57–64, 185–200; Stanley, *Selling Women*, 45–52; Yamamoto, *Nihon kōshōshi*, 4–5, 10–18.

6. Usami Misako, *Shukuba to meshimori onna* (Tokyo: Dōseisha, 2000), 16–19.

7. Kodansha, *Kodansha Encyclopedia of Japan* (Tokyo: Kodansha, 1983), 1:355, 2:267, 3:259–60, 8:259; Usami, *Shukuba to meshimori onna*, 122.

8. Stanley, *Selling Women*, part 1.

9. Here my analysis relies primarily on Stanley, *Selling Women*, part 2. For various forms of women's hardships in brothels, see Sone, *Shōfu to kinsei shakai*, 46–56.

10. On the legal maneuvering related to this incident, see Daniel V. Botsman, "Freedom without Slavery? 'Coolies,' Prostitutes, and Outcastes in Meiji Japan's 'Emancipation Moment,'" *American Historical Review* 116:5

(2011): 1323–47. As Botsman writes, it is problematic to ascribe the issuance of the Emancipation Edict solely to the embarrassment Meiji officials felt in the course of the Maria Luz incident, because the issues pertaining to the indenture of women and children had been discussed among officials in the newly established Meiji government since the late 1860s. See also Sheldon Garon, *Molding Japanese Minds: The State in Everyday Life* (Princeton: Princeton University Press, 1997), 91; Yamamoto, *Nihon kōshōshi*, 74–87.

11. Hagiwara Otohiko, *Tōkyō kaika hanjō-shi* (Tokyo: Mansei-dō, 1874), 2:9; Yoshimi Kaneko, *Baishō no shakaishi* (Tokyo: Yūzankaku, 1984), 21; Hayakawa Noriyo, *Kindai tennōsei to kokumin kokka* (Tokyo: Aoki shoten, 2005), 302–3.

12. Tokyo-fu, *Shōgi geigi kaihō shiryō*, December 1873, NDL; Hayakawa, *Kindai tennōsei to kokumin kokka*, 303–8.

13. Major English-language publications about the background of Japanese migration to the United States include Yasuo Wakatsuki, "Japanese Emigration to the United States, 1866–1924: A Monograph," *Perspectives in American History* 12 (1979): 387–516; Yuji Ichioka, *The Issei: The World of the First Generation Japanese Immigrants, 1885–1924* (New York: The Free Press, 1988), chap. 2. On Japanese migration to Canada, see Audrey Lynn Kobayashi, "Regional Backgrounds of Japanese Immigrants and the Development of Japanese-Canadian Community," Department of Geography, McGill University, *Discussion Papers* no. 1 (May 1986): 1–10; Michiko Midge Ayukawa, *Hiroshima Immigrants in Canada, 1891–1941* (Vancouver: University of British Columbia Press, 2008), chaps. 1–5, especially chap. 1.

14. Andrew Gordon, *A Modern History of Japan: From Tokugawa Times to the Present* (New York: Oxford University Press, 2003), 70–71; Nakamura Masanori, *Rōdōsha to nōmin: Nihon kindai wo sasaeta hitobito* (Tokyo: Shōgakkan, 1998), 44–46.

15. Takafusa Nakamura, *Economic Growth in Prewar Japan*, trans. Robert A. Feldman (New Haven: Yale University Press, 1983), 58; Alan Takeo Moriyama, "The Background of Japanese Emigration to Hawaii, 1885–1894," in *Labor Immigration under Capitalism*, ed. Lucie Cheng and Edna Bonacich (Berkeley: University of California, 1984), 250–51.

16. Ōishi Kaichirō, "Shihonshugi no seiritsu," in *Iwanamikōza nihonrekishi, dai 17 kan* (Tokyo: Iwanami shoten, 1981), 135–39; Nobutaka Ike, "Taxation and Landownership in the Westernization of Japan," *Journal of Economic History* 7:2 (1947): 175; Nakamura, *Economic Growth in Prewar Japan*, 58. Kobayashi, "Regional Backgrounds of Japanese Immigrants," 2–3.

17. Kishimoto Minoru, "Meiji taishōki ni okeru rison chiiki no keisei to toshi jinkō no shūseki katei," *Rekishi chiri gakkai kiyō* 8 (1966): 139–49; Kishimoto, *Jinkō idō-ron* (Tokyo: Ninomiya shoten, 1978), 30–33; Kobayashi, "Regional Backgrounds of Japanese Immigrants," 3.

18. Mikiso Hane, *Peasants, Rebels, and Outcasts: The Underside of Modern Japan* (New York: Pantheon, 1982), 173; Gordon, *A Modern History of Japan*, 95–96.

19. Nakamura, *Rōdōsha to nōmin*, 180–81.

20. For a comparison of daily wages in major industries, see E. Patricia Tsurumi, *Factory Girls: Women in the Thread Mills of Meiji Japan* (Princeton: Princeton University Press, 1990), 105.

21. For an overview of structural changes in prostitution during the Meiji period, see Fujime Yuki, *Sei no rekishigaku: Kōshō seido, dataizai, taisei kara baishun bōshihō, yūsei hogohō taisei e* (Tokyo: Fuji Shuppan, 1997), 97–98.

22. Hane, *Peasants, Rebels, and Outcasts*, 208.

23. Tsurumi, *Factory Girls*, 10; Gordon, *A Modern History of Japan*, 101.

24. Yoshimi Kaneko, "Baishō no jittai to haishō undo," in *Nihon joseishi, dai 4 kan, kindai* (Tokyo: Tokyo daigaku shuppankai, 1982), 230.

25. "Shōgi ni kansuru tōkei," *Toki no koe*, August 1, 1902, 2.

26. Eiichi Kiyooka, trans. and ed., *Fukuzawa Yukichi on Japanese Women: Selected Works* (Tokyo: University of Tokyo Press, 1988), 87–89.

27. More than half of them left elementary school before graduation. Only four women managed to finish elementary school. Yamamuro Gunpei, *Shakai kakusei ron* (1914; repr., Tokyo: Chūkō bunko, 1977), 57–60, 64–70, 83–84.

28. Etsuko Yasukawa, "Ideologies of Family in the Modernization of Japan," in *East Asian Cultural and Historical Perspectives*, ed. Steven Totosy de Zepetnek and Jennifer W. Jay (Edmonton: Research Institute for Comparative Literature and Cross-Cultural Studies, University of Alberta, 1997), 193–94. On the transformation of the *ryōsai kenbo* ideology in relation to various developments after the turn of the century, see Kathleen Uno, "Womanhood, War, and Empire: Transmutations of 'Good Wife, Wise Mother' before 1931," in *Gendering Modern Japanese History*, ed. Barbara Molony and Kathleen Uno (Cambridge, Mass.: Harvard University Press, 2005), 503–13.

29. Hitomi Tonomura and Anne Walthall, "Introduction," in *Women and Class in Japanese Society*, ed. Hitomi Tonomura, Ann Walthall, and Wakita Haruko (Ann Arbor: Center for Japanese Studies, University of Michigan, 1999), 8–9; Sōgō joseishi kenkyū-kai, *Jidai wo ikita onna tachi: Shin nihon josei tsū-shi* (Tokyo: Asahi shuppan-sha, 2010), 82–89, 154, 196.

30. James Francis Warren, *Ah Ku and Karayuki-san: Prostitution in Singapore, 1870–1940* (Singapore: Oxford University Press, 1993), 29–32; Karen Colligan-Taylor, "Translator's Introduction," in *Sandakan Brothel No. 8: An Episode in the History of Lower-Class Japanese Women* (Armonk, N.Y.: M.E. Sharpe, 1999), xviii.

31. Tang Quan, *Umi wo koeta tsuyagoto: Nicchū bunka kōryū hishi* (Tokyo: Shinyōsha, 2005), 173, 175.

32. Nishida Taketoshi, *Nihon jānarizumu-shi kenkyū* (Tokyo: Misuzu shobō, 1989), 355; Kim, *Yūjo, karayuki, ianfu no keifu*, 171–72.

33. Warren, *Ah Ku and Karayuki-san*, 47.

34. Shimizu Hiroshi and Hirakawa Hitoshi, *Karayuki-san to keizai shinshutsu: Sekai keizai no naka no shingapōru-nihon kankei-shi* (Tokyo: Komonzu, 1998), 24.

35. Hiroshi Shimizu and Hitoshi Hirakawa, *Japan and Singapore in the World Economy: Japan's Economic Advance into Singapore, 1870–1965* (London: Routledge, 1999), 26.

36. Warren, *Ah Ku and Karayuki-san*, 47.

37. Nicholas Tarling, "The Establishment of Colonial Regimes," in *The Cambridge History of Southeast Asia*, ed. Nicholas Tarling (Cambridge and New York: Cambridge University Press, 1992), 2:5–46; Robert E. Elson, "International Commerce, the State and Society: Economic and Social Change," in *The Cambridge History of Southeast Asia*, ed. Nicholas Tarling (Cambridge and New York: Cambridge University Press, 1992), 2:141–61; Ian Brown, *Economic Change in South-East Asia, c. 1830–1980* (New York: Oxford University Press, 1997), chap. 2; Shimizu and Hirakawa, *Japan and Singapore in the World Economy*, 8; Eric Hobsbawm, *The Age of Empire, 1875–1914* (1987; repr., New York: Vintage Books, 1989), chap. 3.

38. The male-female ratio among the Chinese in Singapore was five to one in 1881, four to one in 1901, and three to one in 1911. Shimizu and Hirakawa, *Karayuki-san to keizai shinshutsu*, 26.

39. Warren, *Ah Ku and Karayuki-san*, chap. 5.

40. Shimizu and Hirakawa, *Japan and Singapore in the World Economy*, 24; Warren, *Ah Ku and Karayuki-san*, chap. 6.

41. Ronald Takaki, *Pau Hana: Plantation Life and Labor in Hawaii* (Honolulu: University of Hawai'i Press, 1983), x, chaps. 1, 2.

42. Miyamoto Natsuki, "Keiyaku imin jidai no honoruru nihonjin shakai to nihonjin baishunfu," *Hikaku shakai bunka kenkyū* 12 (2002): 48.

43. Alan Takeo Moriyama, *Imingaisha: Japanese Emigration Companies and Hawaii, 1894–1908* (Honolulu: University of Hawai'i Press, 1985), 11, 17.

44. Joan Hori, "Japanese Prostitution in Hawaii during the Immigration Period," *Hawaiian Journal of History* 15 (1981): 115–16.

45. See Okumura Takie, "Fukei ni okersu waga hō no shūgyō fujin," *Fujin shinpō* 4 (May 1895): 28.

46. Hori, "Japanese Prostitution in Hawaii," 113–14, 118–19; Miyamoto, "Keiyaku imin jidai," 52–53.

47. John J. Stephan, *The Russian Far East: A History* (Stanford: Stanford University Press, 1994), 64–65; Barbara A. Anderson, *Internal Migration during Modernization in Late Nineteenth-Century Russia* (Princeton: Princeton University Press, 1980), 129–34.

48. Igor R. Saveliev, "English Abstract," in *Imin to kokka: Kyokutō roshia ni okeru chūgokujin chōsenjin nihonjin imin* (Tokyo: Ochanomizu shobō, 2005), 13–20, 23, 29, 30–32; Kurahashi Masanao, *Kita no Karayuki-san* (Tokyo: Kyōei shobō, 2000), 24–25.

49. On Japanese migrants and prostitutes in the Russian Far East, see Stephan, *The Russian Far East*, 76–77; Nishida, *Nihon jānarizumu-shi*, 346n357; Kuroda Kiyotaka, *Kanyū nikki* (1884), 18–19, NDL.

50. Kikuchi Yūhō, *Nihonkai shūyūki* (Tokyo: Shungakudō, 1903), 290–94, 310–11.

51. Kurahashi, *Kita no Karayuki-san*, 53–54.

52. Song Youn-ok, "Chōsen shokuminchi-shakai ni okeru kōshō-sei," *Nihonshi kenkyū* 371 (July 1993): 52–66; Song, "Chōsen gunji senryō-ka no sei-kanri seisaku," *Sensō sekinin kenkyū* 67 (Spring 2010): 23–25.

53. Kim, *Yūjo, karayuki, ianfu no keifu,* 202–10; Morisaki Kazue, *Karayuki-san* (Tokyo: Asahi bunko, 1980), 102–32; Hane, *Peasants, Rebels, and Outcasts,* 219.

54. Fujinaga Takashi, "Nichiro sensō to nihon ni yoru manshū e no kōshō seido ishoku," in *Kairaku to kisei: Kindai ni okeru goraku no yukue* (Osaka: Osaka sangyō kenkyūjo, 1998), 64–72.

55. One must keep in mind that prostitution itself had existed in Korea before the 1870s. On the history of prostitution in Korea, see Kawamura Minato, *Kiisen: "Monoiu hana" no bunkashi* (Tokyo: Sakuhinsha, 2001), chap. 1.

56. Yamashita Yon'e, "Chōsen ni okeru kōshō-seido no jisshi: Shokuminchi tōchika no sei shihai," in *Chōsen-josei ga mita "ianfu mondai": Asu wo tomoni ikiru tameni,* ed. Yun Jeong-Ok (Tokyo: San'ichi shobō, 1992), 128–67.

57. Fujinaga, "Nichiro sensō to nihon ni yoru," 66, 68–69, 78, 92.

58. Carolyn Podruchny, *Making the Voyageur World: Travelers and Traders in the North American Fur Trade* (Lincoln: University of Nebraska Press, 2006), chap. 8.

59. Rodman W. Paul, *Mining Frontiers of the Far West, 1848–1880* (New York: Holt, Rinehart and Winston, 1963), 136–149; Walter Nugent, *Into the West: The Story of Its People* (New York: Alfred A. Knopf, 1999), 54–57; Richard White, *"It's Your Misfortune and None of My Own": A New History of the American West* (Norman: University of Oklahoma Press, 1991), chaps. 8, 10–12; Robert V. Hine and John Mack Faragher, *The American West: A New Interpretive History* (New Haven: Yale University Press, 2000), chaps. 8–9; Anne M. Butler, *Daughters of Joy, Sisters of Misery: Prostitutes in the American West, 1865–90* (Urbana: University of Illinois Press, 1985), chaps. 1, 6; Charleen P. Smith, "Boomtown Brothels in the Kootenays, 1895–1905," in *People and Place: Historical Influences on Legal Culture,* ed. Jonathan Swainger and Constance Backhouse (Vancouver: University of British Columbia Press, 2003), 120–52.

60. Butler, *Daughters of Joy, Sisters of Misery,* chaps. 4–5; Jef Rettmann "Business, Government, and Prostitution in Spokane, Washington, 1889–1910," *Pacific Northwest Quarterly* 89:2 (1998): 77–83; Marion S. Goldman, *Gold Diggers, Silver Miners: Prostitution and Social Life on the Comstock Lode* (Ann Arbor: University of Michigan Press, 1981), chaps. 5–7; Jacqueline Baker Barnhart, *The Fair but Frail: Prostitution in San Francisco, 1849–1900* (Reno: University of Nevada Press, 1986), chaps. 3, 5–7; Debora Nilsen, "The 'Social Evil': Prostitution in Vancouver, 1900–1920," in *In Her Own Right: Selected Essays on Women's History in B.C.,* ed. Barbara Latham and Cathy Kess (Victoria, BC: Camosun College, 1980), 205–28.

61. Butler, *Daughters of Joy, Sisters of Misery,* 9–10.

62. The act of 1875 was known as the Page Act, the Immigration Act of March 3, 1875 (18 Stat. 477). On the provisions, see Edward P. Hutchinson,

Legislative History of American Immigration Policy, 1798–1965 (Philadelphia: University of Pennsylvania Press, 1981), 65–66. On the Chinese Exclusion Act, see Erika Lee, *At America's Gate: Chinese Immigration during the Exclusion Era, 1882–1943* (Chapel Hill: University of North Carolina Press, 2003), 2, 45–46, 92.

63. The government began to impose a tax on the Chinese in 1885 and increased the amount from $100 to $500 per head in 1903. See Ninette Kelley and Michael Trebilcock, *The Making of the Mosaic: A History of Canadian Immigration Policy* (Toronto: University of Toronto Press, 2010), 145.

64. The executive order referred to here is Executive Order no. 589 issued on March 14, 1907. See Roger Daniels, *The Politics of Prejudice: The Anti-Japanese Movement in California and the Struggle for Japanese Exclusion* (Berkeley: University of California Press, 1977), 43–44. Between 1898 and 1908, 57,000 Japanese left Hawaii for the U.S. mainland. See Andrea Geiger, *Subverting Exclusion: Transpacific Encounters with Race, Caste, and Borders, 1885–1928* (New Haven: Yale University Press, 2011), 105.

65. Kobayashi, "Regional Backgrounds of Japanese Immigrants," 6; Ayukawa, *Hiroshima Immigrants in Canada*, 35; Iino Masako, *Nikkei kanadajin no rekishi* (Tokyo: Tokyo daigaku shuppankai, 1997), 23–24.

66. On the locations of Japanese prostitution in Canada, see Osada Shōhei, *Kanada no makutsu* (Vancouver: Tairiku nippōsha, 1909), frontispiece, 8–19.

CHAPTER 2. HARDSHIPS AT HOME

1. Yamazaki Tomoko, *Sandakan hachiban shōkan: Teihen joseishi joshō* (Tokyo: Bungei shunjū, 1975), 66–76, 255–62.

2. English-language studies of the origins of Japanese immigrants include Yasuo Wakatsuki, "Japanese Emigration to the United States, 1866–1924: A Monograph," *Perspectives in American History* 12 (1979): 389–516; Yuzo Murayama, "Information and Emigrants: Interprefectural Differences of Japanese Emigration to the Pacific Northwest, 1880–1915," *Journal of Economic History* 51 (1991): 125–47; Audrey Lynn Kobayashi, "Regional Backgrounds of Japanese Immigrants and the Development of Japanese-Canadian Community," Department of Geography, McGill University, *Discussion Papers* no. 1 (May 1986): 1–19, app. 1.

3. On the information about the origins of Japanese prostitutes in China and Southeast Asia, see *Toki no koe*, April 1, 1913; Mori Katsumi, *Jinshin baibai* (Tokyo: Shibundō, 1959), 177–81.

4. Between 1890 and 1905, the United States was the largest importer of Japanese silk. Ōkurashō, *Gaikoku bōeki gairan*, 1890, 1895, 1900, 1905 (Tokyo: Ōkurashō shūzei-kyoku, 1912); Sawada Yasuyuki and Sonobe Tetsushi, *Keizaihatten ni okeru kyōdōtai to shijō no yakuwari* (Tokyo: Tōyōkeizai shinpō sha, 2006), 47–48.

5. Norbert MacDonald, *Distant Neighbors: A Comparative History of Seattle and Vancouver* (Lincoln: University of Nebraska Press, 1987), 22–35. By 1900, silk and tea ranked first and second among Japanese products

unloaded in Seattle. Gaimushō, *Tsūsho isan, 59-kan* (1901; repr., Tokyo: Fuji shuppan, 1993–98), 194; Yokohama kaikō shiryōkan, *Yokohama & bankūbā: Taiheiyō wo koete* (Tokyo: Yokohama kaikō shiryōkan, 2005), 9.

6. Yuji Ichioka, *The Issei: The World of the First Generation Japanese Immigrants, 1885–1924* (New York: The Free Press, 1988), 7–9, 51–56; Roger Daniels, *Asian America: Chinese and Japanese in the United States since 1850* (Seattle: University of Washington Press, 1988), 107–9.

7. Department of Interior, Census Office, *Report on Population of the United States at the Eleventh Census: 1890, part 1* (Washington, D.C.: Government Printing Office, 1895), 488; Department of Interior, Census Office, *Twelfth Census of the United States, Taken in the Year 1900*, vol. 1, *Population* (Washington, D.C.: Government Printing Office, 1901), 490–92.

8. Of 4,738 Japanese residents in Canada, 97 percent (4,597) were living in British Columbia. Census Office (Canada), *Census of Canada, 1921*, vol. 1, population (Ottawa: F. A. Acland, Printer, 1924–1927), 354–55.

9. Yokohama shi, *Yokohama shi shikō, fūzoku hen* (1932; repr., Kyoto: Rinkai shoten, 1985), 295, 303–4, 308–13, 315–19, 322–25, 442.

10. Yokohama shinpō sha, *Yokohama hanjō ki* (Yokohama: Yokohama shinpō sha, 1903), 202.

11. Murata Seiji, *Kobe kaikō sanju-nen shi* (Kobe: Kobe kaikō sanjū-nen kinen kai, 1898), 265–70, 408–9; Hitomi Sachiko, "Kōbe fukuwara yūkaku no seiritsu to kindai kōshō-sei," *Nihonshi kenkyū* 544 (December 2007): 30–33, 39–44.

12. Kusayama Iwao, "Kōbe gaikokujin kyoryūchi wo meguru keisatsu mondai," *Kōbe no rekishi* 14 (February 1986): 15–44.

13. Shigetomi Akio, *Yokohama chabuya monogatari: Nihon no mūranrūju* (Yokohama: Senchurii, 1995), 18.

14. Yokohama shinpō sha, *Yokohama hanjō ki*, 366–67.

15. Taizo Fujimoto, *The Story of the Geisha Girl* (London: T. W. Laurie, 1910), 142, 151–53, available in the *Gerritsen Collection*, http://gerritsen.chadwyck.com/marketing/index.jsp (accessed April 29, 2007).

16. Yokohama shinpō sha, *Yokohama hanjō ki*, 187–202, 205–7. On Japanese prostitutes who worked for American customers in Kobe, see Report of Hyogo Prefecture Governor Hayashi Kaoru, March 26, 1890, JFMAD, 4.2.2.10, vol. 1. On Chinese masters who purchased Japanese girls in Kobe, see Report of Hyogo Prefecture Governor Hattori Ichizō, January 19, 1904, JFMAD, 4.2.2.10, vol. 2.

17. *Rafu shinpō*, May 15, 1918, 3, and September 4, 1918, 5.

18. Yokohama shi, *Yokohama shi shikō, fūzoku hen*, 323–24.

19. Report of Kanagawa Prefecture Governor Nakano Takeaki, May 23, 1894, JFMAD, 3.8.8.4, vol. 1.

20. *Asahi shinbun*, December 28, 1898, 4.

21. Ibid., March 25, 1903, 5.

22. Osada Shōhei, *Kanada no makutsu* (Vancouver: Tairiku nippōsha, 1909), 35–36, 90–91, and front matter.

23. *Shin sekai*, September 11, 1907, 3, and August 27, 1912, 3; "Jaguro Ito," case no. 5134, October 1911, RG 21, NARA, San Bruno.

24. *Shin sekai*, September 1, 1907, 4.

25. Ibid., June 2, 1909, 3.

26. This subject will be discussed in more detail in chapter 7.

27. Kanagawa ken, *Kanagawa ken tōkeisho, meiji 22-nen, 23-nen* (Yokohama: Seishi bunsha, 1893), 125, 167.

28. Yūmatu kai, *Kanagawa ken chishi* (Yokohama: Tanuma shoten, 1897), 6–7; Kanagawa ken, *Kanagawa ken tōkeisho, meiji 22-nen, 23-nen*, 127–40.

29. Tomoko Yamazaki, *The Story of Yamada Waka: From Prostitute to Feminist Pioneer*, trans. Wakako Hironaka and Ann Kostant (Tokyo: Kodansha International, 1978), 47, 50–51; Yamazaki Tomoko, *Ameyuki-san no uta: Yamada Waka no sūki naru shōgai* (Tokyo: Bungei shunjū, 1978), 54–55.

30. Yamada Waka, "Sanjū yonen mae," *Fujin to shakai* 105 (1929): 14–15.

31. Yamada Waka, *Renai no shakaiteki igi* (1920; repr., Tokyo: Yumani shobō, 2000), 185; Yamazaki, *Ameyuki-san no uta*, 60–62.

32. Kanagawa ken, *Kanagawa kenshi tsūshi-hen* 6 (Yokohama: Kanagawa ken, 1981), 456, 459, 650.

33. Kanzaki Akitoshi et al., *Kanagawa ken no rekishi* (Tokyo: Yamakawa shuppan sha, 1996), 281; Furushima Toshio, *Shihon seisan no hatten to jinushisei* (Tokyo: Ochanomizu shobō, 1978), 191.

34. Kanagawa ken, *Kanagawa kenshi tsūshi-hen* 6, 714–21.

35. Fujino Yutaka, ed., *Kanagawa no buraku-shi* (Tokyo: Fuji shuppan, 2007), chaps. 3–4, 111–14, 120–22, 126–28.

36. For the quotes, see Yamada, "Sanjū yonen mae," 14.

37. The numbers of male and female agricultural population are as follows: 1890 (181,402:152,870); 1898 (168,893:137,952); 1908 (166,763:115,488). See Kanagawa ken, *Kanagawa kenshi tsūshi-hen* 6, 654.

38. Ibid., 653. On the transition of women's work from unpaid apprentices to wage earners, see E. Patricia Tsurumi, *Factory Girls: Women in the Thread Mills of Meiji Japan* (Princeton: Princeton University Press, 1990), 191.

39. *Asahi shinbun*, July 4, 1899, 5.

40. Yokohama shi, *Yokohama shi shikō, fūzoku hen*, 341. On the Japanese perception of foreigners in the early years of the Meiji period, see Andrea Geiger, *Subverting Exclusion: Transpacific Encounters with Race, Caste, and Borders, 1885–1928* (New Haven: Yale University Press, 2011), 76.

41. Yokohama shi, *Yokohama shi shikō, fūzoku hen*, 375–76; Ōta Hisayoshi, *Yokohama enkaku-shi* (Tokyo: Tōyōsha), 1892), 46.

42. Fujino, *Kanagawa no buraku-shi*, 119. Although these women did what other Japanese women disliked, they were not appreciated by the local people. They were often denounced as a national embarrassment by emperor royalists who wished to expel foreigners (*jōi shishi*) or stripped and tied to trees by the local people. See Yokohama shi, *Yokohama shi shikō, fūzoku hen*, 353–54.

43. Yokohama shinpō sha, *Yokohama hanjō ki*, 194–95.

44. Japanese scholar Kawamoto Yoshikazu argues that the similar idea of using women from marginalized groups for prostitution for foreigners

shaped prostitution policies during the U.S. occupation period after World
War II, including the creation of the Recreation and Amusement Association
(RAA) and "special comfort stations" (tokushu ianjo) for American officers
in Tokyo and near military bases throughout the country. See Kawamoto
Yoshikazu, Kaikō ianfu to hisabetsu buraku (Tokyo: Sanichi shobō, 1997).

45. On the immigration guides that presented a rosy picture of the United
States and facilitated young Japanese men's migration to the country in the
1880s, see Ichioka, The Issei, 11.

46. On the migration from Miho to the United States, see Shizuoka ken
kaigai kyōkai, Shizuoka ken kaigai ijū shi (Shizuoka: Shizuoka ken kaigai
kyōkai, 1979), 66–67.

47. Kishimoto Minoru, "Tōkai chiiki ni okeru jinkō shūseki," Tōhoku
chiri 19:2 (1967): 46–47. Indeed, Shizuoka was one of only five prefectures
producing more than forty thousand out-migrants a year in 1890. The data
come from the statistical yearbooks of twenty-nine prefectures for the year
1890. All volumes are available in NDL.

48. There were fifty-three post stations on the Tōkaidō, nineteen of
which were located in Shizuoka. For a map, see Kodama Kōta, ed., Shukuba
(Tokyo: Tōkyōdō shuppan, 1999), 62.

49. Shizoka ken, Shizuoka kenshi tsūshi-hen 3 (Shizuoka: Shizuoka-ken,
1996), 1389.

50. Umejima Tetsujirō, Kanbara chōshi shikō (Kanbara, Shizuoka Prefecture: privately published, 1971).

51. Takada Shirō, Izu no Ida (Ito, Shizuoka: Izu wo aisuru kai, 1985),
23–26, 46.

52. Report of Secretary Fujita Toshirō, July 30, 1891, JFMAD, 3.8.2.12,
vol. 1.

53. The data come from Nihon keizai tōkei sōran (Tokyo, 1966), cited in
Wakatsuki, "Japanese Emigration to the United States," 449–50.

54. Report of Officer Kawasaki Matsutarō, June 21, 1896, JFMAD,
3.8.2.49, vol. 1.

55. Letter of Yoneda Itsushū, December 14, 1895, JFMAD, 3.8.2.49, vol.
1. On the reports in the local press on Japanese prostitutes and men related to
them, see Butte Anaconda Standard, December 22, 1889, 5; June 18, 1890,
5; December 22, 1892, 5; January 2, 1897, 5.

56. Report of Officer Kawasaki Matsutarō, June 21, 1896, JFMAD,
3.8.2.49, vol. 1.

57. Kudō Miyoko, Kanada yūgirō ni furu yuki wa (Tokyo: Shōbunsha,
1983), 201–2.

58. Strictly speaking, the native village of Torajirō was Ida, located next
to Heda. The two villages were merged into one village and renamed Heda in
1889. I use the name Heda to refer to Ida. Nagaoka Osamu, Me de miru nishi
Izu no rekishi (Fujimiya: Ryokusei shuppan sha, 1986), 114.

59. Kudō, Kanada yugirō ni furu yuki wa, 201–2.

60. Today, his descendants manage an inn in Heda, and the inn's website
introduces the story of Torajirō. I chose not to provide readers with the Inter-
net address in order to protect his privacy.

61. Kudō, *Kanada yugirō ni furu yuki wa*, 202–3.

62. Takada, *Izu no Ida*, 47.

63. Report of Vancouver Consul Yada Chōnosuke and Report of G. L. Milne, Medical Inspector & Immigration Agent, Victoria, June 16, 1909, JFMAD, 4.2.2.27, vol. 3.

64. Shizuoka ken kaigai kyōkai, *Shizuoka ken kaigai ijū shi*, 66–67.

65. Shizuoka ken, *Shizuoka ken tōkei sho, 36-nen* (Shizuoka: Iketsurudō, 1905), 62–69.

66. Kanbara chō shi hensan iinkai, *Kanbara chō shi* (Kanbara: Kanbara chō shi hensan iinkai, 1968), 499.

67. Members of outcaste communities were first permitted to be engaged in farming in the late seventeenth century, and their numbers increased during the late eighteenth and the early nineteenth century for political and social reasons. For more on the subject, see Harada Tomohiko, *Hisabetsu-buraku no rekishi* (1975; repr., Tokyo: Asahi shibunsha, 1990), 133–34.

68. Indeed, dyers (*konya*) had often been considered outcastes until the Sengoku period (1467–1603). Although they were not assigned outcaste status in the Tokugawa period, prejudice against those engaged in handwork persisted well into the Meiji period. See Kobayashi Shigeru, Haga Noboru, Miura Keiichi, et al., *Buraku-shi yōgo jiten* (Tokyo: Kashiwa shobō, 1985), 106; Harada, *Hisabetsu-buraku no rekishi*, 73–74, 77–78, 102, 117–18.

69. Kudō, *Kanada yūgirō ni furu yuki wa*, 204.

70. Statement of Kotaro Ohashi in front of Inspector F. N. Steele, June 9, 1908, JFMAD, 4.2.2.27, vol. 2.

71. Statement of Fusa Ohashi in front of Inspector F. N. Steele, June 9, 1908, JFMAD, 4.2.2.27, vol. 2.

72. Mikiso Hane, *Peasants, Rebels, and Outcasts: The Underside of Modern Japan* (New York: Pantheon, 1982), 31–32.

73. Konosuke Odaka, "Redundancy Utilized: The Economics of Female Domestic Servants in Pre-war Japan," in *Historical Demography and Labor Markets in Prewar Japan*, ed. Michael Smitka (New York: Routledge, 1998), 3:146. As Shimizu Michiko writes, however, there were actually many kinds of domestic servants in large households. See Shimizu Michiko, *"Jochū" imeeji no katei bunka-shi* (Tokyo: Sekai shisō-sha, 2004), 25–28.

74. Murakami Nobuhiko, *Meiij josei-shi* (Tokyo: Kōdansha bunko, 1977), 3:89–90. For more on changes in the image of female servants in the Meiji and the Taisho periods, see Shimizu, *"Jochū" imeeji no katei bunka-shi*, parts 1–2.

75. Murakami, *Meiij josei-shi*, 3:90–91, 94.

76. Statement of Ueda Tomi, in the office of the Yokohama Harbor Police, June 28, 1909, JFMAD, 4.2.2.27, vol. 3.

77. Sasaki Toshiji, *Nihonjin kanada iminshi* (Tokyo: Fuji shuppan, 1999), 105, 108; Kodama Masaaki, *Nihon iminshi kenkyū josetsu* (Hiroshima: Keiseisha, 1992), 457–62, 517–25.

78. Kodama Masaaki, *Nihon iminshi kenkyū josetsu*, 473.

79. For instance, see Josef J. Barton, *Peasants and Strangers: Italians, Rumanians, and Slovaks in an American City, 1890–1950* (Cambridge,

Mass.: Harvard University Press, 1975), chap. 2; Virginia Yans-McLaughlin, *Family and Community: Italian Immigrants in Buffalo, 1880–1930* (Urbana: University of Illinois Press, 1982), 34–35.

80. Kodama Masaaki, *Nihon iminshi kenkyū josetsu*, 65–74, 436–38, 444–45; Michiko Midge Ayukawa, *Hiroshima Immigrants in Canada, 1891–1941* (Vancouver: University of British Columbia Press, 2008), 5, 7–9.

81. Kodama Masaaki, *Nihon iminshi kenkyū josetsu*, 485.

82. Ayukawa, *Hiroshima Immigrants in Canada*, 5, 9–10.

83. Kodama Masaaki, *Nihon iminshi kenkyū josetsu*, 448–50.

84. This analysis draws on statistical yearbooks compiled by each prefecture for the year 1900. If a prefecture had no data for 1900, I used any available data from the period between 1898 and 1901. In total, I could get the data from twenty-seven prefectures.

85. Hirozane Takashi, Masagami Yasunori, and Kaga Hideyuki, "Hiroshima-ken wo chūshin to shita sangyō hatten no rekishi," *Keizai chōsa tōkei geppō* 393 (April 2007): 2–4, 8–12, 15, 20–21; Furumaya Tadao, *Ura nihon* (Tokyo: Iwanami shoten, 1997), 43; Saitō Gunpachirō, *Dainihon teikoku shōgyō chishi* (Kyoto: Wakabayashi Seikichi, 1895), 339–43.

86. Aoki Hideo, "Kindai to toshi buraku: Hiroshima-shi A-machi wo jirei to shite," *Buraku kaihō kenkyū* 3 (1997): 56–77.

87. Report of Vancouver Consul Nosse Tatsugorō, August 30, 1895, JFMAD, 3.8.8.4, vol. 2.

88. A letter from an anonymous resident in the United States addressed to the Hiroshima prefectural police, no date, JFMAD, 3.8.8.4, vol. 4.

89. According to a local history published by Hiroshima Prefecture in 1921, the county of Takata, where the village of Yoshida was located, included the largest number of former outcaste communities (*buraku*) among sixteen counties in Hiroshima Prefecture. Yoshida had the fifth-largest number of former outcastes among the thirty-eight villages in the county. See Hiroshima ken, *Hiroshima ken-shi* (Tokyo: Teikoku chihō gyōsei gakkai, 1921), 1:102–3.

90. *Shin sekai*, May 17, 1908, 3.

91. Kikuyo Zendō is the main protagonist of Imamura Shōhei's documentary film *Karayuki-san* (Imamura Productions, 1973). After the production, Imamura wrote to the town hall in Zendō's native village, and subsequent media coverage of Zendō moved the Hiroshima Prefectural Office and the Foreign Ministry to permit her to repatriate to Japan in May 1973. In this process, the Hiroshima chapter of the Buraku Liberation League played a key role. See Ōba Noboru, *Karayuki-san Okiku no shōgai* (Tokyo: Akashi shoten, 2001), chap. 7.

92. Ōba Noboru, *Karayuki-san Okiku no shōgai*, chaps. 1 and 2; James Francis Warren, *Ah Ku and Karayuki-san: Prostitution in Singapore, 1870–1940* (Singapore: Oxford University Press, 1993), 187, 208, 329.

93. Murakami, *Meiji josei-shi*, 3:189–210; Tsurumi, *Factory Girls*, 132–47.

94. Kodama Masaaki, *Nihon iminshi kenkyū josetsu*, 485.

CHAPTER 3. RECRUITMENT AND PASSAGE

1. *Shin sekai,* September 8, 1931; cited and translated by Yuji Ichioka in his *"Ameyuki-san*: Japanese Prostitutes in Nineteenth-Century America," *Amerasia Journal* 4:1 (1977): 7, n19.

2. Yamada Waka, "Watashi to shūi," *Seitō* 6:1 (January 1916): 108–9, translated in Tomoko Yamazaki, *The Story of Yamada Waka: From Prostitute to Feminist Pioneer,* trans. Wakako Hironaka and Ann Kostant (Tokyo: Kodansha International, 1985), 76.

3. The letter of Fumi Naito, the U.S. District Court's charge against Mukai, and the verdict were parts of a case file, "The United States vs. Y. Mukai alias John Doe," from November to December 1904, United States District Court, Seattle, case no. 2869, RG 21, NARA, Seattle, Washington.

4. "The United States vs. John Doe Naito," December 1904, case no. 2868, United States District Court, Seattle, RG 21, NARA, Seattle, Washington.

5. Transcription of an interrogation of Sumi Teshima, in case file no. 15086, "In the Matter of Sumi Teshima," Circuit Court of the United States, Northern District of California, September 17, 1910, RG21, NARA, San Bruno, California.

6. Lucie Cheng, "Free, Indentured, Enslaved: Chinese Prostitutes in Nineteenth-Century America," in *Labor Immigration under Capitalism,* ed. Lucie Cheng and Edna Bonacich (Berkeley: University of California Press, 1984), 407, 408.

7. *Tairiku nippō,* December 22, 1908, 5. The story of Omatsu appeared in Osada Shōhei, *Kanada no makutsu* (Vancouver: Tairiku nippō sha, 1909), 93–94. It suggests that the author of the article was Osada who conducted a survey on Japanese prostitution in Canada in 1908–9.

8. Ishiwata Takako, "Zasshi *Jogaku sekai* ni miru josei-tachi no kyaria dezain: Meiji kōki wo chūshin to shite," *Ōbirin ronkō, shinri kyōiku kenkyū* 2 (March 2013): 26, 30–32, 34–38.

9. *Shin sekai,* January 23, 1911, 5, and April 6–8, 1911, 3.

10. Yuji Ichioka, *The Issei: The World of the First Generation Japanese Immigrants, 1885–1924* (New York: The Free Press, 1988), 11. On Japanese socialists and labor activists in the United States during the Meiji period, see Josephine Fowler, *Japanese and Chinese Immigrant Activists: Organizing in American and International Communist Movements, 1919–1933* (New Brunswick: Rutgers University Press, 2007).

11. In 1891, when Secretary Fujita Toshirō visited Seattle, he found that about half of the local Japanese prostitutes were working on "long-term contracts" *(nenki bōkō).* See Report of Secretary Fujita Toshirō, JFMAD, 3.8.2.12, vol. 1.

12. For instance, see *Seattle Post-Intelligencer,* March 26, 1892, 3.

13. Report of Shiga Prefecture Governor Kawashima Junki, March 5, 1906, JFMAD, 3.8.5.21, vol. 3. Section 5 of the Regulations for Protecting Immigrants and Detailed Regulations of 1894 required immigration agents to receive licenses from the government, and Section 18 said that violators would be fined. The Immigrant Protection Law of 1896 confirmed

this regulation. Gaimushō, *Imin hogo kisoku oyobi shikō saisoku* (Tokyo: Gaimushō tsūshō-kyoku, 1894); Gaimushō, *Imin hogohō oyobi shikō saisoku* (Tokyo: Gaimushō tsūshō-kyoku, 1896), 2, 5.

14. Murakami Nobuhiko. *Meiji joseishi* (Tokyo: Kōdansha bunko, 1977), 2:337–41.

15. Petra Schmidt, "Law of Succession," in *History of Law in Japan since 1868*, ed. Wilhelm Röhl (Leiden: Brill, 2005), 325; Murakami, *Meiji joseishi*, 2:336–37.

16. "The United States vs. O. Yamamoto," case no. 4026, United States District Court, Northern District of California, October–December 1902, RG 21, NARA, San Bruno, California; *San Francisco Call*, July 24, 1902, 9, and December 12, 1902, 8; *San Francisco Chronicle*, December 12, 1902, 7, and October 22, 1909, 9.

17. Osada, *Kanada no makutsu*, 25–26.

18. Lucie Cheng, "Chinese Immigrant Women in Nineteenth-Century California," in *Women and Power in American History, vol. 1, To 1880*, ed. Kathryn Kish Sklar and Thomas Dublin, 2nd ed. (Upper Saddle River, N.J.: Prentice Hall, 2002), 245–46; Cheng, "Free, Indentured, Enslaved," 412–13.

19. Report of Kanagawa Prefecture Governor Nakano Takeaki, May 23, 1894, JFMAD, 3.8.8.4, vol. 2, and July 6, 1895, JFMAD, 4.2.2.95.

20. On Japanese women hired by or sold to Chinese residents in Yokohama, see "Yokohama no fusei fujin," *Tōkyō fujin kyōfū zasshi* 1 (November 1893): 44–45; *Yokohama mainichi shinbun*, May 12, 1892, 2.

21. Report of Kanagawa Prefecture Governor Oki Morikata, April 27, 1882, JFMAD, 4.2.2.10, vol. 1. This practice obviously continued into the early twentieth century. In 1904, Hyogo Prefecture Governor Hattori Ichizō informed the foreign minister that in Kobe, Chinese men were purchasing Japanese girls under the pretext of "adopting" them into their families. See Report of Hyogo Prefecture Governor Hattori Ichizō, January 19, 1904, in JFMAD, 4.2.2.10, vol. 2.

22. *Asahi shinbun*, November 21, 1894, 3, and March 10, 1899, 5.

23. Ichioka, *"Ameyuki-san,"* 3–4; Itō Kazuo, *Hokubei hyakunen-zakura* (1969; repr., Tokyo: Nichieki shuppan sha, 1973), 887; William M. Mason and John A. Mckinstry, *The Japanese of Los Angeles* (Los Angeles: Los Angeles County Museum of Natural History, 1969), 8; *Sacramento Daily Union*, October 7, 1885, 2, and February 25, 1886, 4; *San Francisco Daily Alta California*, February 24, 1886, 2, March 5, 1886, 2, and September 4, 1887, 1.

24. Ichioka, *"Ameyuki-san,"* 2–3.

25. See *Asahi shinbun*, November 21, 1894, 3; April 15, 1897, 3; August 7, 1897, 4; March 10, 1899, 5; March 12, 1899, 5; May 6, 1899, 5; November 27, 1899; December 1, 1899, 1; June 20, 1900, 5; and July 8, 1900, 5.

26. Miyamoto Natsuki, "Keiyaku imin jidai no honoruru nihonjin shakai to nihonjin baishunfu," *Hikaku shakai bunka kenkyū* 12 (2002): 51.

27. Letter of Vancouver Consul Nosse Tatsugorō, August 30, 1895, JFMAD, 3.8.8.4, vol. 2.

28. See Report of Wakayama Prefecture Governor Kiyosu Ienori, April 15, 1905, JFMAD, 4.2.2.27, vol. 1; Report of Shizuoka Prefecture Governor Yamada Shunzō, December 28, 1906, JFMAD, 3.8.5.21, vol. 3.

29. Ninette Kelley and Michael Trebilcock, *The Making of the Mosaic: A History of Canadian Immigration Policy* (Toronto: University of Toronto Press, 2010), 63–64.

30. Barbara Roberts, *Whence They Came: Deportation from Canada, 1900–1935* (Ottawa: University of Ottawa Press, 1988), 54–57.

31. The act of 1906 defined an excludable person more clearly as a person "who is feeble-minded, an idiot, or an epileptic" or is "deaf and dumb, blind, or infirm" (sec. 26); one "afflicted with a loathsome disease or with a disease which is contagious or infectious and which may become dangerous to the public health or widely disseminated" (sec. 27); a person "who is a pauper, or destitute, or professional beggar, or vagrant, or who is likely to become a public charge" (sec. 28); one "who has been convicted of a crime involving moral turpitude, or who is a prostitute, or who procures or brings or attempts to bring into Canada, prostitutes or women for purposes of prostitution" (sec. 29). Sections 26–29, Immigration Act of 1906, printed in Immigration Commission, *The Immigration Situation in Canada* (Washington, D.C.: Government Printing Office, 1910), 41–42, IA. The act of 1910 added "persons who procure or attempt to bring into Canada prostitutes or women or girls for the purpose of prostitution or other immoral purpose" as excludable persons. Section 3, Immigration Act of 1910, printed in *An Act Respecting Immigration* (Ottawa: C. H. Parmelee, 1910), 5, available at *Early Canadiana Online*, http://eco.canadiana.ca/view/oocihm.9_07184/5?r=0&s=1 (accessed February 5, 2015).

32. From Acting Immigration Officer for British Columbia W. H. Bullock-Webster to Attorney General Charles Wilson, K.C., July 1, 1907, GR0429, Box 11, File 3, Folio 2152/04, BC Archives, Victoria, British Columbia; *Victoria Daily Colonist*, July 1, 1904, 7.

33. From W. H. Bullock-Webster to Hon. K. Morikawa, H.I.J.M. Consul, Vancouver, July 1, 1904, GR0429, Box 11, File 3, Folio 2152/04, BC Archives.

34. For a series of bills aimed at restricting the entry and business activities of Japanese migrants in Canada between 1898 and 1907, see Iino Masako, *Nikkei kanadajin no rekishi* (Tokyo: Tokyo daigaku shuppan kai), 21; Andrea Geiger, *Subverting Exclusion: Transpacific Encounters with Race, Caste, and Borders, 1885–1928* (New Haven: Yale University Press, 2011), 100–104.

35. Kelley and Trebilcock, *The Making of the Mosaic*, 161; Mae Ngai, *Impossible Subjects: Illegal Aliens and the Making of Modern America* (Princeton: Princeton University Press, 2004), 267.

36. Patricia Roy, *A White Man's Province: British Columbia Politicians and Chinese and Japanese Immigrants, 1858–1914* (Vancouver: University of British Columbia Press), 146.

37. Irene Bloemraad, *Becoming a Citizen: Incorporating Immigrants and Refugees in the United States and Canada* (Berkeley: University of California Press, 2006), 23; Kelley and Trebilcock, *The Making of the Mosaic*, 162–63.

38. As early as 1900, a little more than 1,000 Japanese residents in Canada had received naturalization certificates. Roy, *A White Man's Province*, 146. By World War II, about 16 percent of Japanese immigrants had acquired Canadian citizenship. Greg Robinson, *A Tragedy of Democracy: Japanese Confinement in North America* (New York: Columbia University Press, 2009), 11.

39. For instance, Ueda Torajirō, a major procurer, married a woman in 1888, later became a naturalized Canadian citizen, and had remarried twice by 1905. He brought his wife over each time he married, but as it gradually became difficult, when he married his fourth wife, he sent his naturalization paper to his wife and made her carry it when migrating to Canada. After her arrival, an immigration official discovered that he had not followed proper procedures to divorce his previous wife and get a naturalization paper, and Vancouver consul Yada sent Ueda and his "wife" back to Japan. Report of Vancouver Consul Yada Chōnosuke, June 16, 1909, JFMAD, 4.2.2.27, vol. 3.

40. Edward P. Hutchinson, *Legislative History of American Immigration Policy, 1798–1965* (Philadelphia: University of Pennsylvania Press, 1981), 96–97, 101, 103.

41. Erika Lee, *At America's Gates: Chinese Immigration during the Exclusion Era, 1882–1943* (Chapel Hill: University of North Carolina Press, 2003), 151, 171; Yukari Takai, "Asian Migrants, Exclusionary Laws, and Transborder Migration in North America, 1880–1940," *OAH Magazine of History* 23:4 (October 2009): 35–38; Kornel Chang, *Pacific Connections: The Making of the U.S.-Canadian Borderlands* (Berkeley: University of California Press, 2012), chap. 2.

42. Takai, "Asian Migrants," 35–42; Geiger, *Subverting Exclusion*, chap. 5. On Chinese illegal migration to the United States via Canada, see Lee, *At America's Gates*, 152–57. The executive order referred to in this paragraph is Executive Order no. 589, issued on March 14, 1907. See Roger Daniels, *The Politics of Prejudice: The Anti-Japanese Movement in California and the Struggle for Japanese Exclusion* (1962; repr., Berkeley: University of California Press, 1977), 43–44.

43. Report of Seattle Consul Hayashi Sotokichi, August 15, 1901, JFMAD, 4.1.4.34; "Okawara, Tomikichi," case no. 2032, District Court of the United States, District of Washington, Northern Division, June–August 1901, RG21, NARA, Seattle; "Okawara dan no hanzai," *Fujin shinpō* 53 (September 1901): 324.

44. *San Francisco Chronicle*, June 18, 1904, 3.

45. Report of Vancouver Consul Morikawa Kishirō, April 16, 1906, JFMAD, 4.2.2.27, vol. 2.

46. By treaty, U.S. officials were permitted to examine migrants bound for the United States at Canadian ports. The U.S. government had also made a steamship company responsible for sending passengers to their countries of origin at the company's expense if they were refused entry. For more on the implications of these legal policies for Japanese migration via Canada, see Geiger, *Subverting Exclusion*, 112–14; Takai, "Asian Migrants," 38.

47. Lee, *At America's Gates*, 165–79; Takai, "Asian Migrants," 39.

48. William H. Siener, "Through the Back Door: Evading the Chinese Exclusion Act along the Niagara Frontier, 1900 to 1924," *Journal of American Ethnic History* 27:4 (2008): 42–56; Chang, *Pacific Connections*, chap. 2; Lee, *At America's Gates*, 2, 45–46, 152–57.

49. Various pieces of evidence indicate that this migration of Japanese prostitutes and procurers via Canada increased around 1890, especially after 1891, when the arrival of Japanese prostitutes in San Francisco caused a great stir. In Seattle, three cases involving the importation of Japanese prostitutes via British Columbia reached the U.S. District Court in 1896, 1901, and 1903. See case nos. 1015, 2032, and 2868, District of Washington, United States District Court, RG21, NARA, Seattle. Japanese men were also indicted for bribing immigration officials or attempting to import Japanese contract laborers from Canada from 1899 to 1901. See case nos. 1496, 1795, 1796, and 1955 in the same record group.

50. The Page Act referred to here is the Immigration Act of March 3, 1875 (18 Stat. 477). On the provisions, see Hutchinson, *Legislative History of American Immigration Policy*, 65–66.

51. Report of Tacoma Deputy-Consul Saitō Miki, May–June 1896, JFMAD, 3.8.8.4, vol. 2; case no. 1015, June 27, 1896, United States District Court, Seattle, Washington, RG 21, NARA, Seattle; *Seattle Post-Intelligencer*, May 14, 1896, 5, June 6, 1896, 5, June 10, 1896, 5, June 11, 1896, 5, June 12, 1896, 5, June 19, 1896, 5, and June 26, 1896, 1.

52. Roger Daniels, *Asian America: Chinese and Japanese in the United States since 1850* (Seattle: University of Washington Press, 1988), 110.

53. For seaboard states' attempts to control immigration motivated by antebellum European nativism and concerns about the cost of maintaining indigents since the seventeenth century, see Hutchinson, *Legislative History of American Immigration Policy*, 390–93, 397–400, 403; Ngai, *Impossible Subjects*, 58; Hidetaka Hirota, "The Moment of Transition: State Officials, the Federal Government, and the Formation of American Immigration Policy," *Journal of American History* 99:4 (2013): 1092–97. On Chinese exclusion and its significance, see Lucy E. Salyer, *Laws Harsh as Tigers: Chinese Immigrants and the Shaping of Modern Immigration Law* (Chapel Hill: University of North Carolina Press, 1995), 2, 7, 17; Lee, *At America's Gates*, 4, 6, 7, 8, 24–25, 40–43, 246. In 1882, the government enacted an immigration act to levy a tax on immigrants and banned the entry of "any convicts, lunatic, or any person unable to take care of himself or herself without becoming public charges." The 1885 act had outlawed the importation of contract laborers. The 1891 act established a one-year deportation period for those who became public charges after their entry into the country, requiring shipowners to send the indigents to their ports of origin at the companies' expense. See Hutchinson, *Legislative History of American Immigration Policy*, 79–80, 88–89, 102–3.

54. This case was first discussed by Yuji Ichioka in *"Ameyuki-san,"* 5–6, 19. For more on this case, see case file nos. 9175 and 9176, District Court of the United States, Northern District of California, March 1890, RG21, NARA, San Bruno, California; *San Francisco Examiner*, February 18, 1891, 3.

55. Case file nos. 11292–95, Circuit Court of the United States, Northern District of California, May 1891, RG21, NARA, San Bruno, California; *San Francisco Chronicle*, May 14, 1891, 7; March 17, 1892, 10; *San Francisco Bulletin*, May 14 and 15, 1891, 1. Also see Ichioka, "*Ameyuki-san*," 5–6, 11–12. A similar habeas corpus case was filed in Portland in 1892. See *Seattle Post-Intelligencer*, November 29, 1892, 5, and November 30, 1892, 5; case no. 582, District Court of the United States, Division of Washington, Northern Province, November 1892, RG 21, NARA, Seattle.

56. For more on the proceedings, see Charles J. McClain, *In Search of Equality: The Chinese Struggle against Discrimination in Nineteenth-Century America* (Berkeley: University of California Press, 1994), 54–63; Otis Gibson, *The Chinese in America* (Cincinnati: Hitchcock and Walden, 1877), 146–55.

57. Cheng, "Free, Indentured, Enslaved," 409.

58. Lee, *At America's Gates*, 92.

59. Norbert MacDonald, *Distant Neighbors: A Comparative History of Seattle and Vancouver* (Lincoln: University of Nebraska Press, 1987), 47–49, 53; Richard C. Berner, *Seattle, 1900–1920: From Boomtown, Urban Turbulence, to Restoration* (Seattle: Charles Press, 1991), 22.

60. Jef Rettmann, "Business, Government, and Prostitution in Spokane, Washington, 1889–1910," *Pacific Northwest Quarterly* 89:2 (1998): 77–83.

61. Kathryn Brandenfels, "Down on the Sawdust: Prostitution & Vice Control in Seattle, 1870–1920," M.A. thesis, Hampshire College, 1981, 29.

62. "The City of Seattle vs. Mabo—a Japanese," May 2, 1892, Criminal Case No. 552, King County Superior Court, Seattle, Washington; *The Criminal Index, 1899–1923*, King County Superior Court, Seattle, Washington.

63. Report of Secretary Fujita Toshirō, July 30, 1891, JFMAD, 3.8.2.12, vol. 1.

64. Report of Seattle Consul Abe Kihachi, September 26, 1910, JFMAD, 4.2.2.99.

65. Jacqueline Baker Barnhart, *The Fair but Frail: Prostitution in San Francisco, 1849–1900* (Reno: University of Nevada Press, 1986), 73–77.

66. Cheng, "Free, Indentured, Enslaved," 414–15.

67. John A. Eagle, *The Canadian Pacific Railway and the Development of Western Canada, 1896–1914* (Kingston, ON: McGill-Queen's University Press, 1989), 23–26.

68. For an overview of prostitution in the Kootenays, see Charleen P. Smith, "Boomtown Brothels in the Kootenays, 1895–1905," in *People and Place: Historical Influences on Legal Culture*, ed. Jonathan Swainger and Constance Backhouse (Vancouver: University of British Columbia Press, 2003), 120–52.

69. Report of Vancouver Consul Nosse Tatsugorō, July 5, 1898, JFMAD, 4.2.2.99; Report of Vancouver Consul Shimizu Seizaburō, July 5, 1899, JFMAD, 4.2.2.99.

70. *Taihoku nippō*, March 11, 1919, 8, and March 12, 1919, 8; *Tairiku nippō*, March 9, 1920, 7.

71. *Criminal Code, 1892* (Ottawa: Samuel Edward Dawson, 1892), secs. 181–85, 81–82; John P. S. McLaren, "Chasing the Social Evil: Moral Fervour and the Evolution of Canada's Prostitution Laws, 1867–1917," *Canadian Journal of Law and Society* 1 (1986): 130–36; Lesley Erickson, *Westward Bound: Sex, Violence, the Law, and the Making of a Settler Society* (Vancouver: University of British Columbia Press, 2011), 85.

72. *Nelson Miner*, August 22, 1896, 1.

73. In 1911, the total population was 392,480 in British Columbia and 374,295 in Alberta. In 1910, there were 1,141,990 people living in Washington and 672,765 in Oregon. *Census of Canada, 1921*, vol. 1, population (Ottawa: F. A. Acland, Printer, 1924–27), 355; Department of Commerce, Bureau of Census, *Thirteenth Census of the United States Taken in the Year 1910*, vol. 1, *Population* (Washington, D.C.: Department of Commerce, Bureau of the Census, 1913), 30; McLaren, "Chasing the Social Evil," 42, 47; James H. Gray, *Red Lights on the Prairies* (Saskatoon, SK: Fifth House Ltd., 1995); Erickson, *Westward Bound*, 96.

74. Osada, *Kanada no makutsu*, 38.

75. Report of San Francisco Consulate's Deputy Clerk Yokota Saburō, October 16, 1900, JFMAD, 4.2.2.27, vol. 1; *San Francisco Chronicle*, October 16, 1900, and November 13, 1900, 14.

76. Report of Yamamoto Yukiyoshi, May 4, 1906, JFMAD, 4.2.2.27, vol. 2.

77. Report of Seattle Consul Hisamizu Saburō, May 25, 1901, JFMAD, 4.2.2.27, vol. 2.

78. On the brief history of the company, see Takeuchi Kōjirō, *Beikoku seihokubu nihonjin iiminshi* (Seattle: Taihoku nippōsha, 1929), 292.

79. Cheng, "Free, Indentured, Enslaved," 409.

80. Exhibit 15, "Statement of Tadasaburo Umeda, of Seattle, Washington, before Immigrant Inspector Charles L. Babcock of Washington, D.C.," October 25, 1907, in Case File 51701/2A, Investigation of A. H. Geffeney (I.S.), 1907, September–October 1907, *Records of the Immigration and Naturalization Service, Series A: Subject Correspondence Files, Part 5: Prostitution and "White Slavery," 1902–1903*, ed. Alan Kraut (Bethesda, Md.: University Publications of America, 1996), Reel 1. These reels will be cited as RINS reels hereafter.

81. Takeuchi, *Beikoku seihokubu*, 40–43, 566.

82. See *Asahi shinbun*, December 21, 1903, 3.

83. Takeuchi, *Beikoku seihokubu*, 24.

84. A translation of the diary of the procurer, submitted as exhibit 17, in the investigation of A. H. Geffeney in 1907. This letter served as key evidence against Geffeney in the corruption charge. See case file 51701/2, September–October 1907, RINS reel 1; *Seattle Star*, January 10, 1908, 1.

85. Translation by U. G. Murphy, a Methodist minister, who worked in Nagoya, cited in his book *The Social Evil in Japan and Allied Subjects* (Tokyo: Methodist Publishing House, 1908), 26–27.

86. *The Dillingham Commission Reports, Volume 37, Part II: Importation of Women for Immoral Purposes* (Washington, D.C.: Government

Printing Office, 1911), 108–9; for Japanese versions of the two letters, see *Shin sekai*, December 16, 1909, 3.

87. The original Japanese expression for the quoted part is *hai kara sug-ata*, which literally means "wearing a high collar." A high collar was considered "stylish" clothing, a symbol of Western fashion, in Japan at that time; therefore, the expression is translated here as "stylishly dressed in Western clothing." I thank a *Journal American Ethnic History* reviewer for pointing this out. *Shin sekai*, March 19, 1911, 3.

88. Kawaguchi's arrest was reported in articles in *Shin sekai*, March 18, 19, 26, and 27, 1911. *Asahi shinbun*, February 27, 1911, 5. A more detailed, but fictionalized, account of her life can be found in Hara Hiroshi, "Mikaduki Omatsu: Jinniku shijō no ōbosu," *Uramado* 2:2 (March 1957): 238–44.

CHAPTER 4. RACIALIZED, EXPLOITED, AND EXCLUDED

1. Yamazaki Tomoko, *Ameyuki-san no uta: Yamada Waka no sūki naru shōgai* (Tokyo: Bungei shunjū, 1978), 97–98; translated into English as *The Story of Yamada Waka: From Prostitute to Feminist Pioneer*, trans. Wakako Hironaka and Ann Kostant (Tokyo: Kodansha International, 1985).

2. Marion S. Goldman, *Gold Diggers, Silver Miners: Prostitution and Social Life on the Comstock Lode* (Ann Arbor: University of Michigan Press, 1981), 136–48. Similar sexual ideologies were shaping the character of societies in the Canadian West as well. See Lesley Erickson, *Westward Bound: Sex, Violence, the Law, and the Making of a Settler Society* (Vancouver: University of British Columbia Press, 2011), 83, 91.

3. Richard Berner, *Seattle 1900–1920: From Boomtown, Urban Turbulence, to Restoration* (Seattle: Charles Press, 1991), 57.

4. Account of Nellie Fife, superintendent of the Japanese Baptist Woman's Home, cited in Frances M. Schuyler, ed. and comp., *Japanese Women and Children in Seattle* (Chicago: Woman's American Baptist Home Mission Society, 1910), 17–18, courtesy of the Japanese Baptist Church of Seattle.

5. Okina Kyūin, *Okina kyūin zenshū*, vol. 2, *Waga isshō umi no kanata* (Toyama: Okina Kyūin zenshū kankō-kai, 1972), 146.

6. Quintard Taylor, *The Forging of a Black Community: Seattle's Central District from 1870 through the Civil Rights Era* (Seattle: University of Washington Press, 1994), 28.

7. Itō Kazuo, *Hokubei hyakunen-zakura* (1969; repr., Tokyo: Nichieki shuppan sha, 1973), 891; available in English as *Issei: A History of Japanese Immigrants in North America*, trans. Shin'ichiro Nakamura and Jean S. Gerald (Seattle: Japanese Community Service, 1973); Okina, *Okina Kyūin zenshū*, 2:146.

8. Jay Moynahan, *Butte's Sportin' Women, 1880–1920: The Famous Red Light District and a List of Over 1,200 Names* (Spokane: Chickadee Publishing, 2003), 20.

9. These figures come from Herbert Asbury, *The Barbary Coast: An Informal History of the San Francisco Underworld* (1933; repr., New York: Basic Books, 2008), 259.

10. Lucie Cheng, "Free, Indentured, Enslaved: Chinese Prostitutes in Nineteenth-Century America," in *Labor Immigration under Capitalism*, ed. Lucie Cheng and Edna Bonacich (Berkeley: University of California Press, 1984), 411; Judy Yung, *Unbound Feet: A Social History of Chinese Women in San Francisco* (Berkeley: University of California Press, 1995), 31–32; Jacqueline Baker Barnhart, *The Fair but Frail: Prostitution in San Francisco, 1849–1900* (Reno: University of Nevada Press, 1986), 49.

11. Report of San Francisco Consul Mutsu Kōkichi, August 11, 1898, JFMAD, 4.2.2.99; Okina, *Okina Kyūin zenshū*, 2:146; Itō Kazuo, *Hokubei hyakunen-zakura*, 891–92; Itō Kazuo, *Zoku hokubei hyakunen-zakura*, 268.

12. Yuji Ichioka, "*Ameyuki-san*: Japanese Prostitutes in Nineteenth-Century America," *Amerasia Journal* 4:1 (1977): 10.

13. For the reference to Chinese men meeting white prostitutes, see Yong Chen, *Chinese San Francisco, 1850–1943: A Trans-Pacific Community* (Stanford: Stanford University Press, 2000), 76. For the quote, see Ito, *Zoku hokubei hyakunen-zakura*, 176. In Butte, according to Jay Moynahan, "[m]any non-Chinese sportin' women would not sell their services to Chinese men, thus forcing these men to seek out Chinese women." See Moynahan, *Butte's Sportin' Women*, 20. But I must also note that reports of Japanese men meeting white prostitutes occasionally appeared in Japanese-language newspapers and memoirs; for instance, see *Rafu shinpō*, July 8, 1916, 3; Okina, *Okina Kyūin zenshū*, 2:147–49. The reason white men visited Asian brothels often had to do with the cheapness relative to the services of white women. Nayan Shah, *Contagious Divides: Epidemics and Race in San Francisco's Chinatown* (Berkeley: University of California Press, 2001), 86–87.

14. Barnhart, *The Fair but Frail*, 25–33; Mary Murphy, "The Private Lives of Public Women: Prostitution in Butte, Montana, 1878–1917," in *The Women's West*, ed. Susan Armitage and Elizabeth Jameson (Norman: University of Oklahoma Press, 1987), 194–95; Goldman, *Gold Diggers, Silver Miners*, 74–77.

15. Cheng, "Free, Indentured, Enslaved," 411. Marion Goldman found a similar hierarchy among Chinese prostitutes in Virginia City. Goldman, *Gold Diggers, Silver Miners*, 96.

16. Report of Deputy-Consul Mutsu Kōkichi, JFMAD, 4.2.2.99, August 11, 1898.

17. Andrea Geiger, *Subverting Exclusion: Transpacific Encounters with Race, Caste, and Borders, 1885–1928* (New Haven: Yale University Press, 2011), 76–78.

18. Yamada Waka, *Renai no shakaiteki igi* (1920; repr., Tokyo: Yumani shobō, 2000), 188.

19. *Seattle Post-Intelligencer*, April 19, 1891, 8; *Salt Lake Herald*, June 16, 1893, 8.

20. Jef Rettmann, "Business, Government, and Prostitution in Spokane, Washington, 1889–1910," *Pacific Northwest Quarterly*, 89 (1998), 79. On the discrepancy in the enforcement against prostitution in San Francisco, see Barnhart, *The Fair but Frail*, 47.

21. *Seattle Star*, December 16, 1909, 1.

22. *Seattle Post-Intelligencer*, February 24, 1893, 8.

23. *San Francisco Chronicle*, April 19, 1893, 6.

24. *Seattle Post-Intelligencer*, October 24, 1891, 1, December 5, 1891, 2, and March 23, 1890, 4; *San Francisco Chronicle*, February 19, 1891, 2.

25. *Seattle Times*, July 24, 1904, 3.

26. Yung, *Unbound Feet*, 32; *Seattle Post-Intelligencer*, December 12, 1901, 4.

27. Mary Murphy, "The Private Lives of Public Women," 129, 141; Debora Nilsen, "The 'Social Evil': Prostitution in Vancouver, 1900–1920," in *In Her Own Right: Selected Essays on Women's History in B.C.*, ed. Barbara Latham and Cathy Kess (Victoria, BC: Camosun College, 1980), 206; Goldman, *Gold Diggers, Silver Miners*, 15.

28. Goldman, *Gold Diggers, Silver Miners*, 159–61.

29. For the prevailing idea among the Canadian medical community that excessive sexual desires were harmful to human minds, see John P. S. McLaren, "Chasing the Social Evil: Moral Fervour and the Evolution of Canada's Prostitution Laws, 1867–1917," *Canadian Journal of Law and Society* 1 (1986): 144.

30. In 1892, the government built a station on Ellis Island where federal officials examined newly arrived immigrants. In the West, Asians were examined and taken into custody on Angel Island when they were found to be diseased. The Immigration Act of March 3, 1891 (26 Stat. 1084) prohibited the entry of "persons suffering from a loathsome or a dangerous contagious disease." The government provided specific medical grounds on which immigrants could be deported in the act of March 3, 1903 (32 Stat. 1213), adding "imbeciles," "feeble minded persons," and those with mental or physical defects in the act of February 20, 1907 (34 Stat. 898). For more on the subject, see Alan M. Kraut, *Silent Travelers: Germs, Genes, and the "Immigrant Menace"* (New York: Basic Books, 1994).

31. Immigration Commission, *The Immigration Situation in Canada* (Washington, D.C.: Government Printing Office, 1910), 41–42.

32. Shah, *Contagious Divides*, chaps. 1–5; Barnhart, *The Fair but Frail*, 47–58.

33. *Capital Journal*, September 2, 1893, 4.

34. On the similar rendition of Chinese, see Shah, *Contagious Divides*, 27.

35. Kraut, *Silent Travelers*, 83–91.

36. In British Columbia or the prairie regions of western Canada, Japanese prostitutes did not cause a stir, probably due to their small number; therefore, it is difficult to know how local white Canadians responded to Japanese prostitution. Except for occasional Victoria newspaper reports on the arrival of Japanese "slave girls" and procurers' attempts to transport them across the border or Winnipeg reformers' criticism of the Japanese for an increase in human trafficking, the Canadian press or reformers did not develop their discussions about morality, race, and diseases in their writings about Japanese prostitutes. This generalization is based on my reading of

articles on Japanese prostitution published in British Columbia, Alberta, and Saskatchewan from 1890 to 1910 through the following digitized newspaper collections (all accessed January 8, 2015): *The British Colonist, Online Edition: 1858–1920*, University of Victoria Libraries, http://www.british-colonist.ca/; *British Columbia Historical Newspapers*, University of British Columbia Libraries, http://historicalnewspapers.library.ubc.ca/; *Peel's Prairie Provinces*, University of Alberta Libraries, http://peel.library.ualberta.ca/index.html. See also Erickson, *Westward Bound*, 91.

37. Morita Korokurō, *Yankii: Ichimei, sekirara no beikoku* (Tokyo: Shiseidō, 1914), 73–75.

38. Gaimushō, *Nihon gaikō monjo, Taishōki, tsuiho*, vol. 2 (Tokyo: Gaimushō, 1972), 213; cited and translated by Yuji Ichioka in his "*Ameyuki-san*," 11.

39. Asbury, *The Barbary Coast*. Also see Yung, *Unbound Feet*, 315n44.

40. Mrs. E. A. Sturge, "What the Occidental Home is Doing for Japanese Girls," *WOBFM Annual Report*, 1899: 85, SFTS; cited in Ichioka, "*Ameyuki-san*," 11, 20.

41. For a description of a similar practice of displaying Japanese women in the show windows of brothels, see Report of Mutsu Kōkichi, August 11, 1898, JFMAD, 4.2.2.99.

42. Asbury, *The Barbary Coast*, 175. See also "San Francisco Items," *Sacramento Daily Union*, February 25, 1886, 4.

43. The male-female ratio among Chinese in the western states was 24:1 in 1890 and 14:1 in 1900. Department of Interior, Census Office, *Report on Population of the United States at the Eleventh Census: 1890*, part 1 (Washington, D.C.: Government Printing Office, 1895), 488; Department of Interior, Census Office, *Twelfth Census of the United States, Taken in the Year 1900*, vol. 1, *Population* (Washington, D.C.: Government Printing Office, 1901), 492; Cheng, "Free, Indentured, Enslaved," 421.

44. Yung, *Unbound Feet*, 32–33; Cheng, "Free, Indentured, Enslaved," 410, 422.

45. Patricia Roy, *A White Man's Province: British Columbia Politicians and Chinese and Japanese Immigrants, 1858–1914* (Vancouver: University of British Columbia Press), 17.

46. The figure comes from the average amount of money paid in the selling and buying of married women between husbands and masters. It will be discussed in detail later in this chapter.

47. Report of San Francisco Consul Mutsu Kōkichi, August 11, 1898, JFMAD, 4.2.2.99.

48. Joan S. Wang, "The Double Burdens of Immigrant Nationalism: The Relationship between Chinese and Japanese in the American West, 1880s–1920s," *Journal of American Ethnic History* 27:2 (2008): 33–34.

49. Osada Shōhei, *Kanada no makutsu* (Vancouver: Tairiku nippō sha, 1909), 27.

50. Hoshino Tokuji, *Ikyō no kyaku* (Tokyo: Keisei sha, 1903), 149–50.

51. Tengai Kikaku, pseud., *Hokubei musen ryokō* (Tokyo: Daigaku kan, 1906), 174–79.

52. While examining the diary of a Chinese migrant who patronized brothels in 1880, Yong Chen found the special importance the author attached to the word "rest" in describing his experience in brothels. The act of going to a brothel, Chen notes, needs to be understood not just as a means of satisfying his sexual desire but also as part of the relaxation the Chinese man sought after the day's work. See Chen, *Chinese San Francisco*, 76–77.

53. The following are only some of the sources that illuminate American perceptions of Asian-white marriages: *Seattle Post-Intelligencer*, September 22, 1895, 7; *Seattle Times*, February 19, 1903, 7, and March 25, 1903, 8. The marriage of Gunjiro Aoki to Helen Emery, the daughter of the archdeacon of the Episcopal diocese, made a stir in Seattle in 1909. See relevant articles that appeared in the *Seattle Times* from March 3, 1909, to April 10, 1909.

54. Sakaguchi Mitsuhiro, *Nihonjin amerika iminshi* (Tokyo: Fuji shuppan, 2001), 64–65.

55. Ishioka Hikoichi, ed., *Hokubei washinton shū eiryō koronbia shū nihonjin jijō* (Tokyo: Ishioka Hikoichi, 1907); for Washington State, see 32, 35–38.

56. Gaimushō, *Nihon gaikō monjo, Taishōki, tsuiho*, 2:202.

57. *Hokubei nenkan*, vol. 2 (1911) and vol. 6 (1915); cited in Sakaguchi, *Nihonjin amerika iminshi*, 71; Takeuchi Kōjirō, *Beikoku seihokubu nihonjini iminshi* (Seattle: Taihoku nippōsha, 1929), 648; *Tairiku nippō*, July 11, 1908, 2; *Kororado shinbun*, February 25, 1911, 9.

58. Report of Inspector F. N. Steele, August 10, 1908. This is part of the report of a file titled "On the deportation of Kubo Yozo," in JFMAD, 3.8.8.6, vol. 2.

59. *The Dillingham Commission Reports*, Vol. 23, *Immigrants in Industries*, Part 25: *Japanese and Other Immigrant Races in the Pacific and Rocky Mountain States* (Washington, D.C.: Government Printing Office, 1911), 285.

60. Ichioka, "*Ameyuki-san*," 10–11.

61. The laws referred to here are the revised act of February 20, 1907 (34 Stat. 898), the act of March 26, 1910 (36 Stat. 929), and the act of June 25, 1910 (36 Stat. 269). In effect, they granted officials power to deport foreign women who practiced prostitution after entering the United States. On the details of each act, see Department of Commerce and Labor, Bureau of Immigration and Naturalization, *Immigration Laws and Regulations of July 1, 1907* (Washington, D.C.: Government Printing Office, 1910), 1–24, 81–87.

62. *Taihoku nippō*, January 23, 1911, 5; January 30, 1911, 5; and February 6, 1911, 5.

63. *Shin sekai*, March 12, 1915, 5.

64. Ibid., October 26, 1908, 7.

65. Ibid., January 14, 1911, 2.

66. Ibid., October 3, 1909, 8.

67. Department of Commerce, Bureau of Census, *Thirteenth Census of the United States Taken in the Year 1910*, vol. 1, *Population* (Washington, D.C.: Government Printing Office, 1913), 273.

68. Nagai Kafū, "Shakō no ichiya," *Bungei kurabu* 5 (May 1904): 195–99.

69. *Shin sekai*, December 28, 1911, 7.

70. *Tairiku nippō*, July 14, 1908, 5; July 15, 17, 20, 22, 5.

71. Itō Kazuo, *Hokubei hyakunen-zakura*, 954.

72. Itō Kazuo, *Zoku hokubei hyakunen-zakura*, 88.

73. Cited in Sakaguchi, *Nihonjin amerika iminshi*, 67–68.

74. On the feminization of Asian men and its implications for the empowerment of middle-class white women, see Gary Y. Okihiro, *Common Ground: Reimagining American History* (Princeton: Princeton University Press, 2001), 76.

75. Itō Kazuo, *Zoku hokubei hyakunen-zakura*, 99.

76. Ibid., 100.

77. To be more precise, there were 189.8 men to 100 women among the Japanese in 1920. See Department of Commerce, Bureau of Census, *Fourteenth Census of the United States Taken in the Year 1920*, vol. 2, *Population* (Washington, D.C.: Government Printing Office, 1922), 110.

78. Itō Kazuo, *Zoku hokubei hyakunen-zakura*, 107.

79. Nayan Shah, introduction to *Stranger Intimacy: Contesting Race, Sexuality and the Law in the North American West* (Berkeley: University of California Press, 2011), introduction.

80. For a remarkable example in this new type of study of early Asian immigrant communities, see Cecilia M. Tsu, *Garden of the World: Asian Immigrants and the Making of Agriculture in California's Santa Clara Valley* (New York: Oxford University Press, 2013), chap. 3.

81. Interrogation of Takasaki Aki in "The United States vs. John Doe Naito," December 1904, case no. 2868, United States District Court, Seattle, RG 21, NARA, Seattle, Washington. The dollar figure is shown in terms of commodity price. It means that $3–10 in 1904 is worth $81–270 in the price of goods and services sold and bought in the market today (2012). The amount is calculated by multiplying $3–10 by the annual percentage increase in the Consumer Price Index (3.21%) from 1904 to 2012. I used the calculator on the *MeasuringWorth.com* website created by a group of distinguished economists at major research universities in Britain and the United States, http://www.measuringworth.com/index.php (accessed May 3, 2014). Because Japanese sex workers sent money to Japan, we also have to take into account what these earnings meant in the Japanese context during the same period. In 1900, for instance, the average daily wage of farmhands in Japan was in the $0.1–0.25 range. Therefore, earnings of $3–10 a night would have been quite a large sum in Japan. Interrogation of Takasaki Aki in "The United States vs. John Doe Naito," December 1904, case no. 2868, United States District Court, Seattle, RG 21, NARA, Seattle, Washington.

82. Itō Kazuo, *Hokubei hyakunen-zakura*, 490.

83. Osada, *Kanada no makutsu*, 31.

84. Cheng, "Free, Indentured, Enslaved," 414.

85. Yasuo Wakatsuki, "Japanese Emigration to the United States, 1866–1924: A Monograph," *Perspectives in American History* 12 (1979): 449–50.

86. Anne M. Butler, *Daughters of Joy, Sisters of Misery: Prostitutes in the American West, 1865–90* (Urbana: University of Illinois Press, 1985), 55–61.

87. Cheng, "Free, Indentured, Enslaved," 406–7, 412–13.

88. Osada, *Kanada no makutsu*, 25–26.

89. Ibid., 36–37.

90. The data on a Japanese teacher's income come from *Nihon keizai tōkei sōran* (Tokyo, 1966); cited in Wakatsuki, "Japanese Emigration to the United States," 449–50. The salary of a domestic servant is based on the account of Takahashi Takechiyo, the wife of Takahashi Tetsuo, the president of the Oriental Trading Company, which appeared in the Japanese journal *Tobei shinpō*, July 1, 1907; cited in Sakaguchi, *Nihonjin amerika iminshi*, 63, 83n22.

91. The information about the amount of consolation money appears in *Shin sekai*, February 26, 1907; March 8, 1909, 6; September 19, 1910, 4; and February 2, 1911, 3.

92. Ibid., February 13, 1912, 3, and September 3, 1912, 3.

93. Cheng, "Free, Indentured, Enslaved," 412–13. Given the time lag, the market price of Chinese prostitutes and that of the Japanese were probably about the same.

94. *Asahi shinbun*, March 18, 1898, 4.

95. "In the goods of Kato Yasu, deceased," her will (copy), and "In the matter of the estate of Kato Yasu," March 1908, GR-2214, File S2/1908, BC Archives.

96. Osada, *Kanada no makutsu*, 14, 38–39.

97. Information on wages comes from W. Peter Ward, *White Canada Forever: Popular Attitudes and Public Policy toward Orientals in British Columbia* (1978; repr., Montreal and Kingston: McGill-Queen's University Press, 1990), 112.

98. Certainly, other independent prostitutes did not earn as much as Yasu did. For example, Hatsu (Lily) Hosokawa and Tomi (Irene) Takimoto died in Revelstoke on consecutive days in November 1918. Hatsu left one half of a lot (valued at $250) and furniture, personal items, and cash ($242.60 in total). Tomi left the other half of the lot (valued at $250) and furniture and cash ($100 in total). Obviously, they had lived and worked together. The absence of their will and the timing of their deaths suggest that they were murdered. "In the Matter of the Estate of Hatsu Hosokawa," November 23, 1918, GR-2219, Folio 53/1918, BC Archives; "In the Matter of the Estate of Tomi Takimoto," November 23, 1918, GR-2219, Folio 54/1918, BC Archives.

99. *The Dillingham Commission Reports*, Vol. 23, Part 25: 285.

100. *Ōfu nippō*, June 8–9, 1915, 2.

101. According to an immigrant in Seattle, the average monthly earnings of barmaids—including tips and salary—amounted to $100. In February 1913, the *Taihoku nippō* reported that a popular barmaid made as much as $120–130 a month. See Itō Kazuo, *Hokubei hyakunen-zakura*, 954; *Taihoku nippō*, February 25, 1913, 5.

102. Itō Kazuo, *Hokubei hyakunen-zakura*, 441–43.

103. *The Dillingham Commission Reports*, Vol. 37, Part 2: *Importation of Women for Immoral Purposes* (Washington, D.C.: Government Printing Office, 1911), 275, 283, 285.

104. *Nihonjin*, August 24, 1901, 3.

105. For example, see *Tairiku nippō*, May 16, 1908, 3; *Ōfu nippō*, October 20, 1910, 2; *Shin sekai*, January 25, 1914, 6.

106. Mary Murphy, "The Private Lives of Public Women," 198. On homosocial relationships that emerged in the workplace, see Ruth Rosen, *Lost Sisterhood: Prostitution in America, 1900–1918* (1982; repr., Baltimore: Johns Hopkins University Press, 1994), 104–7.

107. Okina Kyūin, *Okina kyūin zenshū*, 2:374; cited and translated in Ichioka, "Ameyuki-san," 10.

108. Itō Kazuo, *Hokubei hyakunen-zakura*, 888–89; Yamazaki, *Ameyuki-san no uta*, 97–98.

109. White prostitutes also turned to alcohol and drug to deal with hard realities. See Rosen, *Lost Sisterhood*, 98–99; Butler, *Daughters of Joy, Sisters of Misery*, 67–68.

110. Ichioka, "Ameyuki-san," 11–12; Itō Kazuo, *Hokubei hyakunen-zakura*, 396.

111. Hasegawa was operating a brothel in San Francisco but was listed as a boardinghouse-keeper in *San Francisco Directory Langley* (1890), San Francisco Public Library. Wakimoto, another brothel-keeper in San Francisco, was serving as a labor contractor for the Santa Fe Railway. See *San Francisco Chronicle*, June 26, 1894, 5; Yuji Ichioka, *The Issei: The World of the First Generation Japanese Immigrants, 1885–1924* (New York: The Free Press, 1988), 59.

112. Ichioka, "Ameyuki-san," 12. Furuya was listed simply as "Japanese goods at 303 Yesler av. res Yokohama, Japan" in *Seattle City Directories, 1891–1893*, published by R. L. Polk & Co., WSADA. On Furuya's relations with prostitutes and pimps, see Takeuchi, *Beikoku seihokubu*, 38–39; Fujioka Shirō, *Ayumi no ato: Hokubei tairiku nihonjin monogatari* (Los Angeles: Ayumi no ato kankō kōenkai, 1957), 277–80.

113. *Ōfu nippō*, January 5, 1908, 8, and January 7, 1908, 8.

114. Interrogation of Takasaki Haki.

115. Yamazaki, *Ameyuki-san no uta*, 96–97.

116. See "Kanashimu beki hōdō kaigai shūgyōsha no arisama," *Tōkyō fujin kyōfū zasshi* 48 (May 1892): 15.

117. Cheng, "Free, Indentured, Enslaved," 416.

118. *Seattle Post-Intelligencer*, December 20, 1892, 1; *Butte Anaconda Standard*, December 22, 1892, 5, and December 23, 1892, 5.

119. I learned from the Spokane County Court that it no longer holds the court record of this case.

120. Hearing of Ogawa Haru and report of Inspector J. H. Barbour, November 23, 1908, in File No. 52241/33, in *Records of the Immigration and Naturalization Service, Series A: Subject Correspondence Files*, Part 5: *Prostitution and "White Slavery," 1902–1903* (Bethesda, Md.: University Publications of America, 1996), reel 1.

121. Butler, *Daughters of Joy, Sisters of Misery*, 61, Goldman; *Gold Diggers, Silver Miners*, 114.

122. See the series of reports on this murder: *Seattle Post-Intelligencer*, May 31, 1899, 12, June 1, 1899, 5, June 10, 1899, 10, June 13, 1899, 6. See also *San Francisco Chronicle*, May 31, 1899, 3.

123. *Seattle Post-Intelligencer*, November 30, 1899, 12, and October 5, 1895, 2; *Los Angeles Herald*, January 24, 1894, 5; *Salt Lake Tribune*, April 22, 1905, 2.

124. *Los Angeles Herald*, April 6, 1892, 1; *Sacramento Record-Union*, February 25, 1897, 7.

125. Constable Upper, "Re murder of Jennie Kiohara at Revelstoke on 19th April, 1905," GR-0429, Folio No. 1403/05, BC Archives.

126. Cited in the context of her analysis in Geiger, *Subverting Exclusion*, 87.

127. Ibid., 79–80; Osada, *Kanada no makutsu*, 151–54.

128. Osada, *Kanada no makutsu*, 155–56.

129. See relevant articles in *Shin sekai*, September 18, 19, 27, 28, 1910. Also see *San Francisco Chronicle*, September 27, 1910, 3.

130. *Ōfu nippō*, August 31, 1907, 3.

131. *Shin sekai*, June 15, 1913, 9, and June 16, 1913, 7.

132. Fujioka, *Ayumi no ato*, 275.

133. Kudō Miyoko, *Kanashii metsuki no hyōryū sha* (Tokyo: Shūeisha, 1991), 195–204.

134. Asano Kōkichi, an immigrant who told an interviewee this story, observed that Kiyo starved to death because she stopped eating after losing all her money. But her registration of death says that the cause of her death was heart disease and pneumonia. "Registration of Death," no. 82-09-00626, Takahashi Kiyo, British Columbia Department of Health Division of Vital Statistics, BC Archives; Kudō, *Kanashii metsuki no hyōryū sha*, 202–4.

135. *Shin sekai*, December 8, 1910, 3.

136. Ibid., October 23, 1915, 3.

137. Information about women who had abortions appears in the following sources: Home, Record 3a., in Oriental Home and School Fonds, UCA; Report of Vancouver Consul Abe Kihachi, February 25, 1916, JFMAD 3.8.2.49, vol. 9, no. 2; *Shin sekai*, September 11, 1909, 5.

138. Osada, *Kanada no makutsu*, 56–57, 71–72, 145, 177–78, 183–84.

139. Studies of prostitution in western mining towns show that white prostitutes also had difficulty raising their children, although their responses varied. Some chose to raise their children in extremely difficult circumstances; others placed them in the care of other families or chose to kill them before or after birth. See Butler, *Daughters of Joy, Sisters of Misery*, 35–36; Goldman, *Gold Diggers, Silver Miners*, 128–29; Mary Murphy, "The Private Lives of Public Women," 197. Japanese barmaids' pregnancies were also occasionally reported in local newspapers. For example, see *Ōfu nippō*, March 7, 1911, 2.

140. Geiger, *Subverting Exclusion*, 80, 89.

141. Yokohama shinpō sha, *Yokohama hanjō ki* (Yokohama: Yokohama shinpō sha, 1903), 195–96.

142. Geiger, *Subverting Exclusion*, 80.

143. In Seattle, according to Bonni Cermak's study, it was only after World War I that the mayor ordered arrests of women suspected of being prostitutes and enforced compulsory medical examinations. See Bonni Cermak, "Closing the Open Town: Prostitution in Seattle, 1910–1920" (master's thesis, Western Washington University, 1997), 48. For an example of a report on the spread of venereal disease in the Japanese community, see *Shin sekai*, May 31, 1906, 5.

144. Exhibit 18, "Statement of Dr. Tatsemaru [*sic*] Uyematsu," October 27, 1907, in Case File 51701/2A, Investigation of A. H. Geffeney (I.S.), 1907, September–October 1907, RINS, reel 1.

145. Ichioka, *The Issei*, 90. For an example of such an advertisement, see *Shin sekai*, September 3, 1910, 8. Similarly, the Chinese immigrant press carried advertisements for curing venereal diseases, which suggests the spread of these diseases in the Chinese community. See Cheng, "Free, Indentured, Enslaved," 417.

146. *Shin sekai*, January 10, 1911, 5; July 5, 1911, 5; and December 24, 1912, 3.

147. Ibid., August 15, 1910, 3.

148. Ibid., May 31, 1906, 5.

149. Report of Kanagawa Prefecture Governor Sufu Kōhei, December 8, 1910, JFMAD, 3.8.8.6, vol. 2; Report of Kanagawa Prefecture Governor Ōshima Hisamitsu, October 2, 1913, JFMAD, 3.8.2.12, vol. 1.

150. Yamamoto Shun'ichi, *Nihon kōshōshi* (Tokyo: Chūō hōki shuppan, 1983), 389–90.

151. Ibid., 390.

152. Kusama Yasoo, *Tomoshibi no onna, yami no onna* (1937), in *Kindai kasō minshū seikatsu-shi* (Tokyo: Akashi shoten, 1987), 283.

153. Report of Seattle Consul Abe Kihachi, January 14, 1911, JFMAD, 3.8.8.6., vol. 2.

154. Rosen, *Lost Sisterhood*, chap. 8. See also a rare firsthand account of a sex worker that illuminates key issues in these women's lives: Maimie Pinzer, *The Maimie Papers*, ed. Ruth Rosen and Sue Davidson (Bloomington: Indiana University Press, 1985). Goldman, *Gold Diggers, Silver Miners*, 35–36; Butler, *Daughters of Joy, Sisters of Misery*, 16; Barnhart, *The Fair but Frail*, 59–63; Nilsen, "The 'Social Evil,'" 215–20; Charleen P. Smith, "Boomtown Brothels in the Kootenays, 1895–1905," in *People and Place: Historical Influences on Legal Culture*, ed. Jonathan Swainger and Constance Backhouse (Vancouver: University of British Columbia Press, 2003), 135–36; Erickson, *Westward Bound*, 105–6.

155. The 1900 Census, cited in Evelyn Nakano Glenn, *Issei, Nisei, and War Brides: Three Generations of Japanese American Women in Domestic Service* (Philadelphia: Temple University Press, 1986), 72–73. For more analysis of the labor market on the West Coast and Japanese immigrant women's work, see ibid., 68–79.

156. Yung, *Unbound Feet*, 26–27, 29.

157. *Ōfu nippō*, October 5, 1909, 2.

158. The hardship American returnees experienced can be linked to that faced by former sex workers in other Pacific regions. For instance, see Yamazaki Tomoko, *Sandakan hachiban shōkan: Teihen joseishi joshō* (1972; repr., Tokyo: Bungei shunjū, 1975), 132–36.

159. *Ōfu nippō*, June 27–29, 1912, 2.

160. *Tairiku nippō*, February 5, 1909, 5, and September 4, 1916, 5.

161. *Shin sekai*, September 3, 1909, 4.

162. Osada, *Kanada no makutsu*, 132–35.

163. Ibid., 136–45.

164. Butler, *Daughters of Joy, Sisters of Misery*, 41–43; Goldman, *Gold Diggers, Silver Miners*, 116–17; Murphy, "The Private Lives of Public Women," 198.

165. Goldman, *Gold Diggers, Silver Miners*, 117–19; Murphy, "The Private Lives of Public Women," 199. For the subculture of prostitution in the eastern parts of the country, see Rosen, *Lost Sisterhood*, 104–5, 163.

166. Takeuchi, *Beikoku seihokubu*, 496

167. Itō Kazuo, *Zoku hokubei hyakunen-zakura*, 268.

168. Itō Kazuo, *Hokubei hyakunen-zakura*, 900.

169. Ibid., 888.

170. Andrea Geiger writes that Japanese officials' sensitive reactions to the clothing of Japanese entertainers and laborers reflected both their status biases rooted in Tokugawa Japan and their concerns about the reputation of Japanese in the United States. See Geiger, *Subverting Exclusion*, 54–55.

171. Itō Kazuo, *Zoku hokubei hyakunen-zakura*, 67–68, Takeuchi, *Beikoku seihokubu*, 495–96.

172. *Taihoku nippō*, February 18, 1911, 5; Sakaguchi, *Nihonjin amerika iminshi*, 109.

173. *Taihoku nippō*, February 28, 1911, 5.

174. *Rafu shinpō*, November 26, 1916, 6.

175. Osada, *Kanada no makutsu*, 20–21. I thank Marlon Zhu for his help in translating the names of Chinese dishes that appear in Osada's account.

176. *Shin sekai*, January 1, 1911, 36.

177. Ibid., January 1, 1911, 36.

178. Ibid., January 1, 1911, 36.

179. Ibid., January 1, 1911, 36.

180. Itō Kazuo, *Zoku hokubei hyakunen-zakura*, 104.

181. Ibid., 107.

182. Ibid., 107, 108.

183. Yamazaki, *Ameyuki-san no uta*, 95–96.

184. For example, Takeuchi Kojirō, in his writing about the early history of the Japanese community in Seattle, clearly distinguished ordinary immigrant women from prostitutes. See Takeuchi, *Beikoku seihokubu*, 43.

185. In answer to questions concerning Japanese prostitution in Seattle at the turn of the century, Tamesa Uhachi observed: "Women in that business—men, too, for that matter—never revealed their names or told where they were born. A woman from Hiroshima would say she was from Osaka and one from Nagasaki might let on that she was from Kyoto. It was natural for

a person in such an occupation to try and hide his or her past." He added that that was the reason why these women used professional names when working as prostitutes and barmaids. See Yamazaki, *The Story of Yamada Waka*, 69.

CHAPTER 5. BREAKING THE SHACKLES OF OPPRESSION

1. Case 22201, March 1917, CSH; "Passenger and Crew Lists of Vessels Arriving at Seattle, WA, 1890–1957," "S.S. HAWAI MARU," April 25, 1916, IA.

2. Case 22201, March 1917, CSH.

3. Case 22201, March 1917, CSH.

4. *Taihoku nippō*, February 24, 1913, 5.

5. Ibid., February 25, 1913, 5.

6. Until 1968 divorce was rare in Canada, and the country maintained one of the lowest divorce rates in Western societies. To get a divorce, one had to either petition the Parliament in Ottawa or file a suit in provincial divorce courts (only British Columbia, Nova Scotia, and New Brunswick had divorce courts before World War I). It was too costly for working-class Canadians to file for divorce: $800–1,500 for Parliamentary divorces and $150–400 for contested divorces in the provincial court in 1911. The only acceptable grounds for divorce was adultery, and the petitioners were required to provide sufficient evidence for their claims. Politicians and Christian leaders harshly criticized divorce as a threat to the family and the nation. See Peter Ward, "Marriage and Divorce," in *The Canadian Encyclopedia,* edited by James H. Marsh, 2nd ed. (Edmonton, AB: Hurtig Publishers, 1988), 1309; Peter Ward, *Courtship, Love, and Marriage in Nineteenth-Century English Canada* (Montreal and Kingston: McGill-Queen's University Press, 1990), 37; James G. Snell, *In the Shadow of the Law: Divorce in Canada, 1900–1939* (Toronto: University of Toronto Press, 1991), chap. 1, 33, 51, 215. In 1916, for example, only eighteen couples were granted divorces in British Columbia, whereas a neighboring U.S. state, Washington, awarded divorces to almost 3,500 couples in the same year. See Snell, *In the Shadow of the Law,* 10–11; U.S. Bureau of the Census, *Marriage and Divorce, 1916, 1922–32* (Westport: Greenwood Press, 1978), 13.

7. Harald Fuess, *Divorce in Japan: Family, Gender, and the State, 1600–2000* (Stanford: Stanford University Press, 2004), 4, 6, 57–67, 82–91, 114–18, 127, 130, chap. 3.

8. *Tairiku nippō*, November 23, 1909, 1; November 24, 1909, 1; April 25, 1912, 1; December 8, 1916, 5.

9. Mary Murphy, "The Private Lives of Public Women: Prostitution in Butte, Montana, 1878–1917," in *The Women's West,* ed. Susan Armitage and Elizabeth Jameson (Norman: University of Oklahoma Press, 1987), 198. Historians of prostitution generally stress competition and fights rather than solidarity among prostitutes. See, for instance, Anne M. Butler, *Daughters of Joy, Sisters of Misery: Prostitutes in the American West, 1865–90* (Urbana: University of Illinois Press, 1985), 41–42; Marion S. Goldman,

Gold Diggers, Silver Miners: Prostitution and Social Life on the Comstock Lode (Ann Arbor: University of Michigan Press, 1981), 116–18. Others found evidence of homosocial relationships among prostitutes that emerged in the workplace. For example, see Ruth Rosen, *Lost Sisterhood: Prostitution in America, 1900–1918* (1982; repr., Baltimore: Johns Hopkins University Press, 1994), 104–7.

10. Immigration Commission, *Importing Women for Immoral Purposes* (Washington, D.C., 1909), 42–43, SUL; *Seattle Star*, November 27, 1909, 1.

11. The institution that housed Kiyo in Seattle appears as the "Protestant rescue mission" or the "Japanese Girls' home" in sources. Considering that Rev. Inoue and Miss Nellie Fife helped her case, it was probably the Japanese Baptist Woman's Home managed by Fife and Japanese helpers.

12. Immigration Commission, *Importing Women for Immoral Purposes*, 43.

13. For the functioning of these photographs and notices of runaway brides in the early Japanese immigrant community, see Kei Tanaka, "Japanese Picture Marriage and the Image of Immigrant Women in Early Twentieth-Century California," *Japanese Journal of American Studies* 15 (2004): 115–38.

14. Etsuko Yasukawa, "Ideologies of Family in the Modernization of Japan," in *East Asian Cultural and Historical Perspectives*, ed. Steven Totosy de Zepetnek and Jennifer W. Jay (Edmonton: Research Institute for Comparative Literature and Cross-Cultural Studies, University of Alberta, 1997), 193–94. As Kathleen Uno writes, however, the transformation of the *ryōsai kenbo* ideology needs to be understood in relation to various issues that emerged in Japan after the turn of the century, including the growth of women's enrollment in secondary education, women's increasing participation in wage labor, the spread of companionate family ideals, and the emergence of the urban middle class. Kathleen Uno, "Womanhood, War, and Empire: Transmutations of 'Good Wife, Wise Mother' before 1931," in *Gendering Modern Japanese History*, ed. Barbara Molony and Kathleen Uno (Cambridge, Mass.: Harvard University Press, 2005), 503–13.

15. Yuji Ichioka, *The Issei: The World of the First Generation Japanese Immigrants, 1885–1924* (New York: The Free Press, 1988), 170–71; Tanaka, "Japanese Picture Marriage and the Image of Immigrant Women," 127–30.

16. As an example, see Secretary Fujita's report on a thirteen-year-old girl who escaped and went to the police after being forced into prostitution in Salem, Oregon, in 1891. Report of Secretary Fujita Toshirō, July 30, 1891, JFMAD, 3.8.2.12, vol. 1.

17. For instance, two girls deceived into prostitution sought the help of Vancouver consul Sugimura immediately after arriving in the port. See "Fujin yūin no chiakkan," *Tōkyō fujin kyōfū zasshi* 40 (August 1891): 15.

18. *Amerika shinbun*, February 16, 1938, JARP; Yamazaki Tomoko, *Ameyuki-san no uta: Yamada Waka no sūki naru shōgai* (Tokyo: Bungei shunjū, 1978), 107–16.

19. *Amerika shinbun*, March 5, 1938. In her book, Yamazaki Tomoko introduces a slightly different version of the account Rev. Sakabe gave then

as follows: "Of course, we prefer that she have nothing to do with you. But it is really she herself who refuses to see you." Tomoko Yamazaki, *The Story of Yamada Waka: From Prostitute to Feminist Pioneer*, trans. Wakako Hironaka and Ann Kostant (Tokyo: Kodansha International, 1978), 86.

20. *Amerika shinbun*, March 5, 1938.

21. *San Francisco Chronicle*, December 16, 1903, 13.

22. Peggy Pascoe, *Relations of Rescue: The Search for Female Moral Authority in the American West, 1874–1939* (New York: Oxford University Press, 1990), 4, 13–17, 50–56, 95.

23. *Amerika shinbun*, March 5, 1938.

24. Report of Donaldina Cameron, *WOBFM Annual Report*, 1904: 56–57, SFTS.

25. See Yamada's recollection of her life in the Chinese Mission Home in Yamada Waka, *Renai no shakaiteki igi* (1920; repr., Tokyo: Yumani shobō, 2000), 108.

26. Report of Donaldina Cameron, *WOBFM Annual Report*, 1904: 57, SFTS.

27. Report of Mrs. E. A. Sturge, *WOBFM Annual Report*, 1905: 68, SFTS.

28. For the quote and Gardener's rescue efforts, see "1887," a letter sent from Rev. J. E. Starr, Metropolitan Methodist Church, Victoria, B.C., to Mrs. E. S. Strachen, president of the Women's Missionary Society, in September of that year, 2–4, UCA. The information about Japanese residents in the Oriental Home can be found in "History of Japanese in Oriental Home," UCA, and Report of Vancouver Consul Nosse Tatsugorō, August 30, 1895, JFMAD, 3.8.8.4, vol. 2.

29. *Tairiku nippō*, April 19, 1909, 5, and October 28, 1910, 5.

30. Home, Record 3a., resident no. 175, UCA.

31. *Tairiku nippō*, January 25, 1910, 1.

32. Home, Record 3a., resident no. 175, UCA.

33. *Tairiku nippō*, October 28, 1910, 5.

34. Home, Record 3a., resident no. 175, UCA.

35. *Tairiku nippō*, August 16, 1913, 1.

36. Ibid., September 19, 1913, 1.

37. Home, Record 3a., resident no. 175, UCA.

38. Report of Mrs. E. A. Sturge, *WOBFM Annual Report*, 1905: 67–68, SFTS.

39. Home, Record 3a., resident no. 37, 89, 90, UCA.

40. Rumi Yasutake, *Transnational Women's Activism: The United States, Japan, and Japanese Immigrant Communities in California, 1859–1920* (New York: New York University Press, 2004), 111–16. See also Eiichiro Azuma, *Between Two Empires: Race, History, and Transnationaism in Japanese America* (New York: Oxford University Press, 2005), 35–39.

41. Itō Kazuo, *Hokubei hyakunen-zakura* (Tokyo: Nichieki shuppan sha, 1973), 891. Japanese Methodists took active part in moral reforms among the Japanese after the establishment of the church in 1904. They also managed their own Woman's Home from 1907. The church's early history can

be found in *Journal, 1904–07*, Blaine Memorial United Methodist Church, Seattle.

42. On the Baptist Woman's Home, see Frances M. Schuyler, ed. and comp., *Japanese Women and Children in Seattle* (Chicago: Woman's American Baptist Home Mission Society, 1910); "Taped Interview of May Herd Katayama by Delores Goto, University of Washington Graduate Student," September 20, 1972; " Japanese Baptist Church, *The 75th Anniversary Booklet* (n.p., 1974), 8, courtesy of the Japanese Baptist Church of Seattle. See also Itō Kazuo, *Hokubei hyakunen-zakura*, 760–61; "Shigeko Uno," September 18, 1998, Segment 7, in *Densho: The Japanese American Legacy Project, 1996–1998*, Wing Luke Asian Museum, Seattle, Washington, http:www.densho.org/archive/default.asp (accessed February 11, 2012).

43. License no. 43914, King County Marriage Certificates, 1855–1990, WSADA; Certificate of Marriage, no.19695, May 11, 1916, Pierce County Auditor, Marriage Records, 1889–1947, WSADA. The cases of the women who appear in these marriage licenses are examined later in this chapter.

44. On Japanese leaders' attempts to control the behavior of immigrant wives and the ideals of womanhood that they expected Japanese women to conform to, see Tanaka, "Japanese Picture Marriage and the Image of Immigrant Women," 127–33; Azuma, *Between Two Empires*, 53–58.

45. Rumi Yasutake suggests that the availability of help from interpreters was a key factor behind the increase in the number of divorces among Japanese immigrants in Sacramento in the early twentieth century. Yasutake, *Transnational Women's Activism*, 124–25.

46. Based on the index of civil cases, in San Francisco at least seventy-four Japanese couples filed for divorce in the Superior Court from 1907 to 1920. Unfortunately, however, all the original pre–World War II case files were destroyed.

47. *Seattle Times*, July 25, 1908, 4.

48. A similar story of a Japanese "slave girl" who escaped from her Japanese masters appeared in the *Seattle Star* in November 1909. In this incident, Rev. Inoue Orio served as translator for the woman when she provided her story at police headquarters, and "Miss Fife" of the "Japanese Girls' Home" in Seattle had offered her protection. Considering that Japanese women often stayed at local Protestant institutions before filing for divorce, the influence of missionaries in women's decisions to file for divorce is not negligible. *Seattle Star*, November 27, 1909, 1.

49. Case 61218, May 1908, KCSC.

50. Case 15192, October 1911–March 1912, CSH.

51. *Ōfu nippō*, extra edition, February 19, 1912. *Shin sekai* reported that Ōta was "prosecuted on the charge of forcing his wife to work as a prostitute." *Shin sekai*, February 21, 1912, 7. The law referred to here would have been California Penal Code 266g, which made the act of forcing a wife into prostitution a punishable offense. As the code said: "Every man who, by force, intimidation, threats, persuasion, promises, or any other means, places or leaves, or procures any other person or persons to place or live, his wife in a house of prostitution, or connives at or consents to, or permits, the

placing or leaving of his wife in a house of prostitution, or allows or permits her to remain therein, is guilty of a felony and punishable by imprisonment in the state prison for not less than three nor more than ten years; and in all prosecutions under this section a wife is a competent witness against her husband." James H. Deering, Walter S. Brann, and R. M. Sims, *The Penal Code of California, Enacted in 1872; As Amended up to and Including 1905, with Statutory History and Citation Digest up to and Including Volume 147, California Reports* (San Francisco: Bancroft-Whitney Company, 1906), 120a.

52. *Ōfu nippō,* April 19, 1912, 3.

53. *Shin sekai,* February 21, 1912, 7.

54. *Taihoku nippō,* January 11 and 12, 1915, 5.

55. Ibid., January 12, 1915, 5.

56. Case 105849, January 1915, CSH.

57. *Taihoku nippō,* January 15, 1915, 5.

58. Ibid., February 2, 1915, 5.

59. Case 105849, January 1915, CSH.

60. Certificate of Marriage, no.19695, May 11, 1916, Pierce County Auditor, Marriage Records, 1889–1947, WSADA.

61. This analysis is based on my examination of 105 Japanese divorce cases in Seattle and 56 similar cases in Sacramento between 1907 and 1920.

62. The newspapers referred to here are *Taihoku nippō* (Seattle), *Shin sekai* (San Francisco), and *Ōfu nippō* (Sacramento).

63. *Shin sekai,* May 27, 1909, 3.

64. Ito Kazuo, *Hokubei hyakunen-zakura,* 897.

65. *The Dillingham Commission Reports,* Vol. 23, *Immigrants in Industries,* Part 25: *Japanese and Other Immigrant Races in the Pacific and Rocky Mountain States* (Washington, D.C.: Government Printing Office, 1911), 274.

66. Ibid., 249–50.

67. For a discussion of the "contradictions" that occurred when Asian immigrant women worked outside the home, see Evelyn Nakano Glenn, *Issei, Nisei, War Bride: Three Generations of Japanese American Women in Domestic Service* (Philadelphia: Temple University Press, 1986), 114–15, 192, 217–18; Gary Y. Okihiro, *Margins and Mainstreams: Asians in American History and Culture* (1994; repr., Seattle: University of Washington Press, 1996), 84; Yen Le Espiritu, *Asian American Women and Men: Labor, Laws, and Love* (Lanham, Md.: Rowman & Littlefield, 2008), 5–6.

68. For information about the wages of barmaids, see *Ōfu nippō,* June 8–9, 1915, 2; *Taihoku nippō,* February 25, 1913, 5.

69. For information about the wages of Japanese male migrant laborers in the first two decades of the twentieth century, see Itō Kazuo, *Hokubei hyakunen-zakura,* 441–43; *The Dillingham Commission Reports,* Vol. 23, Part 25: 275, 283, 285.

70. Case 98795, January 1914, and Case 20447, December 1915, CSH.

71. Key studies that present these models and influenced historians' writings about immigrants include William I. Thomas and Florian Znaniecki,

The Polish Peasant in Europe and America (1918–20; repr., New York: Dover Publications, 1958); Robert E. Park and Herbert A. Miller, *Old World Traits Transplanted* (Chicago: Society for Social Research, University of Chicago, 1921); Milton Gordon, *Assimilation in American Life: The Role of Race, Religion, and National Origins* (New York: Oxford University Press, 1964).

The earliest generation of Japanese American social scientists had graduate training under the guidance of Chicago School sociologists whose influence is evident in their work. On the relation between Japanese American students and Chicago School sociologists, see Henry Yu, *Thinking Orientals: Migration, Contact, and Modern America* (New York: Oxford University Press, 2001), 140–43, 153–58.

72. Major works in this tradition include Harry Kitano, *Japanese Americans: The Evolution of a Subculture* (Englewood Cliffs, N.J.: Prentice-Hall, 1969); Ivan H. Light, *Ethnic Enterprise in America: Business and Welfare among Chinese, Japanese, and Blacks* (Berkeley: University of California Press, 1972); John Modell, *The Economics and Politics of Racial Accommodation: The Japanese of Los Angeles, 1900–1942* (Urbana: University of Illinois Press, 1977); Edna Bonacich and John Modell, *The Economic Basis of Ethnic Solidarity: Small Business in the Japanese American Community* (Berkeley: University of California Press, 1980); and, more recently, Stephen S. Fugita and David J. O'Brien, *Japanese American Ethnicity: The Persistence of Community* (Seattle: University of Washington Press, 1991).

73. Ichioka, *The Issei*, 176–210; Brian M. Hayashi, *"For the Sake of Our Japanese Brethren": Assimilation, Nationalism, and Protestantism among the Japanese of Los Angeles, 1895–1942* (Stanford: Stanford University Press, 1995); Lon Kurashige, *Japanese American Celebration and Conflict: A History of Ethnic Identity and Festival, 1934–1990* (Berkeley: University of California Press, 2002), part 1; Azuma, *Between Two Empires*.

74. Evelyn Nakano Glenn, "The Dialectics of Wage Work: Japanese-American Women and Domestic Service, 1905–1940," in *Labor Immigration under Capitalism*, ed. Lucie Cheng and Edna Bonacich (Berkeley: University of California Press, 1984), 470–514; Glenn, *Issei, Nisei, War Bride*; Susan L. Smith, *Japanese American Midwives: Culture, Community, and Health Politics, 1880–1950* (Urbana: University of Illinois Press, 2005); Cecilia M. Tsu, "Sex, Lies, and Agriculture: Reconstructing Japanese Immigrant Gender Relations in Rural California, 1900–1913," *Pacific Historical Review* 78, no. 2 (May 2009): 171–209; Tsu, *Garden of the World: Asian Immigrants and the Making of Agriculture in California's Santa Clara Valley* (New York: Oxford University Press, 2013), chap. 3.

75. Raymond Grew, "The Comparative Weakness of American History," *Journal of Interdisciplinary History* 16:1 (Summer 1985): 90–100; Peter Kolchin, "Comparing American History," *Reviews in American History* 10:4 (1982): 65; Kolchin, *Unfree Labor: American Slavery and Russian Serfdom* (Cambridge, Mass.: Harvard University Press, 1987), ix. For examples of comparative historical studies of prostitution, see Barbara Meil Hobson, *Uneasy Virtue: The Politics of Prostitution and the American Reform*

Tradition (Chicago: The University of Chicago Press, 1990); Stephanie A. Limoncelli, *The Politics of Trafficking: The First International Movement to Combat the Sexual Exploitation of Women* (Stanford: Stanford University Press, 2010).

76. *Yomiuri shinbun*, November 22, 1901, 4.

77. Hayakawa Noriyo, *Kindai tennōsei to kokumin kokka* (Tokyo: Aoki shoten, 2005), 307–8.

78. For the role of the police in regulating licensed prostitution, see Obinata Sumio, *Nihon kindai kokka no seiritsu to keisatsu* (Tokyo: Azekura shobō, 1992), 290–91, 95, 300–301. For brothel owners' strategies for gaining the favor of the police, see Sheldon Garon, *Molding Japanese Minds: The State in Everyday Life* (Princeton: Princeton University Press, 1997), 103.

79. *Criminal Code, 1892* (Ottawa: Samuel Edward Dawson, 1892), secs. 181–85, 81–82; John P. S. McLaren, "Chasing the Social Evil: Moral Fervour and the Evolution of Canada's Prostitution Laws, 1867–1917," *Canadian Journal of Law and Society* 1 (1986): 125–65; Frances M. Shaver, "Prostitution," in *The Canadian Encyclopedia*, ed. James H. Marsh, 2nd ed. (Edmonton, AB.: Hurtig Publishers, 1988), 1768–69.

80. The Immigration Act of 1903 granted immigration officials the power to deport foreign prostitutes and procurers within two years of their arrival. The revision of 1907 extended the period of deportability from two years to three after arrival. The Immigration Act of 1910 made the period of deportation permanent. See Martha Gardner, *The Qualities of a Citizen: Women, Immigration, and Citizenship, 1870–1965* (Princeton: Princeton University Press, 2005), 63; Hyung-chan Kim, ed., *Asian Americans and the Supreme Court: A Documentary History* (New York: Greenwood Press, 1992), 90; Edward P. Hutchinson, *Legislative History of American Immigration Policy, 1798–1965* (Philadelphia: University of Pennsylvania Press, 1981), 147–48.

81. Deering, Brann, and Sims, *The Penal Code of California*, 120a.

82. On local ordinances and their enforcement, see chap. 3.

83. For example, in 1892, a thirteen-year-old Japanese girl forced into prostitution in Salem, Oregon, escaped from procurers and informed the police of what had happened to her, and officials arrested the procurers on charges of kidnapping and forcing a woman under the age of eighteen into prostitution. See Report of Fujita Toshirō, July 30, 1891, JFMAD, 3.8.2.12, vol. 1.

84. There is no room to discuss other collective actions, but it should be added that licensed prostitutes struck in order to protest against exploitation, especially when employers attempted to impose extra charges on them or force them to work long hours and on holidays. See, for instance, *Yūbin hōchi*, June 23, 1873; cited in Meiji Hennen-shi Hensan Kai, *Meiji hennen-shi, dai ni-kan* (Tokyo: Zaisei keizai gakkai, 1965); Mori Mitsuko, *Harukoma nikki* (1927; rpt., Tokyo: Yumani shobō, 2004), 319–21.

85. *Yomiuri shinbun*, May 22, 1893, 4. For report of a similar strike, see *Asahi shinbun*, December 25, 1890, 4.

86. *Asahi shinbun*, September 18, 1891, 4, and September 22, 1891, 4; *Yomiuri shinbun*, July 22, 1897, 2.

87. Yamamuro Gunpei, *Shakai kakusei ron* (1914; rpt., Tokyo: Chūkō bunko, 1977), 216–28.

88. *Niroku shinpō*, June 30, 1902, 3.

89. Ibid., May 2, 1903, 3.

90. *Kororado shinbun*, July 8, 1915, 3, and July 12, 1915, 3; *Ōfu nippō*, July 17, 1915, 2.

91. *Ōfu nippō*, May 17, 1917, 2.

92. Senior and younger prostitutes often formed intimate relationships. For example, see the rare firsthand account of an unlicensed prostitute, Kaneda Shizuko, *Shishō no sakebi*, in *Baishun mondai shiryō shūsei* (1916; rpt., Tokyo: Fuji shuppan, 1998), 29:188–90. In organized strikes, women also demanded that all prostitutes could charge customers the same amount for their services. See *Asahi shinbun*, May 31, 1891, 4.

93. Hakodate-shi, *Hakodate-shi-shi, tsūsetsu-hen* (Hakodate: City of Hakodate, 1990), 2:1416–17.

94. U. G. Murphy, *The Social Evil in Japan and Allied Subjects* (Tokyo: Methodist Publishing House, 1908), 93–96, 140–43; Okino Iwasaburō, *Shōgi kaihō aiwa* (1930; rpt., Tokyo: Chūkō bunko, 1982), 33–37, 59–60, 255–69; Itō Hidekichi, *Nihon haishō undō-shi* (1931; rpt., Tokyo: Fujishuppan, 1982), 160–61.

95. Itō Hidekichi, *Nihon haishō undō-shi*, 173–76; Okino, *Shōgi kaihō aiwa*, 104–6.

96. Article 5, Rules Relating to the Regulation of Prostitutes, Oct. 1900; cited in Yoshimi Kaneko, *Baishō no shakaishi* (Tokyo: Yūzankaku, 1984), 103.

97. The next few years witnessed a staggering number of prostitutes who submitted notifications. In Tokyo, licensed prostitutes decreased by 25 percent from 1899 to 1901. Keishichō, ed., *Keishichō tōkeisho*, 1897–99 (Tokyo: Kuresu shuppan, 1997), 376–77; Keishichō, *Keishichō tōkeisho*, 1905 (Tokyo: Kuresu shuppan, 1997), 238–39. The overall number of prostitutes in Japan declined from 52,274 in 1899 to 38,676 in 1902. "Shōgi ni kansuru tōkei," *Toki no koe*, 159 (August 1, 1902), 2, *Toki no koe*, 183 (August 1, 1903), 2.

98. For instance, see *Yūbin hōchi*, June 23, 1873; cited in Meiji Hennen-shi Hensan Kai, *Meiji hennen-shi, dai ni-kan*, 50.

99. *Niroku shinpō*, September 3, 1900, 3. *Hokkaidō mainichi shinbun*, January 10, 1900; cited in Hoshi Reiko, "Hokkaidō ni okeru shōgi jiyū haigyō," *Rekishi hyōron* 553 (May 1996): 73–74; *Asahi shinbun*, February 2, 1901, 5, and July 13, 1901, 4.

100. Yamamuro Gunpei, "Shōgi sanbyakunin no kenkyū," *Kakusei* 6:3 (1916): 11–13.

101. See Itō Fujio, "Baishōfu wa katagi ni narieruka," *Toki no koe* 526 (November 15, 1917): 3; Okino, *Shōgi kaihō aiwa*, 137–39.

102. Ichiba Gakujirō, "Baiinfu no matsuro," *Kokka igaku gakkai zasshi* 315 (1913): 59.

103. U. G. Murphy, *The Social Evil in Japan*, 115.

104. Yamazaki, *The Story of Yamada Waka*, 62; Yamazaki, *Ameyuki-san no uta*, 75–77.

105. Andrea Geiger, *Subverting Exclusion: Transpacific Encounters with Race, Caste, and Borders, 1885–1928* (New Haven: Yale University Press, 2011), 166.

106. *Taihoku nippō*, August 9, 1911, 3; Okina Kyūin, *Okina Kyūin zenshū* (Toyama: Okina Kyūin zenshū kankō-kai, 1972), 2:386.

CHAPTER 6. THE EMERGENCE OF ANTI–JAPANESE
PROSTITUTION REFORMS IN THE NORTH AMERICAN WEST
FROM A TRANSPACIFIC AND COMPARATIVE PERSPECTIVE

1. See the reports of Vancouver General Sugimura Fukashi, March 16, 1890, JFMAD, 3.8.5.11, vol. 1, and October 6, 1890, JFMAD, 3.8.2.12, vol. 2.

2. *Victoria Daily Colonist*, March 24, 1891, 8.

3. *Seattle Post-Intelligencer*, April 19, 1891, 8, and April 22, 1891, 5.

4. Report of Vancouver Consul Sugimura Fukashi, May 1, 1891, JFMAD, 3.8.2.12, vol. 2.

5. For instance, see a letter that Consul Sugimura sent to the editor of the *Seattle Post-Intelligencer* to protest an erroneous report on the arrival of Japanese prostitutes. *Seattle Post-Intelligencer*, May 13, 1891, 4.

6. Donald Teruo Hata, Jr., *"Undesirables," Early Immigrants and the Anti-Japanese Movement in San Francisco, 1892–1893: Prelude to Exclusion* (New York: Arno Press, 1978), 82–83. The Slocum report was reprinted in the *San Francisco Chronicle*, February 19, 1891, 2.

7. Gaimushō, *Nihon gaikō monjo, Meijiki, dai 24-kan* (Tokyo: Nihon kokusai rengō kyōkai, 1949), 460–62.

8. For example, see the *Seattle Post-Intelligencer* articles published on February 5, 1890, 1; March 23, 1891, 4; May 2, 1891, 1; and April 21, 1892, 1. The procurers were called "slave dealers." See *San Francisco Call*, August 10, 1897, 7.

9. *San Francisco Daily Report*, May 19, 1891; quoted in Yuji Ichioka, *The Issei: The World of the First Generation Japanese Immigrants, 1885–1924* (New York: The Free Press, 1988), 37. Similarly, the *Salt Lake Herald* editor noted: "[A]s much a disturbing element in the field of labor as their cousins from China, whilst the morals of the Japanese women are of the same low order as those of the Chinese." *Salt Lake Herald*, July 17, 1892, 4.

10. *Victoria Daily Colonist*, May 24, 1895, 1.

11. The Page Act of 1875 banned the entry of "Oriental" prostitutes. The Chinese Exclusion Act of 1882 ended the immigration of Chinese laborers. On Japanese consuls' fear that the Japanese would be confused with the Chinese and their concerns with the passage of discriminatory legislation against the Japanese, see Andrea Geiger, *Subverting Exclusion: Transpacific Encounters with Race, Caste, and Borders, 1885–1928* (New Haven: Yale University Press, 2011), 57–58. The Chinese head tax was originally $50 in 1885, increased to $100 in 1901, and then to $500 in 1903. See Patricia Roy, *A White Man's Province: British Columbia Politicians and Chinese and Japanese Immigrants, 1858–1914* (Vancouver: University of British Columbia Press), 67, 101, 109.

12. Kikuchi Takaiku, "Kanada ni okeru Sugimura Fukashi," *Morioka daigaku tanki daigaku-bu kiyō* 14 (2004): 32–34. See also the articles Sugimura wrote for *Yokohama mainichi shinbun* published August 16, 19, and 20, 1891.

13. On Meiji officials' and immigrants' conceptions of "low class," see Geiger, *Subverting Exclusion*, 65–70, 106–7; Mitziko Sawada, *Tokyo Life, New York Dreams: Urban Japanese Visions of America, 1890–1924* (Berkeley: University of California Press, 1996), 43–44.

14. Report of Secretary Fujita Toshirō, July 30, 1891, JFMAD, 3.8.2.12, vol. 1.

15. For instance, Fujita's entry was included in a major encyclopedia on Japanese American history compiled by the Japanese American National Museum in Los Angeles and edited by Brian Niiya, *Japanese American History: An A-to-Z Reference from 1868 to the Present* (New York: Facts on File, 1993), 140. See also Yasuo Wakatsuki, "Japanese Emigration to the United States, 1866–1924: A Monograph," *Perspectives in American History* 12 (1979): 505.

16. Roger Daniels, *Asian America: Chinese and Japanese in the United States since 1850* (Seattle: University of Washington Press, 1988), 105–9. For more on the content of the Fujita report, see Hata, "*Undesirables*," 72–81.

17. Report of Secretary Fujita Toshirō, July 30, 1891, JFMAD, 3.8.2.12, vol. 1.

18. In May 1896, the *San Francisco Bulletin* published a sensational article titled "'Undesirables': Another Phase in the Immigration from Asia," which reported on the appearance of Japanese prostitutes in the city's Chinatown as well as a Japanese procurer's attempt to release his prostitutes from a federal prison by submitting a habeas corpus petition. *San Francisco Bulletin*, May 4, 1891, 1. Donald Teruo Hata Jr. used this word for the title of his book to illustrate both the American perception of Japanese and the negative image of lower-class Japanese migrants held by Japanese officials and immigrant leaders in the 1890s. See Hata, "*Undesirables*."

19. Yuji Ichioka, "*Ameyuki-san*: Japanese Prostitutes in Nineteenth-Century America," *Amerasia Journal* 4:1 (1977): 16.

20. *Seattle Post-Intelligencer*, March 29, 1892, 4.

21. The members of the Gospel Society in San Francisco were largely reform-minded students (*shosei*) who were pursuing higher education typically while working as domestics in American families. See Hata, "*Undesirables*," 55. G. H. Ando, who brought Japanese officials' attention to the police raids on Japanese brothels in Seattle, was a leading trader who enjoyed an excellent reputation among local Americans. See the references to him in the *Seattle Post-Intelligencer*, October 9, 1892, 8, and January 7, 1893, 4.

22. On Japanese leaders' view of the Chinese, see Eiichiro Azuma, *Between Two Empires: Race, History, and Transnationalism in Japanese America* (New York: Oxford University Press, 2005), 36–38. On the perceptions of the Chinese among Japanese officials in Canada, see Geiger, *Subverting Exclusion*, 59–62.

23. Sheldon Garon, *Molding Japanese Minds: The State in Everyday Life* (Princeton: Princeton University Press, 1997), 98–99.

24. "Kegasaretari! Hinode-kuni! Kyokujitsu-shō!" *Haishō* 5 (October 1890): 1. In this context, an "abolitionist" means a person who wished to abolish licensed prostitution. The newspaper editor was probably referring to articles in the *San Francisco Bulletin,* January 10, 1890, 1, and February 24, 1890, 2.

25. "Kawaguchi Masue-shi no shōjō," *Tōkyō fujin kyōfū zasshi* 28 (August 1890): 6–7. Petitions against the migration of prostitutes came not only from Protestant reformers but also from Japanese businessmen, students, and ordinarily immigrants. The Foreign Ministry continued to receive these letters and petitions well into the 1910s.

26. "Nihon fujo hogo hōan detari," *Haishō* 8 (March 1891): 30.

27. "Baiin fujo no kaigai-yuki torishimari ni kansuru hōritsu tekkai no ken," July 1890 –September 1891, JFMAD, 4.2.2.34, vol. 1.

28. For an example of the argument for prostitutes' migration, see Fukuzawa Yukichi, "Jinmin no ijū to shōfu no dekasegi," *Jiji shimpō,* January 18, 1896, 3. See also Bill Mihalopoulos, "Modernization as Creative Problem Making: Political Action, Personal Conduct and Japanese Overseas Prostitutes," *Economy and Society* 27 (1998): 58–61, and Mihalopoulos, *Sex in Japan's Globalization, 1870–1930: Prostitutes, Emigration and Nation-Building* (London: Pickering & Chatto Publishers, 2011), 96–103.

29. "Kaigai tokō fujo," *Jogaku zasshi* 338 (February 1893): 5–6.

30. Gaimushō, *Imin hogo kisoku oyobi shikō saisoku* (Tokyo: Gaimushō, 1894); Gaimushō, *Imin hogo hō oyobi shikō saisoku* (Tokyo: Gaimushō, 1896).

31. During the Meiji period, numerous reports were exchanged between the Foreign Ministry and governors of prefectures where prostitutes went aboard ships. For example, see the instructions sent from the Foreign Ministry's Commerce Bureau chief to the governors of Kanagawa, Hyogo, and Nagasaki Prefectures on May 13, 1897, in JFMAD, 3.8.8.4, vol. 3.

32. Song Youn-ok, "Chōsen shokuminchi-shakai ni okeru kōshō-sei," *Nihonshi kenkyū* 371 (July 1993): 52–66; Song, "Chōsen gunji senryō-ka no sei-kanri seisaku," *Sensō sekinin kenkyū* 67 (Spring 2010): 23–25.

33. Bill Mihalopoulos notes that this was a common response among Japanese consuls not only in North America but also in China and Southeast Asia. Their primary interest was in maintaining favorable trade relations between Japan and foreign countries for Japan's overseas expansion. Mihalopoulos, "Modernization as Creative Problem Making," 52–57.

34. Iwamoto Yoshiharu, "Kaigai nihon fujoshi no shūbun," *Jogaku zasshi* 265 (May 1891): 1–5. Iwamoto was probably referring to the article "'Undesirables': Another Phase in the Immigration from Asia," *San Francisco Bulletin,* May 4, 1891, 1.

35. The motion was rejected, but, notably, 40 percent of attended members voted for it. "Tokyo-fu haishō-ron," *Jogaku zasshi* 296 (December 1891): 1–4.

36. Admittedly, this generalization was not universally true, because, for Japanese reformers, especially WCTU members, the fight against Japanese prostitution at home and abroad was linked to their broader agenda

of changing gender relations in Japanese society, including their petition campaigns for monogamy. "Teikoku gikai ni oite ippu-ippu no kenpaku no tsūka sen koto wo inoru," *Tōkyō fujin kyōfū zasshi* 44 (December 1891): 2–3. For more on the subject, see Elizabeth Dorn Lublin, *Reforming Japan: The Woman's Christian Temperance Union in the Meiji Period* (Honolulu: University of Hawai'i Press, 2010), especially chap. 4. In the development of transnational networks of Japanese reformers, however, the issue of national honor was probably more important than feminist or religious causes, because those engaged in the process included not only Christians but also a fair number of non-Christians (largely male) such as politicians, businessmen, students, and officials.

37. Indeed, reformers in Japan continued to use the issue of overseas Japanese prostitution to attack licensed prostitution in Japan until the 1910s, although, with the decline of prostitution in the United States, their targets shifted to prostitutes in Japan's East Asian colonies or Southeast Asia.

38. Odagiri Masunosuke, *Gasshūkoku seihokubu ni oite teikoku ryōjikan shinsecchi sentaku ni kansuru hōkoku* (Tokyo: Gaimushō, 1894), NDL.

39. The consulate was moved to Seattle in 1901.

40. The only exception to this generalization was Vancouver. Japanese officials were concerned about the trend against Japanese immigration in the Legislative Assembly of British Columbia located in Victoria, and they thought that the presence of prostitutes would lead to the development of an organized anti-Japanese movement in Canada; therefore, they kept a close eye on the entry of Japanese prostitutes there. See Report of Vancouver Consul Sugimura Fukashi, July 28, 1891, JFMAD, 3.8.2.12; Report of Vancouver Consul Nosse Tatsugorō, August 30, 1895, JFMAD, 3.8.8.4, vol. 2; Osada Shōhei, *Kanada no makutsu* (Vancouver: Tairiku nippō sha, 1909), 16, 18.

41. John P. S. McLaren, "Chasing the Social Evil: Moral Fervour and the Evolution of Canada's Prostitution Laws, 1867–1917," *Canadian Journal of Law and Society* 1 (1986): 130–36, 140–43; Lesley Erickson, *Westward Bound: Sex, Violence, the Law, and the Making of a Settler Society* (Vancouver: University of British Columbia Press, 2011), 85.

42. Barbara Meil Hobson, *Uneasy Virtue: The Politics of Prostitution and the American Reform Tradition* (1987; repr., Chicago: The University of Chicago Press, 1990), 139–41, 150–54; Ruth Rosen, *Lost Sisterhood: Prostitution in America, 1900–1918* (1982; repr., Baltimore: Johns Hopkins University Press, 1994), 14–18, 116–17; Brian Donovan, *White Slave Crusades: Race, Gender, and Anti-vice Activism, 1887–1917* (Urbana: University of Illinois Press, 2006), 2, 18–19, 31–36; McLaren, "Chasing the Social Evil," 140–43.

43. *Seattle Post-Intelligencer*, March 26, 1892, 3; April 5, 1892, 5; April 6, 1892, 5.

44. Cited in Ichioka, "*Ameyuki-san*," 9.

45. Gaimushō, *Nihon gaikō monjo Meijiki, dai 2-kan*, 694–95.

46. Japanese women appear in the *WOBFM Annual Report* from 1892 to 1912, SFTS. On their rescue work with Japanese women, see *San Francisco Chronicle*, February 18, 1899, 9, and October 30, 1900, 8; Mrs. E. A. Sturge, *WOBFM Annual Report*, 1899, 85–86, SFTS.

47. Frances M. Schuyler, ed. and comp., *Work with Japanese Women and Children in Seattle* (Chicago: Woman's American Baptist Home Mission Society, 1910), 10–12, 17–19, courtesy of the Japanese Baptist Church of Seattle.

48. See *Seattle Times*, September 5, 1908, 3. The Methodist Woman's Home was established in 1907. See *Journal, 1904–7*, courtesy of Blaine Memorial Church, Seattle. The San Francisco branch of the Home Missionary Society made a similar effort to protect foreign women from vice, appointing Margarita Lake as a missionary and traveler's aide, who was responsible for contacting conductors at steamships and trains to offer newly arrived women shelter and employment. See *San Francisco Chronicle*, June 26, 1903, 8.

49. "A report upon 'The Home' for rescued Chinese Girls in Victoria, B.C.: The Origin," "History of the Japanese in Oriental Home, Victoria, British Columbia," UCA.

50. Yet it should be added that Japanese women also took an active role in protecting Japanese women from procurers. The women who worked in the Japanese Baptist Woman's Home were equally represented by Japanese and white women. See Japanese Baptist Church, *The 75th Anniversary Booklet* (n.p., 1974), 8.

51. *Criminal Code, 1892* (Ottawa: Samuel Edward Dawson, 1892), secs. 181–85, 81–82.

52. Edward P. Hutchinson, *Legislative History of American Immigration Policy* (Philadelphia: University of Pennsylvania Press, 1981), 65–66.

53. Hyung-Chan Kim, ed., *Asian Americans and Congress* (Westport, Conn.: Greenwood Press, 1992), 142–52; Hutchinson, *Legislative History of American Immigration Policy*, 129–33.

54. See chapter 3 in this book.

55. "The United States vs. O. Yamamoto," case no. 4026, October–December 1902, RG 21, NARA, San Bruno, California. Also see *San Francisco Chronicle*, October 22, 1902, 9, and December 12, 1902, 7.

56. "The United States vs. John Doe Naito," case no. 2868, December 1904, RG 21, NARA, Seattle, Washington.

57. Officials' reports related to these investigations can be found in the Subject Correspondence series of Records of the Immigration and Naturalization Service, RG 85, NARA, Washington, D.C. Many of them are available in a microfilm collection edited by Alan Kraut, *Records of the Immigration and Naturalization Service, Series A: Subject Correspondence Files, Part 5: Prostitution and "White Slavery," 1902–1933* (Bethesda, Md.: University Publications of America, 1996), 7 reels (hereafter RINS reels).

58. Investigation of A. H. Geffeney, 1907, Casefile 51701/2A, RINS reel 1.

59. In this case, immigrant inspectors drew on anti–contract labor laws to deport him. The revised act of 1903 set up a two-year period of deportability for those who become public charges after arrival; therefore, if immigration officials found evidence that Japanese men were living on prostitutes' earnings, they could be subject to deportation or denial of reentry into the

country as persons "likely to become public charges." See case no. 2280, Department of Commerce and Labor, Immigration Service, July 29, 1908; a report of Immigrant Inspector F. N. Steele, August 10, 1908; and the transcript of a meeting of the Board of Special Inquiry, August 12, 1908, JFMAD, 3.8.8.6., vol. 2.

60. Ninette Kelley and Michael Trebilcock, *The Making of the Mosaic: A History of Canadian Immigration Policy* (Toronto: University of Toronto Press, 2010), 14–15.

61. Immigration Commission, *The Immigration Situation in Canada* (Washington, D.C.: Government Printing Office, 1910), 41.

62. "The United States vs. Masataro Yamataya," case no. 2091, July 1901 to July 1902, NARA, RG21, Seattle, Washington.

63. At the same time, federal officials ordered Kaoru Yamataya deported on the grounds that she was likely to become a public charge. Her appeal to the Supreme Court was not successful, but this case established a principle on which immigrants could appeal to the court if their right to due process was violated. Torrie Hester, "'Protection, Not Punishment': Legislative and Judicial Formation of U.S. Deportation Policy, 1882–1904," *Journal of American Ethnic History* 30:1 (Fall 2010): 23–25. On immigration officials' attempts to associate race with immorality in the application of immigration law, see Martha Gardner, *The Qualities of a Citizen: Women, Immigration, and Citizenship, 1870–1965* (Princeton: Princeton University Press, 2005), chap. 3.

64. Report of Immigrant Inspector F. N. Steele with a transcript of his interview with Ogawa Yoichi, April 5, 1909, RINS reel 1.

65. Transcript of an interview with Ogawa Haru and Report of Inspector J. H. Barbour, November 23, 1908, RINS reel 1.

66. Letter of J. H. Barbour, Inspector in Charge, November 25, 1909, RINS reel 1.

67. Letter of Walter H. Evans, Assistant United States Attorney, April 14, 1909; Letter of John B. Sawyer, April 12, 1909; "Certificate as to Landing of Alien," November 23, 1908, RINS reel 1.

68. Letter of Commissioner-General Daniel J. Keefe, April 27, 1909, RINS reel 1.

69. Letter of Assistant Commissioner-General F. H. Larned, April 27, 1909, RINS reel 1.

70. Mark Thomas Connelly, *The Response to Prostitution in the Progressive Era* (Chapel Hill: University of North Carolina Press, 1980), chap. 3; Egal Feldman, "Prostitution, the Alien Woman and the Progressive Imagination, 1910–1915," *American Quarterly* 19:2 (1967): 194–96; Rosen, *Lost Sisterhood*, 139–40; Timothy J. Gilfoyle, *City of Eros: New York City, Prostitution, and the Commercialization of Sex, 1790–1920* (New York: W.W. Norton, 1992), 292; David J. Pivar, *Purity Crusade: Sexual Morality and Social Control* (Westport, Conn.: Greenwood Press, 1973), 137–38.

71. Donovan, *White Slave Crusades*, 29–31, 113–15, 118–19; Rosen, *Lost Sisterhood*, 118–19. On the discussion of the image of Asian men as a threat to white women and children, see Gary Y. Okihiro, *Common*

Ground: Reimagining American History (Princeton: Princeton University Press, 2001), 100–101, 104–7.

72. Rosen, *Lost Sisterhood*, 123; Connelly, *The Response to Prostitution*, 114–15, chaps. 3, 6; Gardner, *The Qualities of a Citizen*, chaps. 3–4

73. Rosen, *Lost Sisterhood*, 60–61, 62, 127, 154, Donovan, *White Slave Crusades*, 64–71; Feldman, "Prostitution, the Alien Woman," 198–206.

74. *Seattle Post-Intelligencer*, January 21, 1892, 8.

75. *San Francisco Call*, July 12, 1907, 3. Also see *Victoria Daily Colonist*, October 5, 1907, 1.

76. Roger Daniels, *The Politics of Prejudice: The Anti-Japanese Movement in California and the Struggle for Japanese Exclusion* (Berkeley: University of California Press, 1977), 27–28, 32–34; Kornel Chang, *Pacific Connections: The Making of the U.S.-Canadian Borderlands* (Berkeley: University of California Press, 2012), 105–6.

77. On sec. 3, Immigration Act of February 20, 1907 (34 Stat. 898), sec. 3, Immigration Act of March 25, 1910 (36 Stat. 263), and Act of June 25, 1910 ("White Slave Traffic Act," 36 Stat. 825), see Department of Commerce and Labor, Bureau of Immigration and Naturalization, *Immigration Laws and Regulations of July 1, 1907* (Washington, D.C.: Government Printing Office, 1910), 6–7, 83–86. Hutchinson, *Legislative History of American Immigration Policy*, 147, 452.

78. *Tairiku nippō*, December 23, 1910, 1.

79. Ibid., December 23, 1910; 1. Report of Kanagawa Prefecture Governor Sufu Kōhei, December 8 and 19, 1910, JFMAD, 3.8.8.6, vol. 2; Report of Kanagawa Prefecture Governor Ōshima Hisamitsu, December 18, 1913, JFMAD, 3.8.8.6, vol. 3.

80. "The United States vs. Frank Yoshida," case 1327, April 1912, RG 21, NARA, Seattle; "The United States vs. Kyutaro Sato and K. Ueda," May–June 1913, file no. 5295, RG21, NARA, San Bruno, California.

81. "The United States vs. Haruzo Nitta," February 1911, file no. 4879, and "The United States vs. Saburo Kudo," October 1912, file no. 5134, RG 21, NARA, San Bruno, California; Report of Kanagawa Prefecture Governor Ōshima Hisamitsu, December 18, 1913, JFMAD, 3.8.8.6, vol. 3; *Shin sekai*, May 10, 1914, 3; *San Francisco Chronicle*, August 15, 1913, 17.

82. Mark Thomas Connelly, *The Response to Prostitution*, 54–64; Rosen, *Lost Sisterhood*, 19, 118–23; Matthew Frye Jacobson, *Whiteness of a Different Color: European Immigrants and the Alchemy of Race* (Cambridge, Mass.: Harvard University Press, 1998), 68–90; Gardner, *The Qualities of a Citizen*, 51–60; Donovan, *White Slave Crusades*, 29–31.

83. Report of Vancouver Consul Abe Kihachi, September 26, 1910, JFMAD, 4.2.2.99.

84. *Tairiku nippō*, February 22, 1909, 1.

85. Sakaguchi Mitsuhiro, *Nihonjin amerika iminshi* (Tokyo: Fuji shuppan, 2001), 71.

86. *The Dillingham Commission Reports*, Vol. 23, *Immigrants in Industries*, Part 25: *Japanese and Other Immigrant Races in the Pacific and Rocky Mountain States* (Washington, D.C.: Government Printing Office, 1911), 285.

87. In Chicago in 1914, a Japanese traveler encountered a man with three prostitutes who had come to the city after working in various interior cities in Washington, Montana, South Dakota, Minnesota, Nebraska, and Pennsylvania. Morita Korokurō, *Yankii: Ichimei, sekirara no beikoku* (Tokyo: Shiseidō, 1914), 277–80.

88. For more on Japanese prostitution in Canada, see Osada, *Kanada no makutsu*.

89. *Taihoku nippō*, May 21, 1917, 5, March 11 and 12, 1919, 8; *Tairiku nippō*, March 9, 1920, 7.

90. It is also worth noting that when antiprostitution forces were growing in the Japanese community, some migrant men were arguing for the protection of barmaids. For instance, see a male reader's letter published in *Taihoku nippō*, April 21, 1911, 3.

91. Department of Interior, Census Office, *Twelfth Census of the United States, Taken in the Year 1900*, vol. 1, *Population* (Washington, D.C.: Government Printing Office, 1901), 492; Department of Commerce, Bureau of Census, *Thirteenth Census of the United States Taken in the Year 1910*, vol. 1, *Population* (Washington, D.C.: Government Printing Office, 1913), 273; Roy, *A White Man's Province*, 269.

92. Ichioka, *The Issei*, 172.

93. In Washington, for instance, small-business owners among Japanese increased by 139 percent in the years between 1903 and 1913. See Yuzo Murayama, "Occupational Advancement of Japanese Immigrants and Its Economic Implications: Experience in the State of Washington, 1903–1925," *Japanese Journal of American Studies* 3 (1989): 142–43.

94. Murayama Yūzō, *Amerika ni ikita nihonjin imin* (Tokyo: Tōyō keizai shinpō sha, 1989), 155–58.

95. Iino Masako, *Nikkei kanadajin no rekishi* (Tokyo: Tokyo daigaku shuppan kai, 1997), 77–83; Geiger, *Subverting Exclusion*, 100–104; Charles H. Young and Helen R. Y. Reid, *The Japanese Canadians* (1938; repr., New York: Arno Press, 1978), 43.

96. W. Peter Ward, *White Canada Forever: Popular Attitudes and Public Policy toward Orientals in British Columbia* (1978; repr., Montreal and Kingston: McGill-Queen's University Press, 1990), 97–107.

97. For example, see the articles published in *Tairiku nippō* on September 1 to 3, 1908, 1; August 13–September 9, 1910, 5; October 13, 1913, 1; September 13, 1917, supplement.

98. Azuma, *Between Two Empires*, 48.

99. *Tairiku nippō*, November 14, 1908, 1.

100. Itō Kazuo, *Hokubei hyakunen-zakura* (1969; repr., Tokyo: Nichieki shuppan sha, 1973), 896–98; *Taihoku nippō*, April 4, 1911, 5.

101. *Hokubei jiji*, May 28, 1919, 4. See also *Tairiku nippō*, May 16, 1918, 5.

102. John Higham, *Strangers in the Land: Patterns of American Nativism, 1860–1925* (1955; repr., New Brunswick: Rutgers University Press, 2002), chap. 9.

103. *Rafu shinpō*, March 5, 1919, 3, and March 16, 1919, 3.

104. Similar assimilationist forces were developing in Canada, where "Anglo-conformity" had become an important element of Canadian citizenship in the early twentieth century. During World War I, English Canadian teachers extended their efforts to "Canadianize" immigrant children. Rosa Bruno-Jofré, "Citizenship and Schooling in Manitoba between the End of the First World War and the End of the Second World War," in *Citizenship in Transformation in Canada*, edited by Yvonne M. Hérbert (Toronto: University of Toronto Press, 2002), 112.

105. It appeared in the issue of *Taihoku nippō*, September 22, 1919; cited in Sakaguchi, *Nihonjin amerika iminshi* 229–30. In 1919, members of the Americanization Committee removed Japanese-language signboards from stores and a major bar-restaurant, Maneki, in Japantown. Itō Kazuo, *Hokubei hyakunen-zakura*, 192–94.

106. In 1916, the Japanese Association of Canada urged Japanese men to serve in the Canadian military, defining their military service as "a golden opportunity to advance the status of Japanese residents" in Canada. In total, 196 Japanese men fought with Canadian forces in France and Belgium. For the recruitment advertisement, see *Tairiku nippō*, January 25, 1916. For the quote, see Ken Adachi, *The Enemy That Never Was: A History of the Japanese Canadians* (Toronto: McClelland and Stewart, 1976), 101–3.

107. Inoue Orio, "Shashi ni okeru kakuseigun no shōri," *Kakusei* 3:6 (June 1913): 262–63.

108. Gary Gerstle, *Working-Class Americanism: The Politics of Labor in a Textile City, 1914–1960* (Princeton: Princeton University Press, 1989); Gerstle, "Liberty, Coercion, and the Making of Americans," *Journal of American History* 84:2 (1997): 544–47; Lizabeth Cohen, *Making a New Deal: Industrial Workers in Chicago, 1919–1939* (1990; repr., New York: Cambridge University Press, 2008).

109. James R. Barrett, "Americanization from the Bottom Up: Immigration and the Remaking of the Working Class in the United States, 1880–1930," *Journal of American History* 79:3 (December 1992): 996–1020.

110. Richard C. Berner, *Seattle 1900–1920: From Boomtown, Urban Turbulence, to Restoration* (Seattle: Charles Press, 1991), 110–12.

111. *Journal, 1904–07*, courtesy of Blaine Memorial United Methodist Church, Seattle.

112. Itō Kazuo, *Hokubei hyakunen-zakura*, 896; *Tairiku nippō*, August 12, 1909, 1; *Seattle Times*, September 5, 1908, 3.

113. *Seattle Times*, April 4, 1908, 1.

114. Okajima Kinya, the president of the Humane Society, served as translator and interpreter for the investigation of a Japanese trafficking ring in 1907. See exhibits 16 and 17, file 151701/2A, RINS reel 1.

115. *Shin sekai*, August 3 and 15, 1906, 5.

116. See relevant articles on page 7 of *Shin sekai*, January 30, and February 5, 6, 7, 1908.

117. About 80–90 percent of urban Japanese residents were reading Japanese-language newspapers regularly in the early 1910s. Sakaguchi, *Nihonjin amerika iminshi*, 92, 94.

118. *Taihoku nippō*, May 15, 1911, 1.
119. See *Tairiku nippō*, June 22, 23, 26, 29, 1911.
120. Ibid., January 31, 1910, 1.
121. Osada, *Kanada no makutsu*, 1–7.
122. Geiger, *Subverting Exclusion*, 88–89. The story of this former prostitute appears in Osada, *Kanada no makutsu*, 149–51.
123. For instance, recall the case of a former prostitute introduced at the end of chapter 5.
124. Osada, *Kanada no makutsu*, 184–86. Osada uses a false name for Nakayama in his book, but the contextual information he provides is enough to identify the man as Nakayama.
125. Geiger, *Subverting Exclusion*, 90.
126. *An Encyclopedia of the Development of the Japanese in Canada* was published by *Taihoku nippō* in 1922. Clearly, by this time, Nakayama had established himself as a major trusted figure in the Japanese immigrant community. The book referred to here is Nakayama Jinshirō, *Kanada dōhō hatten taikan* (Vancouver: Tairiku nippō sha, 1922).
127. See the series of articles in *Tairiku nippō*, May 18–20, 1915.
128. *Shin sekai*, May 23, 1915, 7.
129. See the series of articles in *Tairiku nippō*, July 14–August 14, 1912, 1.
130. *Ōfu nippō*, June 3, 1909, 1.
131. Ibid., September 15, 1909, 3; *Shin sekai*, February 29, 1908, 3, and October 10, 1914, 7; *Rafu shinpō*, August 8, 1915, 3; Report of Vancouver Consul Ukita Satoji, March 15, 1917, JFMAD, 3.8.2.49, vol. 10, no. 1.
132. *Ōfu nippō*, September 27, 1912, 1.
133. Geiger, *Subverting Exclusion*, 20–21. On the various incidents of violence against the former outcaste class in the Meiji period, see David L. Howell, *Geographies of Identity in Nineteenth-Century Japan* (Berkeley: University of California Press, 2005), chap. 4.
134. Letter of Martin Griffin, February 14, 1916, and Letter of Sasaki Minoru, April 17, 1916, JFMAD, 3.8.2.49, vol. 9, no. 2.
135. Letter of Arikado Yatarō, June 8, 1916, and attached documents, JFMAD, 3.8.2.49, vol. 9, no. 2.
136. *Taihoku nippō*, April 2, 1915, 5.
137. *Tairiku nippō*, January 1, 1916, 16.
138. See the articles in *Ōfu nippō*, September 1, 1909, 1, July 8, 1915, 1, and July 9, 1915, 1.
139. Kei Tanaka, "Japanese Picture Marriage and the Image of Immigrant Women in Early Twentieth-Century California," *Japanese Journal of American Studies* 15 (2004): 115–38, especially 127–33.
140. Kei Tanaka, "Japanese Picture Marriage in 1900–1924 California: Construction of Japanese Race and Gender" (Ph.D. diss., Rutgers, The State University of New Jersey, 2002), 221–27.
141. Cited and analyzed in Azuma, *Between Two Empires*, 55.
142. Herbert Asbury, *The Barbary Coast—An Informal History of the San Francisco Underworld* (1933; repr., New York: Alfred A. Knopf, 2008), chap. 12; Bonni Cermak, "Closing the Open Town: Prostitution in Seattle,

1910–1920" (master's thesis, Western Washington University, 1997); Debora Nilsen, "The 'Social Evil': Prostitution in Vancouver, 1900–1920," in *In Her Own Right: Selected Essays on Women's History in B.C.*, ed. Barbara Latham and Cathy Kess (Victoria, B.C.: Camosun College, 1980), 208–15; Mary Murphy, "The Private Lives of Public Women: Prostitution in Butte, Montana, 1878–1917," in *The Women's West*, ed. Susan Armitage and Elizabeth Jameson (Norman: University of Oklahoma Press, 1987), 203; Jay Moynahan, *Butte's Sportin' Women, 1880–1920: The Famous Red Light District and a List of Over 1,200 Names* (Spokane: Chickadee Publishing, 2003), 17.

143. The ratio of Japanese males and females in Oregon, Washington, and British Columbia was roughly two to one by 1920. The number of Japanese restaurants in Seattle decreased from forty-one in the peak year of 1910 to eighteen in 1919. Department of Commerce, Bureau of Census, *Fourteenth Census of the United States Taken in the Year 1920*, vol. 2, *Population* (Washington, D.C.: Government Printing Office, 1922), 110; *Hokubei renraku nikkai*, "Kaimu oyobi kaikei hōkoku," August 20, 1919, to February 29 1920, 76–79; cited in Sakaguchi, *Nihonjin amerika iminshi*, 243; Ward, *White Canada Forever*, 109; Michiko Midge Ayukawa, *Hiroshima Immigrants in Canada, 1891–1941* (Vancouver: University of British Columbia Press, 2008), 35.

144. Beikoku seihokubu renraku nihonjin-kai, ed., *Beikoku seihokubu zairyū nihonjin hatten ryakushi* (Seattle: Beikoku seihokubu renraku nihonjin-kai, 1923), 57–60, NDL.

145. Takeuchi Kōjirō, *Beikoku seihokubu nihonjin iminshi* (Seattle: Taihoku nippōsha, 1929), 43–45.

146. Alain Corbin, *Women for Hire: Prostitution and Sexuality in France after 1850*, trans. Alan Sheridan (Cambridge, Mass.: Harvard University Press, 1990), 219–20; Richard J. Evans, "Prostitution, State and Society in Imperial Germany," *Past and Present* 70 (February 1976): 121–23; Conny Rijken, *Trafficking in Persons: Prosecution from a European Perspective* (The Hague: T.M.C. Asser Press, 2003), 54, chap. 3. On the anti-CDO campaigns in Britain, see Judith R. Walkowitz, *Prostitution and Victorian Society: Women, Class, and the State* (New York: Cambridge University Press, 1980). For a useful comparative overview of prostitution reforms in European countries since the late nineteenth century, see Stephanie A. Limoncelli, *The Politics of Trafficking: The First International Movement to Combat the Sexual Exploitation of Women* (Stanford: Stanford University Press, 2010).

147. James Francis Warren, *Ah Ku and Karayuki-san: Prostitution in Singapore, 1870–1940* (Singapore: Oxford University Press, 1993), 154–57; Hiroshi Shimizu and Hitoshi Hirakawa, *Japan and Singapore in the World Economy: Japan's Economic Advance into Singapore, 1870–1965* (London: Routledge, 1999), 44.

148. Warren, *Ah Ku and Karayuki-san*, 160–64; Shimizu and Hirakawa, *Japan and Singapore in the World Economy*, 40–44; Mihalopoulos, *Sex in Japan's Modernization*, 118–24.

149. See Fujinaga Takashi, "Nichiro sensō to nihon ni yoru Manshū eno kōshō seido ishoku," in *Kairaku to kisei: Kindai ni okeru goraku no yukue* (Osaka: Osaka sangyō kenkyūjo, 1998), 64–74; Kurahashi Masanao, *Jūgun ianfu mondai no rekishiteki kenkyū* (Tokyo: Kyōei shobō, 1994), chap. 5.

150. For the numbers of Japanese prostitutes overseas in China, see table 1.3 in chapter 1 in this book. For the number of Japanese prostitutes in Korea in 1910, see Kimura Kenji, *Zaichō nihonjin no shakai-shi* (Tokyo: Miraisha, 1989), 12–13.

151. Warren, *Ah Ku and Karayuki-san*, 165.

152. Onozawa Akane, *Kindai nihon shakai to kōshō seido: Minshū-shi to kokusai kankei no shiten kara* (Tokyo: Yoshikawa kōbun kan, 2011), 153–74.

153. "Gunjin-ka ni tsuite," *Fujin shinpō* 82 (February 1904): 3–7; "Imon bukuro to reijō," *Fujin shinpō* 84 (April 1904): 5–8.

154. Sidney Xu Lu, "Good Women for Empire: Educating Overseas Female Emigrants in Imperial Japan, 1900–1945," *Journal of Global History* 8:3 (November 2013): 436–60.

CONCLUSION

1. Eric Hobsbawm, *The Age of Empire, 1875–1914* (1987; repr., New York: Vintage Books, 1989), chap. 3.

2. Today, according to Kevin Bales, 27 million persons are living in "slavery," which he defines as "the total control of one person by another for the purpose of economic exploitation," in various industries, not only prostitution but also agriculture, construction, and domestic service. Kevin Bales, *Disposable People: New Slavery in the Global Economy* (1999; repr., Berkeley: University of California Press, 2004), 6–9.

3. For example, Ronald Weitzer, *Legalizing Prostitution: From Illicit Vice to Lawful Business* (New York: New York University Press, 2012).

4. Raelene Frances, *Selling Sex: A Hidden History of Prostitution* (Sydney: University of New South Wales Press, 2007), 294.

JAPANESE-LANGUAGE NEWSPAPERS AND BULLETINS

Amerika shinbun [Japanese American newspaper], San Francisco, 1938

Asahi shinbun [Asahi newspaper], 1884–1920

Fujin shinpō [Women's news], Tokyo, 1895–1904

Haishō [Abolition], Tokyo, 1891

Hawai hōchi [Hawaii news], Honolulu, 1917

Hokubei jiji [North American times], Seattle, 1917–18

Hokkaidō mainichi shinbun [Hokkaido daily news], Sapporo, 1900

Jiji shimpō [Current affairs news], Tokyo, 1896

Jogaku zasshi [Women's education journal], Tokyo, 1891–93

Kakusei [Purity], Tokyo, 1911–18

Kororado shinbun [Colorado news], Denver, 1911–17

Nihonjin [The Japanese], Seattle, 1901

Niroku shinpō [Niroku times], Tokyo, 1900–1903

Ōfu nippō [Sacramento daily news], Sacramento, 1909–19

Rafu shinpō [Los Angeles daily news], Los Angeles, 1914–20

Shin sekai [New world], San Francisco, 1906–20

Sōkō jiji [San Francisco times], San Francisco, 1896

Taihoku nippō [Great northern daily news], Seattle, 1911–20

Tairiku nippō [Continental news], Vancouver, 1908–20

Toki no koe [War cry], Tokyo, 1902–17

Tōkyō fujin kyōfū zasshi [Tokyo woman's reform magazine], Tokyo, 1890–91

Yokohama mainichi shinbun [Yokohama daily news], Yokohama, 1890–93

Yomiuri shinbun [Yomiuri newspaper], Tokyo, 1900–1920

ENGLISH-LANGUAGE NEWSPAPERS

Butte Anaconda Standard, 1889–92

Nelson Miner, 1896

Los Angeles Herald, 1892–94

Sacramento Daily Union, 1885–86

Sacramento Record-Union, 1897

Salem Capital Journal, 1893

Salt Lake Herald, 1892–93

San Francisco Bulletin, 1890-91

San Francisco Call, 1897–1907

San Francisco Chronicle, 1892–1913

San Francisco Daily Alta California, 1886–87

San Francisco Daily Report, 1891

San Francisco Examiner, 1891

Seattle Post-Intelligencer, 1890–1901

Seattle Star, 1908–1909

Seattle Times, 1903–1909

Victoria Daily Colonist, 1891–1907

JAPANESE GOVERNMENT RECORDS

Japanese Foreign Ministry Archival Documents (JFMAD), Tokyo

3.8.2.12. "Zaibei honpō-jin no jōkyō narabini tobeisha torishimari kankei zassan." Vols. 1–2.

3.8.2.49. "Kaigai tokō kankei zakken." Vols. 1–4, 6–11.

3.8.2.250. "Hokubei gasshūkoku narabini eiryō kanada kaigai tokō honpō-jin nyūkokusha kyozetsusha insū chōsa kata kuntatsu hōkoku ikken."

3.8.5.11. "Ryoken hōki oyobi dōhōki toriatsukai tetsuduki ni kansuru kunrei shirei narabini ryoken kafu torishimari zakken." Vol. 1.

3.8.5.21. "Kaigai ryoken kisoku ihan zakken." Vols. 1–3.

3.8.8.4. "Honpō-jin kaigai e mikkō kankei zakken." Vols. 1–5.

3.8.8.6. "Gaikoku ni oite honpō-jin jyōriku kyozetu narabini sōkan kankei zakken." Vols. 2–3.

3.8.8.10. "Fusei gaikoku tokōsha oyobi dō tokōsha shūsen-nin toriatsukai zakken." Vols. 1–2.

3.8.8.22. "Honpō-jin mibun oyobi seikō chōsa—zaigai honpō-jin." Vol. 1.

4.1.4.34. "Gaikoku hōritsu ni junkyo shi shokei seraretaru honpō-jin shimei nado teikoku ryōji yori hōkoku zakken."

4.2.2.10. "Yūkai kankei zakken." Vols. 1–2.

4.2.2.27. "Honpō-jin fusei-gyō torishimari kankei zakken." Vols. 1–4.

4.2.2.34. "Baiin fujo no kaigai-yuki torishimari ni kansuru hōritsu tekkai no ken." Vol. 1.

4.2.2.95. "Fujo mikkō kyōbōsha Yoshino Masashichi ni taisuru kokuhatsu ikken."

4.2.2.99. "Kaigai ni okeru honpō shūgyōfu no insū oyobi sono jōkyō narabini nen nikai hōkoku kata kuntatsu ikken."

Gaimushō. *Imin hogo kisoku oyobi shikō saisoku*. Tokyo: Gaimushō tsūshō-kyoku, 1894.

———. *Imin hogohō oyobi shikō saisoku*. Tokyo: Gaimushō tsūshō-kyoku, 1896.

———. *Kaigai kakuchi zairyū honpōjin shokugyōbetsu jinkōhyō*, 1907, 1914, 1919, 1924, 1929.

———. *Minami manshū ni okeru shōgyō*. Tokyo: Kinkōdō shoseki. 1907.

———. *Nihon gaikō monjo, Meijiki, dai 24-kan*. Tokyo: Nihon kokusai rengō kyōkai, 1949.

———. *Nihon gaikō monjo, Taishōki, tsuiho*. Vol. 2. Tokyo: Gaimishō, 1972.

———. *Tsūshō isan, 59-kan*. 1901. Reprint, Tokyo: Fuji shuppan, 1993–98.

Ōkurashō. *Gaikoku bōeki gairan*. Tokyo: Ōkurashō shūzei-kyoku, 1890, 1895, 1900, 1905.

Kanagawa ken. *Kanagawa ken tōkeisho, meiji 22-nen, 23-nen*. Yokohama: Seishi bunsha, 1893.

Shizuoka ken. *Shizuoka ken tōkei sho, meiji 36-nen*. Shizuoka: Iketsurudō, 1905.

———. *Shizuoka kenshi tsūshi-hen 3*. Shizuoka: Shizuoka-ken, 1996.

Keishichō, ed. *Keishichō tōkeisho*. 1897–99, 1905. Reprint, Tokyo: Kuresu shuppan,1997.

Tokyo-fu. *Shōgi geigi kaihō shiryō*. Tokyo: Tokyo-fu, December 1873.

UNITED STATES GOVERNMENT RECORDS

Department of Commerce, Bureau of Census. *Thirteenth Census of the United States Taken in the Year 1910*. Vol. 1, *Population*. Washington, D.C.: Government Printing Office, 1913.

———. *Fourteenth Census of the United States Taken in the Year 1920*. Vol. 2, *Population*. Washington, D.C.: Government Printing Office, 1922.

Department of Commerce and Labor, Bureau of Immigration and Naturalization. *Immigration Laws and Regulations of July 1, 1907*. Washington, D.C.: Government Printing Office, 1910.

Department of Interior, Census Office. *Report on Population of the United States at the Eleventh Census: 1890*, part 1. Washington, D.C.: Government Printing Office, 1895.

———. *Twelfth Census of the United States, Taken in the Year 1900*. Vol. 1, *Population*. Washington, D.C.: Government Printing Office, 1901.

Records of the Immigration and Naturalization Service, Series A: *Subject Correspondence Files, Part 5: Prostitution and "White Slavery," 1902–1903*. Edited by Alan Kraut. Bethesda, Md.: University Publications of America, 1996. 7 microfilm reels.

United States District Court Case Files, National Archives and Records Administration, Seattle, Washington, Record Group 21.

United States District Court Case Files, National Archives and Records Administration, San Bruno, California, Record Group 21.

The Dillingham Commission Reports, Vol. 23, *Immigrants in Industries, Part 25: Japanese and Other Immigrant Races in the Pacific and Rocky Mountain States*. Washington, D.C.: Government Printing Office, 1911.

The Dillingham Commission Reports, Vol. 37, Part 2: *Importation of Women for Immoral Purposes*. Washington, D.C.: Government Printing Office, 1911.

Immigration Commission. *Importing Women for Immoral Purposes*. Washington, D.C.: Government Printing Office, 1909.

———. *The Immigration Situation in Canada*. Washington, D.C.: Government Printing Office, 1910.

U.S. Bureau of the Census. *Marriage and Divorce, 1916, 1922–32*. Westport: Greenwood Press, 1978.

CANADIAN GOVERNMENT RECORDS

Census Office (Canada). *Census of Canada*, 1891, 1901, 1911, and 1921.

REGIONAL PUBLIC AND INSTITUTIONAL RECORDS

Criminal Case Files, 1892–1903, King County Superior Court, Seattle, Washington.

The Criminal Index, 1899-1923, King County Superior Court, Seattle, Washington.

Divorce Court Records, 1907–20, King County Superior Court, Seattle, Washington.

Divorce Court Records, 1908–20, Sacramento County Superior Court, Center for Sacramento History, Sacramento, California.

Oriental Home and School Fonds, United Church of Canada, British Columbia Conference Archives, Vancouver, British Columbia.

Police Reports, Civil Case Files, Probate Files, Marriage and Death Records, British Columbia Archives, Victoria, British Columbia.

Records of the Japanese Methodist Church, Blaine Memorial United Methodist Church, Seattle, Washington.

Records of the Japanese women's home (Nihon fujin hōmu), Japanese Baptist Church, Seattle, Washington.

Woman's Occidental Board of Foreign Missions Annual Report, 1892–1912, San Francisco Theological Seminary.

ORAL HISTORIES

Densho: The Japanese American Legacy Project, 1996–1998. Wing Luke Asian Museum, Seattle. <URL: http:www.densho.org/archive/default. asp>.

Itō Kazuo, ed. *Hokubei hyakunen-zakura.* 1969, Tokyo: Nichieki shuppan sha, 1973. Available in English as *Issei: A History of Japanese Immigrants in North America.* Translated by Shinichiro Nakamura and Jean S. Gerald. Seattle: Japanese Community Service, 1973.

———. *Zoku hokubei hyakunen-zakura.* 1969. Reprint, Tokyo: Nichieki shuppan sha, 1973.

MEMOIRS, PERSONAL REPORTS,
AND OTHER PRIMARY SOURCES

Fujimoto, Taizo. *The Story of the Geisha Girl.* London: T. W. Laurie, 1910.

Fujioka Shirō. *Ayumi no ato: Hokubei tairiku nihonjin monogatari.* Los Angeles: Ayumi no ato kankō kōenkai, 1957.

Fujita Toshirō. *Kaigai zaijū shihan seiki no kaiko.* 1931. Reprint, Tokyo: Tosho sentā, 1999.

Gibson, Otis. *The Chinese in America.* Cincinnati: Hitchcock and Walden, 1877.

Hagiwara Otohiko. *Tōkyō kaika hanjō-shi.* Tokyo: Mansei-dō, 1874.

Hoshino Tokuji. *Ikyō no kyaku.* Tokyo: Keisei sha, 1903.

Ishioka Hikoichi. *Hokubei washinton shū eiryō koronbia shū nihonjin jijō.* Tokyo: Ishioka Hikoichi, 1907.

Kaneda Shizuko. *Shishō no sakebi.* In *Baishun mondai shiryō shūsei*, vol. 29. 1916. Reprint, Tokyo: Fuji shuppan, 1998.

Kikuchi Yūhō. *Nihonkai shūyūki.* Tokyo: Shungakudō, 1903.

Kuroda Kiyotaka. *Kanyū nikki.* 1884. Held by the National Diet Library, Tokyo.

Mori Mitsuko. *Harukoma nikki*. 1927. Reprint, Tokyo: Yumani shobō, 2004.

Morita Korokurō. *Yankii: Ichimei, sekirara no beikoku*. Tokyo: Shiseidō, 1914.

Muraoka Iheiji. *Muraoka Iheiji den*. 1960. Reprint, Tokyo: Kōdansha bunko, 1982.

Murata Seiji. *Kobe kaikō sanju-nen shi*. Kobe: Kobe kaikō sanjū-nen kinen kai, 1898.

Murphy, U. G. *The Social Evil in Japan and Allied Subjects*. Tokyo: Methodist Publishing House, 1908.

Nagai Kafū. "Shakō no ichiya." *Bungei kurabu* 5 (May 1904): 194–99.

Odagiri Masunosuke. *Gasshūkoku seihokubu ni oite teikoku ryōjikan shinsecchi sentaku ni kansuru hōkoku*. Tokyo: Gaimushō, 1894.

Okina Kyūin. *Okina Kyūin zenshū*. Vol. 2, *Waga isshō umi no kanata*. Toyama: Okina Kyūin zenshū kankō-kai, 1972.

Osada Shōhei. *Kanada no makutsu*. Vancouver: Tairiku nippōsha, 1909.

Ōta Hisayoshi. *Yokohama enkaku-shi*. Tokyo: Tōyōsha, 1892.

Beikoku seihokubu renraku nihonjin-kai, ed. *Beikoku seihokubu zairyū nihonjin hatten ryakushi*. Seattle: Beikoku seihokubu renraku nihonjin-kai, 1923.

Saitō Gunpachirō. *Dainihon teikoku shōgyō chishi*. Kyoto: Wakabayashi Seikichi, 1895.

Takeuchi Kōjirō. *Beikoku seihokubu nihonjin iminshi*. Seattle: Taihoku nippō sha, 1929.

Tengai Kikaku, pseud. *Hokubei musen ryokō*. Tokyo: Daigaku kan, 1906.

Yamada Waka. *Renai no shakaiteki igi*. 1920. Reprint, Tokyo: Yumani shobō, 2000.

———. "Sanjū yonen mae." *Fujin to shakai* 105 (1929): 14–16.

Yamamuro Gunpei. *Shakai kakusei ron*. 1914. Reprint, Tokyo: Chūkō bunko, 1977.

Yokohama shinpō sha. *Yokohama hanjō ki*. Yokohama: Yokohama shinpō sha, 1903.

Yūmatu kai. *Kanagawa ken chishi*. Yokohama: Tanuma shoten, 1897.

ENGLISH-LANGUAGE SECONDARY SOURCES

Adachi, Ken. *The Enemy That Never Was: A History of the Japanese Canadians*. Toronto: McClelland and Stewart, 1976.

Agustin, Laura Maria. *Sex at the Margins: Migration, Labour Markets and the Rescue Industry*. New York: Zed Books, 2007.

Anderson, Barbara A. *Internal Migration during Modernization in Late Nineteenth-Century Russia*. Princeton: Princeton University Press, 1980.

Asbury, Herbert. *The Barbary Coast: An Informal History of the San Francisco Underworld*. 1933. Reprint, New York: Basic Books, 2008.

Ayukawa, Michiko Midge. *Hiroshima Immigrants in Canada, 1891–1941*. Vancouver: University of British Columbia Press, 2008.

Azuma, Eiichiro. *Between Two Empires: Race, History, and Transnationalism in Japanese America*. New York: Oxford University Press, 2005.

Bales, Kevin. *Disposable People: New Slavery in the Global Economy*. Berkeley: University of California Press, 2004.

Barnhart, Jacqueline Baker. *The Fair but Frail: Prostitution in San Francisco, 1849–1900*. Reno: University of Nevada Press, 1986.

Barrett, James R. "Americanization from the Bottom Up: Immigration and the Remaking of the Working Class in the United States, 1880–1930." *Journal of American History* 79:3 (December 1992): 996–1020.

Barton, Josef J. *Peasants and Strangers: Italians, Rumanians, and Slovaks in an American City, 1890–1950*. Cambridge, Mass.: Harvard University Press, 1975.

Berner, Richard C. *Seattle, 1900–1920: From Boomtown, Urban Turbulence, to Restoration*. Seattle: Charles Press, 1991.

Bloch, Marc. *Land and Work in Mediaeval Europe: Selected Papers by Marc Bloch*. Translated by J. E. Anderson. New York: Harper and Row, 1967.

Bloemraad, Irene. *Becoming a Citizen: Incorporating Immigrants and Refugees in the United States and Canada*. Berkeley: University of California Press, 2006.

Bonacich, Edna, and John Modell. *The Economic Basis of Ethnic Solidarity: Small Business in the Japanese American Community*. Berkeley: University of California Press, 1980.

Botsman, Daniel V. "Freedom without Slavery? 'Coolies,' Prostitutes, and Outcastes in Meiji Japan's 'Emancipation Moment.'" *American Historical Review* 116:5 (2011): 1323–47.

Brandenfels, Kathryn. "Down on the Sawdust: Prostitution & Vice Control in Seattle, 1870–1920." M.A. thesis, Hampshire College, 1981.

Brown, Ian. *Economic Change in South-East Asia, c. 1830–1980*. New York: Oxford University Press, 1997.

Bruno-Jofré, Rosa. "Citizenship and Schooling in Manitoba between the End of the First World War and the End of the Second World War." In *Citizenship in Transformation in Canada*, edited by Yvonne M. Hérbert. Toronto: University of Toronto Press, 2002.

Butler, Anne M. *Daughters of Joy, Sisters of Misery: Prostitutes in the American West, 1865–90*. Urbana: University of Illinois Press, 1985.

Cermak, Bonni. "Closing the Open Town: Prostitution in Seattle, 1910–1920." Master's thesis, Western Washington University, 1997.

Chang, Kornel. *Pacific Connections: The Making of the U.S.-Canadian Borderlands.* Berkeley: University of California Press, 2012.

Chen, Yong. *Chinese San Francisco, 1850–1943: A Trans-Pacific Community.* Stanford: Stanford University Press, 2000.

———. "In Their Own Words: The Significance of Chinese-Language Sources for Studying Chinese American History." *Journal of Asian American Studies* 5:3 (2002): 243–68.

Cheng, Lucie. "Chinese Immigrant Women in Nineteenth-Century California." In *Women and Power in American History,* edited by Kathryn Kish Sklar and Thomas Dublin. Vol. 1, *To 1880.* 2nd ed. Upper Saddle River, N.J.: Prentice Hall, 2002.

———. "Free, Indentured, Enslaved: Chinese Prostitutes in Nineteenth-Century America." In *Labor Immigration under Capitalism,* edited by Lucie Cheng and Edna Bonacich. Berkeley: University of California Press, 1984.

Cheng, Lucie, and Edna Bonacich, eds. *Labor Immigration under Capitalism: Asian Workers in the United States before World War II.* Berkeley: University of California Press, 1984.

Choy, Catherine Ceniza. *Empire of Care: Nursing and Migration in Filipino American History.* Durham: Duke University Press, 2003.

Cohen, Deborah, and Maura O'Connor. "Introduction: Comparative History, Cross-National History, Transnational History—Definitions." In *Comparison and History: Europe in Cross-National Perspective,* edited by Deborah Cohen and Maura O'Connor. New York: Routledge, 2004.

Cohen, Lizabeth. *Making a New Deal: Industrial Workers in Chicago, 1919–1939.* 1990. Reprint, New York: Cambridge University Press, 2008.

Colligan-Taylor, Karen. "Translator's Introduction." In *Sandakan Brothel No. 8: An Episode in the History of Lower-Class Japanese Women.* Armonk, N.Y.: M.E. Sharpe, 1999.

Connelly, Mark Thomas. *The Response to Prostitution in the Progressive Era.* Chapel Hill: University of North Carolina Press, 1980.

Corbin, Alain. *Women for Hire: Prostitution and Sexuality in France after 1850.* Translated by Alan Sheridan. Cambridge, Mass.: Harvard University Press, 1990.

Criminal Code, 1892. Ottawa: Samuel Edward Dawson, 1892.

Daniels, Roger. *Asian America: Chinese and Japanese in the United States since 1850.* Seattle: University of Washington Press, 1988.

———. *The Politics of Prejudice: The Anti-Japanese Movement in California and the Struggle for Japanese Exclusion.* Berkeley: University of California Press, 1977.

Deering, James H., Walter S. Brann, and R. M. Sims. *The Penal Code of California, Enacted in 1872; As Amended up to and Including 1905, with Statutory History and Citation Digest up to and Including Volume 147, California Reports.* San Francisco: Bancroft-Whitney Company, 1906.

Donovan, Brian. *White Slave Crusades: Race, Gender, and Anti-vice Activism, 1887–1917.* Urbana: University of Illinois Press, 2006.

Duus, Peter. *Modern Japan.* New York: Houghton Mifflin, 1998.

Eagle, John A. *The Canadian Pacific Railway and the Development of Western Canada, 1896–1914.* Kingston, ON: McGill-Queen's University Press, 1989.

Egal, Feldman. "Prostitution, the Alien Woman and the Progressive Imagination, 1910–1915." *American Quarterly* 19:2 (1967): 192–206.

Elson, Robert E. "International Commerce, the State and Society: Economic and Social Change." In *The Cambridge History of Southeast Asia,* edited by Nicholas Tarling. Vol. 2. Cambridge and New York: Cambridge University Press, 1992.

Erickson, Lesley *Westward Bound: Sex, Violence, the Law, and the Making of a Settler Society.* Vancouver: University of British Columbia Press, 2011.

Espiritu, Yen Le. *Asian American Women and Men: Labor, Laws, and Love.* Lanham, Md.: Rowman & Littlefield, 2008.

Evans, Richard J. "Prostitution, State and Society in Imperial Germany." *Past and Present* 70 (February 1976): 106–29.

Farraday, Fay. "The Debate about Prostitution: A History of the Formation and Failure of Canadian Laws against the Sex Trade, 1867–1917." M.A. thesis, University of Toronto, 1991.

Fowler, Josephine. *Japanese and Chinese Immigrant Activists: Organizing in American and International Communist Movements, 1919–1933.* New Brunswick: Rutgers University Press, 2007.

Frances, Raelene. *Selling Sex: A Hidden History of Prostitution.* Sydney: University of New South Wales Press, 2007.

Fuess, Harald. *Divorce in Japan: Family, Gender, and the State, 1600–2000.* Stanford: Stanford University Press, 2004.

Fugita, Stephen S., and David J. O'Brien. *Japanese American Ethnicity: The Persistence of Community.* Seattle: University of Washington Press, 1991.

Gardner, Martha. *The Qualities of a Citizen: Women, Immigration, and Citizenship, 1870–1965.* Princeton: Princeton University Press, 2005.

Garon, Sheldon. *Molding Japanese Minds: The State in Everyday Life.* Princeton: Princeton University Press, 1997.

Geiger, Andrea. *Subverting Exclusion: Transpacific Encounters with Race, Caste, and Borders, 1885–1928*. New Haven: Yale University Press, 2011.

Gerstle, Gary. "Liberty, Coercion, and the Making of Americans." *Journal of American History* 84:2 (1997): 544–47.

———. *Working-Class Americanism: The Politics of Labor in a Textile City, 1914–1960*. Princeton: Princeton University Press, 1989.

Gilfoyle, Timothy J. *City of Eros: New York City, Prostitution, and the Commercialization of Sex, 1790–1920*. New York: W.W. Norton, 1992.

Glenn, Evelyn Nakano. "The Dialectics of Wage Work: Japanese-American Women and Domestic Service, 1905–1940." In *Labor Immigration under Capitalism*, edited by Lucie Cheng and Edna Bonacich. Berkeley: University of California Press, 1984.

———. *Issei, Nisei, War Bride: Three Generations of Japanese American Women in Domestic Service*. Philadelphia: Temple University Press, 1986.

Goldman, Marion S. *Gold Diggers, Silver Miners: Prostitution and Social Life on the Comstock Lode*. Ann Arbor: University of Michigan Press, 1981.

Gordon, Andrew. *A Modern History of Japan: From Tokugawa Times to the Present*. New York: Oxford University Press, 2003.

Gordon, Milton. *Assimilation in American Life: The Role of Race, Religion, and National Origins*. New York: Oxford University Press, 1964.

Gray, James H. *Red Lights on the Prairies*. Saskatoon, SK: Fifth House Publishers, 1995.

Grew, Raymond. "The Comparative Weakness of American History." *Journal of Interdisciplinary History* 16:1 (Summer 1985): 87–101.

Handlin, Oscar. *The Uprooted: The Epic Story of the Great Migrations That Made the American People*. Boston: Little, Brown & Company, 1979.

Hane, Mikiso. *Peasants, Rebels, and Outcasts: The Underside of Modern Japan*. New York: Pantheon, 1982.

Hata, Donald Teruo, Jr. *"Undesirables," Early Immigrants and the Anti-Japanese Movement in San Francisco, 1892–1893: Prelude to Exclusion*. New York: Arno Press, 1978.

Hayashi, Brian. *"For the Sake of Our Japanese Brethren": Assimilation, Nationalism, and Protestantism among the Japanese of Los Angeles, 1895–1942*. Stanford: Stanford University Press, 1995.

Hershatter, Gail. *Dangerous Pleasures: Prostitution and Modernity in Twentieth-Century Shanghai*. Berkeley: University of California Press, 1997.

Hester, Torrie. "'Protection, Not Punishment': Legislative and Judicial Formation of U.S. Deportation Policy, 1882–1904." *Journal of American Ethnic History* 30:1 (Fall 2010): 11–36.

Higham, John. *Strangers in the Land: Patterns of American Nativism, 1860–1925.* New Brunswick: Rutgers University Press, 2002.

Hine, Robert V., and John Mack Faragher. *The American West: A New Interpretive History.* New Haven: Yale University Press, 2000.

Hirota, Hidetaka. "The Moment of Transition: State Officials, the Federal Government, and the Formation of American Immigration Policy." *Journal of American History* 99:4 (2013): 1092–1108.

Hobsbawm, Eric. *The Age of Empire, 1875–1914.* New York: Vintage Books, 1989.

Hobson, Barbara Meil. *Uneasy Virtue: The Politics of Prostitution and the American Reform Tradition.* Chicago: The University of Chicago Press, 1990.

Hoerder, Dirk, ed. *Labor Migration in the Atlantic Economies: The European and North American Working Classes during the Period of Industrialization.* Westport, Conn.: Greenwood Press, 1985.

Hori, Joan. "Japanese Prostitution in Hawaii during the Immigration Period." *Hawaiian Journal of History* 15 (1981): 113–24.

Howell, David L. *Geographies of Identity in Nineteenth-Century Japan.* Berkeley: University of California Press, 2005.

Hsu, Madeline Y. *Dreaming of Gold, Dreaming of Home: Transnationalism and Migration between the United States and South China, 1882–1943.* Stanford: Stanford University Press, 2000.

Hutchinson, Edward P. *Legislative History of American Immigration Policy, 1798–1965.* Philadelphia: University of Pennsylvania Press, 1981.

Ichioka, Yuji. "*Amerika Nadeshiko*: Japanese Immigrant Women in the United States, 1900–1924." *Pacific Historical Review* 49:2 (1980): 348–54.

———. "*Ameyuki-san*: Japanese Prostitutes in Nineteenth-Century America." *Amerasia Journal* 4:1 (1977): 1–21.

———. *The Issei: The World of the First Generation Japanese Immigrants, 1885–1924.* New York: The Free Press, 1988.

———. "Japanese Immigrant Nationalism: The Issei and the Sino-Japanese War, 1937–1941." *California History* 69:3 (1990): 260–75.

Ike, Nobutaka. "Taxation and Landownership in the Westernization of Japan." *Journal of Economic History* 7:1 (1947): 160–82.

Jacobson, Matthew Frye. *Whiteness of a Different Color: European Immigrants and the Alchemy of Race.* Cambridge, Mass.: Harvard University Press, 1998.

Japanese Baptist Church. *The 75th Anniversary Booklet.* N.p., 1974.

Johnson, Merri Lisa, ed. *Jane Sexes It Up: The Confession of Feminist Desire.* New York: Four Walls Eight Windows, 2002.

Kamphoefner, Walter D. *The Westfalians: From Germany to Missouri.* Princeton: Princeton University Press, 1987.

Kelley, Ninette, and Michael Trebilcock. *The Making of the Mosaic: A History of Canadian Immigration Policy.* Toronto: University of Toronto Press, 2010.

Kim, Hyung-chan, ed. *Asian Americans and the Supreme Court: A Documentary History.* New York: Greenwood Press, 1992.

Kitano, Harry. *Japanese Americans: The Evolution of a Subculture.* Englewood Cliffs, N.J.: Prentice-Hall, 1969.

Kiyooka, Eiichi, trans. and ed. *Fukuzawa Yukichi on Japanese Women: Selected Works.* Tokyo: University of Tokyo Press, 1988.

Kobayashi, Audrey Lynn. "Regional Backgrounds of Japanese Immigrants and the Development of Japanese-Canadian Community." Department of Geography, McGill University, *Discussion Papers* no. 1 (May 1986): 1–26.

Kocka, Jürgen. "Comparison and Beyond." *History and Theory* 42 (2003): 39–44.

Kodansha. *Kodansha Encyclopedia of Japan.* Tokyo: Kodansha, 1983.

Kolchin, Peter. "Comparing American History." *Reviews in American History* 10:4 (1982): 64–81.

———. *Unfree Labor: American Slavery and Russian Serfdom.* Cambridge, Mass.: Harvard University Press, 1987.

Kraut, Alan M. *Silent Travelers: Germs, Genes, and the "Immigrant Menace."* New York: Basic Books, 1994.

Kurashige, Lon. *Japanese American Celebration and Conflict: A History of Ethnic Identity and Festival, 1934–1990.* Berkeley: University of California Press, 2002.

Lee, Erika. *At America's Gates: Chinese Immigration during the Exclusion Era, 1882–1943.* Chapel Hill: University of North Carolina Press, 2003.

Lee, Rachel C. *The Americans of Asian American Literature: Gendered Fictions of Nation and Transnation.* Princeton: Princeton University Press, 1999.

Light, Ivan H. *Ethnic Enterprise in America: Business and Welfare among Chinese, Japanese, and Blacks.* Berkeley: University of California Press, 1972.

Limoncelli, Stephanie A. *The Politics of Trafficking: The First International Movement to Combat the Sexual Exploitation of Women.* Stanford: Stanford University Press, 2010.

Litz, John R. "Chinese and Japanese in the *Seattle Post-Intelligencer,* January 1, 1890 to December 31, 1899." Special Collections, Suzzallo and Allen Libraries, University of Washington, Seattle.

————. "The Japanese in the *Seattle Times*: January 1, 1900 to December 31, 1909." Suzzallo and Allen Libraries, University of Washington, Seattle.

Lu, Sidney Xu. "Good Women for Empire: Educating Overseas Female Emigrants in Imperial Japan, 1900–1945." *Journal of Global History* 8:3 (November 2013): 436–60.

Lublin, Elizabeth Dorn. *Reforming Japan: The Woman's Christian Temperance Union in the Meiji Period.* Honolulu: University of Hawai'i Press, 2010.

MacDonald, Norbert. *Distant Neighbors: A Comparative History of Seattle and Vancouver.* Lincoln: University of Nebraska Press, 1987.

Matsumoto, Valerie J. *Farming the Home Place: A Japanese American Community in California.* Ithaca: Cornell University Press, 1993.

Mason, William M., and John A. Mckinstry. *The Japanese of Los Angeles.* Los Angeles: Los Angeles County Museum of Natural History, 1969.

McClain, Charles J. *In Search of Equality: The Chinese Struggle against Discrimination in Nineteenth-Century America.* Berkeley: University of California Press, 1994.

McLaren, John P. S. "Chasing the Social Evil: Moral Fervour and the Evolution of Canada's Prostitution Laws, 1867–1917." *Canadian Journal of Law and Society* 1 (1986): 125–65.

Mihalopoulos, Bill. "Modernization as Creative Problem Making: Political Action, Personal Conduct and Japanese Overseas Prostitutes." *Economy and Society* 27 (1998): 50–73.

————. *Sex in Japan's Globalization, 1870–1930: Prostitutes, Emigration and Nation-Building.* London: Pickering & Chatto Publishers, 2011.

Modell, John. *The Economics and Politics of Racial Accommodation: The Japanese of Los Angeles, 1900–1942.* Urbana: University of Illinois Press, 1977.

Molony, Barbara, and Kathleen Uno, eds. *Gendering Modern Japanese History.* Cambridge, Mass.: Harvard University Press, 2005.

Morgan, Murray. *Skid Road: An Informal Portrait of Seattle.* New York: The Viking Press, 1951.

Moriyama, Alan Takeo. "The Background of Japanese Emigration to Hawaii, 1885–1894." In *Labor Immigration under Capitalism*, edited by Lucie Cheng and Edna Bonacich. Berkeley: University of California Press, 1984.

————. *Imingaisha: Japanese Emigration Companies and Hawaii, 1894–1908.* Honolulu: University of Hawai'i Press, 1985.

Moynahan, Jay. *Butte's Sportin' Women, 1880–1920: The Famous Red Light District and a List of Over 1,200 Names.* Spokane: Chickadee Publishing, 2003.

Murayama, Yuzo. "Information and Emigrants: Interprefectural Differences of Japanese Emigration to the Pacific Northwest, 1880–1915." *Journal of Economic History* 51 (1991): 125–47.

———. "Occupational Advancement of Japanese Immigrants and Its Economic Implications: Experience in the State of Washington, 1903–1925." *Japanese Journal of American Studies* 3 (1989): 141–54.

Murphy, Mary. "The Private Lives of Public Women: Prostitution in Butte, Montana, 1878–1917." In *The Women's West*, edited by Susan Armitage and Elizabeth Jameson. Norman: University of Oklahoma Press, 1987.

Nakamura, Takafusa. *Economic Growth in Prewar Japan*. Translated by Robert A. Feldman. New Haven: Yale University Press, 1983.

Ngai, Mae. *Impossible Subjects: Illegal Aliens and the Making of Modern America*. Princeton: Princeton University Press, 2004.

Niiya, Brian, ed. *Japanese American History: An A-to-Z Reference from 1868 to the Present*. New York: Facts on File, 1993.

Nilsen, Debora. "The 'Social Evil': Prostitution in Vancouver, 1900–1920." In *In Her Own Right: Selected Essays on Women's History in B.C.*, edited by Barbara Latham and Cathy Kess. Victoria, BC: Camosun College, 1980.

Nugent, Walter. *Into the West: The Story of Its People*. New York: Alfred A. Knopf, 1999.

Odaka, Konosuke. "Redundancy Utilized: The Economics of Female Domestic Servants in Pre-war Japan." In *Historical Demography and Labor Markets in Prewar Japan*, edited by Michael Smitka. Vol. 3. New York: Routledge, 1998.

Okihiro, Gary Y. *Common Ground: Reimagining American History*. Princeton: Princeton University Press, 2001.

———. *Margins and Mainstreams: Asians in American History and Culture*. 1994. Reprint, Seattle: University of Washington Press, 1996.

Park, Robert E., and Herbert A. Miller. *Old World Traits Transplanted*. Chicago: Society for Social Research, University of Chicago, 1921.

Pascoe, Peggy. *Relations of Rescue: The Search for Female Moral Authority in the American West, 1874–1939*. New York: Oxford University Press, 1990.

Paul, Rodman W. *Mining Frontiers of the Far West, 1848–1880*. New York: Holt, Rinehart and Winston, 1963.

Pinzer, Maimie. *The Maimie Papers*. Edited by Ruth Rosen and Sue Davidson. Bloomington: Indiana University Press, 1985.

Pivar, David J. *Purity Crusade: Sexual Morality and Social Control*. Westport, Conn.: Greenwood Press, 1973.

Podruchny, Carolyn. *Making the Voyageur World: Travelers and Traders in the North American Fur Trade*. Lincoln: University of Nebraska Press, 2006.

Rettmann, Jef. "Business, Government, and Prostitution in Spokane, Washington, 1889–1910." *Pacific Northwest Quarterly* 89:2 (1998): 77–83.

Rijken, Conny. *Trafficking in Persons: Prosecution from a European Perspective*. The Hague: T.M.C. Asser Press, 2003.

Roberts, Barbara. *Whence They Came: Deportation from Canada, 1900–1935*. Ottawa: University of Ottawa Press, 1988.

Robinson, Greg. *A Tragedy of Democracy: Japanese Confinement in North America*. New York: Columbia University Press, 2009.

Rosen, Ruth. *Lost Sisterhood: Prostitution in America, 1900–1918*. 1982. Reprint, Baltimore: Johns Hopkins University Press, 1994.

Roy, Patricia. *A White Man's Province: British Columbia Politicians and Chinese and Japanese Immigrants, 1858–1914*. Vancouver: University of British Columbia Press, 1989.

Salyer, Lucy E. *Laws Harsh as Tigers: Chinese Immigrants and the Shaping of Modern Immigration Law*. Chapel Hill: University of North Carolina Press, 1995.

Saveliev, Igor R. "English Abstract." In *Imin to Kokka: Kyokutō Roshia ni okeru Chūgokujin Chōsenjin Nihonjin Imin*. Tokyo: Ochanomizu Shobō, 2005.

Sawada, Mitziko. *Tokyo Life, New York Dreams: Urban Japanese Visions of America, 1890–1924*. Berkeley: University of California Press, 1996.

Schmidt, Petra. "Law of Succession." In *History of Law in Japan since 1868*, edited by Wilhelm Röhl. Leiden: Brill, 2005.

Schuyler, Frances M., ed. and comp. *Work with Japanese Women and Children in Seattle*. Chicago: Woman's American Baptist Home Mission Society, 1910.

Scott, Joan Wallach. *Gender and the Politics of History*. New York: Columbia University Press, 1999.

Shah, Nayan. *Contagious Divides: Epidemics and Race in San Francisco's Chinatown*. Berkeley: University of California Press, 2001.

———. *Stranger Intimacy: Contesting Race, Sexuality and the Law in the North American West*. Berkeley: University of California Press, 2011.

Shaver, Frances M. "Prostitution." In *The Canadian Encyclopedia*, edited by James H. Marsh. 2nd ed. Edmonton, AB: Hurtig Publishers, 1988.

Shimizu, Hiroshi, and Hitoshi Hirakawa. *Japan and Singapore in the World Economy: Japan's Economic Advance into Singapore, 1870–1965*. London: Routledge, 1999.

Siener, William H. "Through the Back Door: Evading the Chinese Exclusion

Act along the Niagara Frontier, 1900 to 1924." *Journal of American Ethnic History* 27:4 (2008): 34–70.

Smith, Charleen P. "Boomtown Brothels in the Kootenays, 1895–1905." In *People and Place: Historical Influences on Legal Culture*, edited by Jonathan Swainger and Constance Backhouse. Vancouver: University of British Columbia Press, 2003.

Smith, Susan L. *Japanese American Midwives: Culture, Community, and Health Politics, 1880–1950*. Urbana: University of Illinois Press, 2005.

Snell, James G. *In the Shadow of the Law: Divorce in Canada, 1900–1939*. Toronto: University of Toronto Press, 1991.

Stanley, Amy. *Selling Women: Prostitution, Markets, and the Household in Early Modern Japan*. Berkeley: University of California Press, 2012.

Stephan, John J. *The Russian Far East: A History*. Stanford: Stanford University Press, 1994.

Takai, Yukari. "Asian Migrants, Exclusionary Laws, and Transborder Migration in North America, 1880–1940." *OAH Magazine of History* (October 2009): 35–42.

———. "Navigating Transpacific Passages: Steamship Companies, State Regulators, and Transshipment of Japanese in the Early-Twentieth-Century Pacific Northwest." *Journal of American Ethnic History* 30:3 (Spring 2011): 7–34.

Takaki, Ronald. *Pau Hana: Plantation Life and Labor in Hawaii*. Honolulu: University of Hawai'i Press, 1983.

Tamura, Linda. *The Hood River Issei: An Oral History of Japanese Settlers in Oregon's Hood River Valley*. Urbana: University of Illinois Press, 1993.

Tanaka, Kei. "Japanese Picture Marriage and the Image of Immigrant Women in Early Twentieth-Century California." *Japanese Journal of American Studies* 15 (2004): 115–38.

———. "Japanese Picture Marriage in 1900–1924 California: Construction of Japanese Race and Gender." Ph.D. diss., Rutgers, The State University of New Jersey, 2002.

Tarling, Nicholas. "The Establishment of Colonial Regimes." In *The Cambridge History of Southeast Asia*, edited by Nicholas Tarling. Vol. 2. Cambridge and New York: Cambridge University Press, 1992.

Taylor, Quintard. *The Forging of a Black Community: Seattle's Central District from 1870 through the Civil Rights Era*. Seattle: University of Washington Press, 1994.

Thomas, William I., and Florian Znaniecki. *The Polish Peasant in Europe and America*. 1918–20. Reprint, New York: Dover Publications, 1958.

Tonomura, Hitomi, and Anne Walthall. "Introduction." In *Women and Class in Japanese Society*, edited by Hitomi Tonomura, Anne Walthall, and Wakita Haruko. Ann Arbor: Center for Japanese Studies, University of Michigan, 1999.

Tsu, Cecilia M. *Garden of the World: Asian Immigrants and the Making of Agriculture in California's Santa Clara Valley.* New York: Oxford University Press, 2013.

———. "Sex, Lies, and Agriculture: Reconstructing Japanese Immigrant Gender Relations in Rural California, 1900–1913." *Pacific Historical Review* 78:2 (May 2009): 171–209.

Tsurumi, E. Patricia. *Factory Girls: Women in the Thread Mills of Meiji Japan.* Princeton: Princeton University Press, 1990.

Uno, Kathleen. "Womanhood, War, and Empire: Transmutations of 'Good Wife, Wise Mother' before 1931." In *Gendering Modern Japanese History*, edited by Barbara Molony and Kathleen Uno. Cambridge, Mass.: Harvard University Press, 2005.

Wakatsuki, Yasuo. "Japanese Emigration to the United States, 1866–1924: A Monograph." *Perspectives in American History* 12 (1979): 389–516.

Walker, Rebecca, ed. *To Be Real: Telling the Truth and Changing the Face of Feminism.* New York: Anchor Books, 1995.

Walkowitz, Judith R. *City of Dreadful Delight: Narratives of Sexual Danger in Late-Victorian London.* Chicago: Chicago University Press, 1992.

———. *Prostitution and Victorian Society: Women, Class, and the State.* New York: Cambridge University Press, 1980.

Wang, Joan S. "The Double Burdens of Immigrant Nationalism: The Relationship between Chinese and Japanese in the American West, 1880s–1920s." *Journal of American Ethnic History* 27:2 (2008): 28–58.

Ward, Peter. *Courtship, Love, and Marriage in Nineteenth-Century English Canada.* Montreal and Kingston: McGill-Queen's University Press, 1990.

———. "Marriage and Divorce." In *The Canadian Encyclopedia*, edited by James H. Marsh. 2nd ed. Edmonton, AB: Hurtig Publishers, 1988.

Ward, W. Peter. *White Canada Forever: Popular Attitudes and Public Policy toward Orientals in British Columbia.* 1978. Reprint, Montreal and Kingston: McGill-Queen's University Press, 1990.

Warren, James Francis. *Ah Ku and Karayuki-san: Prostitution in Singapore, 1870–1940.* Singapore: Oxford University Press, 1993.

Weitzer, Ronald. *Legalizing Prostitution: From Illicit Vice to Lawful Business.* New York: New York University Press, 2012.

White, Richard. *"It's Your Misfortune and None of My Own": A New History of the American West.* Norman: University of Oklahoma Press, 1991.

Yamazaki Tomoko. "From Sandakan No. 8 Brothel." Translated by Tomoko Moore and Steffen Richards. *Bulletin of Concerned Asian Scholars* 7:4 (October–December 1975): 52–60.

————. *Sandakan Brothel No. 8: An Episode in the History of Lower-Class Japanese Women.* Translated by Karen Colligan-Taylor. Armonk, N.Y.: M.E. Sharpe, 1999.

————. *The Story of Yamada Waka: From Prostitute to Feminist Pioneer.* Translated by Wakako Hironaka and Ann Kostant. Tokyo: Kodansha International, 1978.

Yanagisako, Sylvia J. *Transforming the Past: Tradition and Kinship among Japanese Americans.* Seattle: University of Washington Press, 1985.

Yans-McLaughlin, Virginia. *Family and Community: Italian Immigrants in Buffalo, 1880–1930.* Urbana: University of Illinois Press, 1982.

Yasukawa, Etsuko. "Ideologies of Family in the Modernization of Japan." In *East Asian Cultural and Historical Perspectives,* edited by Steven Totosy de Zepetnek and Jennifer W. Jay. Edmonton: Research Institute for Comparative Literature and Cross-Cultural Studies, University of Alberta, 1997.

Yasutake, Rumi. *Transnational Women's Activism: The United States, Japan, and Japanese Immigrant Communities in California, 1859–1920.* New York: New York University Press, 2004.

Young, Charles H., and Helen R. Y. Reid. *The Japanese Canadians.* New York: Arno Press, 1978.

Yu, Henry. *Thinking Orientals: Migration, Contact, and Modern America.* New York: Oxford University Press, 2001.

Yung, Judy. *Unbound Feet: A Social History of Chinese Women in San Francisco.* Berkeley: University of California Press, 1995.

Yung, Judy, Gordon H. Chang, and H. Mark Lai, eds. *Chinese American Voices: From the Gold Rush to the Present.* Berkeley and Los Angeles: University of California Press, 2006.

JAPANESE-LANGUAGE SECONDARY SOURCES

Aoki Hideo. "Kindai to toshi buraku: Hiroshima-shi A-machi wo jirei to shite." *Buraku kaihō kenkyū* 3 (1997): 56–77.

Fujime Yuki. *Sei no rekishigaku: Kōshō seido, dataizai, taisei kara baishun bōshihō, yūsei hogohō taisei e.* Tokyo: Fuji shuppan, 1997.

Fujinaga Takashi. "Nichiro sensō to nihon ni yoru Manshū eno kōshō seido ishoku." In *Kairaku to kisei: Kindai ni okeru goraku no yukue.* Osaka: Osaka sangyō kenkyūjo, 1998.

Fujino Yutaka, ed. *Kanagawa no buraku-shi.* Tokyo: Fuji shuppan, 2007.

————. *Sei no kokka kanri: Baibaishun no kingendaishi.* Tokyo: Fuji shuppan, 2001.

Furumaya Tadao. *Ura nihon*. Tokyo: Iwanami shoten, 1997.

Furushima Toshio. *Shihon seisan no hatten to jinushisei*. Tokyo: Ochano-mizu shobō, 1978.

Hakodate-shi. *Hakodate-shi-shi, tsūshi-hen*. Vol. 2. Hakodate: Hakodate-shi, 1990.

Hara Hiroshi. "Mikaduki Omatsu: Jinniku shijō no ōbosu." *Uramado* 2:2 (March 1957): 238–44.

Harada Tomohiko. *Hisabetsu-buraku no rekishi*. 1975. Reprint, Tokyo: Asahi shibunsha, 1990.

Hayakawa Noriyo. *Kindai tennōsei to kokumin kokka*. Tokyo: Aoki shoten, 2005.

Hiroshima ken. *Hiroshima ken-shi*. Vol. 1. Tokyo: Teikoku chihō gyōsei gakkai, 1921.

Hirozane Takashi, Masagami Yasunori, and Kaga Hideyuki. "Hiroshima-ken wo chūshin to shita sangyō hatten no rekishi." *Keizai chōsa tōkei geppō* 393 (April 2007): 1–12.

Hitomi Sachiko. "Kōbe fukuwara yūkaku no seiritsu to kindai kōshō-sei." *Nihonshi kenkyū* 544 (December 2007): 28–56.

Hoshi Reiko. "Hokkaidō ni okeru shōgi jiyū haigyō." *Rekishi hyōron* 553 (May 1996): 63–80.

Ichiba Gakujirō. "Baiinfu no matsuro." *Kokka igaku gakkai zasshi* 315 (1913): 50–61.

Iino Masako. *Nikkei kanadajin no rekishi*. Tokyo: Tokyo daigaku shup-pankai, 1997.

Ishiwata Takako. "Zasshi *Jogaku sekai* ni miru josei-tachi no kyaria dezain: Meiji kōki wo chūshin to shite." *Ōbirin ronkō, Shinri kyōiku kenkyū* 2 (March 2013): 21–41.

Itō Hidekichi. *Nihon haishō undō-shi*. 1931. Reprint, Tokyo: Fujishuppan, 1982.

Kanagawa ken. *Kanagawa kenshi tsūshi-hen* 6. Yokohama: Kanagawa ken, 1981.

Kanbara chō shi hensan iinkai. *Kanbara chō shi*. Kanbara: Kanbara chō shi hensan iinkai, 1968.

Kanzaki Akitoshi et al. *Kanagawa ken no rekishi*. Tokyo: Yamakawa shuppan sha, 1996.

Kawamoto Yoshikazu. *Kaikō ianfu to hisabetsu buraku*. Tokyo: Sanichi shobō, 1997.

Kawamura Minato. *Kiisen: "Monoiu hana" no bunkashi*. Tokyo: Sakuhin-sha, 2001.

Kikuchi Takaiku. "Kanada ni okeru Sugimura Fukashi." *Morioka daigaku tanki daigaku-bu kiyō* 14 (2004): 30–36.

Kim Il Myon. *Yūjo, karayuki, ianfu no keifu.* Tokyo: Yūzankaku, 1997.

Kimura Kenji. *Zaichō nihonjin no shakai-shi.* Tokyo: Miraisha, 1989.

Kishimoto Minoru. *Jinkō idō-ron.* Tokyo: Ninomiya shoten, 1978.

———. "Meiji taishōki ni okeru rison chiiki no keisei to toshi jinkō no shūseki katei." *Rekishi chiri gakkai kiyō* 8 (1966): 139–49.

———. "Tōkai chiiki ni okeru jinkō shūseki." *Tōhoku chiri* 19:2 (1967): 45–52.

Kobayashi Shigeru, Haga Noboru, Miura Keiichi, et al. *Buraku-shi yōgo jiten.* Tokyo: Kashiwa shobō, 1985.

Kodama Kōta, ed. *Shukuba.* Tokyo: Tōkyōdō shuppan, 1999.

Kodama Masaaki. *Nihon iminshi kenkyū josetsu.* Hiroshima: Keiseisha, 1992.

Kudō Miyoko. *Kanada yūgirō ni furu yuki wa.* Tokyo: Shōbunsha, 1983.

———. *Kanashii metsuki no hyōryū sha.* Tokyo: Shūeisha, 1991.

Kurahashi Masanao. *Jūgun ianfu mondai no rekishiteki kenkyū.* Tokyo: Kyōei shobō, 1994.

———. *Kita no Karayuki-san.* Tokyo: Kyōei shobō, 2000.

Kusama Yasoo. *Tomoshibi no onna, yami no onna.* In *Kindai kasō minshū seikatsu-shi.* 1937. Reprint, Tokyo: Akashi Shoten, 1987.

Kusayama Iwao. "Kōbe gaikokujin kyoryūchi wo meguru keisatsu mondai." *Kōbe no rekishi* 14 (February 1986): 15–44.

Meiji hennen-shi Hensan Kai. *Meiji hennen-shi, dai ni-kan.* Tokyo: Zaisei keizai gakkai, 1965.

Miyamoto Natsuki. "Keiyaku imin jidai no honoruru nihonjin shakai to nihonjin baishunfu." *Hikaku shakai bunka kenkyū* 12 (2002): 47–57.

Miyaoka Kenji. *Shōfu.* Tokyo: San'ichi shobō, 1968.

Mori Katsumi. *Jinshin baibai.* Tokyo: Shibundō, 1959.

Morisaki Kazue. *Karayuki-san.* Tokyo: Asahi bunko, 1980.

Murakami Nobuhiko. *Meiji joseishi*, Vols. 2–3. Tokyo: Kōdansha bunko, 1977.

Murayama Yūzō. *Amerika ni ikita nihonjin imin.* Tokyo: Tōyō keizai shinpō sha, 1989.

Nagaoka Osamu. *Me de miru nishi Izu no rekishi.* Fujimiya: Ryokusei shuppan sha, 1986.

Nakamura Masanori. *Rōdōsha to nōmin: Nihon kindai wo sasaeta hitobito.* Tokyo: Shōgakkan, 1998.

Nakayama Jinshirō, *Kanada dōhō hatten taikan.* Vancouver: Tairiku nippō sha, 1922.

Nishida Taketoshi. *Nihon jānarizumu-shi kenkyū.* Tokyo: Misuzu shobō, 1989.

Ōba Noboru. *Karayuki-san Okiku no shōgai.* Tokyo: Akashi shoten, 2001.

Obinata Sumio. *Nihon kindai kokka no seiritsu to keisatsu.* Tokyo: Azekura shobō, 1992.

Ōishi Kaichirō. "Shihonshugi no seiritsu." In *Iwanamikōza nihonrekishi, dai 17 kan.* Tokyo: Iwanami shoten, 1981.

Okino Iwasaburō. *Shōgi kaihō aiwa.* 1930. Reprint, Tokyo: Chūkō bunko, 1982.

Onozawa Akane. *Kindai nihon shakai to kōshō seido: Minshū-shi to kokusai kankei no shiten kara.* Tokyo: Yoshikawa kōbun kan, 2011.

Pedlar, Neil A. *Yokohama Ehagakisho.* Translated by Ōtsu Kanya. Yokohama: Yūrindō, 1980.

Saeki Junko. *Yūjo no bunka shi.* Tokyo: Chūō kōron sha, 1987.

Sakaguchi Mitsuhiro. *Nihonjin amerika iminshi.* Tokyo: Fuji shuppan, 2001.

Sasaki Toshiji. *Nihonjin kanada iminshi.* Tokyo: Fuji shuppan, 1999.

Sawada Yasuyuki and Sonobe Tetsushi. *Keizaihatten ni okeru kyōdōtai to shijō no yakuwari.* Tokyo: Tōyōkeizai shinpō sha, 2006.

Shigetomi Akio. *Yokohama chabuya monogatari: Nihon no mūranrūju.* Yokohama: Senchurii, 1995.

Shimizu Hiroshi and Hirakawa Hitoshi. *Karayuki-san to keizai shinshutsu: Sekai keizai no naka no shingapōru-nihon kankei-shi.* Tokyo: Komonzu, 1998.

Shimizu Michiko. *"Jochū" imeeji no katei bunka-shi.* Tokyo: Sekai shisōsha, 2004.

Shinpo Mitsuru. *Ishi wo mote owaruru gotoku.* Vancouver: Tairiku nippō sha, 1975.

Shizuoka ken kaigai kyōkai. *Shizuoka ken kaigai ijū shi.* Shizuoka: Shizuoka ken kaigai kyōkai, 1979.

Sōgō joseishi kenkyū-kai. *Jidai wo ikita onnna tachi: Shin nihon josei tsū-shi.* Tokyo: Asahi shuppansha, 2010.

Sone Hiromi. *Shōfu to kinsei shakai.* Tokyo: Yoshikawa kōbun kan, 2003.

Song Youn-ok. "Chōsen gunji senryō-ka no sei-kanri seisaku." *Sensō sekinin kenkyū* 67 (Spring 2010): 20–29.

———. "Chōsen shokuminchi-shakai ni okeru kōshō-sei." *Nihonshi kenkyū* 371 (July 1993): 52–66.

Suzuki Yūko, ed. *Nihon josei undō shiryō shūsei, dai 8–kan.* Tokyo: Fuji shuppan, 1997.

Takada Shirō. *Izu no Ida.* Ito, Shizuoka: Izu wo aisuru kai, 1985.

Tang Quan. *Umi wo koeta tsuyagoto: Nicchū bunka kōryū hishi.* Tokyo: Shinyōsha, 2005.

Umejima Tetsujirō. *Kanbara chōshi shikō.* Kanbara, Shizuoka Prefecture: Privately published, 1971.

Usami Misako. *Shukuba to meshimori onna.* Tokyo: Dōseisha, 2000.

Yamamoto Shun'ichi. *Nihon kōshōshi.* Tokyo: Chūō hōki shuppan, 1983.

Yamashita Yon'e. "Chōsen ni okeru kōshō-seido no jisshi: Shokuminchi tōchika no sei shihai." In *Chōsen-josei ga mita "ianfu mondai": Asu wo tomoni ikiru tameni,* edited by Yun Jeong-Ok, 128–67. Tokyo: San'ichi shobō, 1992.

Yamazaki Tomoko. *Ameyuki-san no uta: Yamada Waka no sūki naru shōgai.* Tokyo: Bungei shunjū, 1978. Available in English as *The Story of Yamada Waka: From Prostitute to Feminist Pioneer.* Translated by Wakako Hironaka and Ann Kostant. Tokyo: Kodansha International, 1985.

———. *Sandakan hachiban shōkan: Teihen joseishi joshō.* 1972. Reprint, Tokyo: Bungei shunjū, 1975. Available in English as *Sandakan Brothel No. 8: An Episode in the History of Lower-Class Japanese Women.* Translated by Karen Colligan-Taylor. Armonk, N.Y.: M.E. Sharpe, 1999.

Yokohama kaikō shiryōkan, *Yokohama & bankūbā: Taiheiyō wo koete.* Tokyo: Yokohama kaikō shiryōkan, 2005.

Yokohama shi. *Yokohama shi shikō, fūzoku hen.* 1932. Reprint, Kyoto: Rinkai shoten, 1985.

Yoshimi Kaneko. "Baishō no jittai to haishō undō." In *Nihon joseishi, dai 4 kan, kindai.* Tokyo: Tokyo daigaku shuppankai, 1982.

———. *Baishō no shakaishi.* Tokyo: Yūzankaku, 1984.

INDEX

Abe Kihachi, 128, 194
agrarian sector: agricultural
  laborers, 41; cash crops, 61–
  62; commercialization of, 61;
  disintegration of, 202; farmer
  displacement, 20–21, 48–51,
  54, 62, 204; marginalization
  in, 52; and overseas migration,
  130; population gender ratios in,
  219n37; and ryōsai kenbo ideology,
  24–25; tenancy of agricultural
  lands, 21, 22t1.1, 50
Alien Land Law of 1913, 186, 196
Americanization, 187–89, 196,
  257n104, 257n105
anti-Asian sentiments: anti-alien
  prostitution movements, 168, 182;
  anti-Chinese sentiment, 103–4,
  170; anti-Japanese prostitution
  movements, 203; anti-Japanese
  sentiment, 186, 188, 193, 196–
  97, 200; antimiscegenation laws,
  196; exclusionary legislation,
  103, 183–84; hostility towards
  Asians, 33, 179, 200, 204; and law
  enforcement, 99; and segregation,
  97
antiprostitution reform, 168, 203,
  256n90; in Europe, 197; influence
  on overseas Japanese prostitution,
  176; in Japan, 149; in Japanese
  immigrant community, 7, 148, 185–
  89, 188; and Japanese immigrant
  leaders, 189–97; in Japanese
  territories, 200; in North American
  West, 176–85; overview, 14–15;
  transnational approach, 173–76
Aoki Shūzō, 174
assimilation, 188–90, 195,
  257nn104,106
Australia, 26t1.3, 199t6.1, 203

Azuma, Eiichiro, 195

bar-brothels (chabuya), 41, 44, 152
barmaids (shakufu): and antiprostitution
  reform, 196, 256n90; barmaid-
  prostitutes (meshi-mori onna), 41,
  52; children of, 238n139; and class
  status, 99; and deportation, 165;
  and divorces, 151–52; everyday lives
  of, 134–35; income, 117, 236n101;
  and Japanese men, 204; Japanese
  overseas, numbers of, 26t1.3; job
  description, 105–8; in Korea, 29,
  175; leisure activities of, 132–35;
  in Maneki restaurant, 107f4.1;
  married women as, 108, 135–
  36, 194; in official reports, 185;
  payment system, 117; recruitment
  of, 108–9, 110f4.2; response to
  exploitation, 137–67; runaways,
  144f5.1; suicides, 130; tanka
  writing, 135; wages, 236n101
bar-restaurants: brothel comparison,
  112; decrease in, 259n143; increase
  of, 184–85; and Japanese immigrant
  leaders, 192–93; management of,
  147, 205; men's perspectives of,
  111, 204; in North American West,
  105–14; prohibitions on, 189
beauty contests, 118–19, 147, 190
blacks (African Americans): biracial
  children, 126; black customers,
  126; black prostitutes, 33, 97, 100,
  111
Britain: antiprostitution reform, 197;
  British Malaya, 27, 197; Criminal
  Law Amendment Act of 1885, 178
British Columbia, 34–35, 46, 218n8,
  242n17; and anti-Japanese
  sentiment, 186; brothel-keepers,
  117; and Chinese prostitutes,

domestic work, 59–60, 62–63, 112, 129, 146, 174, 204, 236*n*90, 250*n*21; female domestics (*jochū*), 59–60
double standards, 96, 175

economic contexts: and barmaids, 108; debt payment, 139–41; economic constraints, 65–66; and independence, 205; inflation, 20–21; of Japanese sex work, 114–19; and labor migration, 61, 199; of local economy, 18; in Meiji Japan, 13, 16; of North Americans West, 84–88; in North American West, 31, 32, 36, 94, 120, 204; in Pacific regions, 202; in post-Meiji Restoration, 20; and prostitution, 24, 32, 32–33, 120, 199; and recruitment, 94; and women's migration, 16, 50
education, 24, 41, 129, 143, 195–96, 214*n*27
Emancipation Edict of 1871, 50, 213*n*10
Europe: and antiprostitution reform, 197; European colonialism, 26, 27, 197, 203; European prostitutes in North American West, 33, 97, 99; France, 27, 197; Germany, 27, 197; Japanese prostitutes in, 26*t*1.3, 199*t*6.1; Netherlands, 26–27; Russia, 26*t*1.3, 28–29, 198, 199*t*6.1, 200, 204
exclusionism, 183, 188, 196. *See also* legislation, exclusionary
exploitation, 12, 95; economic, 137–67; and informal regulation, 120–21; and Japanese entrepreneurs, 120; and law enforcement, 99–100; by procurers, 115; responses to, 14, 165–67, 247*n*84; sexual, 137–67, 168, 178; slavery, modern-day, 260*n*2

family formation, 108–9, 120, 186, 188, 190, 197
family ideology, 25, 242*n*14
Fife, Nellie, 177–78, 242*n*11, 244*n*48
filial piety, 18, 59, 130
Florence Crittenton Refuge House, 181
foreigners: foreign trade, 18, 54, 61; and prostitution, 51–53, 219*n*42; and sexual violation danger, 52–53; in treaty ports, 41–44; in Yokohama, 51–52
Fujita Toshirō, 171–72, 176, 223*n*11, 242*n*16, 250*n*15
Fukuzawa Yukichi, 24

Furuya Masajirō, 120

Geffeney, A. H., 180, 229*n*84
Geiger, Andrea, 13, 124, 126, 166, 191, 211*n*29, 240*n*170
geisha, 23, 46, 106–7, 159, 163, 175
gejo hōkō (girl-servants' jobs), 59–60, 112, 204
gender issues: gender constraints, 48–49; gender inequality, 129; gender oppression, 7, 203; gender roles, 194; in Japanese society, 252*n*36
gender ratios, 28, 29, 32, 129, 185, 196, 204, 215*n*38, 219*n*37, 233*n*43, 235*n*77, 259*n*143
Gentlemen's Agreements, 35, 47, 148, 185
geographic origins, 13, 38*t*2.1; Hiroshima Prefecture as, 38, 38*t*2.1, 61–66; Hyogo Prefecture as, 38, 38*t*2.1; of Japanese procurers, 38*t*2.1; of Japanese prostitutes, 37–38, 38, 38*t*2.1, 39, 48–49, 49*m*2.2, 240*n*185; Kanagawa Prefecture as, 38, 38*t*2.1, 48; Kumamoto Prefecture as, 38, 38*t*2.1; Nagasaki Prefecture as, 38; Osaka Prefecture as, 38, 38*t*2.1; Shiga Prefecture as, 38, 38*t*2.1; Shizuoka Prefecture as, 38, 38*t*2.1, 219*n*47; and social origins, 37–38; Tokyo Prefecture as, 38, 38*t*2.1; Yokohama as, 38, 46–48, 56, 108, 179
"good" vs. "bad" women, 96, 103, 194–95
Gospel Society, 172, 250*n*21
graft, 99–100, 114, 172

harimise (display practice), 103, 158
Hasegawa Genji, 120
Hawaii, 16, 28, 33, 41, 130, 217*n*64
Hayashi-Lemieux Agreement of 1907, 35
head tax, 35, 80, 104, 170, 217*n*63, 227*n*53, 249*n*11
Heda, 53, 54–55, 57, 57–58, 220*n*58, 220*n*60
Hiroshima (city), 63
Home Missionary Society, 178, 253*n*48
honor, Japanese, 15, 203; importance of, 200, 252*n*36; and international reputation, 14, 168, 170–71, 173, 175, 199; and Japanese immigrant community, 186–87; and liberation order, 19; Matthews, Mark A., 148; national honor of, 15, 203; and social stigma, 130; and status

The Great Columbia Plain: A Historical Geography, 1805–1910,
by Donald W. Meinig

*Mills and Markets: A History of the Pacific Coast Lumber Industry
to 1900,* by Thomas R. Cox

*Radical Heritage: Labor, Socialism, and Reform in Washington and
British Columbia, 1885–1917,* by Carlos A. Schwantes

*The Battle for Butte: Mining and Politics on the Northern Frontier,
1864–1906,* by Michael P. Malone

*The Forging of a Black Community: Seattle's Central District from 1870
through the Civil Rights Era,* by Quintard Taylor

Warren G. Magnuson and the Shaping of Twentieth-Century America,
by Shelby Scates

The Atomic West, edited by Bruce Hevly and John M. Findlay

Power and Place in the North American West, edited by Richard White
and John M. Findlay

Henry M. Jackson: A Life in Politics, by Robert G. Kaufman

Parallel Destinies: Canadian-American Relations West of the Rockies,
edited by John M. Findlay and Ken S. Coates

*Nikkei in the Pacific Northwest: Japanese Americans and Japanese
Canadians in the Twentieth Century,* edited by Louis Fiset
and Gail M. Nomura

Bringing Indians to the Book, by Albert Furtwangler

Death of Celilo Falls, by Katrine Barber

*The Power of Promises: Perspectives on Indian Treaties of the Pacific
Northwest,* edited by Alexandra Harmon

Warship under Sail: The USS Decatur *in the Pacific West,*
by Lorraine McConaghy

Shadow Tribe: The Making of Columbia River Indian Identity,
by Andrew H. Fisher

*A Home for Every Child: Relinquishment, Adoption, and the Washington
Children's Home Society, 1896–1915,* by Patricia Susan Hart

Atomic Frontier Days: Hanford and the American West,
by John M. Findlay and Bruce Hevly

*The Nature of Borders: Salmon, Boundaries, and Bandits on the Salish
Sea,* by Lissa K. Wadewitz

*Encounters in Avalanche Country: A History of Survival in the Mountain
West, 1820–1920,* by Diana L. Di Stefano

*The Rising Tide of Color: Race, State Violence, and Radical Movements
across the Pacific,* edited by Moon-Ho Jung

*Trout Culture: How Fly Fishing Forever Changed the Rocky Mountain
West,* by Jen Corrinne Brown

Japanese Prostitutes in the North American West, 1887–1920, by Kazuhiro
Oharazeki